A Man's LIFE
THE COMPLETE INSTRUCTIONS

ALSO BY DENIS BOYLES

The Modern Man's Guide to Life (coauthor)
The Modern Man's Guide to Modern Women
African Lives
Man Eaters Motel

A Man's LIFE

THE COMPLETE INSTRUCTIONS

Animal Magnetism · Beer as Food · Careers · Day Care for Men · Exercises that Work · Firing Your Boss · Growing Tomatoes · How to Change a Diaper with One Hand · Inspirational Sex · Junk-Food Diets · Killer Hoop Tricks · Landing a 747 · Married Women · Nasty Neighbors · Outwitting Fish · Pension Plans · Quick Cleans · Rural Real Estate · Screws · Travel · Urban Tenting · Vested Options · What to Do to Your Thumb After You Whack It with a Hammer · and More.

DENIS BOYLES

with lots of help from
GREGG STEBBEN

and a whole bunch of other guys

Illustrations by A. R. B.

HarperPerennial
A Division of HarperCollinsPublishers

Some portions of this book have appeared in *Men's Health*. Other portions have appeared, in different form, in *Esquire* and in *A Man's Life* on the World Wide Web at www. manslife.com.

HarperCollins books may be purchased for educational, business, or sales promotional use. For information please write: Special Markets Department, HarperCollins Publishers, Inc., 10 East 53rd Street, New York, NY 10022.

FIRST EDITION

Designed by Laura Lindgren

Library of Congress Cataloging-in-Publication Data

Boyles, Denis.
   A man's life : the complete instructions / by Denis Boyles ; with lots of help from
Gregg Stebben ; and a whole bunch of other guys.
     p.   cm.
   Includes index.
   ISBN 0-06-095141-9
   1. Men—Conduct of life. 2. Men—Psychology.   I. Stebben, Gregg. I. Title.
BJ1601.B66   1996
646.7'0081—dc20   96-15766

96 97 98 99 00 ❖/RRD 10 9 8 7 6 5 4 3 2 1

To
Claude
and
Donald
Boyles
· · · · ·
*Two perfect examples
of how a man's life ought to be lived.
Thanks for the lessons.*

Contents

Acknowledgments

While a great deal of this book depends on the kindness and generosity of strangers, some of it owes a lot to people I actually know.

My wife, April, took a big pile of debts, a humdrum wardrobe, an irritable personality, a reasonable measure of potency, and out of it fashioned this man's life. Nice work, too. I rather like what she did.

Every time I do one of these collections, I count on lots of other guys to bail me out. This time, while many correspondents chipped in useful stuff, Gregg Stebben did a whole bunch of legwork, filling in the holes, picking up the pieces, calling famous guys to get their take on the details of a man's life, and generally doing whatever it took to get the book assembled as well as help out a friend.

Also Mike Lafavore and my editorial pals at *Men's Health*—especially Dave Zinczenko, Peter Moore, Steve Perrine, and Jeff Csatari—did lots of heavy lifting, since they not only provided me with stuff I needed, but also helped shape much of the material that appears here. Other chums—Harry Stein, Eric Boardman, Dave Hirshey, Joe Queenan, Cary Schneider, Fred Schruers, Gene Stone, Steve Wiest, and the monstrously prolific William Boot—all donated small pieces of their own livelihoods to this large piece of mine, and I appreciate it. To test some of this stuff out in the loftier reaches of thin air, my friends at Novo McKinley in San Francisco—Kelly Rodriques, Philip Dzivelis, Selino Valdes, Shelley Blockhus, Arno Harris, David Thatcher, Kim Garretson, Annie Nelson, and J. Mario Flores—indulged my whim to clutter a corner of the Web with souvenirs of A Man's Life. As ever, my hat's off to my brother, David, and my nephew, Jeremy. I also owe all my cousins and uncles, big-time.

Mostly, though, I'm obliged to strangers. Men—and not a few women—from all over the dry-land part of the planet sent tips, hints, observations, and advice from the ashes of their own experience, and what they didn't supply, Gregg did. For years, I've been badgering readers to send me stuff they think other guys need to know to make life a happier passage. Many, many responded. Thanks to these contributors, we have thoroughly covered exactly as much of the waterfront of a man's life as you can see from here.

Regarding these many generous, sometimes anonymous contributors, a few comments:

1. If something you sent in has been included here, but you didn't say where you got it, we tried like dickens to determine its provenance. When we were successful, we said so. When we weren't, we assumed you came up with it yourself. If we were wrong, please accept our apologies—and our thanks.

2. If you're one of the many who contributed a chunk of your life to this book, I thank you very much. You'll see you've been noted by initials in the text and identified by name in the back of the book. I promised you each a hearty handshake in exchange for your wisdom, and I mean to pay you each just as soon as we get together.

    Some portions of this book first appeared, in different form, in *Men's Health* magazine. For those who gave me information for use in the magazine columns in which some of this content first appeared, I have tried to give you your due here—a little late, but still heartfelt.

3. If you're one of the many who have contributed a chunk of your income to buying this book, I thank you very much, indeed. Having already given me money, you might as well go all the way and send me whatever you think might be useful for the next book like this.

4. If, however, you're one of the vast number who have contributed neither money nor experience to this small enterprise, I beg you to reconsider. My address appears below.

Denis Boyles
Modern Man Books
c/o Rex's Barber Shop
116 W. Jefferson St.
Mankato, KS 66956

Introduction

For lots of guys, life is a VCR. I mean, most of us can get along just fine making stuff up as we go. Life, for most of us, works swell, up to a point. But then one morning you wake up and find you have to set the timer on life's VCR, and that's when things start to fall apart—the marriage disintegrates, the belly sags, the kids go to juvie. You find you just don't know what to do next. So what do you do when all else fails? You read the instructions. Welcome to this book.

A Man's Life is dedicated to a favorite theme of mine, one that informed the last book of received wisdom on which I worked, *The Modern Man's Guide to Life*: It's the proposition that in a world full of too much information, there's only so much a guy really needs to know, and most of it's not terribly modern. Like modern men everywhere, I very much doubt the value of the latest idea, because like most ideas, the latest idea is usually a bad idea. The best ideas, of course, are tried-and-true ideas. They have a lovely simplicity to them. They can be understood because they look and feel just like common sense.

All most of us want to know is what works and what doesn't. We want to know the Main Thing about everything, because we sense that once you get a lock on the Main Thing, the little things will fall in line. The Main Thing is the thing that has always worked. It worked for your uncle, your dad, and your granddad. And if you can find it, it'll work for you, too. This kind of dope used to be passed from generation to generation. No more. These days, generations aren't on speaking terms.

However, just because I admire useful, tried-and-true avuncular advice such as that found in this precious volume, that doesn't mean I'm insensitive to really inane, cockamamie, oddball tips. There's a lot of that in here, too. In fact, this book is full of information from everybody about everything. All of it has been tested by the science guys in the Man's Life lab, and all of it works just fine.

This book is only one small part of a vast, impersonal, ozone-eating global empire of products related to this man's life. For example, there's A Man's Life, the Web site, at http://www.manslife.com. There's *A Man's Life,* the occasional newspaper, published from the spacious corporate offices of A Man's Life at Rex's Barber Shop, 116 W. Jefferson St., Mankato, KS 66956. And, finally, there's A Man's Life, which I am living at the moment, and hope to continue doing so for the foreseeable future. I hope you enjoy this part of it.

A DISCLAIMER

Like many men of my generation, I have been somewhat tardy in accepting responsibility for my own life. I have no interest in accepting any responsibility for any part of yours. Therefore, allow me to say clearly and plainly that the contents of this book are for information only. This book is not a shrink, a medical doctor, a lawyer, a car mechanic, so obviously it's not a substitute for the kind of professional advice you can get from shrinks, doctors, mechanics, lawyers, and all the others. But it's a lot cheaper.

1. Hardware and Machinery

The reason a man's life starts with hardware and machinery is that most men's lives are like complicated machines with plenty of moving parts. Most of the time, life just hums along. But one day, you hear a cough and a sputter, and suddenly there's smoke and fire everywhere. That's when it pays to know a little about hardware, because once you understand hardware, the only thing standing between you and bliss is finding the right tool for the job.

Hardware

HOW TO PUT TOGETHER ANYTHING

Here's the bad news on those L'il Tad model 12G5 wind-up kiddie swings: The elbows at the top of pole assemblies 12 and 14 go inverse to the cross-member and motor-mount housing.

Look, we were all single once, so you can just wipe that smirk right off your face. For your information, mister, the L'il Tad 12G5 happens to be a high-performance, self-propelled, child-bearing, pendular device that, *when properly assembled,* will enable you to give that special small treasure of yours all the excitement and adventure of travel on almost no money and without luggage. But if you reverse those pole assemblies on the 12G5, and then wind her up, what you get is your basic torqued-child fault, in which the kid, instead of going front to back, goes wonky in a kind of front-to-side-to-upside-down motion, real fast. Cool, huh? Women and children hate that, though. See for yourself. Give it a try, and your wife will come along behind you with a pair of pliers and straighten out all the pieces you had carefully reengineered to fit the way you thought they were supposed to fit.

You may think the lesson in this little tale is that it always pays to read the directions, but you're wrong. The lesson here is that there are only so many ways to put together *anything,* and that once these fundamental principles of what we can call civilian engineering have been mastered, there is nothing you cannot join together, no assembly you cannot assemble, no tabs you cannot insert, no slots you cannot fill, no act you can't get together.

What follows are:

The Master Assembly Instructions

After you read these directions once—design flaws, emotional trauma, and manufacturing errors notwithstanding—*you'll never have to read any directions for anything ever again.*

GET THE BIG PICTURE

This is the most important step of all, which is why it comes first: **Look at the box.**

No matter what you're putting together, the parts look nothing like the whole. If you spread out the parts for the 12G5, for instance, you'd think it was something you, personally, might like—a sit-down vaulting pole, for instance (would that be *great* or what?) where you could just, like, run along until you got to the thirty-foot crossbar, plant your pole, take a seat, and ride the crest in style, waving to the crowd and taking pictures as you go—instead of whatever it is for the tyke. One look at the box will set you straight.

This particular assembly instruction—looking at the box—is critical because it has universal application. To illustrate why, let's take something not normally associated with hardware. For instance, you take Mexico and a cheeseburger and put them together, you wouldn't think you'd get a taco. You have to see it before you can build it. Like a field of dreams.

Use Your Mental Wrench. So look at the picture, imagine how it's assembled, then, mentally, *disassemble* the thing. In fact, a good set of instructions contains an exploded diagram. That's really all you need. Spill all the parts out of the box onto a smooth surface—the floor, maybe. Place them on the living room carpet so they appear in the order shown on the exploded diagram. From here on, it's just a matter of tightening things up. (But not too tight.)

RECOGNIZE A LIE WHEN YOU SEE IT

Unless nature has blessed you with a Phillips-head fingernail, you *always* need tools, always, no matter what. Just in case, better get power tools. New ones, and lots of them.

DON'T READ THE DIRECTIONS

Except, of course, those you're reading just now. You already knew this one, right? Besides, the people who write directions do not make the objects the assembly of which they describe. They know much less about how to put something together than you will five minutes after you finish the job. Why? Because engineers can't write worth a damn, and because writers can barely assemble their thoughts, let alone something as complicated as a Soloflex.

An Exception: Always read the instructions accompanying any product made in China, for, while the directions apparently have nothing to do with the product, they do provide a great deal of admirable practical advice. An example, from a package of bottle rockets made in the People's Republic: "1. Point up to cloudy sky. 2. Match fire will ignite fuse. 3. Do not hover. 4. Listen carefully for report."

IF YOU'RE CONFUSED, SIZE THE PARTS

When you're putting something together, remember there are *three basic types of parts out of which all unassembled products are made:*

1. Little parts.
2. Really important parts, including the Main Thing.
3. Big parts.

The key to proper assembly is to start small and work your way up.

The Little Parts. You can't skip the small stuff. This causes frustration, I know, but here it is: Little pieces almost always have to be put together before big pieces. Except in *Mad Max* movies, most assembled objects do not have their innards hanging on the outside. As a rule, the little stuff gets put together in small assemblies. These, in turn, become part of a larger assembly.

It's the little things in a big thing that make everything go a little more smoothly. In that regard, little things do indeed mean a lot. Take sex, for instance. For most of us, it's a big thing, yes? But without that little thing, you got nothing.

The Really Important Parts. What we mean here is the one piece—technically, the Main Thing—without which no other piece will be able to stay in place. The L'il Tad 12G5 has that wicked crossmember, for example. That's the thing you have to worry about, because if you get that wrong, nothing else will be right.

Every Assembly Has a Main Thing That Holds Together All the Other Things.

Witness:

- Washing machines: Tub armature. If the tub armature bends, no more whiter than white.
- Wagons: The axles. If an axle's upside down, those tires are goners.
- Balkan conflicts: Crazy Serbs. Crazy Croats. No Croats, no Serbs, no war.
- Thursday nights: If Jerry quits *Seinfeld,* you're stuck with *Matlock.*

There's always one thing that makes sense of everything else. Find it, feel it, understand it. It's the key to your universe.

Assembly tip: How to spot the Main Thing. It's usually a medium-sized piece, not the biggest, and not one of the little pieces of shrapnel stapled in the little plastic bag. There's usually a hole in it—often, two, one at each end.

Big Parts. Here's an important rule about big parts:

THE BIG THING ISN'T NECESSARILY THE MAIN THING.

In fact, the biggest thing is often the least consequential, because it simply wraps up everything else. On a car, for instance, the hood is a big thing, but it certainly isn't any of the main things that make the car go. Since, in most assemblies, the Main Thing is usually the thing that takes up the most room, you'll want to get it out of the way first. Trying to put together the Big Thing first is an understandable mistake, of course, since by putting together the Big Thing first, you'll also make a giant step toward making all those parts look like that picture. But here's a promise: If you build the Big Thing first, you'll have to take it apart when you start building all the little things. Then you'll have to dismantle everything when you finally figure out the Main Thing.

A note on electronic stuff: Everything that has to do with electronic goods comes in pairs. It's a yin-yang thing. Every part is a positive or a negative, a red or a gray, an input or an output. Abstractly, these things all form a big circle that isn't complete until all the positives and negatives are joined together. To assemble any pile of electro-junk, all you have to do is keep track of the pluses and the minuses. You have to keep the inputs going in and the outputs going out.

TIGHTEN NOTHING UNTIL IT'S ALL OVER

Tightening all the screws and bolts is the last thing you do in any assembly process. Give everything a little elbow room, let it all settle. Once you're sure, then you can commit.

WHEN IN DOUBT, GET EXPERT HELP

Never be ashamed to seek outside advice. Brain surgeons ask for outside opinions—not when they're doing brain surgery, maybe, but when they have to rig up a new computer or a VCR-cable box-stereo combo.

There are a number of ways to get an expert's point of view.

- *Building a cabinet or bookshelf?* Go to an antique shop or a fine furniture showroom and look for examples of how the job ought to be done. Grab a drawer out of an old dresser. See the way that dovetailed corner has been joined? Check out the pegged assembly on that chair brace.
- *If it's a consumer product,* ask to talk to the guy who put together the store's display model. Even better: Buy the display model.
- *Become an expert yourself* by convincing your neighbor to buy one first, then kibitzing as you give him a hand.
- *Marry an expert.* If you're putting together something as technologically sophisticated as a 12G5 and your wife offers a suggestion, listen carefully, but do not express even the slightest degree of comprehension. Instead, ask her to demonstrate. Then try again, but get it wrong. For most wives or girlfriends, the threshold of domestic jerk-tolerance is extremely low.

Very quickly, you'll hear the expert words of advice you really need, which go something like this: "For crying out loud, get out of the way. I'll do it myself."

THE FAMILY TREE OF HAND TOOLS

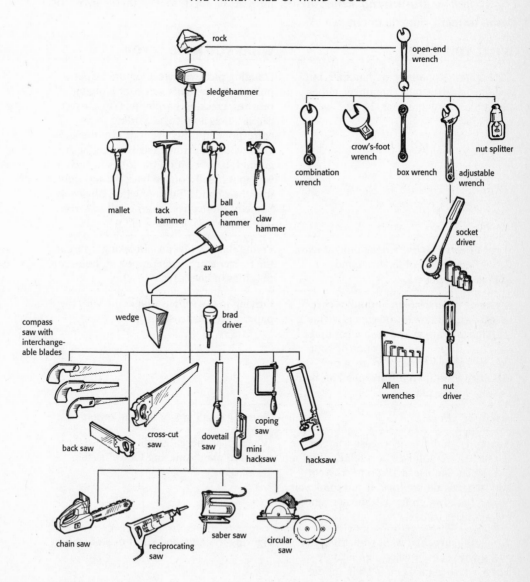

How to Equip a Toolchest

Before you start anything major, figure out one thing first: Are you labor? Or are you management? Lots of guys are handy fellows, patching up life as they live it. Others are just as clever with tools but lack the time or the inclination. Still others like to watch.

If you're the hiring kind, here's all you'll need to do those jobs too small to merit outside talent:

WHAT YOU NEED	WHAT YOU NEED IT FOR
A hammer. Not a framing hammer, but not one of those "lady" hammers, either. Just a basic claw hammer, 16 oz. minimum.	Hanging pictures, retacking the carpet, pulling out the nails you bent hanging pictures, cracking hazelnuts. (SF) Or you can use it as a yo-yo, according to one correspondent: "Believe it or not, there are guys who can throw their hammer at the ground, have it hit on the tongs in such a way that it will bounce back up and right into their hands. Takes practice, obviously. Some of these guys are so good they can do this *while they walk.*" (TD)
A set of screwdrivers, including at least two different sizes of flat-head and Phillips-head drivers.	Prying the lids off cans, breaking up ice in the freezer compartment, poking holes in the sides of beer cans. (TMcD)
A power screwdriver, and not a cheesy, cheap one, either. Get the expensive kind, with lots of power. And grab a handful of bits, too. If you count the value of your time, it's always cheaper to use a new screwdriver bit than it is to spend an hour looking for the old one.	Driving in the screws that come with the paper towel dispenser.
A pair of pliers.	Opening small jars of martini onions.
A saw. If you have any excuse whatsoever, go for a power job (see next table). But for general civilian use, a 10-point crosscut handsaw will do the trick. If you think you need a hacksaw, go for a 10-incher, since it's less likely to flex.	When great carpenters die, they use these things to play "Amazing Grace" at the burial service.
Tape measure. You want something that will stay erect even when significantly extended, so get a ¾ in. × 16 ft. model. Tell your wife it's a 12 in. compact model.	Figuring the long and short of stuff. (SF)

If you're the DIY kind, you already know what you need. Here's the workshop inventory of a pro carpenter:

THE BEST MAKE/MODEL AND THE UGLY PRICE IT BEARS	WHAT IT DOES BEST
• Powermatic 5 hp single-phase table saw with a Biesemeyer 50 in. commercial fence, model 1660791. $2,050.	For cutting solid wood and sheets of plywood, etc. You need to run the stock against the Biesemeyer fence as you send the wood into the saw's blades. A Biesemeyer fence has a built-in tape measure, making cutting more accurate.
• Griggio 12 in. joiner with tenoning/mortising attachment. Around $4,500.	For milling solid stock. The joiner flattens one surface and gives lumber two true, flat, perpendicular surfaces. Removes any irregularities from wood and gets it to lay dead flat. The tenoning/mortising attachment makes joinery for furniture that is similar to tongue-and-groove, but deeper.
• Powermatic 15 in. planer, model 1791209. $1,300.	After you run wood through the joiner you take it to the planer, which trues the wood and takes it to the dimensions you want.
• Elu 3 hp plunge router with fence, model 3339. $280.	For making shapes in the edge of wood, like a rounded edge on a tabletop or at the nose of a stair.
• Porter Cable 1½ hp D-handle router, model 691. $160.	Portable model.
• Powermatic spindle shaper, model 1270100. $2,050.	A spindle shaper does the same thing as a router, but on a larger scale. Of all the tools on this list, this is the one that the average guy in a workshop is least likely to buy because of cost. But the spindle shaper, and the feeder, are great for working with laminate coatings and when working with a lot of tongue-and-groove or wood inset. Also, unlike a router, a spindle shaper will cut both sides of the wood at the same time. Worth it, right? Except if you're going to buy yourself a Powermatic 1270100, you're also going to need a 1790807—see below.

THE BEST MAKE/MODEL AND THE UGLY PRICE IT BEARS	WHAT IT DOES BEST
• Powermatic single-phase stock feeder, model 1790807. $930.	Feeder for the spindle shaper, gives you safety, accuracy, and consistency. Works like the paper feeder on a computer printer.
• Powermatic 6 in. × 48 in. belt/12 in. disk sander, model 1310001. $1,300.	Used to prepare wood for final sanding. The belt part is for quickly getting machine mill marks off wood. The disk part is for cleaning up curves you've cut on your band saw (see below).
• Powermatic oscillating spindle sander, model 1791208. $300.	As above, but the 1791208 works on concave surfaces.
• Jet 17 in. floor drill press, model JDP 17MF. $430.	Drills holes in things.
• Delta 14 in. wood-cutting band saw, model 28283KB. $800.	Two functions: 1. Resawing (ripping—with grain) lumber or cutting veneers. 2. Cutting irregular shapes and curves.
• Hitachi 10 in. slide compound saw, model C10FS. $750. With blade, model LU91M010. $60.	For cut-off (across grain), miters, and compound miter joints. Because of the slide, it eliminates the need for a radial armsaw. So you're saving money right there.
• Makita 9.6 V cordless driver/drill, model 6095DWE. $140.	For drilling holes and driving screws.
• Makita ⅜ in. 9.6 V cordless angle drill driver, model DA391DW. $180.	Like the above item, but designed to work in hard-to-reach places. The drawback is that it is not as comfortable to work with as the 6095, and it doesn't have as much torque. Otherwise, it would be the only tool you'd need for this kind of work.
• Milwaukee ½ in. hammer drill kit, Model 53771. $210.	For handling large-size bits and for drilling in harder surfaces like concrete and masonry.
• Freud biscuit (plate) joiner, model JS-102. $180. Or go for the original, the Lamello Top 10 plate joiner, model TOP10—if you can afford it at $620.	Lets you attach two pieces of wood parallel or perpendicular to each other. The biscuit is the fastener. Freud is the shrink.
• Baldor industrial duty "Big Red" grinder, 7 in. ½ hp, model 712R. $200.	For sharpening hollow-ground edge on your hand tools—like chisels and planer irons—and drill bits.

THE BEST MAKE/MODEL AND THE UGLY PRICE IT BEARS	WHAT IT DOES BEST
• Biesemeyer T-square cut-off saw stop. $70.	Provides accurate measuring for miter saw.
• Milwaukee fast-cutting orbital jigsaw, model 6266-6. $180.	Like a band saw, but portable. Great for concave and convex cuts. You can take it to your wood so you don't have to lug your wood to it.
• Porter Cable 5 in. VS random orbital sander with carrying case, model 330. $140.	For finish sanding.
• Porter Cable 4 in. × 24 in. belt sander with bag, model 362. $205.	For rough sanding. It's the portable version of the stationary disc sander.
• DeWalt heavy-duty laminate trimmer kit, model DW673K. $210.	For trimming plastic laminate and doing veneer work.
• De Vilbiss 4 hp 20 gal. tank, model IRF420. $380.	For driving pneumatic fastening tools, using spray-finishing accessories, blowing away debris, and screwing around. To get your money's worth, aim it at a cat.
• Jet 12 in. VS wood lathe with stand, model JWL-1236. $570.	For doing bowls and spindles and other cylindrical parts.
• Powermatic 75 1900 CFM dust collector, model 1791071. $680.	For collecting wood chips and dust, primarily from the joiner, planer, and table saw. Like a grass catcher, it's a vacuum system that attaches to the exhaust chute of those machines. Saves you from sweeping and from having dust all over tools. It also keeps you from breathing sawdust all day.
• Senco full round head framing nailer, model SN60. $450. • Senco brad nailer with case, model SLP20. $280. • Senco narrow crown stapler, model SLS20. $280.	All for nailing and stapling stuff at full speed.
• Flat-head screwdriver. $1.29.	For prying the lids off cans, breaking up ice in the freezer compartment, poking holes in the sides of beer cans. (TMcD)

Other Tools, Other Uses: It's a crazy world out there. And guys with tools can go as crazy as anyone else.

TYPE OF TOOL	CONVENTIONAL USE	ALTERNATE USE
• Chisel	Flat-edged cutting tool	Chisel chicken: Takes two or more to play. Flip your chisel into the air and let it stick, blade-first, in the ground. The object is to get closer to your opponent's foot than he gets to yours. If you hit his foot, you lose points.
• Variable speed router	Rotary cutting tool	Car polisher
• Adjustable wrench	Nut-adjusting tool	Hammer
• Hammer	High-impact driving tool	Attitude-adjuster on difficult-to-repair items
• Large hand sander	Finishing tool	Sex toy (remove sandpaper)
• Band saw	Stock cutting tool	Deer processor
• Handsaw	Stock cutting tool	Machete (TD)

How to Hammer a Nail

If you're looking for the animal tracks of a previous generation, start here. At no other time in the history of man have so few men known so little about such a completely obvious thing as how to drive a nail into a board. If you know, fine. You're a manly man. If you don't, keep it to yourself—and learn this three-step process:

Step one: Drill it, dull it, drive it. If the nail is going to be driven any-place where it's likely to split the wood, drill a small pilot hole first. If you're on the fence about the likelihood of splitting the wood, buy some insurance by turning the nail upside down and tapping it a few times on the point. A dull nail is far less likely to split wood than a sharp one. (KD)

Step two: Set the nail. Hold it between your thumb and forefinger and give it a sure-thing tap. Don't girl out on this: Hit the thing hard enough that you're not going to have to set it again. You want it to stand up all by itself.

Step three: Nail it. Hold the hammer at the end of the handle. Keep your wrist fairly stiff, and whack it. You use your whole forearm for this: A good hammer blow is very much like a good overhead slam in tennis. You want to pound right *through* the nail's head. Practice this for five minutes, and you should be able to set an eightpenny nail with one tap and drive it into a two-by-four with three good, solid, no-jive shots.

Notes: Lots can happen between the first tap and the last whack:

- If you bend the nail more than a little, don't fool with it. Yank it out and take it from the top.
- Don't miss. There are two telltales of a bum carpenter: bent nails, of course, and scarred wood. If you see a nail head surrounded by what appear to be miniature elephant tracks, you know a rube has been at work.
- If the wood's green, or if it's ungodly hard, soap the tip of the nail with a bar of Ivory.
- If you're doing any kind of finish work, don't drive the nail home with the hammer. Instead, hold it back from the surface of the board a bit and use a nail punch to finish the job. (KD, KN)

How to Keep Your Thumbnail on Your Thumb After You Whack It with a Hammer

This really works:

Step one: Whack your thumb with a hammer while you're trying to drive in a nail.

Step two: Gas it. Before you can count slowly to thirty, get your thumb under a can of gasoline.

Step three: Slowly trickle gasoline over the banged-up thumbnail. You don't need a gush of gas; a trickle slow enough to last about a minute will do the trick. No blue nail, no aching thumb.

Step four: Stop smoking. (DER)

Once you figure out how to drive in a nail, take your knowledge to grad school.

How to Perform Stupid and Life-Threatening Tricks with Nail Guns

Hey, here's some good news: You can do anything with a nail gun that you can do with a .22, including lots of truly terrifying and dangerous stunts. A correspondent has sent us some of his faves.

Before you can play any of these games you have to disassemble the safety on your gun. It's designed to ensure that you only nail into something solid, so it requires that you be pressing the nose of the gun down onto a rigid surface before you fire it. Every safety is different. Unload your gun and then give it the once-over: You'll figure something out. What you've got to do is figure out how to press down on the safety and hold it there as if the nose were pressed against a solid surface while you are swinging it around in the air looking for something to shoot.

NAIL GUN SPORTS

- *Shoot the lackey.* Every construction site has a lackey. Take turns shooting at him as he goes about his chores. Make sure he isn't close enough that it would hurt if you actually hit him, and make sure you don't aim for the eyes. Deduct points if you shoot at him while he has run off to get you a beer.
- *Target shooting.* Put up a wedding photo from your first marriage or a snapshot of the site foreman. Fire away. Bull's-eye wins. With a nail gun you've got, say, thirty feet. Therefore, when you aim you have to aim high because the nail will go straight for only a foot or two and then start dropping. In a way, that means you can have a lot more fun with a nail gun because you can fire it off over here and not worry about hitting some lady sitting in her living room a half mile away.
- *Indoor skeet shooting.* One guy throws up a chunk of wood, the other guy draws and shoots. If you're a little slow on the upswing, play with a Styrofoam coffee cup; it will float to the ground much slower and therefore be much easier to draw a bead on.
- *Pest control.* Mouse or rat or—if you're working construction in the Bronx—cockroach hunting.
- *Catch.* You hold the gun, your buddy tries to catch the nails in his baseball glove. (TD)

A small note: While we're pleased to get tips and hints on how to make the workday go a little faster, we really don't recommend any of these fascinating pastimes. In fact, hard to believe, but the lackey-shoot might even be illegal. It's an OSHA thing.

HOW TO GO TO THE HARDWARE STORE

What is it about the subsonic cry of spare parts and hex nuts that makes us crazy? What is it in a man that drives him to saber saws and bell-housings?

Answer: hardware hormones. Men are loaded with the stuff: Hardware lust virtually fills the crotch of our Y chromosomes. Hardware is the bare bones of a modern man's life, the unassembled machinery of the masculine soul. Hardware is our congenital obsession, our shared affection, our gender responsibility, our primal yearning. Hardware is also fun to fool with.

So you're walking down Broadway, thinking, maybe, new necktie, when suddenly a hardware store reaches out, grabs you, and pulls you in. There you are, surrounded by strangely seductive bits of metal and plastic. You realize you've stumbled into a hidden corner of patriarchal holiness, where **two Main Things** are always assumed:

1. *Everything has its place.*
2. *Everything has a name.* Of course, that's where the hardware problem starts. While you may not know the name of every two-bit outside miter cap in the joint, you also want other guys—especially the guys in the hardware store—to think that you sure as hell would know exactly what to do with one if you had one on you. This, of course, can all be a bit overpowering for a do-it-yourself-if-it-looks-easy-enough kind of guy. Which brings us to the meat of our ministration here, the loin of our little lesson: how to hang with hardware.

First, you will note that *there are only two ways to visit a hardware store.*

1. *As a household paramedic.* Let's say the thing fell off the thing and you need a new thing right away. You know what it looks like—even though you don't know what it's called—so you cruise aisles until you find the right thing, and you're out of there.
2. *As a browser.* If you don't have a cover—such as searching for something you actually need—go as a tourist. Touch everything. See the way things work. Grab one of those anodized jobs and screw one of these on over the top, then press that lever, there. Push them plungers, retract them tapes. Pretend you just happened to wander in while your wife was across the street reaming out the Goodwrench guy who, as you understand it, countersunk your muffler bearing while the Olds was in for an oil change. Saunter slowly and enjoy the sights.

Talk Hardware

If you go into a hardware store and admit that you don't know the name of the doohickey you're looking for, not only will you be *girlified* by the clerk, you're also likely to walk out with a double-ringed doohickey instead of the plier-bolt doohickey you needed.

A better way: ***Simply describe the task you wish to accomplish.*** Instantly, all important hardware-store chores become not-your-problem. Let the clerk name the unknowable and introduce you to it properly. If he steers you wrong, you own the moral edge when you bring the wrong doohickey back to exchange it for the right doohickey.

Get in Touch with Your Needs

There's a lot in life you want, but only a few things you really need. You should know what they are before you get close to hardware, or you'll leave with a ten-pound bag full of whatever it takes to make a passing thought into a defeated ambition. Next stop: depression. Go slow if you're a hardware rookie. Remember, most of what you want in life may be found in a hardware store, not counting sex.

Organization Is Everything

This is what gives that warm glow to hardware aura, the one thing that distinguishes a hardware store from a big pile of junk. For, if we looked deep inside ourselves, we'd have to admit that for many of us, a good hardware store is not so much about home improvement but about *life* improvement, and most of us lead lives that could be improved with a little organization.

Hardware is improvement disassembled. For instance, men love to watch *This Old House* and *Home Again* and other Fixit Channel favorites. Why? It's ***makeovers for men*** . . . progressions of improvement, man-style. For instance, take an old car and redo it. Take an old house and redo it. Take your marriage and make it better. That's how men do makeovers. (TA)

At a hardware store, everything you need to fix a leaky household budget, repair a broken family value, or mend a tired metaphor is laid out in perfect order. Those long aisles filled with bins of screws, nails, bolts, nuts, nestled next to hinges and flanges and casters are the mesmerizing *Wesen* of a hardware store. This, you think, is what creation must have looked like before God tucked the first Tab A into the first Slot B. Thousands, no, millions, no, billions and billions of nameless pieces of the Great Puzzle—the microbes, fungi, bacilli of existence carefully disguised as washers, chalk lines, and dowel jigs—a whole world of widgets named, classified, and put in *exactly* the right place. If you really want to straighten up the government's mess, hire a bunch of hardware guys, because nobody knows organization like an ironmonger.

So, in a way, a hardware store is the perfect planet, where all we really need in order to find our way around is a little, tiny map showing its various continents.

Hardware World's Seven Continents

- *Tools*
- *Fasteners*
- *Paints and stains*
- *Electrical stuff*
- *Plumbing stuff*
- *Masonry stuff*
- *All other stuff*

Each of these is divided neatly into smaller units, until common sense leads you to the little box of fuses or whatever it is you've come to find.

Note: In most hardware stores, what distributors call "associated products" are next to each other—hinges are next to latches, and so forth. Odd and unusual items, however, are usually placed in a spot that's convenient for busy hardware guys. Since most oddball pieces have to be asked for anyway, there's no reason to scatter them throughout the store. (TZ)

Here are the landmarks:

TOOLS

Hand tools and electric tools both have this in common: Each of them is just what you need for some jobs, but *none of them is what you need for all jobs.* This is why manufacturers make it easy to tell the difference between an adjustable wrench and a ball peen hammer. Also, most hand tools have a venerable look to them: You can tell what they do and how they do it by just glancing at them. Some power tools—circular saws, for example, or hand drills—also have this quality, but the newer stuff—the sonar tapes, the .22-caliber hammers, and all that—have a sporting aspect that begs for additional insight beyond that available to most unhandy chaps.

FASTENERS

The fastener department is the fertile crescent of all hardware, the screws, nails, bolts, hinges, and hooks that make up the swampy ooze of the manufactured universe. The best way to navigate here is to comprehend the use of each type of fastener. Some are obvious: Hinges hinge and braces brace. The nuances come in the details surrounding such commonplace things as nails, screws, and bolts. For example, since all of these things—nails, screws, bolts—are used to join one thing to another, intention is everything.

Next, you want to understand how these things are classified.

- **Common nails.** I worked in a pub in London the year England gave up on shillings and half crowns and went Euro-decimal. Today, only common nails still have the charm of an almost completely logic-free system of measurement: They sell 'em by weight, and, no doubt purely for the sake of convenience, they measure 'em in units designated in old-style English pennies: 2d (a twopenny—but *not* tup'ny—nail, the smallest, at one inch), and 80d (a mega-spike). Sizes increase from 2d in quarter-inch increments (for example, a 3d nail is one and a quarter inches long) until you get to three-inch 10d nails; then the increments grow larger. Common nails hold better than headless finishing nails. At least on the planet of nails, there will always be an England.

- **Screws** are sold by length and gauge, which is expressed as an arbitrary number starting with two—teeny, skinny things of virtually no nondental use—and ending with giganto twenty-fours. The most useful wood screws are eights, tens, and twelves—between an eighth- and, say, a quarter-inch thick. Because they are required to fasten different types of materials, the three main types of screws aren't interchangeable: Wood screws generally have flat heads, shallow threads, and pointed tips. Metal screws have a thread running the entire length of the shank and a slightly deeper thread pattern than that found on a wood screw. They're used to hold sheet metal together. Machine screws are round-topped and flat-bottomed; they are actually small bolts, in that they accept a nut and washer.

- **Bolts** are arranged straightforwardly by length and width, all in inches. Ditto the nuts that go with them. Japanese and European products use metric sizing—which means a new set of wrenches to go with the nuts and bolts. Outrageous, really.

PAINTS AND STAINS

Here's all you really need to know: When it comes to paint, spend as much as you can and always go for latex. When it comes to other materials, such as preservatives and sealants, be specific when you describe what you wish to preserve. Decks are one thing; caskets are something else. To paint a wall, see the section of this chapter entitled "How to Hide the Handwriting on the Wall."

ELECTRICAL AND PLUMBING STUFF

All of this stuff is completely standardized, so there is no excuse for getting the wrong thing if you bring along whatever it is you're seeking to replace. But don't get carried away: If you're putting in a new kitchen drain, for example, leave the basin home. Just take along the plug and a good set of measurements.

MASONRY STUFF

This stuff isn't useful on anything but masonry. Don't try to put together a treehouse using masonry nails, for instance, and don't use Thoroseal as a caulk.

ALL OTHER STUFF

The last continent, *the miscellany department,* is where the heart and valve of a good hardware store can be found. The most obscure, rarefied tasks have a welter of metal and plastic components that, like bottom feeders in the Marianas Trench, only exist in one place, at one time. A great hardware store has them all. This is also where you can find the sash for your window of hardware opportunity: If you really want to talk ironmongery, specialize in mender fittings or compression joints. Since generalists are always in awe of specialists, this sort of narrow focus will buy you immediate respect—as well as a great deal of forbearance when you talk about mallets while holding a sledgehammer.

Ultimately, of course, nobody—not Bob Vila, not Tim Allen, and certainly not John Madden—knows everything about hardware, for if that were so, there would be no inventions left to invent, no hinges that squeaked, no faucets that dripped. The cool thing about hardware is that, given the right combination of time and tools and nuts and bolts, the unhandiest man in the world can stumble across a better—no, the best!—mousetrap imaginable while building himself a brand-new life.

Or he can just build a better bookcase.

HOW TO BUILD A BOOKCASE IN A REALLY SMALL APARTMENT USING PRACTICALLY NO WEIRD TOOLS

Men and wood are a matched set. For example, made properly, this bookshelf will outlast its maker, but made hastily, clumsily, it will mirror a life grown precarious with carelessness. You are what you make; thus is existence a hectoring thing, full of little lectures and lessons.

This is a quintessential bookshelf, a familiar classic. As it's designed, it's a masculine sort of piece—solid, practical, capable of bearing its responsibility without complaint. And, since it shelters so much of what we hold close, maybe it's right that we should make the thing ourselves.

Our bookcase is designed to be built by a woodshop rookie. It will take him eight to ten hours. A master carpenter can do the job in less than four hours.

What you need: Toolwise, the list of tools you'll need for this project is tiny, and, for the sake of the downstairs neighbors, excludes the use of power tools.

1. *A saw.*
2. *A square*—a tri-square or a combination square is best.
3. *A hand drill* with a quarter-inch bit.
4. *A hammer.*

You'll also need some furniture glue and some sandpaper—120 for the rough stuff, and 220 for finishing work. The rest are items from around the house: a yardstick maybe, and a pencil.

LUMBER

Go to your local version of Woodville with this list:

QUANTITY	DIMENSIONS	LENGTH
1	1 in. × 4 in.	37 in.
2	1 in. × 4 in.	34½ in. ea.
2	1 in. × 12 in.	60 in. ea.
5	1 in. × 12 in.	34½ in. ea.
1	1 in. × 8 in.	34½ in.
2	¼-in. dowels	36 in. ea.

Make sure you ask for clear-grade white pine. Clear-grade wood will have no knots. It costs a *lot.* If you want a more rustic look, ask for number two–grade wood.

Note: A first-rate lumberyard in a large city may cut these pieces to length for you.

Another note: Remember, a one-by-four-inch piece of wood isn't one inch thick, nor is it four inches wide. A one-by-four-inch measures three-quarters of an inch thick and three and one-half inches wide.

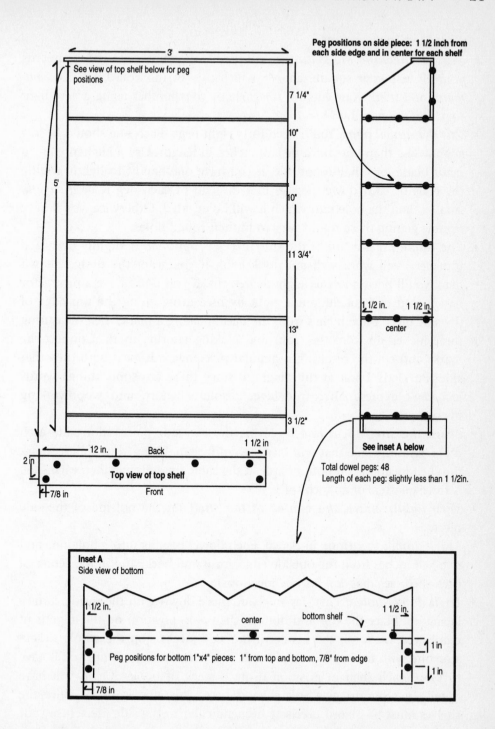

Peg positions on side piece: 1 1/2 inch from each side edge and in center for each shelf

See view of top shelf below for peg positions

3'

5'

7 1/4"

10"

10"

11 3/4"

13"

3 1/2"

1 1/2 in.   1 1/2 in.
center

See inset A below

Total dowel pegs: 48
Length of each peg: slightly less than 1 1/2in.

12 in.   Back   1 1/2 in
2 in
Top view of top shelf
7/8 in   Front

Inset A
Side view of bottom

1 1/2 in.   center   bottom shelf   1 1/2 in.

Peg positions for bottom 1"x4" pieces: 1" from top and bottom, 7/8" from edge

1 in

1 in

7/8 in

Step-by-Step Instructions

- Start by **checking the square of all pieces.** If you have to cut the boards yourself, use your square, choose which side of the board will face *out-ward*, and mark your cuts on that side of your lumber using a very light touch on the pencil.
- **Cut the dowel pegs.** You'll need forty-eight pegs. Each one should be just slightly less than one and one-half inches in length. Use a kitchen knife, a razor blade, or a half-round file, if you have one handy, to lightly whittle the ends of each dowel peg so that the end of each peg is *very slightly* smaller than the hole into which it will be inserted. Otherwise, you'll have trouble getting these round pegs to fit their round holes.
- **The angle on the top** of the side pieces is optional. A slightly oversized top piece will work well and look cool. If you want the design shown here, you'll need a twenty-eight-degree cut. If you don't have a protractor handy, you can get the angle right by measuring along the top edge of the side piece three inches from the back, making a mark, then measuring three inches up from the front and making another mark. Connect the marks and cut the resulting triangular piece away. Repeat with the other side. Puzzled? Look at the diagram, since there are some things words just can't express—like true love, absolute beauty, and woodworking instructions.
- **Mark the shelf locations** by laying the two side pieces alongside each other, with the side that will face inward faceup. Using your square, mark the shelf locations on both boards at the same time. Remember, each shelf is three-quarters of an inch thick.
- **Very lightly mark the center of the shelf** on the outside of the side pieces.
- **Mark dowel locations** in pencil. Each dowel peg fits into a hole one and one-half inches from the outside edge, front and back, and in the center of each shelf (see diagram for peg locations).
- **Drill dowel holes.** First, lay one side piece down with the inside surface facing up. Place the top and bottom shelves in position on the alignment marks you made on the inside of the side pieces. Top the whole rickety structure with the other side piece. If you don't have a clamp, you'll have to brace each shelf in position using a stack of books. Or, if you have friends, get one to give you a hand here. This step is tricky, since the shelves must be placed precisely perpendicular to the side piece (use your square to check), and they must be held in place as each hole is drilled.

- *Glue as you go.* After you drill the three holes for the bottom shelf, squeeze a small amount of glue into each hole. Then coat the inside of each hole with the glue using a toothpick or matchstick. Finally, insert the dowel peg. The peg should be flush with the side piece. If it requires coaxing, take a wood scrap, put it on top of the offending dowel, and tap it into position using a hammer or the heel of a shoe. Be careful not to hit the dowel so hard that the wood flares. Repeat this with the upper shelf. Then repeat with the three intermediate shelves and the top shelf. Then turn the structure over and repeat with the other side.
- *Neatness counts.* Should any glue ooze out of the hole after the dowel is inserted, wipe it away using a moist paper towel. If you leave any glue, the stain won't adhere to the surface, and the result will be a sloppy little halo around each messy peg hole.
- *Let the piece dry* overnight.
- *Sand* the piece so that the edges are eased and smoothly rounded. Use the coarser-grade sandpaper for this. Make sure all the dowels are flush and that the surfaces are smooth. Remove all dust.
- *Apply the stain* to the bookshelf using a rag to rub it in. The longer you let the stain set, the darker the stain will be. Caution: "Stain varnishes" are difficult to control. Get a simple stain in a color and shade you like. Let the stain dry according to the manufacturer's instructions.
- *Apply a semigloss or satin varnish* to the bookshelf. After it has dried thoroughly, sand the piece of furniture lightly with 220-grade sandpaper or soft steel wool. Dust thoroughly. Then apply another coat of varnish. Let dry.

That's it. But remember, a whole life fits into a good bookshelf, a piece of furniture that, unlike perhaps even our bed, contains the things we love and with which we'd *never* part. (KD)

HOW TO HIDE THE HANDWRITING ON THE WALL

Don't confuse painting a wall with painting a masterpiece. The difference between a wall painted by a household Picasso and the one you paint yourself is minimal. Just get it covered.

Latex, Please

Unless you have a specific need for enamel paint, skip it. The prep work and the cleanup are mindless time-eaters. Latex paint is the best thing to happen to paintbrushes since Tom Sawyer cut his toe.

How much latex paint should you buy? The rule of thumb is one gallon of paint per 450 square feet of wall space. That's assuming you can do the job in a single, thick coat.

For next to nothing, you can buy one of those cheap, plastic kid's pools downtown. For a big painting job, just fill the wading pool with water and toss the brushes, trays, and rollers into the pool as you go. Give everything a final squirt with the hose when you're ready to go.

By the way, if you end up using enamel despite our warnings and you get some of the paint on your skin, olive oil will take it right off. Works with latex, too, of course. (JS)

How to Prepare a Wall

- *Scrape off loose paint* with a scraper or putty knife.
- *Use spackle* to fill in holes and cracks, and to smooth out dents and rough spots. Even old paint can make a wall too rough to paint.
- *Sand down all rough surfaces.* A coat of primer on sanded spots will save you two coats of paint later.
- *Cover water-stained areas with a stain killer.* Stains on walls live forever, and unless you "seal" them, they'll show through the new coat of paint as well as they do through the old paint.
- *Remove all dust* from the walls, ceiling, and floors. Painting over dust is begging for trouble.
- *Cover window and door sashes with masking tape.* If you're painting down close to a narrow baseboard, remove the trim. Then tape newspaper along the floor and an inch or two up the wall so that when you replace the baseboard, only new paint will show. (JS)

How to Paint a Wall

- *Take it from the top*—ceiling first. Use a brush to paint a narrow strip around the perimeter of the ceiling.
- *Load the roller* with paint evenly, but be sure it is not saturated to the point where it will drip. If you see a thick bead of paint along the edge of the roller's track of color, you're using too much.
- *Work in small patches.* Cover three or four square feet at a time in a zigzag motion—first away from you and then back to cover the parts you missed. Once you have covered several adjoining patches, crisscross over the entire area to make sure that the paint is applied uniformly over each section.

- *Always paint toward the light source,* never painting more area than you can easily reach. Faraway chunks of wall tend to get short shrift, so move your ladder frequently. Start in a dry area and work toward an area that has already been painted. If you try to do it the other way around and feather the color out toward the unpainted part of the wall, you'll only create a big patch of paint surrounded by lots of barely painted wallboard.

- *Use a brush* not only to paint around the edges of the wall at the ceiling, but also in the corners and around doors and windows.

- *Shield it.* If the color you are painting is different from that on the other walls or the ceiling, use a piece of cardboard to protect those surfaces as well as moldings and baseboards.

- *To avoid drips,* make sure the first stroke after you reload the roller is an upward one.

- *Work quickly*—or as quickly as you can without making a huge mess. Semidry paint looks different from wet paint, so if you work at a brisk pace, you'll have a much easier time judging how much paint you need to cover the wall and where touch-ups are needed. (JS, GSte)

If wall painting is too *basic,* too mundane, too down-to-earth, you can elevate your newfound hardware expertise with this small exercise in aeronautical engineering.

HOW TO BUILD A BOMBER USING A MATCHSTICK AND A BUNCH OF FROZEN FLIES

This is the kind of handyman derring-do that made America great:

- *Take a wooden matchstick* and slice a thin sliver down one side. Then cut the remaining stick in two, lengthwise. Make sure you leave a little of the red tip intact for effect. Discard half the 'stick.

- *Make the aircraft* by gluing the sliver of wood—the wing—across the remaining part of the matchstick—the fuselage. If you want, you can use little scraps to make a tail section. Or you can make a biplane. Or you can use a couple of thin slices of balsa to make a huge wing, one that will carry maybe *twenty* engines. Indulge your aeronautical whims. Think of lift, think of thrust, think of innovation without benefit of an industrial policy.

- *Catch a bunch of flies.* Put them in a jar and put the jar in the freezer. In a few seconds, the flies will be chilled out completely. (Male honeybees also work swell, but sexing bees can be tricky work.) This is called cryogenics, and it has its drawbacks. For example, the flies will be *dead flies* if you freeze them for too long. Dead flies are no good. So if you're a slow tinkerer, simply refrigerate your flies. It takes longer to make them comatose, but they have a much higher rate of recovery than the ones you leave in the freezer.

- *Meanwhile, put a tiny drop* of rubber cement at each place along the wing where you want an engine.
- *Take the flies out of the freezer.* Attach the abdomen of one frigid fly to each drop of glue. *Make sure all the flies are facing the same direction.*
- *Breathe life into the flies.* A miracle: A gentle puff of your warm breath will resuscitate the flies.
- *Launch the aircraft.* It should fly like a charm, and, far from being cruel to the flies, you'll be teaching them a new and valuable thing, one which brings us to the virtue of this exercise. For we see that while flies have a great deal in common, think a lot alike, share many hopes and dreams, they never act in concert, as a team, with regard for the worth of other, neighboring flies, *until forced by grim circumstance*—as, for example, when they are harnessed to fly and either first experience the exhilaration of high-altitude cooperation or die. Redeemed by such a critical choice, they'll soar like a glider, race like a Stealth, and, when overflying a barn-yard or kennel, turn into an awesome-wicked dive-bomber.

Machinery

When you combine hardware with a full tank of gasoline, you get an alchemy all men understand. For when it comes to essential information, there are some things guys just *know.* For example, men *know* baseball, the same way they *know* how to change tires in the rain while maintaining a casual conver-sation with their wives, the way they can make a clothesline peg from third to first without warming up, the way they can kill anything that flies or crawls, the way they can operate anything that burns gas or oil. Right? Somewhere in our genetic baggage, there's an old manual that contains the instructions to all these things, and if we've lost track of it, well, who needs directions, anyway? Right?

Right—up to a point. In fact, it's the common acceptance of what must be called manly skills that sharpens the competitive edge among men and makes them hotdog like maniacs in front of women.

Take heavy equipment.

You get two guys standing around a tractor, and you get big-time testosterone-talk. Chain saws do this, too. So do motorcycles, welding tools, and pit bulls. Backhoes do it big-time. Men were *born* to backhoe. Blenders and juicers would do it if they were powered by Briggs & Stratton eight-horsepower OHV single-stroke engines and had a decent transmission. In fact, anything in the physical world not feminized is contested territory among men—especially if there are women around.

HOW TO MAKE THE EARTH MOVE

Now, a tractor is a loud, massive piece of machinery dedicated to the constructive exercise of *power.* Men understand work, and tractors are built for work. *Ergo,* real men understand tractors. Big Olivers and old Hart-Parrs, modern Deeres and lightweight Kubotas are beautiful pieces of iron and steel. Guys slap the metal on these monsters the way they grip a brother's shoulder. They're big, strong, and *functional.* Like Brigitte Nielsen, I guess. Around heavy equipment, gauntlets are everywhere. One guy tosses the keys to the other guy and says, "Try her out?"

You're the other guy. What do you do?

Mount Up

The thing that gets guys who don't know heavy equipment in trouble is their expectation of speed. You'd think that because something's big and loud, it ought to have speed, too. But that's where you'd go wrong. Any man can drive any piece of equipment if he just takes his time. It's all in what kind of expectations you have. When it comes to heavy equipment, just don't expect speed.

Skid shovels, 'dozers, and other kinds of grading equipment—stuff that pushes: Work slowly, from top to bottom. Say you've got a wall of dirt in front of you. You're not going to get far trying to dig from the bottom; you'll never lift the whole thing. So take it off the top, a bit at a time, and pretty soon you'll make a molehill out of that mountain. (LL)

A skid shovel lifts, a 'dozer pushes. But they both steer like a tank—with sticks that are essentially brakes used to stop the treads on one side of the machine or the other.

Backhoes and other similar kinds of excavation machinery can dig and lift. You're moving the arm up and down, scooping with the bucket, and turning the arm to drop what you've scooped. Go slowly, no matter how good you get. Some guys are like sculptors with these things. But they never hurry: Swinging a bucket into another guy's head will kill him *right now.* (FE)

The value of a backhoe can be determined by looking at two things: the hydraulics and the supports. Other stuff comes second. Tires, for example, don't matter at all. (JD)

Sod Busters
Farm tractors are the cabriolets of heavy equipment—kind of sporty compared to big, yellow earthmovers. Some general tractorial principles:

- *Gravity:* If you're pulling weight and you have to go downhill, use a gear one step lower than the one you think you'll need. If the weight starts pushing the tractor, whatever you do, don't step on the clutch. You'll only go flying. Most tractor accidents are caused by pulling too heavy a load behind too light a tractor. You're fine on level ground, but when you head downhill, you'll lose it. (FSO'R)

- *Steer with the brakes*—one for the right wheel, one for the left—as well as with the steering wheel. In fact, you can drive a tractor with complete control using nothing but the brakes, provided you take it slow.

- *Narrow front-end tractors*—with a wheel configuration like a tricycle—are great for farming crops in rows. But you can flip one of these on level ground at five miles per hour by just turning too sharply.

The most perilous tractor is the Oliver 70, made from 1935 until the 1950s. The entire tractor—with the exception of the transmission pan—sits above the center of gravity.

Be especially cautious using a front-end loader on a trike tractor; lifting the bucket raises the center of gravity, and if you're on even a slight slope, you can flip. Wide front-end tractors are essential for utility work and for use on hilly ground. (KJ)

CARS
How to Assemble a Collection of Good, Reliable, American Cars
There are four good reasons that God made three major American auto companies:

- *For hauling:* Get a Ford truck if you want unspectacular dependability. In Pennsylvania, there's a 1965 Ford with 300,000 miles on it. It used to belong to a guy who drove through the Alleghenies once a week from farm to farm picking up chickens, then drove them 150 miles to a chicken soup factory in Baltimore. Ford doesn't make ritzy trucks, but its trucks do deliver the goods, and that's what counts. (HJ)

- *For women:* Wives love sporty little coupes until they become kid toters, at which time they want the mom equivalent of a Ford truck—namely, a Chrysler Corporation sedan, the kind you can start on a thirty-below morning and race off down the street after letting it warm up for all of three seconds. Dream car: a 1987 Plymouth Caravelle with less than 45,000 miles on it. These are the most dependable cars in the history of man on Earth. If you find one, buy it and kiss it full on the lips. (HJ, BE)

- *Family value:* For general, all-purpose family cartage, go for a Chevy Suburban, in which the back seat is far enough removed from the front seat to make the loudest of kids look damned cute. Suburbans aren't real fancy, but they're real big.
- *Manly motors:* Bonus! A souvenir of a Big Four era: a 1981 Jeep Scrambler—a kind of short-bed pickup built for swamp walking. A Scrambler is exactly what every chap needs to provide testicular transportation when riding the road just isn't dangerous enough: Going full-throttle across the furrows of an overgrown cornfield is the way we used to do kidney surgery in this country, back when men were men.

How to Buy a Used Car

With as much *sangfroid* and *insouciance* as you can muster (although never use words like those around used-car guys, lest you become encumbered with Renaults). Buying used cars should be like buying tropical fish. They may be stupid, and they may be useless, and they may die tomorrow, but they're sort of cool and sort of fun, for a while. Here's how to do it. If you follow this advice, you'll end up with a really interesting stable of horsepower.

- *Fifteen-grand Cherokee:* First, buy one really good, dependable, get-you-there car.
- *Make sure it's something no more than two years old,* with as much warranty left on it as possible. But don't be a chump: Never buy a new car. A one- or two-year-old car, with a warranty, is a much, much better deal.
- *Pay attention* to what you're buying, and *spend what it takes.* In order to be free to buy what you want, you must first buy what you *need.* Once that's out of the way, you're ready to go used-car shopping.
- *Bicmobiles:* Buy a bunch of fooling-around cars, but never spend more than a thousand dollars on any one of them, and never spend more than twenty minutes contemplating each purchase because it just doesn't matter.

A personal observation: My first fooling-around car was a 1954 Merc with only one forward gear and no reverse. Cost: twenty-five dollars. This was in 1965, maybe. Me and another guy towed it across the Mojave with the intention of pushing it into the Grand Canyon just to see it happen, but it got totaled in Brawley when a semi ran the red light, missed me, but got my fooling-around car broadside. Not long ago, when my normal car was in the shop for major rehab, I blew five hundred dollars on a 1972 Cadillac Eldorado Sedan de Ville de Luxe, or something. It was powered by a 750-cubic-foot engine that sounded like it was running on grizzlies. It weighed twenty-two tons, got five gallons to the mile, was three feet longer than the shortest Winnebago, had a rear landing dock for choppers, and would plow through five-foot snowdrifts, no sweat. You could sublet the trunk to Miata drivers looking for a safe place to stow their children. It was seriously loaded; the headlights dimmed themselves, and you could change radio stations with a little foot-button on the floor. The interior was done up in seasick green, streaked with tobacco residue, and it had matching silk-brocade upholstery on seats longer than most convertible sofas. Once, before I became a responsible married man, I held open the door for a date who took one look inside and said, "I don't know. Getting into this car is like checking into a cheap motel," which was sort of what I had in mind. I drove it for a year, then gave it to Bob Friedman so his band, the Mambo Combo, could use it to cart around amps and marimbas—although now I wish I'd kept it for livestock.

There are lots of cars you can buy for less than a grand, and some of them are cars you always meant to own but never did because your dad or common sense wouldn't let you. Like a Chevy II with a 327, or a Marlin. Last week, I almost spent six hundred dollars on a 1975 Lincoln Town Car that had been made into a kind of convertible, but the yard's full.

Remember, though, we're talking Bicmobiles here, lads, so drive as if you'll blow the tranny in a week, no problem. Look around small lots or in the classifieds for these babes. Auctions are good. Or drive down to Wheeling. The entire state of West Virginia is devoted to pompous pork politicians and the gaudy, sawdust-packed, STP-filled, nearly stationary limos they rode in on.

HOW TO READ IDIOT LIGHTS

They blink, you blink, and it's not love. It's trouble. But the trouble with idiot lights on a dashboard is they don't tell you what little they know. Not only are they idiot lights, they're flat outright *dumb*. If they could talk, though, here's what they'd say.

Hot

The message here is that the engine is, well, *hot*. Way too hot to drive, so pull over, shut it down, turn on the radio, and wait for exactly two innings.

Problem: The car's overheated because the engine isn't getting sufficient coolant. That's probably it. But it could also be overloaded; slow down, turn off the a/c, and see if that helps. No? Then it could be the thermostat.

What you do: When the motor cools down, open the radiator cap. If you do this before the engine's cool, you'll steam-blast the skin right off your face and spend the rest of your life looking like the front-page star of *Weekly World News.* So the first thing to check is the temperature of the engine. Is it cool? Cool. Check the water level; if you can see metal inside the radiator instead of fluid, you're dry. Need some water? Add some—but not until you've first checked all the hoses and belts. Grab the fan and try to wiggle it front-to-back. If it seems slightly loose, you need a new water pump. Medium bucks. Maybe it's the thermostat. You'll find it right where the big hose from the radiator comes into the engine. Check it out. If everything looks jake, but the car still overheats, don't drive it. Call Mr. Holmes. Never drive a car without coolant in it. You may get a mile or so down the road, but the whole engine will seize up and you'll be out of pocket a grand or two.

Alt

This means the alternator's not charging the battery. You can putt along for a few miles, but you're running on Delco alone, so don't press it.

Problem: Belt's loose. That's if you're lucky. If you're not, the belt's broken. Or the alternator's shot. If it's neither, the problem's in the electrical system. If you smell something weird in the engine compartment—say, burned wire insulation—take the keys out of the car so you don't accidentally put juice through the system, causing the damaged wire to spark, igniting the gas in the engine, spreading fire and mayhem through the car until the gas tank gets a flicker, then—you get the picture.

What you do: Replace the belt; replace the alternator; replace the wire. If the problem is just a loose belt, you can tighten it by using a wrench and a prying bar and a little common sense. (NG, DD)

Oil

There's no oil. Don't drive.

Problem: Probably you. When was the last time you checked the oil?

What you do: Add some. Check the dipstick. If the level's still low, look under the car for the quart of oil you just poured in. Engines need oil to run. Don't try anything funny.

Brake

The emergency or parking brake is on.

Problem: The brake isn't releasing completely. Or maybe you're low on brake fluid.

What you do: Jiggle the brake handle. If that doesn't work, drive forward and backward a bit. Or, if you can spot it, check the emergency brake cable; on older cars—especially on older Ford trucks—the thing freezes up for no good reason. If none of this has any effect, check the brake fluid in the reservoir under the hood. (GR)

HOW TO DO DOWN-AND-DIRTY DIAGNOSTICS

If coolant flush were tea leaves, you'd know exactly what the immediate future holds for your jalopy. Here's how to read the alarming puddles of liquid under your broken-down car.

PUDDLE COLOR	LOCATION	DIAGNOSIS
Greenish bluish	Front end	Antifreeze. Something's leaking someplace—or you've overheated to the point where coolant is running out the vent. Keep the pooch away, incidentally. Dogs love lapping antifreeze. In fact, they *die* for it.
Black, dark brown	Front, probably	Oil leak. Check the plug on the oil pan.
Red	Front	Transmission or power-steering fluid. If it's tranny fluid, you'll probably see it leaking out from around the transmission fluid pan, just behind the car's oil pan. If it's power-steering fluid, you'll see it leaking out from one of the hoses running between the power-steering pump and the steering gearbox.
Clear	Anywhere	Hmm. Brake fluid's clear. Check the level in the master cylinder. Is it gasoline? Smell it. Gas leaks are a real mess—and dangerous, too. If you don't know how to track the fuel line and check the fittings, get it towed to somebody who does. Maybe it's just water. This is America's most common under-car puddle. Take the kids, load them in the car, drive around, and see for yourself: On a hot day, cars are dripping sweat like an indicted Arkansas banker. It's condensation from the air conditioner.

PUDDLE COLOR	LOCATION	DIAGNOSIS
Clear	Anywhere	Could be windshield-washer solution. Check the reservoir. It always made of plastic, so leaks aren't uncommon. Stuff's toxic, by the by.
Brown	Front	Power-steering juice, probably. Could also be oil. Could even be dirty water.
Yellow	Tires	Dogs. (GR, NG)

TRANSPORTATION TOOL KIT

When you're on the road, your trunk should contain:

- A jack and a spare, of course.
- Jumper cables.
- A few wrenches, screwdrivers, and a pair of pliers.
- A quart of oil and a jug of windshield-cleaning solvent.
- Paper towels.
- Flashlight.
- Fire extinguisher. (GR)
  Semidissent: You're better off with an extinguisher *inside* the car. (DD)

HOW TO HAVE FUN WITH CHAIN SAWS

Hardware in bins may be fun. But you stick enough hardware together to make yourself a loud and dangerous machine, and, buddy, you're having man-sized fun.

This isn't a universal appreciation, by the way. In urban areas, danger isn't normally associated with machines. It's associated with lawyers and women. In fact, if you actually need evidence that it is no longer a man's world, allow me to point out that you could evacuate the entire New York Stock Exchange, turn the building upside down, and not find a single chain saw—proof the World of Work has been thoroughly feminized.

Outside Manhattan, where work actually involves *labor*, it's different. Chain saws are everywhere. Every guy's got a 'saw. I hang mine from my rearview. Guy down the road uses his as a key ring. We have lots of them because, even if we don't need them, we love them. Why? Well, for one thing, they're noisy. For another, they're dirty. And for another, they're *really* dangerous. And, for those city dwellers who may at this point be confused and in need of help to distinguish chain saws from bad wives, cranky bosses, and congressional Democrats, there's one other thing about chain saws: They're a good time.

How to Make an Indian out of a Tree

According to our correspondent, if you want to carve a wooden Indian, you've got to look deep into the heart of an ancient coastal forest and *see* the wooden Indian you want to make: "I use old-growth redwood to do my carving because I live in Big Sur and that's what's around. It's perfect for me because it's a soft wood and, also, it's big and I like making big stuff. But if you're living back East, you might want to use a lot of white pine or cedar. Stay away from the harder woods. It's rough on the equipment. Working with wood is just like working with marble or anything else: You've got to see the sculpture in the raw materials you're working with and then take away everything that doesn't belong."

BASIC KNOWLEDGE

If you want to carve, you've got to know three things:

1. *How to operate the saw.*
2. *How to stay safe.* You'll want to know how to keep your fingers and toes, arms and legs, and head intact.
3. *How to look at a piece of wood.* You've got to know how to visualize things and then get your hands to work with your head to create them. Any idiot can carve wood with a chain saw, says our tree-sculpting source, just like any idiot can make a newsletter with a computer. Power is not the answer. Artistry is.

TAKING PRECAUTIONS

- *Assuming you know how to operate a chain saw* and are comfortable handling one, take all the usual precautions: Before you start the saw, swing it around your head in every direction and in a 360-degree circle around your body and work space to clear the area and make sure you're not going to hit something with the blade.
- *Assuming you don't know how to use a chain saw* and you aren't comfortable handling one: Wood sculpting is suicide. First things first. Put in some time with a saw and some trees before you start contorting your body into strange positions trying to make a wooden Indian's nose look right.
- *Wear the right safety equipment:* That's goggles, ear muffs, dust mask, chaps for your legs. "The chaps, they tell me, will make the chain saw

blade bind up if you screw up and run the blade against your leg. I've never tried it, and don't ever intend to. Some guys wear a helmet, but I save that for when I'm roller blading and making love." (SB)

SIZE COUNTS

The size of the saw you use depends on the size of the wood and the kind of detail work you're doing. You start with a big saw to take away the big chunks of wood, and as you start working in finer and finer detail you use a smaller and smaller saw. Some saws have special carving bars with fine tips. They range in size from one with a four-foot bar all the way down to one of the smallest, which has a twelve-inch bar and a tip on it that's about as big around as a quarter. Some guys stop there, where chain saws end, but you can keep going and do even finer detail work with a die grinder and big drummel tool that has a bunch of different bits you can use to finish things off. There are all kinds of sanders and sanding burrs you can use for the finest detail work.

If you're working with big enough wood, you can just lie it down on the ground and it will pretty much stay where you put it. If you're working with smaller wood, take a piece of plywood and drive a screw through it and the wood you want to carve. Then screw the plywood into an old log stump or something, and have at her. (SB)

How to Build a Small Livestock Shelter in Three Hours

Here's a final project that combines everything you need to know about hard-ware *and* machinery:

What you need: Three poles, each at least twenty feet long. A pallet-load of cheap lumber. Eight two-by-four-by-eights, cheapest, roughest stud-grade you can buy. A post-hole digger. A nail gun. A chain saw. Some tin. A cooler full of cans. Two friends.

- *Step one:* Take the chain saw and cut eight feet off the end of each post.
- *Step two:* Dig six holes three feet deep in two rows. You want the posts to be about seven feet apart from each other, so you have a rectangle measuring approximately fourteen by seven.
- *Step three:* Drop the shorter poles into one set of holes, and the longer ones into the other. Fill in the holes with concrete, if it's handy, or dirt if it's not.
- *Step four:* Run the two-by-fours around the top and bottom on three sides of the rectangle. Just bang them in place with the nail gun. Bang-

bang-bang. Three nails on each board at each post. Then run the lumber side by side. Keep the bottom a couple of inches off the ground. Don't worry about the tops.

- **Step five:** Trim off the excess with the chain saw. Among fine cabinet-makers, this is called "finish carpentry."
- **Step six:** Nail board "headers" across the top of the tall posts and across the top of the short posts, one on each side of the post. Make the boards on the front of the posts slightly higher than the boards on the back. Then bang in boards connecting the two sets of headers, one every two feet or so. If you really want some structural soundness, nail these rafters in place on edge. Trim off the ends with the chain saw.
- **Step seven:** Nail the tin to the rafters and feed the horses.

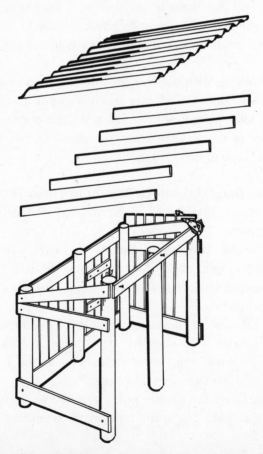

How to Keep Rain off a Donkey's Back: This thing goes together in a morning, especially if you have a nailgun and a couple of pals. Use the chain saw to do the delicate finish work.

2. Technology

For those who like technology, there are two complementary views of everything that beeps, whirs, and updates in the night. One view sees all technological advancement as a manifestation of man's spiritual progress toward God, in which that which is bad—famine, disease, boredom, ignorance—is defeated by that which is good—more efficient agriculture, better medicine, livelier entertainment, more accessible information. And while I encourage all of you lads to reflect on progress only in those terms, I am forced to admit that there is another, perhaps less exalted way of looking at our relationship to technology: We think gadgets are really cool.

How to Find Appropriate Technology

Many men are gadget freaks. Good thing, too, for technology is everywhere, and yet we still feel like we could use a little more. These are complex times, so the notion that you can buy a little control by plugging in the right chip makes more and more sense to more and more men.

THE ANTHROPO-TECHNO-TRUTH

The above phenomenon is understandable only in anthropological terms. After all, there are two ways you can make any chunk of the physical universe instantly desirable to a modern man: You can either put a blond wig on it and dress it sassy, or stick a small, red LED on it and call it cellular. Either way, you take something perhaps quite commonplace—your average woman, maybe, or a small box made of PVC plastic—and elevate it to something you're certain holds great potential for making your life better, easier, more pleasurable, maybe even more useful.

There's a downside to that short upside, for the things that promise to make everything better usually break that promise right after the warranty's up. Most laborsaving devices generate much more labor than the labor they were supposed to save.

But as easily as we are driven to want to possess that which has either long, golden hair or a suppresser-clad power cord, we are just as easily disappointed by that gaudy trinket we so ardently wish to make our own. When we first spot the object of our desire, we see that it will make a tremendous difference to the way we live. Whether it's a blonde or a PowerMac, we figure if we can just hold on to it, keep up with it, maintain it, it will make us better than other men. It will give us a kind of value-added edge. Not only can we be who we are, but we can also add a whole layer of new stuff to our already impressive selves. So we pay for it and plug it in. But sooner or later, after building you way up, that little widget you had to have is going to let you way down. And when the tumble comes, it hurts.

WHAT MEN WANT

Let's start by making some useful observations about men. Ultimately, men are interested in only two things: finding the meaning of life and scoring with women. It is extremely taxing to make a continuous inquiry into the meaning of life, so instead we spend way too much time doing that which comes easier—although no man will ever suggest that living with women is easy. But it is easier than finding God.

Now, let's talk about machines. There are only two reasons we like machines. One, they promise to save us work. Any guy loves that. Two, they impress women. How? By making us more powerful. A guy with a PowerPC 604 in his noggin, a RAM doubler in his shorts, and a backhoe for a mitt has what it takes.

So this little men-and-machines problem has a certain algebraic charm to it, no? By cross-multiplying, we can see that the best machines are those that give us easy access to women.

That's why the Internet is so wildly popular. The Internet's World Wide Web does for PCs what Pamela Anderson does for TV sets. That is, not only can you enjoy sparkling repartee from the bimbos of cyberspace, but you can also check 'em out, right there on your monitor. Boys like to imagine owning X-ray specs in the hope that a little technological advancement will help them properly objectify women. But when they grow up, they realize technology has trumped their desires: Grown-ups can *monitor* women—they can download 'em and digitize 'em and store 'em in a hard drive. Once, the best you could get from a PC was an interoffice memo and a balanced checkbook. Now you can get Estelle's Lingerie Homepage. That's why most of us think the Internet represents progress. If you equate enhanced technology for objectifying women with progress, then that's exactly what you've got.

Wrong, of course. This is nothing but a betrayal of progress. And it serves us right, for while progress may save us work or amuse us, new gadgets also come with a whole set of new technical—and moral—problems: Technically, the measure of value they promise to give to us is directly proportional to the amount of work they require to set up, take down, upgrade, and maintain. This isn't universally true, of course—witness the tire jack and the bike pump. But it's usually true of virtually all technology, and it's expressly true of virtual technology, in which there is no gadget with fewer than two moving parts. Morally, any tool that permits us to do all we can do without a clear awareness of what we ought to do is plain dangerous.

The fact is there are many things we don't need at all.

GO LUDDITE

Instead of buying a new gadget, see what you can avoid buying.

- *Upgrades.* Unless you have a technical application for a computer, the thing is nothing but a combination typewriter/slide rule. If you're a writer, say, a new computer won't help you type faster or wisecrack better. It won't buy you lunch at Morty's, and it won't convince HarperCollins that if they'd just stop nagging you, maybe the damn book would get done. So why upgrade? A ten-year-old computer will do all the word processing and household record keeping any civilian needs. On the other hand, if you use your computer for any technical application or for graphics or design work, figure a three- to five-year lifespan for even the most sophisticated system, and buy accordingly.

- *Printers.* Attention, add-on nuts: You can buy special computer printers for envelopes. People have discovered that even though they've spent ten grand on a new high-speed laser printer, they still can't get the thing to put the electric company's address on an envelope. One chap's solution: Pick up a Remington portable—ten bucks, tops—at a yard sale. The dynamic impact of letterforms pressed through a cloth ribbon is unique and compelling.

- *Satellite television.* Even with five hundred choices, there's still nothing good on TV. So forget satellite television, and while you're at it, yank the cable, too. If you really need to watch TV, you can watch it the way God intended for it to be watched: On a black-and-white portable with a coat hanger sticking out the back.

- *Engine-compartment computers.* Here's the makings of a good class-action lawsuit brought by backyard mechanics everywhere: To do a tune-up on any car made within the last, oh, ten years or so, you have to have a computerized rig capable of reading the computer installed in the car by the manufacturer. Each manufacturer requires a different computer, and some require many different computers. The solution is to buy precomputerized used cars. An old car with low miles is better than a new car with no miles, dollar for dollar, every time, almost. That's a guarantee. You have it in writing.

WHAT MEN NEED

Essential technology can actually be as much fun as the stupid stuff. The problem is, the technology we really need isn't yet on the market. But where there's a demand, there's a supply, so stay tuned for the following:

- *Smart Willy.* We need new technology in the stupid decisions department. For example, Jockey needs to come up with a little peter-Pentium, something that will make a racket like a beat dog when you start to tell your secretary about your lanky friend, Mister Johnson.

- **Moral compass.** This has been much discussed lately. William Bennett and Mother Teresa have both been talking up the need for this kind of tool, and now even the president, General Bill, has noticed that he gets completely turned around every time he sets foot in the wilderness of modern ethics. Should be priced right so it's a good value. And it ought to be portable, maybe a small handheld number, like the Apple Newton, with a little arrow that always points to "Right," the reciprocal of "Wrong."

  User tip: Point the thing at Barbara Boxer, the Chuck Barris of the U.S. Senate, as she defends late-term abortions on Friday, then anguishes over a decision to remove the dolphin-safe label from tuna cans on Monday. But watch for meltdown.

- **Danger replicator.** It would be nice to have something that would suggest the adrenaline-pumping presence of life-threatening danger where there really isn't any. This is the principle on which roller coasters and *Friday the Thirteenth* movies operate. One suggestion: An alignment buster you can attach to the front end of your car to give it a wild shimmy at speeds in excess of, say, seventy-five miles per hour. Or something that would make the car careen like crazy while taking a corner in a normal suburban neighborhood. Of course, you can always just hire a teenage boy to drive you to work, but talk about high maintenance!

- **Dialectical technology.** This is where you create a gadgetary life-form by taking two or more middlin' gadgets, combining them, and getting one huge, life-changing mega-gadget. Then you take that gadget and go full-Hegel with it: Attach it to other gadgets, thus yielding yet another über-gadget, and so on.

  For instance, the only reason men watch TV is there's a good chance you can spot a good-looking woman every thirty seconds or so. So TV is a piece of technology we can all love. But how do you make it into a technological expression of an entire lifestyle? Simple. You take a twenty-five-inch TV set that shows nothing except the babe scenes in *Baywatch.* You mount that on top of a 750-watt Panasonic microwave with a slow-mo turntable in which you've custom-installed a few red-hot bean burritos and cheddar cheese, and what do you have? A technological replacement for that women's studies major you've been dating. But that's just the start. Add a Bud-laden club refrigerator to the bottom tier, and you're talking technolife as it was meant to be lived. The good thing about dialectical technology is that it has endless possibility for modification. Some guys—and they're writing letters to the editor right now—are superior human beings and don't wish to be known as couch-mounted butt watchers. Who knows why? Relax, all you Michael Kinsley lookalikes. With an understanding of dialectical technology, you can make a few mods—remove your *Baywatch* module and slam in a PBS card with a *Dr. Quinn* override, yank the bean bombs and sub a box of Weight Watcher's spaghetti with white clam sauce, and ditch the brew and slide in a box of Aussie white. Now, add a copy of the *New Yorker* to keep the goo off the coffee table, and you've got a whole new senso-guy model gadget.

Rule of thumb: Qualified service repairs on any household appliance are much less expensive than the best alimony arrangement known to man.

How to Surf the Web

Bitchin.' Here's the techno-board you need to wax before you shoot a curl:

- *A computer, of course.* But you don't need a *great* computer. A fair-to-middling computer will do just fine.
- *A high-speed modem.* At press time, 28.8 was the standard. But by the time you read this, high-speed Internet access may be much more commonplace.
- *An account with a flat-rate Internet access provider,* such as AT&T or MCI.

    Rule of thumb: If your Internet-access bill exceeds your cable TV bill, you're doing it all wrong.
- *A Web browser*—the software that allows you to view the graphic part of the Internet. Each browser "sees" the Web differently. Some—like Netscape—see it as it was designed to be seen. Some—like AOL's bowser of a browser—are dreadful.

    What you don't need:

    An oversized monitor.

    Big stereo speakers.

    Your own home page.

How to Read AFEs

Every computer chat board is cluttered with abbreviations designed to save space and time in communicating. Trouble is, there are now so many of these

AFEs—acronyms for everything—that Internet tourists need a phrasebook in order to communicate with the natives.

AAMOF	As A Matter Of Fact
AFAIK	As Far As I Know
AWGTHTGTTA	Are We Going To Have To Go Through This Again?
AWGTHTGTATA	(. . . Through *All* This Again?)
BBFN	Bye Bye For Now
BIOYA	Blow It Out Your A**
BIOYIOP	Blow It Out Your Input-Output Port
BRB	Be Right Back (generally used on chat systems)
BTA	But Then Again
BTW	By The Way
BYKT	But You Knew That
BYKTA	But You Knew That Already
CMIIW	Correct Me If I'm Wrong
CYL	See You Later
DNPM	Darn Near P***ed Myself
EOD	End Of Discussion
EOL	End Of Lecture
ESOSL	Endless Snorts of Stupid Laughter
FDROTFL	Falling Down Rolling On The Floor Laughing
FITB	Fill In The Blank. . . .
FOTCL	Falling Off The Chair Laughing
FWIW	For What It's Worth
GD&R	Grin, Duck, & Run
GOK	God Only Knows
IAC	In Any Case
IITYWYBAD	If I Tell You, Will You Buy Another Drink
IITYWYBMAB	If I Tell You, Will You Buy Me A Beer
IMCDO	In My Conceited Dogmatic Opinion
IMHO	In My Humble Opinion
IMNSHO	In My Not So Humble Opinion
INPO	In No Particular Order
IOW	In Other Words
KCBIWIYWI	Keep Coming Back, It Works If You Work It
LLTA	Lots and Lots of Thunderous (or Thundering) Applause
LOL	Laughing Out Loud
LMAO	Laughing My A** Off
MUNG	Mash Until No Good
NICBDAT	Nothing Is Certain But Death And Taxes
NIMBY	Not In My Backyard
NIMTO	Not In My Term of Office
NPLU	Not People Like Us
NQOS	Not Quite Our Sort
OIC	Oh, I See
OTOH	On The Other Hand
PGY	Post Graduate Year (PGY-1, -2, etc.—used in PGY Med.)

PMETC	Pardon Me Etc.
PMYMHMMFSWGAD	Pardon Me, You Must Have Mistaken Me For Someone Who Gives A Damn
PTO	Patent and Trademark Office
ROFL	Rolling On Floor Laughing
ROFLAHMSL	Rolling On Floor Laughing And Holding My Sides Laughing
ROTBA	Reality On The Blink Again
ROTFL	Rolling On The Floor Laughing
ROTFLASTC	Rolling On The Floor Laughing And Scaring The Cat
ROTFLMAAOBPO	Rolling On The Floor Laughing My A** And Other Body Parts Off
ROY G. BIV	Red Orange Yellow Green Blue Indigo Violet (colors of the spectrum)
RSN	Real Soon Now
RTFM	Read The F**** Manual
SWAG	Simple Wild-A** Guess
SYT	Sweet Young Thing (Thang)
TANJ	There Ain't No Justice
TANSTAAFL	There Ain't No Such Thing As A Free Lunch
TIC	Tongue In Cheek
TINALO	This Is Not A Legal Opinion
TINAR	This Is Not A Recommendation
TIWTGLGG	This Is Where The Goofy Little Grin Goes
TJATAW	Truth, Justice, And The American Way
TLA	Three-Letter Acronym
TRDMC	Tears Running Down My Cheeks
TTBOMK	To The Best Of My Knowledge
TTFN	Ta Ta For Now
TTYL	Talk To You Later
TYVM	Thank You Very Much
WAMKSAM	Why Are My Kids (or Kittens) Staring At Me?
WIBAMU	Well I'll Be A Monkey's Uncle
WYSBYGI	What You See Before You Get It
WYSIWYG	What You See Is What You Get
YAP	Yet Another Ploy
YMMV	Your Mileage May Vary (GS, KEW)

How to Watch Television

Once, when this was a God-fearing nation, you could ID your neighbors by their religious affiliation. You had your next-door neighbor, the Methodist, and the guy next to him who was a Baptist, and so on down the block, past Presbyterians, Jews, Catholics, Episcopalians, and the Zen guy with the great fish pond down on the corner. Nobody went to the same church, but one thing everybody had in common was religion. You could almost tell what their belief was by just looking at the front yard.

Now, much to our peril, we are less concerned with religion than we were, say, fifty years ago. Today our shared heritage isn't spiritual, it's electronic. The one thing we all have in common is this: We all watch TV. With a million channels knocking at the front door, we don't all watch the same thing, but we're all tuned in, nonetheless.

TELEATHEISTS

A guy who tells you he doesn't watch television is lying, sort of the same way guys used to say they were *sure* there was no God in heaven, but guarded their doubts carefully, just in case. *Not* watching TV is so astonishing a thing that a genre of magazine journalism, called culture slumming, has grown up around the phenomenal number of articles written by putatively shocked, appalled, or bemused elitists tuning in to TV for the first time, ever.

No way. Everybody watches TV all the time. You may not know whether your next-door neighbor is Orthodox or Unitarian, but you can bet your last dollar he believes in watching TV.

THE SOURCE OF LIFE FOR ALL MANKIND

What makes TV so irresistible? For men, the answer to that small question provides a whole lesson, since, for us, television gives us a life without the trouble and hassle of actually going out and living one. Again, this applies to men only, mostly because men and women differ appreciably in their viewing methodologies. Women, of course, already have real lives, some more complex than others. Single women build whole lives around their relationship with cats. If you have that much imagination, you don't need TV. For evidence that women aren't driven to TV in the reckless way men are, you have to look no farther than to the circulation figures for *TV Guide*. The fact is, many more women than men read *TV Guide*. On Mondays, they look up "Monday" in *TV Guide* and read the little blurbs that describe their prime-time lives. There's no room—and no need—for spontaneity in a woman's viewing pattern. For women, TV is merely an orderly adjunct to real life.

Men wing it. When we sit down in front of the TV, anything can happen. Sure, there are a few time slots we have booked. You've got your news slot or maybe your NFL slot. But for most guys, the details of a night with TV are up for grabs. If we're feeling good, all the sitcoms are funny and all the TV movies are blockbusters. If we feel bad, everything's QVC. We don't go out to look for good TV. We surf from channel to channel, figuring that if something's really all that good, it'll find us. We're looking to TV to give us a life by telling us what we feel like watching. Is that so much to ask of an important household appliance? No.

THE SAMSUNG PIPELINE

Because of our admittedly casual desire to find something resembling an epiphany on TV, men are far better channel surfers than women. For one thing, women actually pause long enough on each channel to figure out what's on. If two people are talking, women want to know what they're talking about. Men don't care. "Two people talking," you say to yourself, and you're gone. For another, women have a powerful relationship memory. A woman scanning channels will hit *The Love Boat,* see John Davidson and Lauren Tewes on the pool deck, and recall *instantly* the fact that they *almost* slept together but decided not to because he still had some things to work out. Men just see John Davidson, and that's enough.

Men like to do what we call the "Samsung Pipeline," which is what a guy does when he surfs from channel 1 and goes *straight through* to channel 2,000, with nanosecond stops along the way for beer and pretzels. Bam, bam, bam. Really good TVs are equipped with one of those Chinese assault remotes you use when you want to wipe out the security cameras down at the post office. You just throw it into automatic, kick off the safety, aim, and hold the button. The sucker runs off of two car batteries and an old Husqvarna chainsaw engine. When you want to hit the telecurl, you paddle your way through the sports channels, then start slowly rolling through the networks. You can really pick up speed through the basic stuff—CNN, Nashville, and the Weatherdweebs (True Weather Channel quote from Dave Schwartz: "If you live in these areas, please, I beg you, *for the sake of meteorology,* don't go outside!")—take a smooth rail change through the shoppers, cut back and down the face of Showtime, Cinemax, and the other premiums, out the inside of the music channels, go backside past the Spandex people on the health and fitness channels (Jake: "C'mon, kids, raise that *buttisimo!*"), trim through the TV preachers, almost wipe out on the Hitler and Lizard channels—A & E, Discovery—and wind up exhausted, with your remote smoking, at the other end of the telebeach on a white, sandy stretch of desolate infomercials. Most women say this kind of thing gives them motion sickness and makes them a little nauseous. The remedy? Dramamine and a half hour on the home-and-garden channel.

QUALITY-CONTROL TIPS

Obviously, a master surfer knows what to avoid and what to look for. Sometimes, for no apparent reason, a TV show'll reach out and grab you by the paunch and yell, "Watch me!" Careful. Could be a ruse. Here's how to tell in ninety seconds or less whether a TV show's worth watching:

Ditch it if there's

- A talking animal—dog, horse, cat, politician.
- A close-up of insects.
- A telephone number superimposed at the bottom of the screen.
- A man and a woman in bed—with blankets over them.
- An interview with Madonna.

A note on sitcoms: Men are often caricatured as attention spendthrifts, living on the deficit-disordered fringe of electronic consciousness. True. So what? This is the five-year decade of short attention spans. Even the people who write most half-hour TV shows can't pay attention for a full half hour. That's why network sitcoms are only twenty-two minutes long. In general, watch *no* sitcoms, except Tim's, Jerry's, and John's.

Stick around if there's

- A car in midair and upside down.
- A guy with his leg practically stuck in the mouth of a bass.
- A wide receiver in midair and upside down. You can blow an afternoon here.
- Guys with jet-packs on their backs.
- Someone saying, "Quick! Let's get out of here!"
- A guy on a fire escape.
- A guy walking down a dimly lit street.
- Psycho music.
- A woman's voice behind a door, saying, "I'll be right out."
- A white Bronco driving down the freeway followed by seven police cars and a squadron of choppers. There's something about snapshots of a wealthy society in cultural despair that makes a guy want to pause and linger.
- Skin.

There it is. That's the unicorn you're looking for: Women. The *surfer girls* who decorate Surf City. All channel surfers are unconsciously homing in on the women on the electronic beach. If you're shooting the pipeline, you realize that every channel that had a women doing something sort of personal— taking off her silk stockings, if it's HBO, or taking off her Birkenstocks, if it's

PBS—will embed itself in your transponder memory. On color televisions, there's a certain skin tone that is unmistakable. It exists nowhere else in nature or on TV. That color on your video screen in sufficient quantity can mean only one thing: Somebody's naked.

If you're on the remote and your wife's along for the ride, you don't want to actually *stop* when you see skin, but it's there, you spotted it, and you know where to find it later, after you've worked up some stupid excuse: "Hey, hon! Wait a sec! Lemme go back. Did you see that bearskin rug? Is that Kodiak or Grizzly? Jeesh, I wish they'd get that undressed *person* out of the way."

To a guy riding his remote solo, of course, that telltale expanse of fleshy-beige is like a concrete bridge abutment: *Bam,* news. *Bam,* sports. *Bam,* weather. *Bam,* skin, *bam!* You can blow the transmission in a power remote by slamming it into reverse for one of those Hawaiian Tropic bikini contests.

Is that bad? Well, yes, as a matter of fact. Too much TV life is no life at all. True story: There's a correspondent in Los Angeles who, for the last several years, has had an entire relationship with an inventory of rental videotapes. If he wants a hot meal, he talks softly to his microwave. In his own mind, he has made women technologically obsolete. As he says, if he wants sensitivity and compassion, he can always get that from Oprah, and if he wants unexpected thrills and excitement, he can get tipsy, turn on the Breeder's Channel, and, with one untimely phone call, have a whole herd of Herefords in the front yard by morning, bull included.

Is it a life? "It's not bad," he says, "considering it's all TV."

HOW TO CHOOSE PROGRAMMING

Let's say your wife wants to watch old black-and-white movies on AMC, but you want to see the armored cars. In our house, possession of the remote is nine-tenths of the law—and I'm there first. It's hard for us men to get into a movie with Katharine Hepburn and Spencer Tracy, for example, that's just about personal relationships, when we could be watching a movie like *T2*, which has a robot from the future that can morph. (TA)

3. Housework

Cleanliness. You know it's around here someplace. Check over there in the corner, next to that big pile of
Godliness.

The different parts of personal hygiene unfold like the delicate
petals of a glorious and beautiful flower in the hands of a man bent
on beating dust and grime. But through all the suds and all the
steam, there's one thing—**the Main Thing about cleaning anything**—that all men must know: Always, no matter what you're
scrubbing, no matter what you're scouring, whether it's a Chevy or
your own filthy habits, always, always *start at the top and work
down.*

Note to women readers: You're right. This is the shortest chapter
in the book.

How to Clean the Upstairs: The Attic Laws

These are the **Main Things** to know about how to clean an attic—or any area used primarily for storage.

THE RULE OF TWO AND FIVE

It is possible, barely, to clean an attic without disturbing its so-called primary function, provided the attic

- is in a house you have occupied for less than five years and
- has not already been cleaned at least twice.

Let's run the numbers on this one:

First attic clean? No sweat. Just stack boxes and the job's done. If you're a married guy cleaning the attic, you'll find the inspector-general will probably confuse organization with cleanliness.

Second clean: You have to unstack the boxes and repack them, compressing the contents of two boxes into one. But you still don't have to chuck anything out.

Third and subsequent cleanings: After two cleanings, things get tight. Why? Because after two cleanings or five years, whichever comes first, the laws of physics—which do not allow two objects to occupy the same space at the same time—get in the way. After five gloriously retentive years, or after two ersatz cleanings, there's nothing left but to go through each box and separate the wheat—the items of value—from the chaff—the box they came in.

That brings us to another law:

ZIMMERMAN'S LAW OF PACKAGING

There is a fixed percentage of waste available to you on the third cleaning: You can figure by repacking everything of value and disregarding its extraneous elements you will gain 20 percent more space. How do we know this? Because it was so stated by a Mr. Tom Zimmerman, a man who owns a hardware store and therefore comprehends perfectly all the many parts of existence, if not its sum. According to brother Zimmerman, about 20 percent of his store is devoted to harboring the cartons and bags products come in when they arrive from the factory. Therefore, it stands to reason that *if you are discarding more than 20 percent of what you have in the attic, you're throwing away some good stuff*—like the hand-drawn map your chum, Lenny, drew at summer camp, or the colony reordering instructions for an ant farm—and so you're ditching not only some stuff you'll want to have later on, but also a lot of really good stuff you're actually going to *need*.

Another way of looking at the problem:

THE 40-PERCENT REDLINE

The cosmic cleanometer is clearly graduated to offer maximum analysis. Let's watch the needle:

Less than 10 percent: If you discard almost nothing from an attic after five years of cramming stuff into it, your wife is right: You *are* an anal lunatic. Or maybe your wife is right: You *are* lazy. Or maybe your wife is right: You *want* to live like an animal.

From 15 to 20 percent: This is factory-recommended maintenance. Chucking out the unnecessary stuff in an attic—all that junk your wife and kids accumulate, for starters—is a sign of discipline and maturity.

From 20 to 40 percent: If you find you're throwing away between 20 and 40 percent of your attic's contents, you're going through a crisis, midlife or otherwise. You're going to later regret your zeal, of course, but men have recovered from 30 percent cleanings. Even 40 percent can be a survivable loss, especially if you're prepared for the inevitable cycle of denial, anger, and grief.

From 50 to 60 percent: If you're throwing away between 50 and 60 percent, you're moving out, even if you don't realize it. You could be cleaning yourself right out of the house.

More than 60 percent: You can figure *your permanent record has been erased.* You are a nonperson, a man without a history, a guy born yesterday. Your soul has been lost in the lather of good intentions.

So what are you to do? Clean the attic despite your conviction that to do so is to do that which is against your own interests? No. But how can a civilized man argue against cleanliness? This is, after all, an age in which *littering* is viewed with greater moral certainty than abortion. Nevertheless, you have to give it a shot.

This conjures another attic law:

IF YOU CAN'T AVOID CLEANING THE ATTIC, AVOID CLEANING THE ATTIC WITH YOUR WIFE

Not only will having your wife or girlfriend involved result in some *actual* cleaning, but you run the risk of exposing her to evidence of past transgressions, including premarital love-crimes. For example, you're working your way, layer by layer, box by box, through a six-strata carton escarpment when, oh-oh, someplace in the middle of your own late Jurassic period—early college, say—you come across a forgotten fossil that provides positive proof that you *did* take Wanda Joy to a motel outside St. Louis in 1969, despite your years of denial.

You can't throw it out. It's good stuff. So what do you do? You put the evidence in your best friend's attic and hope for the best.

That, of course, brings us to the last attic law:

THE EASIEST ATTIC FOR YOU TO CLEAN IS ANOTHER GUY'S ATTIC

If it's not your attic, you can figure about 2 percent of the clutter is worth keeping.

The rest is junk.

How to Clean a Three-Storey House in One-Storey Time

Start high, work low. The trick is to use the attic and the basement as the two storage areas sandwiching the living area. Clutter the storage areas if you like, but keep the living area clear.

- *Pack your attic.* Put big stuff around the edges, little stuff in the middle. Remember, you don't need to actually be able to reach anything in the attic instantly; it's okay to have a course or two of boxes between you and what you want.
- *Label everything.* Make sure you can see what's in a box by looking at it. This is one of the most important things about organizing an attic: Use paper flags, thick markers—anything that will mark the contents of a box so the tag can be read from a distance.
- *Don't put dirty clothes in the attic.* Moths and other bugs love sweat-covered sweaters and jackets. (TF)
- *Put clutter into storage.* If your blankets hang low enough, the space under a bed makes dandy space.
- *Clean the rooms before you clean the hallway.* Whatever won't fit under the bed, in a dresser, or into a closet goes into the hallway.

- *Gut the hallways.* Everything in the hallways on the top two floors goes to the attic, which is best used for storing personal stuff—clothes, pictures, all that. The basement is for kitchen, hardware, and other stuff.
- *Clear the decks.* The secret to making living and cooking areas look clean is to leave long stretches of countertop and other flat, horizontal surfaces clear of clutter. If you can't get stuff into the cupboards, put it in the basement.
- *Go high.* You can't get as much stuff in a typical basement as you can in a typical attic. The reason? The heating plant needs space and access. Also, basements actually provide a way in and out of a house, so that knocks out the use of a whole wall, virtually. Worst of all, they flood. (JD, JG)

How to Mop a Floor

Broom it out first. Don't fool around. Get a thirty-second aerobic workout. Stretch those arms, stretch those arms, move those legs, move those legs, then bend at the waist, one, two, hold it, breathe, start at the top, broom out the cobwebs in the corners. Knock all the dirt down to the floor. (FDG)

TWO WAYS TO MOP

One way is to keep the water in the bucket and use the mop as a sort of big, wet dusting cloth. Cover the floor in three- to four-foot-square sections, keeping the exit from the room and the nearest sink to your back. When the mop gets dirty, rinse. When you reach the door, step out of the room and finish the job, then rinse your mop and leave it standing to dry with the mop-head up.

The other way is to grab a bucket of warm water and spill it here and there in the center of the floor. Work from the center out to three of the walls, keeping your line of retreat open. Soak it up, rinse it out, soak it up some more.

If you need a serious cleaning, use two mops and two buckets. First cover a section of the floor with water and a cleaning solution, then rinse that section with the second mop and plain water. Repeat. (PJH)

A plug: Mop n' Glo is a great one-step, bachelor-tested floor cleaner. It has been used under quasi-clinical conditions on industrial carpeting to remove beer scum, and it worked just fine. (FDG)

How to Wash a Week's Worth of Dishes During Commercial Breaks

Sunday through Friday, keep your sink uncluttered. Rinse off your dishes as you use them, then arrange them on the countertop according to size: Big plates on big plates, little plates on little plates, cereal bowls in cereal bowls. Pots and pans together. Keep a plastic Stadium or Big Gulp cup next to the sink. Put your silverware in there.

On Saturday afternoon, fill the sink with hot water and soap. Put a stack of plates into the water to soak. Fill the Big Gulp and the pots and pans with soap and water and leave them on the counter next to the sink.

Go away for at least a half hour. Come back, run a little hot water across the plates as you swipe at them with a soapy sponge. Dunk them; then stack them in the drainer. It shouldn't take more than two-and-two to do a week's worth of one kind of plate. Fill the sink again, and after a half hour, come back and repeat the process. After all the dishes are done, wipe off the silverware, rinse out the pot, and you're ready for a whole new week. (PE)

How to Clean a Filthy Refrigerator

Let's say you, like our correspondent, won a refrigerator at a poker game. But then your father-in-law pointed out that if you took an appliance as filthy as that into your house, your wife—his daughter—would leave you and return to him. Here's what you do:

- *Load the refrigerator above the wheels* in the back of the pickup. Make sure it's secure, but you're going to need lots of room on all sides, so put it square in the middle of the bed. Don't lay a 'fridge on its side, either. Bad for the pipes.
- *Drive the 'fridge* to a do-it-yourself car wash.
- *Soap and steam* the refrigerator. Take your time, but five minutes ought to do the trick. Secure the door in an open position for the final leg of the trip home. Should be clean and dry by the time you hit the driveway.

Feeling ambitious? Pop in a few more quarters and go to the next instruction. (MB)

How to Wash Your Car

This ought to be instinctive by now, yes? No. Our instincts are to do jobs such as this one as quickly and easily as possible. There's a better, if partially nonintuitive, way:

- **Hose it.** Wash the car down with plain water first to remove dust and loose dirt.
- **Soap it.** Choose a detergent with a low pH and cover the car thoroughly, starting, of course, at the top. If it's a hot day, and there's a chance the soap will dry on the surface, work in smaller areas.
- **Use only clean, soft cloths.** Even the smallest amount of dirt or grit can scratch the paint, especially on late-model cars.
- **Scrub tough spots** with baking soda or a soft plastic netlike dish scrubber.
- **Never wash your car in direct sunlight** or it will streak.
- **Rinse the car starting at the top** and working down.
- **Use commercial products to remove tree sap,** heavy bird droppings, gasoline and oil, and road tar.
- **Dry it.** Wipe your car clean with terry cloth towels.
- **Clean your windows** with undiluted vinegar. Rinse with water and dry with clean rags.
- **Clean the windshield wipers** with a cloth and a solution of water and antifreeze, mixed half-and-half.
- **Scrub the tires.** A touch of tire black helps. Clean, black tires make a huge difference to the appearance of a car. (JFo)

How to Clean Up Your Entire Act

Here's a batch of bits and pieces from men everywhere who—judging from the subject of their correspondence—are sick and tired of the way I've been running this so-called life of mine and want me to clean up my act fast.

HOW TO PERMANENTLY BAN ROACHES FROM THE HOUSE

Variety's the spice of death: Every time you buy a new can of roach poison, buy a different brand. Why? Because roaches are adaptable. By buying a different brand every time, you are getting a different poison formula every time, thus making it harder for the roaches to adapt and easier for you to kill them. (TF)

HOW TO CLEAN UP YOUR IMMEDIATE ENVIRONMENT

Is everybody in the office talking behind your back? Maybe it's because you stink. According to a recent study, more than half the men you work with, and an even greater number of women, will not tell you that you smell like dead pets. Here's how to reduce your emissions:

- *Dog breath.* Eat parsley, brush your tongue, swallow chlorophyll tablets, chew on a lemon, eat antacids, use a mouthwash containing zinc.
- *Pit bull.* Dial 1-800-903-7374 and ask whoever answers the phone how you can get a Shower'N Towel, a twelve-by-twelve baby wipe with aloe and a deodorizing antibacterial. Or save the $1.99 and take a shower. (AMcLL)
- *Garlic.* Squeeze lemon juice over your hands and then rinse them in cold water to remove the smell of garlic from your hands. (UG)

HOW TO LIVE A CLEAN LIFE

You are your own rain forest. Keep your biosphere pristine.

Carbon Monoxide

After tennis star Vitas Gerulaitis was found dead in his bed, carbon monoxide became famous as the killer it is. What you can do:

- *Inspect.* Have all gas, oil, and wood-burning appliances inspected once a year. The best time to do it is just before you need them for the winter.
- *Detect.* Buy a CO detector and radon tester that have the Underwriter's Laboratory sticker on them. Make sure the results of both tests meet Environmental Protection Agency standards.
- *Disinfect.* Get your chimney swept and cleaned annually. (DM)

Get the Lead Out

This holds true especially if you have children. The stuff practically eats brains alive. Important question: When was your house built? Even though lead-based paint was banned in 1978, your house could still have it and you and your family may be inhaling it and younger kids may be eating chips of it. In either case, this can lead to damage to the nervous system. Not just a little damage, either: Some historians believe that the addled state of the populace, most of whom drank water through lead pipes, was responsible for the collapse of the Roman Empire and the election of Barbara Boxer.

If your house was built before 1978, hire a professional tester or buy a kit to check for yourself the lead content in your interior paint. If there is lead in the paint, have a removal contractor treat the surface or area on which the lead was found. He'll give you a choice between seal it or remove it. Go for the seal-choice. It's cheaper, simpler, cleaner, and therefore safer. (DM)

Clean the Water Supply

What lurks in your tap water? For many people, the answer is a lot of different pollutants that can lead to gastrointestinal problems, birth defects, and cancer. What to do? Ask your water company to test the water or to send you a self-test kit. If you find a problem, it's the water company's, not yours. The company will have to fix it.

If you have your own well, have the water tested every few years—especially if the well is vulnerable to surface runoff.

Install a water filter. (HTD)

Clean the Can

You're not the only one who loves hanging out in the latrine. As the coziest, warmest, and wettest room in your house, you'll always have plenty of company; mildew and bacteria, especially, love bathtubs, sinks, and bathroom walls.

What to do?

- *Crack the window* when you take a bath, shower, and shave.
- *Install an exhaust fan* to remove steam. (RSR)

Clean the Air

If you use a humidifier, you must clean it daily to avoid bacterial and fungal buildup.

Forced air heat? Electrostatic air filters cost a bundle, but they actually work. (Anon.)

4. Clothes

What crazy thing makes us get up every morning and put on a suit and tie? Perhaps the thought that if we didn't, we might think we were unemployed.

Suits, for instance, are admittedly a retro idea, the kind of cloak of anonymity many of us have been avoiding since the summer of 1967. But in an age of barbarous informality, where dressing "down" is seen as a progressive notion, suits can be a reassuring thing. Why? Because guys without jobs *never* wear suits.

So. Suits signify: A suit is the dress uniform of the working man. A suit says we are all dogfaces in the war on irresponsibility. We earn money. And we wear suits to prove it.

However, if we're all going to suit up, maybe we ought to take a sec to make sure we've got the right stuff—in the right size and in the right order—and that it's on the right way around.

How to Buy a Suit

You have three **Main Things:**
  1. Name
  2. Price
  3. Appearance.
  Common sense screams, "Three!" while fear whispers, "Uno, bello, uno." So we split it down the middle and end up with neither.

WHAT'S IN A NAME?

A name on a suit is important to guys who wear "fashion"—as the tonier men's mags call what any regular guy would call expensive clothes. For most of us, there are only two reasons to buy a suit because of the name that's on it:

  1. *The contract says you have to.* If you make a deal to pitch for the Indians, the name on the suit's everything. But you'll notice Giorgio Armani doesn't have a franchise.
  2. *Proof of good taste.* The other reason to buy a suit because of the name on it is that you're an insecure guy who needs to be able to point to the "Giorgio" on the jacket lining so others will know that no matter what their eyes are telling them, you're actually well-dressed.

  Either way, you get no guarantee the thing will fit. Here's the bottom line on **why the name on a suit means nothing:**

  • *You can buy the name.* Lots of designers license their names to manufacturers and thereby sign away any control they have over what the suit looks like or how it fits. (HG)
  • *The names you can't license,* ironically, are names such as Wal-Mart's and other mass retailers. As many as three-quarters of all suits sold in the United States are sold in discount houses. Small wonder; the $99 suit you get down at SootCity may have started out as a $400 beauty at Nordstrom or Bloomie's. It may have survived a $200 tag at a specialty discount retailer, such as Men's Warehouse, and ended up at the local discount barn for no worse reason than that the manufacturer made too many suits. On the other hand, the $99 suit you've been looking at may have started as a $1.25 suit in some remote corner of the Philippines or Ecuador. (DS)

  How can you tell the difference?

HOW TO SPOT A CHEAP SUIT

Postcard from an honest haberdasher: "The same factory that makes a $600 suit also makes a $200 suit. And it's the same suit." Here's **how to tell if it's a good suit selling cheap** or a cheap suit worth exactly what you'll pay for it:

Wrinkles: There are two places where wrinkles matter. One is in the fabric itself; if you grab a handful of the material and crunch it, does it stay wrinkled? If it does, it's a cheap suit. Twisting an arm is a good way to gauge this, by the way.

Wrinkling of the fabric around seams is another surefire indicator of a ten-dollar prison-issue suit. Usually, it's a sign of cheap fabric *and* cheap manufacture, in which a robot machine made a seam by squirting a line of glue and squishing together all the layers of fabric. A guy in a glued-suit looks like Lurch. The only other way to finish a suit lapel is by hand. How to tell the difference? Rub the lapel between your thumb and forefinger. If the fabrics have a little play and rub against each other a bit, you're holding a hand-finished suit. If the lapel has no play, you're holding a fused-fabric special.

Count the stitches: A well-made garment will have a fairly dense stitch. If you can count more than twelve stitches to an inch of seam, you're okay. Less is bad; more is good.

Weave: Check the fabric under good light. See if there's a bunch of missing threads.

Match: Here's something else everybody forgets to check: Does the coat match the trousers? Very often, there are subtle differences because the two garments may be made by different third-world manufacturers— sometimes even on different continents.

Collar: Does the lapel lay flat, like it should, or does it roll and buckle, like it shouldn't?

The shoulder should lay neatly. The line of the shoulder seam should be flat, without waves or bulges.

The patterns should meet neatly at the shoulders, on the back, and under the arms. The pattern on the lapel and on the sleeve should match the pattern on the torso.

Lining: Except for all-cotton leisure wear, all suit jackets should be fully lined in the sleeves and at least halfway down the back. Trousers should be lined at least to the knee.

Fasteners: Check out the button that will hold your trousers closed. It should have a hand-finished loop behind it to keep it from popping off.

The buttons on a cheap suit will be—well, cheap looking. They'll also be loosely attached.

The sleeves on a cheap suit won't have a miter-cut to them. They'll be more like a shirt sleeve—and a lot harder to alter than a good suit sleeve.

The pockets on a good suit will have a coin pouch, and maybe other inside pockets.

Front: Look for a good French-fly front, with the drape of the cloth disguising any closures. It's a no-fail sign of a well-made suit of clothes. (DS, REM)

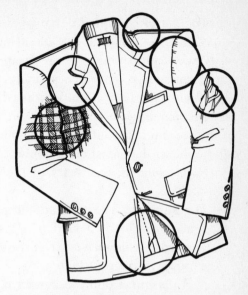

How to Spot a North Korean sportcoat: Watch for curling lapels and mismatched fabric patterns. A cheap shoulder pad will break the line of the shoulder. Puckering around the seams results from bad manufacturing. If you twist the sleeve and it stays crushed, it's cheap fabric. Large stitches inside won't hold for long.

HOW TO SPOT A READY-MADE RIP-OFF

If you spend $1,500 on a custom-made suit, you're actually getting more suit, more value for the money than if you bought a ready-made suit for the same price. The reason is, with the ready-made suit you pay a 50 percent markup from both the designer and the store, which means you're probably getting a suit that originally cost $350 to make. With a custom-made suit, you only pay the designer's markup, which means you're getting a suit that cost about $750 to make. (PF)

HOW TO MEET YOUR MATERIAL NEEDS
Why Ray Charles Always Looks Cool

You can actually tell the difference between cheap fabric and expensive stuff by feel alone:

Cheap fabric is stiff and has a slight papery feel to it. When you put on a jacket made of cheap stuff, it hangs stiffly; sometimes, there's an unseemly crease at the bottom of the lapel; sometimes, the thing just hangs on you, like a drunk date.

The better the fabric, the softer it feels. Expensive suiting has a sort of springiness—a nonmale way of saying resilient flexibility. But don't get carried away with "springiness": A cheap fabric with a loose weave will possess more "springiness" than a cheap mattress.

The best fabric for a suit is worsted wool, which is to suiting material what aspirin is to drugs: a miracle. You can wear it in winter and stay warm, and in warm weather, the stuff breathes enough to keep you cool. Worsted wool also drapes better than most other fabrics.

Runners-up: If you weary of the usual worsted suit, try some of these alternatives:

- *For summer:* The standard beige or khaki summer suit (also called a "traveling suit") is a kind of classic and makes for a nice break in the worsteds. Avoid seersucker. A seersucker suit is what guys in the know call a "novelty suit." (PO'T)

  A dissent: Cotton seersucker is a great fabric for summer suits. But be careful here: Seersucker is acceptable between Memorial Day and Labor Day, especially in hot-summer cities. But seersucker is to suiting material what bow ties are to neckwear: It's just a tad too cute for most men's lives. (More on bow ties later in this chapter.) If you have to get in touch with the frat-brat inside you by wearing suits with stripes of light blue, gray, or *pink,* then by all means make the suit a single-breasted number, make the shirt a solid Oxford-cloth button-down, and make the tie a Madras one. Add penny loafers, no socks. If you're going to go fey, go fey all the way. (REM)

- *For spring:* Silk and silk blends. Linen is also a good spring suit fabric. (But watch those wrinkles! See below.)

- *For winter:* Pure wool tweed is timeless—and wearless. A good tweed will last two lifetimes.

Linen Lament

Whoever said linen was a good hot-weather fabric must have been selling the stuff. The shapes of linen's peculiar fibers actually traps hot air. Silk does the same. Both of them wrinkle faster than a thumb in dishwater. (REM)

Synthetic Sympathy

Polyester blends help keep a suit looking fresh. Polyester also resists wrinkling. If you're a traveling kind of Wilbury, you can't do without a good poly-blend suit. (PO'T)

A dissent: If God had wanted us to wear chemicals, we'd all be wearing trash bags and runway foam. Polyester doesn't exist in nature. Adding it to a natural fabric, such as wool, is a great way to cheapen the appearance of a suit. If you're traveling and wrinkles are a worry, bring along one of those little fabric steamers, or take along a lightweight wool suit and let it hang in the john while you shower. Pure poly suits stick to your body. They stretch and bag, and look as cheap as they feel. (SCJ)

RULES FOR ALL SIZES
The Length Rules
The standard length of a suit jacket is thirty-one inches. When your arm's at your side, the sleeves should end at the narrowest part of your wrist. Your shirt sleeve should extend no more than a half inch beyond that point. (FGMcF)

- *Waistcoat wearers:* Your vest ought to cover the waistband of your trousers. The bottom button must be left unbuttoned. (GRD)
- *Trouser length:* The crease of the trousers should break gently when the cuff is resting on the shoe. Without the break, you'll look like a washout survivor.

The Oversized Rule
Heavyset men should avoid vests, unless they're part of a three-piece suit. Big, bold guys should also avoid big, bold plaids. Better bets: vertical stripes and small herringbone patterns. (FGMcF)

The Suit-to-Alteration Rule
Unless you're a peg-legged, piratical kind of guy, your new suit shouldn't need radical alterations. Assuming you've purchased something roughly your size, the most the store's tailor should have to do is hem the pants cuffs, adjust the waistband, fix the length of the sleeves, and, possibly, take in the jacket a bit under the arms or on the sides. That's it. So *if the store wants to charge you more than, say, fifty dollars for all this, you can take your business elsewhere,* safe in the knowledge that if it was willing to rip you off on the alterations, it was willing to rip you off on the suit, too. (FGMcF)

CUFFS AND BUTTONS
Cuffs
Cuffs should never be thinner than an inch or wider than one and three-quarters inches.

Shorter men need shorter cuffs: If you're five-foot-ten or less, go for a cuff about an inch and a half wide.

Button Bits

The top button of a *two-button suit jacket* should button at the waist. No post-modern man wears a jacket with fewer than two buttons, of course, unless he's got his own lounge act. And no matter how many buttons *more* than two a jacket has, the bottom one is never buttoned. (FGMcF)

Trad note: Button either the top two or just the middle button of a three-button suit coat. (PO'T)

How to Dress to Suit

A few notes from everywhere about how to wear a suit to achieve a specific effect:

- *Elegance:* If you want that 1940s sense of style and elegance, wear the waistband of your trousers just *slightly* above your actual waist—quite high on most men—and allow for a generous break in the trousers at the cuff. Wear your jacket buttoned, your tie tight. Your legs will look five yards long. (DEW)
- *Rough affability:* Wear the waistband of your trousers well below your waist, so that if you actually had a beer gut, it would hang over your belt. Leave your jacket open and your tie loosely knotted.
- *Serious competence:* Most serious men are brain-dead, so dress like a mortician. Or like Dan Rather. Dark suits only. Wear the waistband of your trousers just ever so *slightly* below your waist. Hold it there with braces. Add a waistcoat when it's in style. But no matter what, keep your jacket buttoned. White shirts only, please, and make a small floral gesture with your necktie your only sign of life—plant or otherwise. (JGF)

How to Take Care of a Suit

- *Hanging hint:* Always hang your suit jacket on a wooden or plastic hanger—the kind that offers a wide shoulder support and a slight curve forward at the shoulders. Your jacket will keep its shape twice as long. (TF)

- *Hanging on empty:* Don't leave stuff in your pockets when you hang up your suit coat. It'll just bag out *right now.* Also: Leave it unbuttoned when you hang it up. This allows the lapel to roll naturally. (DFC)
- *Don't crowd* your suits in the closet. Give them some air and some space. (SCJ)
- *Rotate:* A suit should have forty-eight hours off for every twelve hours of work. It's like a union-suit thing. (TF) Letting the suit hang for a couple of days will restore the fabric, prevent bagging, and keep the suit looking fresh. (SCJ)
- *Death press:* When you take a suit or sport coat to the dry cleaners, always spend the extra two or three dollars to have it hand finished rather than run through the pressing machine. The pressing machine kills 50 percent of the garment. The heat causes the glue in a fused garment to separate, and it comes back puckered. (FGMcF)

How to Dress for the Road

- *Pack right:* When packing, you can reduce the amount of clothing you have to take by sticking with the same three colors. If everything you take with you is blue, gray, and white, for instance, you can wear every shirt with every suit with every tie, and you'll have much more flexibility with your travel wardrobe. (HPh)
- *Pack light:* If your business trip is for more than three days, take one less shirt and one less tie than you think you'll need. (GE)
- *Pack tight:* If you jam-pack your suitcase full of clothes, you'll end up with a wrinkled wardrobe at the other end of the plane ride. Better bet: Pack your suitcase tightly, but not jammed. If you leave too much room in your suitcase, you'll have the same wrinkled mess you'd have with a crammed 'case. A closely packed suitcase will keep clothes from bunching and wadding. (HPh)

How to Dress for a Midnight—or Midlife—Crisis

Who came up with the idea that formal wear should be rented, but bowling shirts should be owned outright? *If you need a tux, buy the thing.* Why? Because there are at least **five more reasons to own one than the reason you think.**

You need your own tux:

1. to properly drink a martini;
2. to have something reasonable to wear on the beach at night;
3. to wear when driving a small, yellow convertible through Manhattan;
4. to add a small whiplash to a regular date with your wife;
5. to wear to breakfast the next morning. (GY)

HOW TO IDENTIFY THE PARTS OF A TUXEDO

This small list may seem obvious to some, but anyone who's ever seen a chap wearing a rented tux with a brand-new brown leather belt knows there's somebody out there who needs it.

- *Jacket:* The color should be black. Of the three collar styles available in most shops—peaked, pointed, or shawl—only the latter two are completely acceptable.

  Single-breasted jackets with a peaked lapel are the most versatile and work best with a vest or cummerbund. Center vent, if any.

  Double-breasted jackets with peaked lapels should be worn with neither a vest nor a cummerbund. You ought to be younger than thirty-five and older than twenty-eight to wear one of these, and a perfect physical specimen. Fat guys, short guys, old guys beware. Double-breasted jackets with shawl collars are bizarre. Side vents, but ha! ha!

  Single-breasted jackets with a shawl collar should be worn only in the evening, if at all. No vents—or, if you need the air, a center vent.

- *Trousers:* These may have a small black strip of piping down the leg, but they won't have cuffs. Right?

- *Shirt:* Easy on big pleats and ruffles. Keep it simple; you don't want to look like a guy wearing a doily. The purpose of a tux is to make every guy look like every other guy so the women all look dazzling. Don't compete with the scenery, please. (GY)

- *Tie:* Black. Tie it yourself (see instructions later in this chapter).

- *Jewelry:* Black, gold, or silver studs, depending on the color of your watchband or eyeglasses. No other jewelry should be visible. That means no necklaces, please, lest somebody think you're King o' Porn or an off-duty sommelier.

- *Simple cummerbund* in black—or red, if you just have to be wild. A couple of ancillary cummerbund notes:

  Never wear a cummerbund with double-breasted formal wear.

  Wear those cummerbund pleats up. (Long ago, men out on the town used to keep their tickets to the opera tucked in the pleats of their cummerbund.)

- *Shoes:* Black patent-leather oxfords or pumps. (GY, TFK) Black tassel loafers with a high shine do fine. (GY)

HOW TO ACTUALLY WEAR A TUX

1. **The Richest Man in the Room Ploy:** A young lawyer named Bagge noticed something peculiar at corporate black-tie dinners. The oldest and most powerful partners invariably wore white button-down shirts under their tuxedos. No studs, no links, no nothing, leaving all the wing-collared preening to the Young Turks. The theory: It makes the tux feel more like a business suit. After adopting the style, young Bagge figured he'd better talk to the other guys who looked like this. He was right. Now he's in charge of three hundred other lawyers for a bank.

2. **The Tatty Gambit:** The Swedes are impeccably formal, the Spanish proudly so, but nobody lives in black tie better than the Brits. They wear it even in the country. They wear their dinner jackets till their elbows shine. The message is that the tatty tux should not be donated to the thrift shop; it should be worn proudly. The tatty tux is your rank, your party stripes.

3. **Mr. O's Sting:** The crafty Mr. O is a baseball club owner who spends a lot of his time going to banquets around the country. Sometimes he doesn't have his tux with him, but because of the heavy-caliber company he hangs with, he must prove to his peers that he is a class guy. Mr. O says rhetorically: "Never rent a tux. But when you do have to rent one, rent it so it looks like you own it. Rent one two sizes too small."

4. **The Reptile Encroachment:** Nancy, a fashion editor in New Orleans, claims that the most entertaining play in her town of late is the replacement of the cummerbund with a black alligator belt. She says black lizard will do. She says it works because these large reptiles have a graceful disregard for everything, and their skin lends that quality to the wearer. But you can never tell about fashion. It may just be that the boys around New Orleans had a great 'gator crop last year.

5. **The Heir Apparent:** Look to your ancestors. Not only did they wear terrific clothes, but the truth is, some of those fellows are bound to be dead and their clothes available to you free of charge. If you're careful, you can assemble the basic Five-Man-Tux: Grandfather's collars and studs, father's peaked-lapel jacket, stepfather's cummerbund, and a stolen bib-front shirt. Mix and match with elements of your own purchased gear. There's

nothing like wearing the clothes of four or five people at once to give you a sense of tradition with the secret larceny of a disguise. (WB)

HOW TO TIE A BLACK BOW TIE

The planet is increasingly a dress-down kind of place; you can wear your Silver Bullet windbreaker to church, or your Speedo to a bowling alley, and nobody'll pay much attention. Then comes June. Just as the weather starts to warm, the icy curtain of formal occasions rises. At weddings, receptions, parties, and graduations, guys who have been clip-on cool all year long suddenly turn into loosely knotted nerds. Who would have ever thought it would be the job of *bow ties* to separate the men from the boys?

A Whole Bunch of Ways to Tie the Knot: Around the border, from the top left corner: A figure-eight, a pair of wedding bands, a square knot, engagement-ring-and-band set, overhand knot, clove hitch, lariat loop, mid-shipman's hitch (we're in the middle of the bottom now), bowline, cat's paw. In the center on the left is a batwing bow tie, and on the right is a butterfly bow tie. In between is how you tie either one.

- *Warm up* by using your date's thigh as a temporary neck. Tie the necktie around the leg just as if you were tying your shoe, and you'll get the hang of the knot. (LEW)

- *Neck it:* Drape the tie around your neck with one end hanging just slightly below the other.

- *Square:* Next, tie a simple square knot, the knot you were born knowing how to tie.

- *Pull the bows into shape* by tugging at them until they're arranged in the shape and pattern you want.

- *Three knot notes:*

  1. A black tie will have a smaller, tighter knot than a conventional bow tie.

  2. If you avoid looking in the mirror and just tie the damned thing as if you were tying your shoe, you may have better luck.

  3. A perfectly proportioned tie will have ends that stick out on the sides about as far as the ends of your jaw, but no farther. (JY)

How to Hold Up Your Trousers

Use belts and braces.

The old-fashioned kind of B & D is really the only one we ever understood. Yes, yes. You can dress up your wife in this stuff. But at a certain age, the belt looks better on you than it does on her.

Given its traditional use—separating your belly from your thighs—and considering a belt is sometimes all that stands between you and indecent exposure, it pays to know a good one from a bad one.

BRACING FOR BELTS

Braces are a bit pompous if worn ostentatiously, but any will do. Avoid clip-ons, though.

Meanwhile, for the belted masses, look for the following commonsense qualities:

- *Good leather.* Feel it. Is it soft and smooth? Or is it cardboardlike and rough? Give it a little twist. If it seems both sturdy and supple, you're jake.
- *Check for tanning flaws.* Irregular spots and blemishes mean cheap goods.
- *Watch out for oil* and polish on an inexpensive belt. Before you buy, take a tissue and run it along the length of the belt. If oil or die comes off on the tissue, you can be sure it'll come off big-time on your trousers. (FEW)
- *Buckles* should be smooth, heavy, and free from pits, flaking, and other obvious indicators of low quality.
- *The edge* of the belt shouldn't have many rough spots, even if it's a work-type belt. On a more formal belt, the finish should be smooth to the touch. Watch out for small, unfinished areas.
- *The stitching* should be neat and tight—but not so tight that the stitches will pop if they're forced to stretch around your waist.
- *The lining* should be full-grain leather (see below). A vinyl lining will crack. (FEW, MG)

HIDES WE SEEK

A good belt shop has enough skin to make a more-or-less complete barnyard:

- *Cow.* Cows come from the manufacturer packed inside a hide that is heavy, durable, easily dyed, and easily embossed. Cowhide is the amateur leatherworker's favorite.

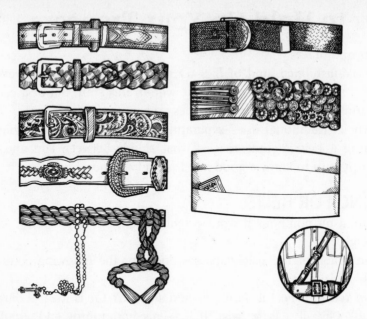

How to Separate Your Belly from Your Trousers: The wide world of belts, from top to bottom, left-hand column first: Texas Ranger, braided, Western, concho belt, cincture (with rosary), D-ring, gaucho, cummerbund (pleats up, please), and a Sam Brown, the belt most men secretly would love to wear to work.

- **Pig.** Pigskin is used to make cheap belts and expensive footballs. The easily recognized characteristic: Small, deep pinpoints, and lots of them.
- **Lamb.** Soft and supple? You bet. Condoms are made from this stuff, if that's an indicator.
- **Calf.** The best leather for dress belts. It's firm, it's mellow, and it takes a shine easily.
- **Eels, snakes, 'possum, gators,** and the rest of Creation also yield leather of varying degrees of durability. Even *sea bass* leather shows up on belts— cool for guys who insist on wearing seafood.

Price alert: Because belts made from hamsters or whatever are usually fashioned from small, individual pieces of leather, they are usually much more expensive. (FEW)

SKIN TRADE

The alternate leather glossary:

- **Top-grain and full-grain leathers** are made from the hair-side of the animal, the part generally thought to be most attractive—perhaps because it's the only part we see. Look for small "pores," which are actually hair cells, where follicles once bloomed.

Watch out for repeating patterns or for leather that has been cosmetically altered by the tannery to cover a badly bruised or otherwise damaged chunk of hide.

- *Split leather* is the part left after the top grain has been stripped away. The stuff's good for suede, or for embossing, since it has no grain.
- *Bonded leather* is the particle board of Hide World. Lots of inexpensive junk belts are made out of this stuff. Stiff as a party drunk. (MG, FEW)
- *E-note:* For more belt lore, go to http://www.fashionmall.com/htmledit/editors/bill/doc/belts.htm.

THIRD HOLE RULE

To fit properly, a belt should buckle at the third hole in from the end. On most belts, this will be the middle hole of five. (SA)

BIBLE OF BELTS

The best width for a belt is one inch. It's a width that always seems to work. Wide belts and skinny belts come and go, but the one-inch belt is the postmodern man standard, the width to buy if you want to buy only one. Dark brown or cordovan if you want universality. (RFD)

How to Drape a Torso

There are two kinds of shirts: dress shirts and all other shirts. What you wear off-duty is anybody's guess and nobody's concern. So let's rush through the notes we've got on fatigues first, and get down to business later.

BASIC T-SHIRT BASICS

There's a reason they're called "T-shirts" and not "tea shirts." We're talking underwear here, chaps. Far be it from me to defend the tattered flag of formality, but anybody who was irritated by Madonna's stage clothes during the late 1980s wasn't looking carefully at his own wardrobe.

- *The collar is the Main Thing* on a tee. You can tell by feel how thick and well-made a T-shirt collar is. As long as that stays together, the rest of the shirt can fall apart and you'll still look jake. But a shirt with great weave and a lousy, sagging, blown-out collar is a lousy shirt. (DES)

- *As undershirts.* Just because T-shirts are underwear doesn't mean you should actually wear them under anything. There's something about a T-shirt visible under a dress shirt that screams "Weenie" at the top of its lungs. Colored shirts are especially goofy looking under dress shirts. However, T-shirts can look fine under a casual shirt. But we're talking crew neck here. No V-necks no place.

  An unconvincing dissent: A cotton undershirt worn under a dress shirt can help make the shirt last longer and look better. On a hot day, the added cotton keeps you cooler, believe it or not.

- *Long-sleeve mock turtleneck.* T-shirts look great under a blazer or jacket. They stay neat and trim and make your shoulders look wider than they really are. Color is a matter of preference. (RFW)

  An instant dissent: Turtlenecks of any kind, whether worn under jackets or not, are the rough above-the-waist equivalent of SansaBelt trousers. But if you're going to wear one, wear a good one—something made from cashmere or at least lamb's wool. A turtleneck under a jacket looks like lounge-lizard leisure wear, and if you have even a 5 percent body-fat problem, a snugly fitting knit shirt only provides cheap fabric for all that abdominal upholstery. (EQ)

- *King-sized censor.* T-shirt lit is a colorful genre. But, a correspondent writes, "Can I ask other guys a favor? I have two little kids, just now getting to be able to read. If you wear a T-shirt with an obscenity on it, I see that the same as screaming cuss words at my wife and kids, and I'll object.

  "PS—I'm 6'3" and I weigh 240." (HTR)

WORK SHIRT WICK

If you really have to work for a living and you have to dress for work, work in a cotton shirt. Even the smallest amount of synthetic added to the weave will reduce cotton's natural ability to breathe efficiently and wick away moisture. Guys working in hot climates know that a heavy cotton shirt can provide a kind of wearable air-conditioning: The shirt works just like a swamp cooler. (HTR)

HOW TO SHOOT A CUFF

Get this: Guy goes out, blows six hundred on a suit and twenty bucks on a shirt, then can't figure out why the suit looks so lousy.

If your dress shirt doesn't fit properly, all the effort you put into getting your suit tailored to fit you well will go to waste.

So here, well pressed and chock full o' starch, is what you need to know about dress shirts:

- **Buy dress shirts from a reputable maker.** Men don't like to shop around for shirts—or most other items of clothing. Once they find a good shirtmaker, they stick with the label. If they're let down even once, it's adios. Shirtmakers know this and mind their buttons and closures. (HE)
- **Buy your shirts in an exact size.** S-M-L-XL is too vague for grown-up shirt sizes. Even two-inch variables—16 by 32–34, for example—are the sure sign of a cut-rate shirt.
- **Get a fresh measurement every year.** This is because all things change, including you. Necks, especially, fluctuate. Your collar should fit snugly when buttoned—not so loose that your tie hangs away from your neck, not so tight as to be pinching the skin. In fact, plastic surgeons are having a boom right now doing a new surgical procedure that takes away excess skin from the neck in men that is not naturally occurring, but the result of wearing a collar that is far too tight and has therefore stretched the skin of the neck for hours and hours each day. (EQ)
- **Sleeve length:** The sleeve should end about five inches above the tip of the thumb. Another landmark: With a jacket on, your shirt's sleeve should extend about a half inch below the edge of your jacket cuff when your arm is at your side. More than an inch showing? Your jacket sleeve is going to look mighty short.
- **Fit.** Buy shirts that hang about six inches below your waist before you tuck them in. This extra length will be enough to stay tucked in without bulging around the midsection from the creep of excess fabric.
- **Cotton only.** Unless you're dressing for a novelty act, 100 percent cotton should be your only shirting choice. Why? Because a cotton shirt, well-pressed, well-laundered, perfectly sized, is one of the few things a man can wear that deserves the term "exquisite." Cotton is also the most comfortable shirting fabric. (EQ, NSA)
- **Collars:** When you look at a shirt in a clothier's, you have to remember that when you put it on, your head and neck will be sticking out of the top. So remember to choose a collar that complements your head. If you have a short neck, get a collar that sits low. If you have a long neck, get a collar that is higher.

    Collar rise: A good rule of thumb is that the collar should stand about a half inch above the back of your jacket collar. Look for stitching around the outer edges that makes the collar rigid. A well-made collar is less likely to sag and flatten with wear. Some of the more expensive shirts have hand-stitched collars. This stitching should always be subtle or almost invisible.

Closure: The two sides of the collar should *meet* at the neck and form a perfect V. Don't count on a necktie to bring the two together. Even a small gap—say a quarter inch—will make your shirt look like the ill-fitting, shabbily made thing it is. It'll also make your necktie look wonky.

Points: When you're wearing it, the points of the collar should touch the chest of the shirt. (See the discussion of types of collars, below.)

- *Stitching:* The better the shirt, the more stitches on the collar there will be per inch. (NSA)
- *Select the shirt to match the suit.* To choose a shirt to go with a particular suit, consider the image the suit portrays. A casual tweedy or woolen suit calls for a casual button-down or rounded collar. A conservative pinstripe suit calls for a shirt with a stiffer collar with sharp points. Button-down collars are never appropriate as evening wear. (EQ)

How to Dissect a Shirt

A good corporate soldier should be able to break down his shirt and reassemble it in thirty seconds under fire at a stockholders' meeting. Know the parts, know the shirt:

- *Cuffs:* Pick one: Barrel? Or French?

  Barrel cuffs are those with one or two buttons and buttonholes.

  French cuffs are twice the length of a barrel cuff, and then folded in half over the outside of the shirt and held together with a cuff link. (Anon.)

- *Plackets:* The area of the shirt that the buttonholes are sewed into. In the good old days, the placket was a separate piece of fabric. Today, the placket is just simulated by folding the fabric of the shirt over. Plackets are generally an inch and a half wide. (EQ, KEL)

- *The yoke* is a piece of fabric sewed across the back of the shirt, at the shoulders. It is used to attach the front and the back of the shirt together. An added touch is a split yoke, or a yoke for the back left and another for the back right, where both half-yokes are sewed together in the middle. A split yoke is a sign of quality. A bad yoke isn't funny.

  See? (EQ)

- *A gauntlet* is the term for a sleeve placket, or that area of the shirt before the cuff where the sleeve is split. A higher-quality shirt will have a button on the gauntlet. Why add a gauntlet button? So you can close the gap

HOW TO TELL WHAT'S ON YOUR BACK

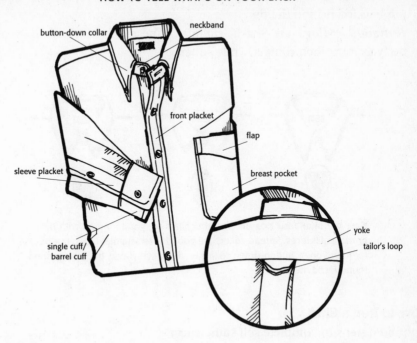

button-down collar

neckband

front placket

flap

sleeve placket

breast pocket

single cuff/
barrel cuff

yoke

tailor's loop

when buttoning the sleeve of the shirt, and open the gap to roll up your sleeves when washing. (EQ, BNS)

Neck Notes

The collar on a traditional dress shirt has regular points. Everything else is everything else:

- *Windsor collars* have points that are cut at a wider angle than the regular straight-point collar. They also sit lower, thus exposing more of the shirt at the neckline. The Windsor collar goes particularly well with double-breasted suits, but worn with more informal blazers or tweed jackets, it looks like a cheap shirt.
- *English spread collars* show more of the shirt at the neckline than the traditional dress-shirt collar and less than the Windsor. It is considered dressy while still giving an indication of the wearer's sense of style. Prince Charles and his pop are two fans of the English spread collar.
- *Pin collars:* These prissy jobs, with a pinhole on each side for a tie pin, are for men with longish necks. (EQ, NSA)

- **Tab collars** are much like pin collars, except they come with a snap or tab buckled behind the tie.
- **Rounded collars** are—well, *rounded*. These are as close to wearing a doily as most men can get while sober.

How to Collar Your Noggin: Straight collars are good for guys with oval or triangular faces. Spread collars are good for rectangular faces, but bad for round ones. Button-down collars work for everybody, but look best on round-faced men.

How to Iron a Shirt

Eight little steps to complete self-sufficiency:

1. **Start with a clean shirt,** something flat that resembles an ironing board, and an iron.
2. **Water it.** Get out a spray bottle or an old squirt gun and moisten the shirt.
3. **Begin with the collar.** Iron only the back, and iron it flat. Let your tie handle the job of putting in the fold. If you do it, it'll look squirrely.
4. **Next, iron the yoke** of the shirt. That's the part of the shirt that goes over your shoulders in the back. (See above.)
5. **Attack those sleeves.** If you like a crease, make sure you flatten the material out so that the crease on the shoulder matches the inside seam. The guys who work at expensive clothing stores will tell you that a good shirt will never have a crease on the sleeve; if you buy their advice, you can forgo the crease by stuffing a towel inside the sleeve before ironing.
6. *Don't forget the placket on the sleeve*—that's the part of the sleeve where the button and buttonhole are. Technical term (as noted earlier): the gauntlet.
7. *Next, finish off the back* of the shirt, **then the front**—which is the most important part.

8. *Complete the job by ironing the placket* down the front of the shirt—get around those buttons good—and **then the cuffs.** (SE)

HOW TO BUY A SWEATER

Only sheep look good in skintight sweaters. Make sure yours is big enough that you'll have room to move your arms and take a deep breath. Some sweaters will shrink when you wash them (cotton will practically disappear, unless you hand-wash), while other fabrics (such as alpaca or cashmere) won't. Sweaters generally come in four sizes and it is best to try one on in the store before you buy it, since the standard for sizing is much more lax than it is with, say, shirts or jackets. (RDY)

Heavy men should avoid sweaters that have a lot of cabling or detail. They should also stay away from sweaters that are too long: The extra fabric will just gather at the waist. Tall and thin men have it easier when buying sweaters, although if they choose a sweater that is too tight or too long, they might look unnaturally thin.

If you're going to own only one sweater, make it navy blue or gray. Synthetic fabrics itch. So do cheap woolen sweaters. They don't look very good, either.

If you plan to wear a sweater under a sport coat, it should fit tighter so that you don't bulge and so you can still move with both the sweater and jacket on. (SE, EQ)

How to Invest in Clothes

1. *Plan.* Never buy one piece of clothing without first considering how you will use it with the rest of your wardrobe.
2. *Consolidate.* Only buy clothes within a narrow range of colors so that everything you buy will go with many other things you own.
3. *Rotate inventory.* Supplementing your wardrobe on a regular basis will make your money go farther than large, widely spaced shopping sprees.
4. *Stay down-to-earth.* If money is tight, try to buy colors and fabrics that can be worn year-round. That means plenty of earth tones, such as browns and greens. (FD)

What to Buy Yourself for Christmas and Father's Day

- *Cotton and wool socks* are the standard. They wick like crazy. But even a tiny touch of synthetic junk will turn your socks into feet-swamps.
- *Silk and cashmere* socks are a grand extravagance. (EΩ)
- *Black socks* with brown shoes or sneakers are a no-no.
- *Blue socks* look dorky with brown shoes, especially if they match your necktie.
- *White socks* are not to be worn with black shoes or a business suit regardless of the color of the shoe.
- *Short socks:* When worn for business, socks should always go over the calf to avoid showing skin when you cross your legs.
- *Difficult socks:* If you choose to wear socks with an elaborate design or pattern, make sure they somehow match the rest of your clothes, either in color or texture or both.
- *Old athletic socks:* Don't throw them out when you wear holes in them. They're great for buffing your shoes. Just stick your hand in and get to work. You can also use them to pack shoes by slipping one shoe in each sock. (HT, MDW)

How to Ring a Neck

At least once a day, somewhere, somebody turns to a perfectly happy chappy and asks, "Hey, mister. Whatcha wearing a tie for?"

What in the name of heaven has caused this epidemic of informality? Since when do you treat life as though it were a big come-as-you-are party?

Like a simple suit, a necktie is a badge of honor, the battle ribbon of a veteran of the Great Game, the consolation prize of existence, the oriflamme of our gender. A reasonable necktie proclaims your seriousness about the business of being a man. Hang a necktie around your neck, and you're saying, "The Doctor Is In," you're saying, "Take a Number, Please," you're saying, "Do Not Talk to the Driver While the Bus Is in Motion." You're marking yourself as a man to be reckoned with.

THE LANGUAGE OF NECKTIES

A necktie is not a throwaway garment. As much as your suit, your shoes, and your shirt, a necktie makes a statement about you that is loud and clear. That's why a tie should be worn with the same insouciant sassiness normally associated with hats. A necktie has its own rakish tilt, its own dark threat, its own open innocence. A florid spectacle afloat on a sea of gray flannel can be worn only by men who are supremely confident of themselves.

But there are notable exceptions. And all of them are bow ties.

How to Remake Al Franken (left to right): bolo, colonel, Apache scarf. Bottom: A "Poet's Tie." Just say no.

BOW TIES

For most men, formal occasions requiring formal dress provide sufficient justification to wear one of these poseur-ribbons. But prom night and the occasional wedding apparently aren't enough for those who aspire to a kind of daily vamp of poofy superciliousness. On a regular basis throughout this great nation, bow ties are worn everywhere by men who are both terrified and deeply affected.

Why? Who knows. Maybe it's because fifty, seventy-five years ago, bow ties were worn by radio wiseguys and newspaper columnists who traded barbed comments with good-looking dames across a round table. Now every jack with a bow around his neck thinks he's F. P. Adams. As the millennium pales, bow ties have gone one step beyond casual sassiness to something much more depraved: the empty emblem of eccentric cuteness. A bow tie apparently proclaims a man to be witty, brilliant, perhaps a chap of Thurberesque genius. The trouble is, so many men who wish to be seen as Thurberesque geniuses are now wearing bow ties that the claim of brilliance made by that cheap square of gaudy cloth obviously cannot possibly be universally true. Instead of smart men making witty remarks, all we have are a bunch of boring dorks wearing bow ties.

There are only two men in America who may wear bow ties as a badge of merit: George Will and Charles Osgood. Nobody else. All other bow-tie guys are just faking wit. Failing to find a cute thing to say, they try instead for a cute thing to wear. And the very best they can come up with is a lousy bow tie. (JS)

What is being said of importance here is that if you wish to call attention to yourself, paint your face red and die your hair blue, but don't get stupid with neckwear, since people looking at obnoxious men in silly ties see only a rope where the tie ought to be, and secretly they smile to themselves.

But if you must, here's how you tie one. Imagine your head is your shoe, and imagine your bow tie is your shoelace. Tie the tie the same way you'd tie your shoe. Stick out your tongue, if you have to. (DY) (See also above, under "How to Tie a Black Bow Tie.")

NEVER MIND THE QUALITY
Width

In the last twenty-five years, ties, like the men who have worn them, have put weight on and taken weight off. When JFK was president, cool guys wore skinny little exclamation points around their necks. By the time LBJ was out of there, ties were *five inches wide.* Good pilots could set an F-14 down on the neckties of the early 1970s. When God made the first tie, he made it three and one-half inches wide, and he condemned to perpetual ridicule anybody who wavered more than three-quarters of an inch either way. American-made box suits like those from Brooks Brothers and standard-issue neckwear are a timeless combo, the kind of thing that will do for a lifetime for those men who have no need to pursue late-breaking fashion. (DY)

A dissent: The cheapest, easiest way of making sure your wardrobe is up-to-date is to update your necktie collection on a regular basis. Don't throw away the old ones, though, since they'll be in fashion again within ten years. (LA)

Length

Ties vary in length, generally from fifty-four to fifty-eight inches, so it can be difficult to get one to land at the top of your belt buckle, as it should. Here's how to end that dilemma in your life, once and for all: Always take with you, when you go shopping for ties, one that you already have that is the right length. (DY)

TIE TELLS

It's not hard to tell a bad tie from a good one:

When a tie refuses to land dead center at a man's neck, it may be that the tie was made off-center. How to tell: Drape the middle of the tie over one hand and let the two ends fall; the small end should land directly in the middle of the thicker end. If not, the stitching of the tie is off-center. (See also the next section, on knots.) (RES)

Used to be that guys in the know would turn a necktie inside out and count the yellow or gold bars woven into the interlining. Five bars was tops, two was worst, everything else was in between. But all that told you was how good the interlining was, and if you wore all your neckties inside out, everybody'd know how cool your ties were. Of course, some silk ties have no interlining to speak of at all, and many of the best ties are sewn closed and to peek at the guts of the tie would require pocketknife surgery. Men's shops hate that.

So, *to find out how good a tie is, tie one on.* This is a **Main Thing** if ever there was one. There are other things the quality of which you really can't estimate until you tie the knot, but neckties, even expensive neckties, are cheaper. Make one really terrific necktie a part of your closet existence. If you pay attention, it may be just enough to help you build an entire wardrobe—no, an entire *life*—around such a thing.

KNOT NEGOTIABLE

There are three knots every self-respecting man ought to be able to tie before he dies: a square knot, a clove hitch, and a knot we can call *the Single* (or Half-) *Windsor.*

New tie knots show up from time to time, usually to accommodate some oddity in neckwear design. But the knot that most men use never changes, and they usually call it a "Windsor" of some sort, but it usually isn't. Whatever it is, however, it's the knot they live with, at least until the undertaker ties that loose confection called the Mortician Special.

The Knot to Know: The Single Windsor

Sometimes mistakenly called a "Half-Windsor," the SW is tied by simply passing the end of the tie beneath a first cross throw. It is a simple knot and it is superior to all others. The genius of this little tangle is that it allows for easy adjustment and, more important, for a balanced, well-proportioned knot. In a moment of feverish lust, it can be removed, completely untied, with one hand, and looped around a willing wrist in a nanosecond. Because the knot is so compressible, it can be used with ties of almost any fabric: Big, bulky ties can be made to look sleek with a smallish knot, while flimsy, silk flutterers can be given the substance of a larger knot. Properly tied, the Single Windsor will provide a small pleat just off-center and below the knot. A fabulous knot, and the result of Darwinianism, too: The Single Windsor is a more manageable version of a Double Windsor, the knot Larraine Day taught to Cary Grant in *Mr. Lucky* because the knot he'd been wearing was too goiteresque for a swell.

Are Knots Important?

As important as the tie they bind. The peculiar look some English people and some New Jersey automotive retailers bring to neckwear—with knots to the right and knots to the left and knots bulging beneath their throbbing ruby-red necks like smuggled grapefruit—is a result of overzealous neck tying, of throwing a Double Windsor into a tie that just can't stand that much complication. Most ties need only a simple knot firmly, but not tightly, wound, and centered close where the collar meets, with no shirt visible above.

Here's a rule of thumb: If your tie crisscrosses itself more than four times, total, you're a man with a neckwear problem—*knot*. And above all, the knot ought not be the focal point of the tie. When you look at a man's tie, your eyes should be drawn to a point approximately three inches *below* the knot, or about an inch below the point where the pleat stops.

MORE NEWS FOR NECKS

Color

Forget worrying about colors. Of all the things that can possibly go wrong with your choice of a necktie, color is the least. Wear orange with yellow or blue with purple; so long as you don't let your necktie match your shirt or jacket or anything else, you'll be cool, colorwise. Besides, not to get obscure, but tint and shade mean more than color. If you have a muted, chalk-blue shirt and wear a kelly-green tie, you're ugly. But a green tie muted to the same degree as the shirt is beauteousness. (Anon.)

Pattern

More critical than color is pattern and fabric. Here's a tie matcher's checklist:

- *Pinstripe shirts.* Let's say shirtwise you've got a cute little crowded pinstripe number, something in an Oxford, and you want to wear a tie with polka dots. Just *say*, okay? If you make sure the polka dots are tiny, you're in business, so long as some color in the necktie complements the color of the stripe on the shirt. But the scale of the pattern matters, too: If the stripes are big wide refugees from a barber pole and you wear a tie with a huge print on it, you'll look like a man wearing carpet remnants. *The scale is the main thing here.* The rule is big-pattern shirt, little-pattern tie, and vice versa.

- *Plain talk.* For those men looking for an easy way through life, plain shirts and plain ties don't do so well together. A plain tie with a large-scale print shirt looks hopeless, especially if the color of the tie is a dead match with a color in the shirt's pattern.
- *Stripes.* Unless the car rental company you work for requires them, *avoid all striped ties*, for striped ties are the sure sign of a wife-bought tie. (JC)
- *Novelty patterns* defy all rules, so let's put it this way: If you own a necktie with a big picture of a cow on it, you may be assured it goes perfectly with everything else you own. (JS, DY)

Fabric

Few men pay much attention to fabric choices, so here's where your inner clown gets his best shot. Imagine you're wearing a thick, tweed jacket and a rough cotton twill shirt. Then, somehow, your hand involuntarily grabs a silk satin necktie, shiny and smooth as ice, and you put it on. Bells go off, sirens sound, and the dork alarm summons a clothes cop who slaps you around a little until you regain your senses. You look at yourself in the mirror. Of course—wrong tie.

The fabric of a necktie is as subject to mismatch as its pattern, and much more so than its color. A slick suit needs a slick tie. That professorial, burgundy-colored, woolen job with the little square bottom won't work with a smoothly textured jacket or a silk shirt. You'll look like an Irish immigrant who borrowed a suit from Don Trump. On the other hand, a corduroy jacket is just begging to be bedecked with a tweedy, woven necktie. (DY)

The Suit-to-Tie Breakdown
- *Slick suits* (silk, sharkskin, linen, worsted): Slick ties—silk is best.
- *Regular suits* (flannel, linen, cashmere): Silk foulards, tightly woven wool.
- *Avuncular suits* (tweed, wool, corduroy): Knit ties, woolen paisleys.

How to Dress for Weather

OUTERWEAR
The Overcoat

Here is the Main Thing you need to know about this garment:

The overcoat is used primarily to fend off the cold when your suit jacket or blazer is not enough.

- *Color:* Black, navy, or camel.
- *Material:* Wool, cashmere, or camel.
- *Size:* Big enough to fit over a suit jacket or blazer, but not so large that it looks like you're camping in it for the night.
- *Length:* Sleeves should extend slightly past the shirt sleeves. Bottom should go well below the knees.
- *Style:* Overcoats are not a yearly renewable in the ecoforest of your wardrobe. Go for something traditional and, if you're over ninety, you'll wear the same overcoat for the rest of your life. Anything "fashionable" or trendy will make you look like a fool when next year's fashions and trends hit the street. Something simple, single-breasted, and without a belt (which you will lose) fits the traditional bill. (RD)

Another tip for keeping your overcoat for a long time: Avoid one that is fitted around the waist. (EQ)

Trench Coat Dispatch

- *Color:* God intended all trench coats to be beige or tan.
- *Fabric:* High-quality woven cotton.
- *Style:* For once in your life, indulge yourself and pick out the same one that Bogey would have worn. You'll be glad you did. Gunflaps, belts, epaulets, and wristbands all serve a useful purpose: They keep out the wind and rain.
- *Lining:* Want a zip-out lining? Before you buy a coat with a removable lining, make sure the lining and zipper are well made, since this is where most of the wear and stress will occur. When you remove the lining, look for a strip of fabric inside the outer garment that will hide the zipper when you wear the shell without the lining.

  Also, when you send the coat out to be cleaned, send the lining as a separate garment. (RD)

Jacket Copy

Like a hat or a pair of trousers, the jacket you wear should have some relationship to the body that's wearing it:

- *Short, heavy men* should wear longer jackets.
- *Short, slim men* should wear short jackets.
- *Tall, heavy men* should wear midlength jackets.
- *Tall, slender men* can wear anything they want. (EQ, VES)

Another jacket tip: Make sure you have enough room in a new jacket to move. Think of your jacket as the principal thing in your wardrobe when you want to dress up to catch a baseball or pick up a child or change a tire. (SDW)

HOW TO LOOK CRISP ON A WILTING-HOT DAY

Nothing like a bracing dip in the swollen, wet heat of an August day in hell to make you realize that the difference between you and Jacques Cousteau is the accent. You know, it doesn't always have to be like this. You can go through life as a dry human being, a man with crisp pleats and an actual crease, a chap with a honker from which no drop of sweat ever drops. All you have to do is be cool and dress for hot.

Evaporation's the Main Thing

You need natural fibers, such as cotton, if you really want to wear cool clothing. Cotton allows air to pass through the weave, even as it seeks out the smallest possible pool of perspiration, wicks it away from the skin, and uses the moisture for air-conditioning. (EQ)

Avoid Linen, Silk, and Wool

Linen is Hot! How it ever got a rep for being a cool, summer-weight fabric is a matter for the courts. As you perhaps already know from personal experience, not only is linen hot and ugly, it wrinkles pronto: Put on a crisp linen suit and in five minutes you'll look like Columbo's body double. Silk? Same deal. Wool? You bet; wool is for winter. Linen, silk, and wool all have tubular fibers that keep the fabric from breathing and lock in the heat your body produces. Linen and silk are even worse than either one alone. Ironically, however, if you weave silk and wool together, you're okay. (RD)

Lighten Up

To look cooler than you feel, seek out the lightest colors with which you're comfortable. Tans are good, and so is a light khaki. Light blue is cool, but if it makes you feel strange to go around dressed like the host of a TV kiddie show, skip it. Try olive, but a light olive, not a dark olive. (RD)

Loosen Up

Pleated trousers, a loose-fitting 100 percent cotton shirt, and a thin, silk tie is a cool-looking combination. If you want to try something slightly more casual, seek out a fabric called, alternately, pigment-dyed or chemically-washed or enzyme-washed cotton. It's perfect for hot weather. Another surprising twist: A long-sleeved cotton-knit sweater, with the sleeves pushed up, conveys a sense of casual cool. (YR, RD)

Cut It Close
The shorter your hair, the cooler you'll look. When it's one-ten outside, you can't look cool and still be cool, hairwise. (YR, GFS)

HOW TO DRESS FOR COOL
Bond James Bond has the right idea when it comes to clothes: Quality counts; flamboyance and flashiness don't. Here's the generic breakdown on zip-zip-seven's wardrobe:

- *Suit:* Standard issue, dark blue. Look to the weather to be your guide, but when it comes to fabric you only have three choices: serge, alpaca, or tropical worsted.
- *Shirt:* White, cotton, grabber collar—that is, a collar with a pin, tab, or other device to keep the points down.
- *Socks:* Very dark blue.
- *Tie:* Dark, knit, silk. And there's only one Bond knot: a regular-round-over-and-through—a.k.a. a Half-Windsor.
- *Shoes:* Plain black, moccasins for ease of movement, maybe? Well polished. What does all this tell you? Next to attitude, wardrobe means nothing.

(HTh)

How to Become an Optical Illusion

The magnificent seven: "Oh, no!" you say to yourself, "time to either get myself in shape or get my wardrobe in shape." We know the answer. Here are slightly more than a half-dozen ways to help you *look* thinner than you really are:

1. *Breathe.* Wear a shirt with a collar that's not squeezing that extra chin up and out of your throat. Pointed collars make your chin look longer.
2. *Wear a loose-fitting jacket* with shoulders wider than your hips.
3. *Subdue!* Avoid eye-grabbing neckties.
4. *Choose a fabric that drapes smoothly.* Gabardines and worsteds are good.
5. *Wear deeply pleated trousers high on your waist.* The extra drape and length will help guys with large bellies and thick thighs.
6. *Use a conventional-width cuff.* Anything between an inch and an inch and a half will do.

7. *Shine your shoes.* Or, if they're wide and thick-soled, toss 'em in favor of a new pair with a thin sole. (AMcLL)

How to Keep Your Feet Dry

For the hard-jogging, aerobically enhanced man, shoes are where the rubber meets the road, unless you're going to the office. In other words, the shoe you choose has a lot to do with where you're going.

SWEAT SHOES

If you wear athletic shoes as a fashion statement, you don't need our advice. But if you wear them to take care of yourself, you'll want to consider the following before you fork over five grand to buy your next pair.

There's a shoe for every game. Want a pair of tennis shoes? No problem. Golf shoes? Got those. Bowling shoes. Yep. Bingo shoes. See? That's the point: If the game requires mobility, you have to guard your wheels.

Why you shouldn't jog in sneaks. Two different beasts:

- *Tennis shoes* provide lateral stability and support. In tennis, the stress can come from any direction, so you need a shoe that will help you make quick moves from side to side and from front to back.
- *Solid insteps:* Nike's Air Cross-Trainers, with their flat, solid instep and their firm, slightly rounded toe, give great traction to tennis players on the run. But to really stop the skids, try cutting up the old tires off your mountain bike and sew them into the soles of the shoes you're wearing. This gives max traction.
- *Running shoes* are designed for a guy going in one direction: forward. There's a slight heel elevation in a running shoe not found in a tennis shoe. The running shoe is designed not so much for support, but for protection from impact. The kind of impact, however, is what creates a subset of running shoes:

    Long-distance runners bang down their heels with every step, so their running shoes have a slightly elevated heel.

    Middle-distance runners are all over the place, depending on their personal style: Some are heel-first runners, like the marathon men, but others run on the balls of their feet or even on their forefeet. There are running shoes to accommodate each of these styles.

- *Skateboarding* poses a special shoe dilemma, one apparently solved best by Airwalk. The cool-shoe one-two-three among indy nose pickers every-where? Blue Suedes, Tony Hawks, and GTOs.

- *Hacky-sackers* agree that the best bets for footbaggers are the Rod Laver model made by Adidas, the Le Coq Sportif Super Ashe, and Teva sandals. Teva sandals are best for freestyle stuff. One big advantage of the Tevas: You can actually make contact with the bag by using your toes. (RS, BS)

HOW TO DRESS A FOOT FOR WORK

Real-life conversation:

First chap: "The guy from Harvard, did he get the job?"

Second chap: "You kidding? Did you see those *shoes*?"

The lesson: When it comes to sizing you up, you just never know how low a guy will go. Sometimes, out of the whole cosmic soup of a wardrobe, the last thing ends up being the **Main Thing.**

The Seven Sole Sisters

1. *The plain cap-toe* and the perforated cap-toe. These are the dressiest business shoes money can buy. They come in black and various shades of brown, and they are the staple of the business world. They are only appro-priate with business wear, particu-larly of worsted wool and flannel. Ironically, these shoes were origi-nally designed for men in the mil-itary. (GFL)

2. *Wing tips:* In the world of busi-ness, they come in just three colors: black, brown, cordovan. Because of the additional detail, they can be worn with textured fabrics like tweeds and cheviots, as well as worsteds and flannels.

3. *Slip-ons,* or dress loafers: Go easy on the giant, flapping chunks of metal. You could hurt somebody.

4. *The monk strap:* Plain-toed, with a buckle on the side, it allows the wearer to show a bit of style beyond traditional foot-

How to Talk to Al Bundy: The known universe of men's shoe types: Top: monk strap, wingtip, cap toe. Second: tassel loafer, suede shoes, loafer. Bottom: Topsider-type boating shoe.

wear. The classic version is made of suede and was originated by the church.

5. *Suede shoes:* Originally intended only to be worn in the English countryside. If your business environment will let you get away with it, these shoes look great with a casual suit and even better, in contrast, with more severe and conservative suits.

6. *The tassel loafer:* Originally thought to be unacceptable for business, but that thinking has changed in some circles. Here's a rule of thumb: If a blue blazer isn't dressy enough for where you are going, this shoe isn't either. Be careful your tassel is reasonable. If it looks like you mugged a stripper for footwear, you've gone too far.

7. *Summer shoes:* These shoes are for men who can't bear to wear the same style year-round. Essentially, summer shoes are shoes in colors lighter than black, brown, and cordovan to go with lighter-colored summer suits. (GFL, BS)

Technical data: For business shoes, the soles should be a quarter-inch thick or less. The job of the sole is to protect your feet and give support. Heels should be low and follow the line of the shoe. Both should be close-clipped to the rest of the shoe. The welt is what the sole is attached to; a fine pair of shoes will use stitching. The vamp is the leather part of the shoe that covers the top of the foot; a low vamp makes for a sleeker looking shoe. (BS)

HOW TO SHOP FOR SHOES

- *Wait until later* in the day, when your feet have had a chance to swell to their largest size.
- *Wear the same socks* you will be wearing when you wear the shoes you are about to buy.
- *Break:* It may be helpful to also wear the type of trousers you will be wearing the shoes with, to see how they will look in action. (RD)

HOW TO TAKE CARE OF YOUR SHOES

Get into the habit of having your shoes repaired regularly. Your shoes will last longer for two reasons: First, they will never get run down to the point where the repair is pointless. Second, your shoe repair man will get to know you and take better care of you. Other wing tips:

- *Polish your shoes before you wear them* for the first time. This will help them stay clean and maintain a good coat of polish.
- *Don't wear the same pair* of shoes two days in a row. Let them rest, air out, snap back into shape between wearings.

- **Keep your heels in good repair.** Wearing shoes with worn heels causes the leather to stretch in ways that it shouldn't.
- **Polish shoes often** to keep the leather fresh.
- **Keep shoe trees in shoes** to help them retain their shape.
- **Clean suede shoes** with a suede brush or an artist's gum eraser. (BS, VP)

Banana spit: Great execs know time is money. If you're in need of a quick shine, but don't have the time to find a can of polish, try this time-tested ploy: Go to the zoo. Visit the monkeys. Take off all your clothes and sneak into the monkey cage. When some baboon isn't looking, swipe his banana. Climb out, get dressed, knock the dust off your shoes, then rub your leather uppers with the inside of the banana peel. Remove any particles left behind. Then give the shoe a good buff with a napkin. Now you're ready to make *decisions*. (AMcLL)

How to Cover Your Other End: Hats you've heard of, caps you love. From most formal to least:

Top: Top hat, hamburg, cowboy
Second: Fedora, boater, derby
Third: Eight- and six-part caps, seamed cap
Fourth: Flat-top, Fudd-the-hunter, fur cap (Detroit shape)
Bottom: Standard American ball cap

How to Shop for Blue Jeans

In retail, there's a confusing helix of jeans, with prices ranging into serious three-digits for what are supposed to be rough work trousers. But when it comes time to dress-down, don't dumb-down for the occasion. Simply follow this **Main**

Thing rule: *It's unnecessary for any pair of blue jeans to cost more than a pair of Levi's 501s.*

It's not that other jeans might not look better on a chap than a pair of standard-issues; 501s look especially weird on some bodies. It's just that there's no reason for anybody to need to charge more for theirs than Levi Strauss does. You can't get better denim, and you can't get better manufacturing. So no matter how many years have passed since this book's first appearance, to find the very latest going price on a good pair of jeans, price a pair of 501s and go from there. (HEW)

5. Fitness, Health, and Grooming

Once upon a time, the men women admired the most were fat Ottoman Turks, huge guys with beer guts and a swarm of dependents crammed into a seraglio someplace guarded by a bunch of thin, lithe eunuchs. No more. Now women like guys who look like the eunuchs, so it's good-bye big belly, and hello Tony Little.

The benefit of this, of course, is that we're leaner, meaner, and healthier men-machines. Why? Because we learned the little secret disclosed below—and behind a million magazine coverlines:

How to Get Fit Fast!

This little instruction is a dual **Main-Thing**, two-step gem:
  1. Eat less.
  2. Exercise more.

There are, however, some really ugly details, from food to fitness. We'll cover them all.

THE FOUR ROADS TO SWEAT

There are *four basic types of exercises.* Since most men don't have a whole lot of time for exercise, anyway, it's smart to choose a type of exercise that goes directly to your least favorite problem:
  1. *Aerobics.* Great for cardio-circulatory strength. Pretty good at stretching and increasing metabolic rates. Lousy at muscle building.
  2. *Endurance exercise.* The goal of an endurance routine is to get organs like your heart and lungs and other muscles to be able to work for longer and longer periods of time. An endurance exercise can be anything you do from running to walking to racquetball. Each specific activity will deliver its own virtue, but the point of an endurance exercise is to simply increase stamina.
  3. *Strength training.* Building muscles can be more than just piling a heap o' bicep onto your upper arm. You can also strengthen things like your back and feel better for it.
  4. *Flexibility exercise.* Yoga with a dash of anger. The emphasis in flex exercises is to loosen joints and tone muscles. (JTh, GEF)

GETTING STARTED

The most important thing is simply realizing that not only can't you be lazy, you actually have to look for ways to be active. Try these, for starters:
  • *Park a few blocks from work,* walk the rest of the way. And when you walk, try to be conscious of the exercise you're getting. Feel the strength in your legs, loosen your back as you go. Swing your arms freely. Feels good.
  • *Take the stairs,* instead of the elevator.
  • *Use your feet instead of the phone.* When you need to talk to someone down the hall or on another floor, go there. You might walk a few miles every day doing this alone.
  • *Leave your car at the office* or in the garage and walk when you can.
  • *Take the dog for a walk.*

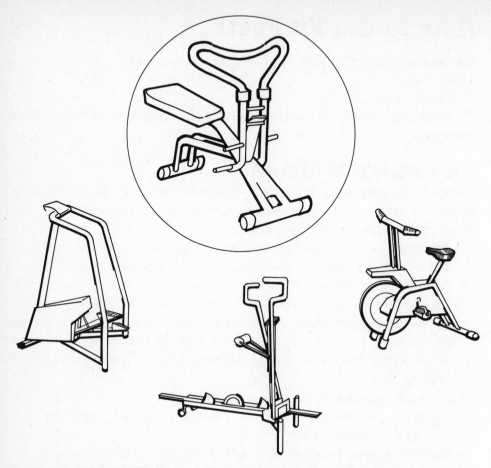

How to Lose Weight Watching "Baywatch": Across the bottom, from right to left: A climber, cross-country skier, exercise bike. But the machine that's tops for most purposes is the rider.

- *Take the wife for a walk.*
- *Turn off the TV* and the computer games and play a game outside with your kids.
- *Make two trips.* Forget efficiency. Whenever you have to get multiple items from one place to another, thumb your nose at time-saving techniques and deliberately carry one thing at a time.
- *Go to the grocery store with your wife.* Push the cart. Carry the groceries to the car one or two bags at a time. Make multiple trips with them into the house, as well. Your wife will think you're a gent. You'll think you're getting exercise. Only one of you will be right.

- *Let older neighbors know you are available* for carrying things like groceries and taking out the garbage. No, don't drive over there when they need help—start your workout by walking there. (JTh)

HOW MUCH EXERCISE DO YOU NEED?

The minimum weekly workout for a healthy person is three times a week, at least twenty minutes per workout. (CV) This must qualify as a **Main Thing**, yes?

How long should you exercise? For however long it takes. According to Uncle Sam, if you're a 150-pound guy, here's what you're going to have to do for one solid hour to burn off calories.

ACTIVITY	CALORIES BURNED PER HOUR
Running	900. We're talking flat-out, here. This is not jogging. See below.
Rowing	800
Cross-country sking	600
Riding a bike	550
Jogging	550
Swimming	550
Tennis	
Singles	550
Doubles	In doubles, obviously, the less you run, the lower the number of calories you burn. But even if you loaf, you're looking at, say, 350 calories, plus or minus.
Backpacking	550
Racquetball	500
Stair climber	400
Mowing the lawn	
with a push mower	400. It really ought to be higher than this, yes? Think about it: Hot day, big sweat, rotten job. And *riding a bike* gives you a higher burn? A bitter injustice.
Lifting weights	400
Golf (no cart)	375
Gardening	350
Aerobics	350
Walking	275
Ping-Pong	275
Cleaning house	250

But don't let this little list fool you. Remember, *the more exercise you do, the faster your body burns calories.* (GS, GEF)

HOW TO WARM UP

In many ways, *all the stuff you do before you do the hard part of any exercise or workout is the stuff that counts most.* You have to steadily increase your heart rate in preparation for a long-term exercise session, and you have to stretch your muscles so they don't tear with the exertion of whatever you're going to do next.

HOW TO STRETCH

Be careful, lads. *The two biggest candidates for injury are those who stretch too little and those who stretch too much.*

One stretch to avoid: the old toe-on-a-step-and-the-back-of-the-foot-hangs-off stretch. When you drop your weight down to stretch your calf muscle, you run the risk of overstretching both the calf and the Achilles. (DSA)

Here is a list of great stretches:

- *Calf stretch.* This stretch treats one leg at a time. Take your time. Stand with one foot in front of another, about two to three feet from a wall. Your back leg should be straight, your front leg should be bent, and both feet should face the wall. Your hands are against the wall. Hold this position for ten seconds, then switch legs. Do this ten times.
- *Hamstring stretch.* Straighten one leg out in front of you and rest it on a footstool, with your knee locked. Bend at the waist and try to touch your head to your leg. Hold for ten seconds. Switch legs and repeat. Repeat ten times. Don't bob and bounce. Take it slow and easy and make all your movements smooth as peanut butter.
- *Knee and lower back.* Lie on the ground. Bring both knees to your chest. Hold for ten seconds. Repeat five times.
- *Push-up.* Come on. You know how to do this. Lie on the ground. Put your hands flat on the floor below your chest. Raise yourself by pushing up with your arms. Hold for ten seconds. Repeat five times.
- *Backward bend.* Stand straight. Put the palms of your hands against the small of your back. Tighten the muscles in your butt and bend backward. Hold for ten seconds, then relax. Repeat five times.
- *Shin stretch.* Sit on a clifftop with your legs hanging over the side. A table will also work. Put a light weight—say three, maybe five pounds—on your toes. Like, maybe a lightweight brass bell. Joke. Okay. Raise your foot at the ankle. Hold for six seconds. Repeat five times. (GEF)

HOW TO KEEP GOING ALL YEAR LONG

One reason nobody considers working out a "sport" is that the season never ends.

Monthly Allowance

Allow for change: Nevertheless, trying to maintain a steady workout pattern through changing seasons can sometimes backfire. Experts recommend taking ten to fourteen days to acclimate yourself to warmer weather by combining exposure to higher temps with more moderate exercise. Then gradually build back up to your usual level. Once you adjust to the hotter temperatures, you'll sweat more, sweat faster, and have a lower body temperature and heart rate during exercise. (AMcLL)

Hot-Weather Runs

Some tips for the heat beat:

- *Timeless:* Leave the watch at home. Trying to beat the clock in hot weather will only cause you to beat yourself to death.
- *Marathon mariner:* Drink lots of fluids because you are sweating more and those fluids need to be replaced. Start with a full glass before you begin running and then drink another glass of water every fifteen to twenty minutes while you run. Careful: Very cold water will give you a mega-cramp.
- *Add salt to the water* you drink to help quench your thirst. If you're running on an empty stomach, skip the salt or it may cause you to get stomach cramps. Gatorade works.
- *Beware of falling blood pressure* that may come as a result of slower blood circulation. When your circulation slows in the heat, your heart has to work harder to get its job done. So it may be a bad time to put an excess burden on it by running full-out. (JTh, LKO)
- *It's not worth dying over.* Here's what **heat exhaustion** looks like:
  You start to feel dizzy.
  You feel extremely dehydrated while running.
  Your breathing gets more rapid than your pace would normally dictate.
  If any of these describes you, stop running *immediately*, get out of the sun, get something cool (but not cold) to drink, and rest.
- *Heatstroke* is even more serious. It can kill you. Watch for these nine symptoms:
  Absence of sweating even though you are very hot.

Skin red and flushed.

Burning in the legs.

A sudden chill, dizziness, or deliriousness.

Difficulty thinking clearly.

Difficulty running straight.

Sudden headache.

A burning sensation in the chest.

Difficulty breathing.

If you think you are experiencing heatstroke, you have to get your temperature down immediately. Lie down with your legs high and your head low as if you were in shock. Drink cool water and, better yet, have someone pour liquid over you, regardless of what it is. Ice is the best thing—rub it all over yourself or have someone else do it. Rub the skin to open the pores so they will let the cooler air under the surface of the skin. Do not cover yourself, for that will only raise your temperature. If you are near someone else and you suspect he is suffering from heatstroke, get the person to the hospital immediately if he is not lucid or conscious. (LKO)

Icy Difference

Cold-weather runs require special attention. Here's 90 percent of a ten-point checklist:

1. *Stretch.* Warm up before you start up.
2. *Avoid ice and snow.* If you have to choose, take the ice.
3. *Slow down* and shorten your stride.
4. *Wear a hat* to keep your body heat where you need it—in your body. The woolen kind are best, because they wick moisture without letting heat escape. At the other, nonverbal end of your body, try wearing a thin sock beneath a thick one.
5. *Wear insulated shorts.* Polypropylene and Gortex are great, breathable fabrics for running.
6. *Don't forget about the windchill* you're creating by running. Run into the wind when you start so that you're running with it when you return full of sweat.
7. *Wear sunblock.* The sun's rays reflecting off the snow can be harsh and even dangerous.
8. *Drink plenty of fluids.* Even though it's cold, you still have to replace the juice you've lost while running.

9. *Make sure your winkie is well-protected.* This is the truth: There are cases of penile injury caused by running in the cold. (JTh, VGS) *What?* It freezes and breaks off?

HOW TO RUN AROUND

You think about running and you think about a million long-stride steps between you and fitness. In reality, if you want to start running, there are only three steps, and they're all quite small:

Warm Up

Don't leave home without a decent stretch. And don't start stretching until you've loosened up a bit. A short walk will help, along with some twisting and bending exercises. Want the full limber-lore rundown? See earlier mention, under "How to Warm Up."

Run

When you run, run easy. The secret: You want to sweat, you want to get your heart beating, but you want to do it without bringing yourself to the point of heavy-breathing, Darth Vader-like exhaustion.

- *The ideal pace:* You'll know it when you find it. It'll be comfortable, and not something that will have you huffing and puffing. Try whistling a few bars of "It's a Small World, After All." If you can't, then either you're running too fast, or you've never been to Disneyland.
- *When you start,* run at least three times a week but not more than four. Make each run last at least twenty minutes; twenty minutes is what it takes to get your heart pounding, your lungs pumping, your glands sweating. And that twenty minutes doesn't include the time it takes you to warm up and cool down. It only includes the hard part.
- *Be a train. Run on time.* It's important to be consistent in scheduling your runs when you first start out. For instance, if you run every other day for three weeks, and then you run three days in a row, and then you skip the next four days, you're only making things hard on yourself. The best thing to do is to schedule your running dates and times on your calendar and keep to the schedule.

IF YOU'VE NEVER RUN BEFORE . . .

Begin by walking. Stretch your arms and legs out in front of you as you go. (GEF)

TOE AND HEEL

Put some spring in your step. Sometimes, the world passes you by. Here's how to catch up:

- *Saunter:* The speed of the average person ambling over to the office watercooler is twenty minutes per mile (m/m), or three mph.
- *Stroll:* Your basic boulevard walker—a guy on his way to a job he enjoys, for example—is fifteen m/m or four mph.
- *Hell-on-leather:* A man with a mission—arms flying, heel-and-toe, and lapping the field—is cruising at a pace of 12 m/m. Figure five mph. (TY)
- *City speed:* Midtown Manhattan traffic at rush hour moves at two to three mph. On a Manhattan avenue, there are approximately twenty blocks per mile. The moral: You can hoof it to work faster than a cabbie can floor it. The benefit: A wonderful aerobic workout, especially on a fine, spring morning. (AMcLL)
- *Next, jog slowly.* Despite its speedy rep, a jog is more of a fast walk than a slow run. Step on your heels, not on your toes, and rock as you would if you were walking at a normal pace. If you can't carry on a conversation as you jog, you're going too fast.
- *Speed it up.* When you feel comfortable at a jogger's pace, try running a bit. The difference between running and jogging or walking has as much to do with speed as it does with how your feet hit the ground and how long they stay there. Try it, come on. Stand up. When you walk, you put one foot down before you pick the other up. Right? See? Down. Up. Down. Up. When you run, you are pushing off with one foot as you place the other. If you try walking that way, you'll run.

    Over time, increase the amount of time in a workout you spend running *versus* jogging or walking. (TY)
- *Make goals for yourself,* as to how much time you will spend actually running during the course of one workout. Start with something small, say, two minutes of running near the beginning of the workout, two more minutes of running in the middle, and two more minutes at the end. But always remember that your heart should dictate how hard you press yourself. (STE)
- *So slow down!* When you're getting started with a new running program, you'll make quicker progress if you mix a little walking in with the running: Run until you're tired, then take a walk. When you're rested, run again. The main thing is to make sure your run or walk workout lasts at least thirty minutes. (AMcLL)

Cool Down

When you are tired out from running, return to a jog—or, if it's more comfortable, return to a walk.

After your run, repeat some or all of your stretches.

After cooling down, lie on the ground or grass and stare at the sky for a short breather. Some guys pray. Some guys don't have a prayer, so they meditate. (TY, EMcG)

First Step, Second Step

Next day: The hardest part of starting to run isn't doing it the first time. It's doing it the second time. Therefore, if you make it your goal to continue running on a regular schedule for, say, *four weeks,* it will be a lot easier for you to slip into your sneakers as part of a routine, rather than a one-time, two-time thing. Why? Because, you reason, anything as unpleasant as the first run just has to get easier. That isn't true, of course, until the tenth or twentieth run, but at least you can see the top of the hill, after which everything is gravity-fed. (EMcG)

- *Madness:* Some people discover the feeling of joy in running. They are insane, of course. But it is possible to get to the point where you would miss it if you stopped running. (LW)

How to Tell Where You Stand

The difference between a beginner, intermediate, and advanced runner is this:

- *A beginner* will only be able to run a very small part of a twenty-minute workout. In some cases, the amount of time spent running will be only a few minutes, while the remainder of the time is spent walking or jogging.
- *An intermediate runner* will be able to run for twenty or thirty minutes without having to jog or walk.
- *An advanced runner* can run for thirty minutes or more without having to walk or jog. Marathon runners can go forever, which is why they are loved by all women. (LW)

HOW TO RIG A BARE-BONES GYM
All You Really Need

If you've got more ambition than bucks, here's the get-by, two-part minimum for putting together a workout facility designed primarily to raise your body's metabolism:

- *Sneakers*
- *Jump rope*

That's it. Everything else is optional. Run and skip your way to boy-god-hood.

Ten minutes with a jump rope is worth two days in the sack with Anna Nicole Smith, if burning fat is what you're after. (RMcD)

Cinder blocks in various sizes, some two-by-fours, and a pulley are all you need to rig a cut-rate, cutthroat lifting station. (GDO'H) Yow! How about going deluxe and adding a bale of hay?

Add-ons

If, however, you're, like, *married* to Anna Nicole, money means nothing. For rich guys and fat cats, add

- *A cross-country skiing machine or a treadmill*
- *A rowing machine*

Multifunctional, Nautilus-type equipment is nice, but not essential. Ditto those riding machines, although they're fun and low-impact. (JS) You can play wildman rodeo on those things if you want to really burn it: Buy a Hank Williams, Jr., CD, turn it up, and *pump.* The best is the Cardio-Fit series sold by Sears. (FLD)

- *A set of weights.* Building muscles is an excellent way to really pump up your body's metabolic rate. Also, muscles eat calories *alive.* (JS) (See also "How to Get Psycho-Fit," later in this chapter.)

Test Drive

Want to buy your own workout machine, but don't know which one to buy? Here are two easy and cheap ways to test them:

- *Health clubs* (see next section) offer free trial memberships. Take them up on it, but just long enough to try out the various kinds of machines and equipment. Remember the stuff you use at home won't be as heavy-duty as the machines in a gym, so concentrate on a *type* of machine, not on finding a specific model.
- *Spend the weekend with your wife* at a hotel that has a well-equipped gym. Sweat all day, sweat all night. You may end up forgetting about the hardware altogether. (TP, EP)

HOW TO SPEND A LOT OF MONEY GETTING FIT

Join a health club. Talk about money! And if you're like most guys who join, check out the babes, give it a shot for a few weeks, then disappear, you might as well buy a self-help diet book you can ignore after a week. It would be a heck of a lot cheaper. (TD)

The Upside

There *are* some valid reasons for joining a gym:

- *Camaraderie.* Sign up with a bud. The chances of slacking off are halved. Besides, it's more fun.
- *Instruction.* Most gyms have a trainer or therapist handy.
- *Tools.* Make sure the gym has a full range of equipment and services. Whatever it has, it's likely to be better equipment than most of us can afford. (GEF, TD)

THE PAINFUL WORKOUT

The Downside

You're gonna get screwed, say a couple of correspondents:

- *Price paranoia.* No two people at a health club pay the same price for membership, and you are probably not the guy who's getting the best deal. A correspondent writes, "A friend of mine, with whom I play handball three times a week, just discovered that even though he travels around the country leading corporate seminars on negotiating, he pays 20 percent more a month for his membership to the club than I do." (SG)
- *Availability.* The other downside is for guys with screwy hours. Unless you live in the big city, you may not be able to go at the times you most want—in the middle of the night, for instance.

  Travel alert: If you travel a lot, make sure the club will let you stop and start your membership so you aren't paying for a lot of time when you're not even in town. (GEF)

What to Look for in a Gym

Okay. Besides that.

- *Location.* You want a club close to work or home. Halfway between would be best. Stop in for your workout on the way to work or on the way home. If you have to go too far out of your way, you'll probably stop going pretty quickly.
- *Ambiance.* Sounds stupid, but it can mean a lot. Check out the culture of the place. Different clubs have different atmospheres. For instance, are you into dressing up or dressing down to work out? Are you likely to be intimidated by others who are bench pressing more than you could safely lift

with a car jack? Will scantily clad women be too much of a distraction for you? Okay, okay. (TD)

Check it out. Ask for a free trial membership. Make sure you go at the time you would be most likely to be there, since that's the only way to assess how busy the place will be. Take a good look at the facilities and exercise equipment. Is everything clean and in good repair? Are there lots of machines with "out of order" signs hanging on them? Take a good look at the locker room. Is it clean? Is there enough room, enough showers, and are the lockers secure? Talk to other members and find out if they are happy or not. (GEF)

- *Value.* Get what you pay for, and don't pay for what you don't want. If all you want to do is lift weights and shower, don't pay for the juice bar, the pool, the sauna, and the Friday nighters. (SG)

Specials. Never join unless the club is offering a "special." And if it's not offering a special today, don't worry—it will be again, soon. It's probably worth your while to wait. Or you can just tell the salesperson that you won't join unless you get to pay the same price as that offered in the last special.

Payment plans. If you go for the payment plan, watch out for the finance manager. He'll have you paying a heavier interest rate than anyone can lift. Paying monthly at 18 or 20 percent interest is no bargain. On the other hand, if you have the cash to pay for a full year in advance, ask for a *hefty* discount. And if you are going to pay for a year in advance, consider calling the Better Business Bureau about the club in question before you do.

- *Transferability.* What if you move? Are you limited to transferring your membership to an affiliated club if one is in the area? In some contracts, the answer is yes—even if you don't like the affiliated club or it is out of your way. If it's a franchise, can you go from club to club and city to city? If not, find out if you can sell your membership if you decide to move or jump ship before it runs out.

A final note: Read the contract as if you were a lawyer. If the club's staff won't let you take it home to read in the privacy of your own home, tell them to stuff it and walk away. (TD)

See also, "How to Be Polite in a Gym," in Chapter 13.

HOW TO GET TO BUFF FROM FLAB IN A FLASH

Life is short. That's the really bad news. The good news is your list of essential exercises—the ones you really have to do if the object of your game is keeping your belly off your belt—is also short. There are exercise freaks out there, of course. But face it, you can exercise all day long and go from buff to more buff, but then you die fit and you miss life along the way.

The better bet: Figure out what part of your body needs fitness first aid, then focus on it. Here's your list:

THE MAIN-THING EXERCISE FOR EACH BROKEN-DOWN BODY PART

BODY PART	NO-FAIL EXERCISE
	(FOR EACH OF THESE, START WITH EIGHT REPS AND GO FROM THERE.)

Legs   **The squat.** Start with your feet slightly apart and a barbell across the back of your shoulders. Now, hunker down, duck-style, like a bear in the woods, until your thighs are parallel to the floor, then slowly raise up.

Calves   **Calf raise.** Grab a dumbbell and hold it in your left hand, arm down, palm facing in. Step onto a riser—a crate or a small bench, maybe, or something else that's at least six inches high. Stick your right foot behind your left heel and rise up on the toes of your left foot. Don't take a tumble; you can use your right hand to brace yourself against a wall or a girlfriend. Next, lower yourself until your heel is a couple of inches below the top of the box. Do this eight times, then do it again with your right leg, and the dumbbell in your right hand. Ow.

Butt   **Kneeling back kick.** Climb up on the end of a workout bench, grasping the sides. Hug it like you love it. Next, raise and extend your right leg directly behind you, until your foot is a few inches higher than your butt. Lower it back down to the bench, and repeat it seven more times, then switch to your other leg.

Chest   **Bench press.** Lying faceup on an exercise bench, grip a barbell with your hands slightly more than shoulder-width apart. Lower the bar slowly until it touches your chest. Leave it there. No, no! Just kidding. Slowly raise it back up. Eight reps.

Back   **Seated row.** You need a machine with a low pulley bar for this one. Sit on the floor in front of the bar, bend your knees a little, then reach out and grab the pulley bar with both hands. Pull it slowly to your chest, keeping your back straight and—as much as possible—perpendicular to the floor throughout the movement.

Shoulders   **Military press.** 'Ten-hut, para-jocks. Stand up or sit on an exercise bench. Grasp a barbell with your hands slightly farther than your shoulders. Raise the 'bell above your head, then lower it until it touches the back of your shoulders.

Triceps   **Triceps pushdowns.** Grab hold of a bar attached to a high-pulley cable. With your hands about six inches apart and with your elbows against your sides, bring the bar down until your forearms are parallel to the floor. That's where you start. Now, push the bar down until your arms are fully extended. Return to the starting point.

Biceps   **Dumbbell preacher curl.** You need the preacher curl station of your multi- for this one. Rest your upper arms on the pad, palms up. Curl the dumbbells up to your shoulders and down again slowly.

BODY PART	NO-FAIL EXERCISE
	(FOR EACH OF THESE, START WITH EIGHT REPS AND GO FROM THERE.)

Abdominals *Belly-sag* is a four-exercise problem. The best of these is the classic crunch, below, but the others can also help big-time.

> • **Crunch.** On your back, with your knees bent, feet together and about a foot from your rump. Cross your arms comfortably over your chest and curl your body upward until your shoulders are maybe six inches off the carpet. Stay there for a sec. Feel that burn? Good. Back down slow and easy.

> • **Twisting crunch.** On your back, with your knees bent, feet together and about a foot from your rump. Cross your arms comfortably over your chest and curl your left shoulder toward your right knee until your left shoulder blade comes off the floor. Then come back down slowly and repeat from the other side. Remember to freeze for a couple of seconds at the top of each rep.
>
> • **Seated barbell twist.** Sitting on the end of an exercise bench, place a barbell across the back of your shoulders. Keep your lower body facing forward and twist your torso to the left, back to the center, to the right, and then back again.
>
> • **Side bend.** Stand with a dumbbell in your right hand. With your back straight, slowly bend to the right as far as possible. Return to the starting point and bend to your left. Do this eight times, then switch sides. (GS)

Noggin See the section "How to Get Brain Buff" in chapter 7.

HOW TO CARRY YOUR OWN WEIGHT

Metaphorically, this would be a **Main Thing** to know. But we're dealing with the literal side of life in this chapter. Alas.

- *First, don't rush.* Position yourself close to the thing you want to lift.
- *Keep your feet shoulder-width apart.*

- *Bend at the knees*—not the waist.
- *Tighten your stomach muscles* as you lift to relieve the pressure on your lower back.
- *Never twist* your body while carrying a heavy load. (AMcLL)
  Okay. Now you're fit. So let's get *crazy.*

HOW TO GET PSYCHO-FIT

If you haven't seen a doctor, if you're in lousy shape, if you have any reason to believe pushing your body beyond the limits God intended might cause you harm, *skip this section* and go straight to the section "How to Pick Up Women in Aerobics Class." But if getting fit, to you, is more than just an extension of lifestyle eccentricities, more than just a subject of sweaty fanaticism, you'll be pleased to note that there's a guy out there who agrees with you. He's the guy who thought up what he calls "psycho-training," in which you die looking your best. Here, for the edification of us all, is how health clubs in America might operate if we handed over our towels and locker keys to North Koreans.

The Bifurcated Buffer

According to our correspondent, there are two parts to the psycho-trainer method of getting really huge really quickly:

1. **A sadistic partner.**
2. **Some sadistic exercise methods.**

Make no mistake about it, this workout is going to hurt, and it will hurt a lot (you'll learn later that this is a good thing). There are a few general benchmarks to the workouts that will let you know if you're doing them correctly.

Signs of a Good Set

Don't go for glory. Go for broke:

- *A good set really sucks and hurts.* (This is a general guideline; later on, we'll outline what constitutes proper suck and proper hurt.)
- *You can't move very well* the day after doing an exercise.
- *You can't move very well* two days after doing an exercise.
- *During an exercise* you hear weird animal noises, then realize you're the one making them.
- *Your face changes more than four shades of red,* purple, or black during a set.

- *You see stars,* get tunnel vision, and then come-to with a bar resting comfortably on your neck.

Don't Go Psycho Alone

The first thing you'll need is a good workout partner or two. Two is better than one, for it reduces the possibility of one person wimping out and dragging the intensity of the workout down to a sane level. Whether the partner is stronger or weaker than you is irrelevant. However, attitude is everything: the more sadistic, the better.

And don't forget to take your turn when it's time to be a psycho-partner yourself. This will allow you to push your partner harder, thus making him seek revenge later. Revenge is a great motivator for these types of workouts.

Pain Counts

Just lifting more is not enough to be psycho. You need to go for the big hurt. This can be achieved by upping the intensity of each exercise. There are two recommended ways for reaching psycho-intensity levels: preexhaustion and breakdown.

PREEXHAUSTION

This technique works well on complex exercises like the bench press and the military press. Let's look at the bench press:

- *Warm up.*
- *Get dumbbells* that you would normally use for flat-bench dumbbell flys. Know what a flat-bench dumbbell fly is? You lie on your back, dumbbell in each hand, your arms out on each side. Now squeeze your arms together back up at the top. After a while, it hurts good. Try it with about 40 pounds and see what happens. That's a "flat-bench dumbbell fly." Now ratchet it up to psycho-level:
- *Load the bench press* with slightly more than warm-up weight—maybe 150 pounds. With the 40-pound weights, do a set of dumbbell flys until you fail, and fail hard—but do at least twelve reps.
- *When you finally flag, immediately* drop the weights and start bench-pressing the 150-pound weight. This will suck and hurt. This is good. This is great for developing the chest, especially when the shoulders and arms are already tired from the week's previous workouts.

Preexhaustion uses an isolation exercise—the flys—to fatigue the chest to failure, then uses the relatively fresh shoulders and arms to force even more stress on the chest during the bench press. This is also a great exercise for those guys who fear they may die of heart failure at an early age, because they find out *right away* whether their fear has any basis in fact.

BREAKDOWN

The breakdown is a great way to increase the intensity and can be used on almost any exercise. It is generally best used in conjunction with your normal workout.

- *Go back* to the bench press.
- *Warm up.*
- *After a few sets* of your normal routine, load about 90 percent of your max onto the bench, or about what you can do for, say, two unassisted reps. Bench-press the weight for *four* reps, getting help as you need it from your sadistic spotter, who should note that the lifter should be just about purple by the time the weight gets back on the rack.
- *After putting the weight on the rack,* *immediately* strip off about 60 percent of it and keep benching, getting at least eight reps.

  You need to strip off a good chunk of weight to make this principle work. If you are benching 150 pounds, fail hard, and then pull off only 20 pounds, the weight isn't going to feel any lighter, and you'll never be able to get the reps that you need.
- *In the last stage of a breakdown,* you should be able to bench at least six reps unassisted to make it work. The psycho-partner is very important in the last stage of the breakdown lift. The weight is light, but the lifter is tired. The partner uses psycho-principles to focus the lifter's effort on lifting and get his mind off the awesome hurt he's feeling (he's doing it right). Two breakdown sets per exercise are usually enough.

Frequency

Three psycho-days per week of weights is enough. More will get you less. *Lifting seven days a week like a psycho is too much stress for your body to handle.* You will work yourself into a bad cycle of overtraining, in which you actually see negative results.

Harder, not longer, is the goal of these workouts. Doing a bzillion sets of an exercise may make you better at that exercise, but not improve the body part as much as doing fewer and harder sets. *Psycho-training should be used in conjunction with sensible planning.* Train psycho for a week, and use your normal training routine for a week, or alternate psycho and normal workouts. As always, let your body be the guide.

Rest is key. The body can't heal the massive amounts of stress you've placed upon it in a single day. In fact, sometimes it will take two or three days to fully recover.

The following are a couple of sample workouts and ways to divide your body up to maximize the psycho principles. These are general workouts and can be modified to suit your tastes. Remember, superior effort brings superior results. Get psycho and have fun. Or die.

Psycho-Workout Plan 1

The principle here is to go for more weight and fewer reps and the sets will progress. In psycho-training, eight to four reps at 60 to 80 percent of max is your standard coed stuff.

MONDAY: CHEST AND BACK

- *Bench press:* Three sets of eight to four reps, 60 to 80 percent of max. Two of the previous sets should combine preexhaustion and breakdown (as specified in the previous section).
- *Incline bench press:* Three sets of four to twelve reps, 50 to 100 percent of max.
- *Lat pulldowns.* Three sets of twelve to four reps, 50 to 80 percent of max. Two sets of breakdowns.
- *Cable rows:* Three sets of four to twelve reps, 50 to 80 percent of max. Two sets of breakdowns, from 90 percent to 60 percent of max. One set double breakdowns—fail, drop 60 percent, fail, drop 60 percent.

WEDNESDAY: SHOULDERS AND LEGS

- *Hack squats:* Three sets of fifteen to eight reps, 50 to 80 percent of max. *Then* one set of thirty-plus reps with warm-up weight.
- *Leg curls:* Three sets of twelve to eight reps, 50 to 80 percent of max.
- *Leg extensions:* Three sets of twelve to eight reps, 50 to 80 percent of max.
- *Military press:* Five sets of twelve to eight reps, 50 to 80 percent of max. Three sets preexhaustion using lateral dumbbell raises first.
- *Shoulder shrugs:* Two sets, 50 to 90 percent of max. Two sets double breakdowns. Ten to four reps.
- *Calf raises:* Three sets of ten to twenty reps, 50 to 90 percent of max; breakdowns on all sets.

FRIDAY: ARMS

- *Preacher bench curls:* Three sets of fifteen to eight reps, 50 to 80 percent of max.
- *Straight bar curls:* Three sets, all breakdowns.
- *Concentration curls:* Two sets of *double* breakdowns.
- *Lying French presses* (skullcrushers): One set normal of fifteen to eight reps, 50 to 80 percent of max. Two sets of breakdowns.
- *Triceps pushdowns:* Two sets normal of fifteen to six reps, 50 to 80 percent of max.
- *Triceps kickbacks:* Three sets of twelve to ten reps, *with good form.*

Psycho-Workout Plan 2
MONDAY: CHEST AND BACK

- *Bench press:* Three sets with preexhaustion and breakdown (as specified above).
- *Incline bench press:* Three sets of four to twelve reps, 50 to 100 percent of max; breakdowns on all sets.
- *Lat pulldowns:* Two sets of twelve reps at 50 percent of max, four reps at 80 percent of max. *Then* do a breakdown immediately after the last set at 80 percent.
- *Dead lifts:* Two sets of fifteen to ten slow reps (two to four seconds up and two to four seconds down).

WEDNESDAY: SHOULDERS AND LEGS

- *Squats:* Three sets of fifteen to thirty reps, 50 to 80 percent of max.
- *Leg curls:* Two sets of twelve to eight reps, 50 to 80 percent of max.
- *Leg extensions:* Two sets of twelve to eight reps, 50 to 80 percent of max.
- *Military press:* Three sets of twelve to eight reps, 50 to 80 percent of max. Two sets preexhaustion using lateral dumbbell raises first.
- *Shoulder shrugs:* Two sets, 50 to 90 percent of max. Two sets double breakdowns.
- *Calf raises:* Three sets of ten to twenty reps, 50 to 90 percent of max. Toes in and out on at least two of the sets.

FRIDAY: ARMS

- One sixty-second slo-mo chin-up (thirty seconds up, thirty seconds down), followed by straight bar curls (eight to twelve reps). Do this cycle twice. Then:

- *Concentration curls:* Two sets of double breakdowns.
- One sixty-second slow-mo dip (thirty seconds up, 30 seconds down), followed by *lying French presses* (skullcrushers). Do this cycle twice.
- *Triceps pushdowns:* Two sets normal of fifteen to six reps, 50 to 80 percent of max.
- *Triceps kickbacks:* One set of ten to twelve reps, *with good form.* (JP)

You are now psycho. So what's left for a guy who's both buff and bonkers? Aerobics, of course.

HOW TO ATTEND YOUR FIRST AEROBICS CLASS WITHOUT LOOKING LIKE A DWEEB

- ***Do homework.*** Buy or rent a tape and practice at home until you get the hang of it.
- ***Hang.*** Go to the club and hang out at the back of the class. You can watch the teacher and all the students in front of you, but most of them will be unable to watch you—that is, until the instructor has everyone turn and face the opposite direction, in which case you will then be in the front of the class on exhibit before all.
- ***The Main Thing: Don't worry about it.*** Everyone had to start somewhere, and (almost) everyone there will be friendly and eager to help you. Take a beginner's class and enjoy yourself. Do the parts that you can pick up easily, stop when you get confused, and watch the teacher and students in front of you. Lousy at dancing? Try to pick up the steps one piece at a time. The truth is, once you get a few basic moves down, you'll be able to do anything the instructor dishes out. Aerobics is not ballet. It's not even ballroom dancing.
- ***How long:*** The minimum one would want to exercise on a weekly basis is for twenty minutes, three times a week. The goal is to reach 60 to 90 percent of what therapists call your "age-specific maximal heart rate" during the exercise period.

    To determine maximal heart rate, use the following formula to determine a high and low rate between which you want your ticker to tick. To figure the high rate, take 220, subtract your age, and multiply the result times 60 percent. The low rate is 60 percent of the high rate. (RDL)

HOW TO PICK UP WOMEN IN AEROBICS CLASS

Since aerobics class isn't where a guy goes to get buff, there are only two valid reasons for signing up. Either you have a medical condition and need therapy, or you're there to meet women dressed in leotards. Let's assume you're pursuing reason number two:

- *Take your time.* In an aerobic romance, only the bodies move quickly. All relationships develop much more slowly in an aerobics class than they do in real life. Why? Remember, you've got her in a vulnerable spot. Unless she's one of those few women who is completely unself-conscious about her body, she is bound to be aware of the fact that you are checking her out while she is, sort of, kind of, partially undressed. For some women, aerobics is also a very private time. Invade it at your own risk. You're looking at a twice-the-street-average rate of rejection here, anyway.

- *Make eye contact first.* A smile will go a long way the first time you see her in class.

- *Speak.* Next day, smile and say hello. Progress a small step each time you see her. When it's time for conversation, make it about something neutral, something you both have in common. Events at the club. The aerobics class. Nonthreatening current events in your town. Don't talk about her thong-'tards. No thigh talk.

- *Lean into it.* Pick up on her body language. This is a good time to let what you perceive to be "no" mean "*no!*" and "yes" mean "probably not." If you think her demeanor is all green lights, proceed as if she were giving you a yellow. And remember, just because she smiled at you, just because she made small talk with you, doesn't mean she's available. She might just be friendly—and married. (JEH, Anon.) Or she might be the girlfriend of the guy doing psycho-training. In the next room.

WHAT TO DO ONCE YOU'VE BUILT A BETTER BODY

There are only two things you can do with a body once you've got it sculpted. First, you can *find a regular maintenance program and stick with it.* Especially if the focus of your fitness program has been to develop muscle, you have to keep it in shape forever. (JP)

The other thing you can do with your body is *take it to the beach.*

How to Go to the Beach

A beach is where all you have going for you is whatever you got from the manufacturer. You check all accessories at the door. You can leave all those Armani body wraps hanging in the closet, you can forget all those power ties and Eye-tie loafers with stupid tassels when a guy like you goes coastwise.

Nowhere to hide: The big sign at the entrance to every beach says,

"Nothing allowed." Winning personalities, great senses of humor, big-buck mega-jobs, sensational SAT scores are almost completely invisible in the bright light of a sun-bleached beach. On the beach, what you see is what you get, and, for all they know, what others see is what you are. That's why important diplomatic meetings are never conducted in a luau setting.

VIRTUE'S REWARD

There's also a certain amount of naturally occurring justice on every beach. All the bills you ran up all winter come due in the heat of summer: For guys who spent the whole winter reading about fitness while choking down brews and chili-dogs, the beach is where you pay the tab for six months of backsliding, for instance. Every extra helping of pasta, every last gotta-have-it Oreo is displayed prominently just above your trunks. On a beach, you become a walking museum of your own personal natural history of gluttony and indolence, as if you were wearing a sandwich board reading, "Will eat for work."

The men who thought ahead, who lived every winter day as if it were the day before the first day of summer, are easy to spot. For guys who kept their Nordics on track and their Solos flexed, a trip to the shore is, in every respect, a day at the beach.

DESIGNER BIRTHDAY SUITS

Dressing down and out: In terms of fashion and society, an afternoon on the beach is just down the ladder a rung or two below garage sales and basement floodings. What you have on a crowded beach is a skivvy party, a get-together for strangers who all show up in their underwear. Men and women both react to this reality with astonishing hypocrisy. A power broker who spends all week in a gray suit making prudent financial decisions, and a women's studies professor who spends all week institutionalizing prudery, will both turn up at the local surf club wearing shoelaces—and then not only demand to be taken seriously, but also deny, often vehemently, that their close brush with nudity creates any prurient response. People truly concerned with nonobjectification go to a public beach wearing a floral print muumuu over a vast, black, one-piece bathing suit. They carry a big umbrella and a small chair. They read, and never, ever look up, lest they objectify somebody else.

NUDE BEACHES

Scandinavians love taking off all their clothes. But Scandos also have the world's highest suicide rate, so be careful. **The Main Thing** to remember about nude beaches is that *everybody* **is expected to get nude.** Since most guys like spectator sports more than participator sports, this can be a problem. Nudists say after you're around a bunch of naked people for a while, you forget they're naked. That's because most people don't look fabulous without clothing on. A person who looks great clad, however, will also look great unclad, and that's when you'll remember she's naked.

Let's change the subject.

Health

There's only one **Main** health-related **Thing** we all want to know:

How to Live Forever

Never get sick. On the other hand, there's nothing like a bout of acute hypochondria to put the fear of God into an otherwise healthy man.

THE HYPOCHONDRIA CHECKLIST

Feeling lousy? Like there's some ugly tumor growing just inside your forehead? Could be brain cancer. Or it could be hypochondria. Here's how to tell the difference:

1. When your doctor makes a diagnosis, do you feel it's probably wrong?
2. After you read or hear about a new illness or disease, do you find that the symptoms describe what you're suffering?
3. Have you ever gone from doctor to doctor because you felt your old one wasn't taking you—and your grotesque illnesses—seriously enough?
4. If you asked your friends how often you talk about your health, would they laugh out loud?
5. Do you feel sick if your doctor discovers that what ails you is really something very much less significant than the ebola variant you had imagined?
6. Are you often on the phone with your doctor to describe new symptoms of new illnesses?
7. Did you answer yes to one or more of the above? If so, the next illness you talk to your doctor about ought to be hypochondria. The nice thing is, this time the doctor's bound to listen and be enthusiastic about

helping, and also have plenty of experience with your problem. Hypochondria afflicts as many as half of all visitors to a typical family doctor's office. (GF)

DEATH'S DIRTY DOZEN

On the other hand, here are the actuarial all-stars, the twelve horses upon which the grim reaper rides. Say hello now. You may become better acquainted later.

Although, note: *Mike Lafavore once told me that if science discovered tomorrow the magic bullet that could cure all known cancers, our average lifespan would increase just slightly more than two years. But if science found a cure for all forms of heart disease tomorrow, we'd all get an extra decade or more.*

1. *Heart disease/heart attack*

Symptoms: Intense pain in the chest, feels like a heaviness or intense pressure. It may extend beyond your chest into your left shoulder and arm or into both arms, or to your back, neck, teeth, and jaw. At first it may feel like intense indigestion and may be accompanied by nausea, vomiting, a shortness of breath, and intense bouts of sweating.

2. *High blood pressure/hypertension*

Symptoms: No outward symptoms, but if you have a family history of hypertension, eat a lot of salt, drink a lot, are obese, are African-American, get little or no exercise, have problems sleeping, or are often stressed out, you are a good candidate.

3. *Prostate cancer and prostatitis*

Symptoms of prostate cancer: Problems urinating, which include an inability to urinate or start urinating, blood in the urine, a weak or interrupted flow, a flow that is painful to stop, burning sensations when urinating. Increased need to urinate at night. Lower back pain, and pain in the upper thighs and pelvis.

Symptoms of prostatitis: Fever, problems (burning, bleeding) urinating, lower back pain, pain in the upper thighs and pelvis.

The two illnesses aren't the same thing. Both are painful, but while prostate cancer can kill you, prostatitis hurts more. While some researchers have suggested hormonal imbalance or immune system disorders as causes for prostatitis, the chances are it's a bacterial or viral illness. Doctors aren't sure yet, since they can't find a specific infection in most sufferers, but the routine prescription is for antibiotics, since that's what seems to work best.

Guys over forty ought to get to know their doctors on this one: A yearly checkup—called, with delicate poetry, a "digital-rectal exam"—is mandatory for midlife men. Besides, the self-exams are a pain.

Five wisecracks every urologist loves to hear: Does this mean we have a relationship? I suppose now you've lost all respect for me. I know you: You won't even call me tomorrow. We never talk.

4. *Diabetes*

Symptoms of insulin-dependent diabetes: Frequent urination, sudden weight loss, excessive thirst and hunger, weakness, fatigue, irrational behavior or irritability, nausea, vomiting.

5. *Stroke*

Symptoms: A sudden feeling of weakness on one side of the body—in the face, or on the hand, arm, or leg; loss of speaking ability or loss of the ability to understand what others are saying; double vision, loss of vision in one eye or a dimming of vision in one eye; headaches without a cause or a change in a normal pattern of headaches; dizziness, vertigo, unsteadiness, proneness to falling; an awkwardness or clumsiness with one limb or more—a symptom which may first be detected as an unexplained change in handwriting.

6. *Emphysema*

Symptoms: Shortness of breath; chronic, persistent, often mild cough.

7. *Lung cancer*

Symptoms: Persistent coughing that contains phlegm, which may be blood-streaked. Shortness of breath, chest pain, hoarseness, loss of appetite, loss of weight.

8. *Pneumonia*

Symptoms: Painful cough with or without bloody phlegm, pain in the chest, difficulty breathing, fatigue, chills, high fever.

9. *Tuberculosis*

Symptoms: Begins with mild cough and fever; followed by chronic fatigue. Also, weight loss, cough with bloody phlegm, fever, and night sweats.

10. *Liver disease and cirrhosis*

Symptoms: Loss of appetite and/or weight loss, nausea and vomiting, fatigue, weakness, jaundice, pain in the abdomen and intestinal bleeding, easy bruising, broken blood vessels under the skin that look like tiny red spiders, loss of interest in sex and/or impotence, itching, swelling of legs and abdomen.

11. *Skin cancer*

Symptoms: Sores that don't heal, lumps or growths that are firm to the touch and that grow or bleed, moles that are black or brown, have a splotchy appearance or an uneven border; moles that change size or shape; moles that itch or become sensitive. (GS, GF)

God willing, you'll never have any of the diseases listed above. But a cold? Guaranteed. Unless you follow directions.

HOW TO PREVENT THE COMMON COLD

There's no cure yet, but while you're waiting try a few of these relief techniques:

- *Take lots of Vitamin C.*
- *Take beta carotene:* 50,000–100,000 units a day in divided doses.
- *Cut out booze and coffee* during cold season.
- *Eat lighter and eat less* during cold season. If you eat a lot, your body has to work harder to digest the grub. But that same energy you're using to digest could be used to fight off any hideous cold cooties that try to invade the temple of your manhood.
- *Chop up two to four cloves of raw garlic* and swallow them with water. And stand over there, please.
- *Go to France.* The leading cold and flu medicine in Europe is Oscillococcinum. It stimulates the body's defense mechanisms and helps you fight off bugs.
- *Herbal medicines* like echinacea, goldenseal, and yarrow will help you fight off a cold.
- *Go classical:* Ancient Romans used to soak an onion in water, then sip the broth. Of course, they're all dead.
- *Go Revolutionary:* Similarly, eighteenth-century Americans drank a tea made of sage, hyssop, yarrow, black cohosh, buckthorn, goldenseal, coltsfoot, and bloodrot. A revolting brew, by the way.
- *Visit the juiceman* and drink lots of celery and grapefruit juice. Carrot juice. Carrot, celery, and parsley juice. Carrot and cucumber or carrot and beet, or mix all three. (RET, GF)

Treatment
- *Drink a tea* of onion and garlic.
- *Breathe a steam* of water from a pot containing water with oil (or leaves) of eucalyptus, pine, cloves, or thyme. (GF)

- **Do a blue-bath healing:** You need a blue candle and some blue healing bath salts. Fill your tub with water and add a couple, three tablespoons of salts. Put one foot into the tub and feel the sickness drain from your body into the water. Repeat with other foot. Sit in the tub and feel the illness drain from your entire body. When the water becomes cool, drain the tub—don't get out—and watch your illness go down the drain. Use the shower to wash the remainder of the illness from your body. (HGR)
- **New tea:** Garlic, green onion, basil, ginger, and mustard or cinnamon— boil for five minutes. (JAS)
- **Take a fever bath** using marigold, thyme, lavender buds, pennyroyal, elder flowers, mugwort. Mix a quarter cup of each and soak it all in a quart of water. Once the mix is saturated, boil, then let it simmer for twenty minutes. Pour the liquid off into a bowl and pour that into a hot bath. Wrap the solids in a towel and rub over body while lying in tub. (WO)
- **Pray:** Orthodox Christians pray for help from St. Nectarios and St. John Maximovich, among other saints. Holy water and holy oil are also useful in effecting cures. Skeptics note: Medical researchers—including some at Harvard and the NIH—are researching the statistically significant, inexplicably efficacious effects of prayer as a healing agent. Eventually, who knows? They may find God. (DB)

DO-IT-YOURSELF POST-OP MAINTENANCE

If you want to lose a Band-Aid but keep all that attractive body hair, do this: *Point a hair dryer at the bandage for a few moments.* When the adhesive melts, you can pull the strip off easily. (ES)

HOW TO BLAME SOMEBODY ELSE FOR YOUR BAD MOOD

Specifically, Pop: According to a researcher in Pennsylvania, as much as 40 percent of the cause for an irritable personality can be laid at the feet of genetics. (AMcLL)

HOW TO MAKE EVERYBODY IN CHINA ITCH

Urushiol oil, that colorless stuff that gives poison ivy, oak, and sumac its special charm, is so potent that a mere *one-billionth of a gram* is enough to give sensitive folks an itch. You could squeeze enough to infect everybody in China on the tip of your finger. Plus, the oil stays potent for up to five years, so last year's work gloves still have what it takes to make your skin crawl.

The good news is you can defeat poison ivy by simply washing the affected area with soap and water. You have about fifteen minutes to come clean, so hurry. If you've stumbled on poison ivy someplace in the waterless expanse of, say, the Sahara, a moist towelette will do the trick. Even slo-mo washers have a shot at avoiding the rash: One researcher found that wiping exposed skin with a moist towelette within a half hour and every half hour after that can decrease the severity of the outbreak by up to 80 percent. (AMcLL)

HOW TO DEMOLISH YOUR DENTURES

Looking for the wrong tool for the job? Try your teeth. They make a lousy wrench, a chintzy nutcracker, a completely unreliable C-clamp. Want some better ways to ruin a good set of choppers?

Dental experts cite the following as major causes of large dental bills:

- *Chewing ice cubes.* Cracks teeth and fillings. Duh.
- *Sucking lemons.* Citric acid damages your tooth's surface.
- *Brushing like crazy.* Overbrushing is the major cause of gum recession.
- *Using a toothpick.* Floss does it better and with less risk of injury. (AMcLL)

ACHES, PAINS, AND OTHER COMPLAINTS

A small but eccentric collection of gripes:

How to Gracefully Wend Your Way down the Aisle

After a two-hour movie? Make sure you've spent your time with your feet flat on the floor, or, if that's too tight, with your ankles crossed. Either of these positions will relax the pressure on your legs. The worst position? One ankle over the thigh. It looks damned manly—and gives a nice presentation to those tube socks—but you're also temporarily shortening the leg muscle, curving your spine, and pinching the nerves in your leg. The result? Shooting pains from your heinie down to your toes. (AMcLL)

How to Ride in Style

Walkin' like a cowpoke but ridin' a bike? Could be those sores are caused by a poorly adjusted saddle. Your bike's seat should be level and at a height where your knee is just slightly bent at the bottom of your pedal stroke. Also, trade those Lycra shorts in on some good, old-fashioned, 100 percent cotton briefs. Cotton absorbs moisture and makes for a more comfortable ride.

If your discomfort is coming at the other end of your body, take a look at your helmet. It should fit straight around your noggin and the straps should make a nice V just below your ears. Finally, shake your head. If the helmet shakes more than your head, adjust it. (AMcLL)

How to Prevent Kidney Stones

Pass the stones, please. Life just too sissified for you, Arnold? Need a man-sized pain challenge? Looking for a way to recapture the moral edge after your wife's gone through childbirth? Then forget rock climbing, say no to hang gliding, and skip the bungee. Go straight to *kidney stones!* What better way to show your woman you're a man than to pass some of those glasslike slivers right out the old willie?

The good news is you only have to show her once. After that, prevention is your likely choice. Here's what to know before you go:

- *Keep your piss watered down.* Drink water. Lots of it, too. Eight glasses a day. Give your whole body cavity a nice hydroponic environment. What's good for tomatoes is good for kidneys.
- *Add calcium.* The lab boys at Harvard studied 45,000 men—a stadium-full—and found those who consumed the most calcium had the *lowest* risk of peter-rocks.
- *Bogart that beef.* Vegetarians have only half as many stones as the rest of us. However, they have twice as much self-righteousness.
- *No salt.* That sodium crystal on your eggs is tomorrow's weenie-Gibraltar.
- *Up to your potassium in 'taters.* The same Harvard study that made the paradoxical calcium finding also discovered that high levels of potassium lower the risk of stones. Good sources: oranges, nectarines, spuds, and, of course, *bananas.* (ATR)

Five Foolproof Ways to Cure Hiccups

1. *At last! The cure for hiccups!* According to a gastroenterologist from Philly, all you have to do is plug your ears with your fingers for twenty seconds.
2. *No, no. Wait! Try this!* Hold your breath for sixty seconds. Breaks the spaz cycle in your diaphragm.
3. *No! This!* Slowly sip water for two minutes. You'll drown, but you'll stop the hiccup.
4. *No! Not that! This!* Breathe into a paper bag for a couple of minutes. This is especially elegant as well as effective at formal dinner parties.

5. *Or this!* If you just can't stop, use your affliction to your advantage: Pretend you're a Latin scholar. Here are some useful hiccup phrases: *Hic et ubique; hic et nunc; hic jacet . . . ; hoc opus, hic labor est;* and the best of all, *hic, haec, hoc.* (AMcLL)

How to Have a Date with a Coma

The planet's all-time favorite complaint? *I'm tired!* Fatigue following a good night's sleep can be a symptom of anything from obesity to depression to alcoholism. But not being able to fall asleep—well, that's an Everyman kind of problem.

Four golden solutions:

1. *Don't toss and turn* for more than twenty minutes. Get up and do something useful, but nothing strenuous.
2. *Hide the clock* and turn on some white noise. A small room heater turned to the "Fan Only" setting will even out extraneous noise.
3. *Exercise early* in the day. Revving up your body just before you park it doesn't do much to help induce a temporary coma.
4. *Use a relaxation technique.* Some guys count, some guys have sex, some guys pray. Some guys pray for sex—but that's no way to get sleep. Or sex. Or religion. (TFR)

How Long to Pack a Twisted Ankle in Ice

First comes the icy walk, then comes the twisted ankle, then comes even more ice. But how much ice? And for how long? The answers: lots. For the second question, exactly twenty-five minutes, no more, no less. Researchers in Chicago found that if you take a gallon-sized plastic bag, fill it with ice, wrap it around the joint completely, and tape it in place, healing will start within five minutes and peak at twenty-five. After that: trouble. Icing for longer than a half hour can cause damage to the tissue and the nerves. (GS)

How to Give a Warm Round of Applause

To quickly warm up cold hands, swing your arms downward behind your body, then upward in front of you, like a crazed softball pitcher. Do it fast: About eighty swings per minute is what you want. The exercise drives blood to the fingers by using both gravity and centrifugal force. (DMcI)

How to Improve Everything

It's a **Main Thing** if ever there was a **Main Thing:** *Stop smoking.*

According to various experts, all working in tight harmony with your girlfriend and your mom and everybody else who's trying to get you to breathe easier, there are more reasons to stop smoking than you ever dreamed of. Here's a quick dix:

1. You'll have better sex, since blood will flow easier to your penis.
2. You'll drive better. Smokers are one and a half times more likely to wreck than nonsmokers.
3. You'll heal faster after the wreck. Up to 80 percent faster, docs say.
4. You'll smell better.
5. You'll have quicker reflexes.
6. You'll sleep better, plus—
7. You'll have sweeter dreams.
8. You'll produce more sperm.
9. You'll cut your risk of stroke in two.
10. You'll be calmer and more focused. (FAC)

How to Add Three Inches to Your Height

Research suggests that *your posture is one of the first three things people notice about you.* Slouch and your world slouches with you, because, according to experts, you're sending a signal that you feel badly about yourself. Stand straight up for yourself, however, and you signal self-confidence. You also increase your energy by making it easier for your lungs to expand, help strengthen your abs and lower back muscles, and add up to three inches to your height. (AMcLL)

How to Test for a Ruptured Achilles Tendon

Touch-football vets know how easy it is to rupture an Achilles tendon. The only good news is that it's even easier to test for one. This rupture test is almost always accurate—and you can do it at home. Here's how:

1. *Sit in a chair* with another chair in front of you. Extend your leg so your ankle is suspended over the edge of the second chair. Completely relax your leg.
2. *Squeeze the back of your leg* firmly just below the widest part of your calf muscle. If your tendon's in working order, your foot will automatically extend forward. If it doesn't, you may have a tear. (FF)

How to Dress Better for a Hernia

No truss, no muss. Say so long to that good-looking chunk of elasto-girdle you've been using to hold back the hernia time forgot. Doctors are using a mesh plug in place of old-fashioned in-patient hernial repair techniques. The advantages: lower cost, less cutting, less pain, less chance of recurrence, less time in the hospital. Disadvantages: less truss. (KR)

How to Make Your Wife Stop Snoring

There are a number of things—five, to be exact—you can do to douse a noisy spouse.

1. *Teach her tricks.* Teaching your wife to roll over on command requires patience and clear thinking. One women's magazine suggested sewing a tennis ball on the back of a pajama top, but that's needlessly wasteful, especially in view of the rising cost of tennis balls. Try this: When she starts honking, lean over and gently blow a little night breath across her face. Odds are, she'll turn away pronto. There's also an off chance she'll spring out of bed and call the fire department. Or, if she's a new mom, she may also try to wrap your head in a diaper, on sheer instinct.

2. *Get her to sleep sitting up.* Start by plumping a pile of pillows *under* your wife's head. (Piling pillows *on* your wife's head will certainly cause her to stop snoring, but you'll do time for sure.) Then get sensitive; tell her about your hopes and dreams, your feelings about your life and your job. Talk about the melancholy march of time and the insane interest rates Citibank puts on its credit cards. Read aloud your favorite magazine columnist. Talk about cars and football. When you're sure she's asleep, talk about communitarianism. That'll put you to sleep. Alternative: Tilt the bed. Second alternative: Tilt the room.

3. *Get her on the straight-and-narrow.* If she's started mixing highballs with her bon-bons, rush her down to Betty Ford's clinic and dry her up. Alcohol helps induce snoring. (So does smoking, of course, and so does taking drugs, such as sleeping pills. Unless you take a *lot* of sleeping pills.) When you've finally got her sober, invite Richard Simmons over for dinner. For a small fee, he'll be the one who tells her fat people snore more than skinny people. Then he'll sell her a Deal-a-Meal. It's worth it. Another fitness-related cause of wifely snoring: According to the American Academy of Otolaryngolgy, *bad muscle tone in the tongue and throat.* Getting your wife on a good tongue-and-throat fitness regimen will ultimately be good for both of you, of course, but explain that it's not an overnight thing. Say right up front that it may take months, even years, to get the perfect tongue-and-throat tone, that you're willing to help all the way, and that once she starts these kind of exercises, she should never stop.

4. *Call an ambulance* and have her carted over to Loyola University Medical Center in Chicago, where a laser surgeon will point a phaser down her throat and blast away the excess tissue that causes snoring.

5. *Take her to Toronto.* The U.S. Patent Office has hundreds of inventions on file all designed to filter decibels out of a crowded bedroom. They have stuff you sleep on and stuff you strap on. If you always dreamed of sleeping with Darth Vader, the boys at Patent Central can fix you and the missus right up.

One device sure to be a hit with almost any woman is called a Nozovent. The Nozovent is a little plastic tube your wife jams down her nostril. It was invented in Sweden by a guy who claims that snoring starts when "the nasal wings are sucked in against the septum of the nose." Clip them little nasal wings with a Nozovent, and you'll have a bodaciously snoreless wife. Does the Nozovent work? Just ask a certain Englishperson named Switzer. Patient Switzer got a Nozovent because, according to the *Guiness Book of World Records*, the Switzer snore was clocked at 87.5 decibels—roughly what you get if you park a Honda Shadow in the boys' bathroom, then rev 'er up. The nonsnoring Switzer, by the way, went deaf in one ear because of this little problem, and only a timely Nozovent intervention saved the other ear. If your wife wants her own Nozovent, send her up to Canada with a purchase order, because so far, the U.S. government's FDA has said no, no, Nozovent—apparently fearful somebody might OD on the suckers. (TES)

If your mate expresses a little reluctance to plunge headfirst into antisnoring therapy, you can tell her it's for her own good. Snoring, according to the otolaryngological academicians of the nation, causes sleep disruption in the snorer—her—as well as in you, the victim. Besides, snoring is associated with stroke and hypertension and also indicates the possibility of a condition called obstructed sleep apnea, and *sleep apnea can kill.*

S.A. is snoring at redline, when your wife's snoremaker is running at top speed, full-out. Then, suddenly, everything shuts down. The throat jams closed right there at the back of the mouth, where the hard palate meets the soft tissue of the throat. Instantly, no snoring—but, sadly, no breath, either. Blood oxygen levels plummet and the heart starts beating irregularly, ka-ka-ka-boom-chuck-a-luck-a-luck. Sleep apneasts can suffer these attacks as many as three hundred times a night. They wake up feeling like hell, until one night they snore themselves to death, and don't wake up at all. If your wife's sleep apnea attacks come more than seven times an hour and last for more than ten seconds each time, wake her up, then wake up an otolaryngolist, stat! (TES)

WHY MEN SNORE

Even men occasionally snore, but only because we dream about chain saws, Harleys, and 'dozers. Overall, men have superior dreams, very vivid dreams, with lots of awesome special effects. Tell your wife, however, that guys who dream about stamps and baseball never snore. And, you can add, neither do guys who dream about women. That'll keep her up all night, snore-free. (DB)

How to Groom the Beast

Covered with hair and worry, it's easy to forget how nice monkeys have it: Imagine, living in trees with whole tribes of cosmetologists, just picking and grooming.

Let's take this small subject from the top, starting with the all-time classic of instructional lit:

HOW TO USE PRELL
Directions:
1. Lather.
2. Rinse.
3. Repeat.

Unfortunately, there's more to it than that. You have to know your hair.

- *Dry hair* is dry the entire length of the shaft to the scalp, which may itch and develop flakes. It seems like it never needs to be shampooed, and the ends look split, unkempt, and uneven. The texture of the hair is coarse. Often, gray or very curly hair is dry. Use a gentle shampoo every other day or so. Use an extra-rich conditioner.
- *Normal hair* is smooth, usually free from breakage, and feels as if it has its own natural oil or source of moisture near the scalp. Shampoo when you like, using whatever you like.
- *Oily hair* has a tendency to feel damp. It has a shiny, silky texture, and by the end of the day, it's sticking to your scalp like a bad rug. It has to be washed every day. Unfortunately, frequent washing makes the problem worse, since the scalp will produce more oil to counteract the dryness resulting from the shampoo. (JH)

HOW TO TELL IF YOU'RE GOING BALD
Sorry you asked. If your hair has just begun thinning noticeably, you've already lost half of what you once had.

Digits from dandruff:
- Normal hair loss is 10–50 hairs per day.
- Slightly abnormal hair loss is 50–100 per day.
- Definitely abnormal hair loss is 100–150 per day.
- Almost toupee time: 150 or more per day.

How soon? Depends:
- On the average blond head: 120,000 hairs.
- On the average brunette: 100,000 hairs.
- On the average redhead: 80,000 hairs.

Other ugly signs:
- Acne, now or ever.
- A flaky scalp (seborrhea).
- Development of bald patches (called alopecia areata).
- An increase in body hair or the appearance of body hair in unusual places.
Nine reasons guys go bald:
1. Poor scalp hygiene.
2. Low levels of estrogen.
3. Overuse of the wrong shampoos.
4. Too much dieting or rapid loss of weight.
5. High vitamin intake—vitamin A, in particular.
6. Too much brushing too hard.
7. Poor blood circulation—to the scalp especially.
8. Genetics.
9. Karma. (JH, HDS)
- *One more reason:* So they'll never have to be middle-aged with their hair in a ponytail. However, *if you have a ponytail,* bald guys don't want you in their ranks. So use a coated rubber band to hold your hair instead of a clip. Clips will break and crease your hair. (HDS)

HOW TO SHAVE
How to Brush on Lather
You have to have a badger-fur shaving brush. If you don't have it, you have to go out, find a badger, and negotiate. Once you run this luxurious fur across your face in the morning, you'll know you're never going back to a shaving creme can or gel.

The bulb of the brush fits into your hand like the joystick of an F-16. Stroke the bristles across your shaving soap, and then paint the lather across your face with to-and-fro strokes, letting the soft, water-soaked bristles of the brush massage open the pores of your skin for a much much better shave. You'll find badger-fur shaving brushes at a good department store, barbershop, or an old-fashioned neighborhood pharmacy. Expect to pay at least fifty bucks. (TF)

Face Facts

- The average male face has between 10,000 and 30,000 whiskers.
- Facial hair grows about fifteen-thousandths of an inch every day. That's as much as six inches a year.
- Over a lifetime, the average man will spend 125 days—3,000 hours—shaving.
- Collectively, men will spend $80 million this year on razors, $900 million on replacement blades.
- Thirty percent of that will be on electric shaving devices.
- Sixty percent of wet-shave razors sold are disposables. (TF)

How a Barber Gives a Shave

The widespread abandonment of America's barbershops by American men willing to pay one, two hundred dollars for a haircut to foreigners with one name is one of the red flags of growing national idiocy, and a reliable measurement of how deeply eroded common sense has become.

While barbers no longer get much respect, you have to remember that not too long ago, barbers did brain surgery, thus working both sides of the cranium. So just maybe we owe it to ourselves to reacquaint ourselves with these *noggin-istes.* Also, barbershops are one of the few citadels of unsullied manhood left in this country: Big jars filled with blue Barbasol, the endless snip of scissors, the smell of shaving cream—in a barbershop, you've got everything a man needs, except women. Plus, you've got a normal guy there who will cut your hair pretty well. Maybe not great—but maybe your head of hair isn't all that great anyway.

Here's what you'll get from a barber—along with a healthy dose of your own self-respect back:

- *First, he'll cover your face with hot lather.* If you want to try this at home, throw your shaving cream into a sink full of hot water while you take a shower.
- *Next, he covers your face—lather and all—with hot towels.* This removes the fat and oils from your face.
- *Then he relathers your face.* Soap and a brush are more traditional, but the point of the lather is to get your skin and facial hair follicles moist.

Soap dries too quickly to keep the moisture contained. Today's creams and gels are more effective.

- *Then he starts to shave*—using a straight razor if he's any kind of barber at all.
- *On the first pass, he'll go with the grain.* Then he'll come back sideways. Going against the grain is a good way to donate blood. Going with the grain spares your skin, but spares your hairs at the same time. Thus, the second pass going sideways.
- *After the shave,* he applies menthol to your face and another hot towel.
- *To close your pores and prevent infection,* he'll give you a couple of slaps of astringent lotion.
- *A dash of talcum* finishes you off. (LB)

How to Give Yourself a Perfect Shave if You Can't Get to a Barber

Unless you're the Rockette of the watercooler, your face is about as much skin as company policy permits you to show around the office. Women? They've got those legs. But nobody makes pantyhose *specifically* for guys' faces, so it pays to take care of the mug you've got. How? By being careful how you use the mug you shave with. Here's how to scrape that winter beard off your face and make your skin smile at the prospect:

- *Get it clean.* Wash your face with warm water and mild soap. Use the occasion as an excuse to give yourself a kind of mug-massage by gently rubbing the soap into the skin. Rinse with warm water; you want to keep those pores wide open and happy.
- *Set it up.* The warm water will also keep your beard soft. Add a thick cream or a gel to lubricate your skin.
- *Cut it off.* In your ruthless ambition to cut every follicle's son, you'll want to shave against the grain. You'll be wrong. To avoid irritating your skin, shave with the direction of hair growth. Best razor? A double-bladed job with a pivoting head. (STu)
- *Thanks. You Needed That.* Think of shaving as petty surgery; the recuperation is as important as the way you wield the blade. So get tough: After you rinse the cream residue away, slap yourself around a little. Rubbing your skin dry is bad; patting your skin dry is good.
- **Use a weather sealant.** Not a deck finish, exactly, but maybe something that will both moisturize your skin and give it a little sunscreen at the same time. (SF)

6. Food

Eat it, play with it, throw it, but whatever you do, before you actually put it in your body, *get to know it.*

Nutrition is to food as reproduction is to sex: When you're right in the middle of a Big Mac, the last thing you want to think about is how it all works. But this is an age of safe eating, after all, when a sensible guy won't just rush into a relationship with chow. Instead, he'll take his time. He'll read its label and calculate its values. He'll get to know his lunch as *nutrient,* not just food. And only then will he consummate the relationship. And, like so many relationships in a man's life, this one will eventually turn to something foul and repugnant.

So what difference does it make? Simple: Bad food will kill you. How do you know what's bad? What's bad is usually what tastes great. Therefore, eating is an adventure in discipline and discernment. Happily, the road is well marked.

How to Get Skinny

- **The Main Thing.** For those of us still toting some body fat, remember this:

3,500 CALORIES = ONE POUND OF FLESH.

In other words, if you need to gain a pound by tomorrow, grease down a half-dozen Whoppers today, and you're there. Unfortunately, it doesn't work the other way around: To lose a pound by tomorrow, you have to work really hard today.

- *Here's why.* The average guy needs a couple thousand calories every day just to make the plant run: Your body's life-support system needs fuel to make the lungs breathe and the heart pump. So to lose a pound by tomorrow, not only do you have to eat nothing, you also have to burn up an additional 1,500 calories. So starve and spend the day on a marathon jog.

Sensible men simply eliminate a burger or a brew and reduce their calorie intake by maybe 500 calories a day. At that rate, you'll lose a pound a week. Stay on this diet long enough and you'll cease to exist.

- *No deal!* It doesn't work that way, unfortunately. It's Zeno's dietary paradox: The more you lose, the harder you have to work to lose it. You cut back on the calories and your brain thinks you're losing weight and that that's good. But your body, the brainless idiot, thinks, "Starvation!" So it slows down your metabolic rate to make sure the rations you're supplying will be enough to go around.

- *Here's the diet cycle.* You diet. Your body slows down to counter the effect of the diet. You get frustrated because dieting doesn't work and so you go back to your old chow-hound ways and what happens? Your metabolism rate decreases to a rate that is even slower than what it was before you started dieting so what you ate before now causes you to add even more weight.

And that's why, if you want to lose weight, you need to exercise as well as reduce calories. The more you exercise, the higher your body's metabolic rate. (FG, EWR)

- *It's common sense all the way.* The federal government has a whole bunch of bureaucracies set up to tell you that the right way to get along with food looks like this:

Eat a variety of foods.
Maintain a healthy weight.

Choose a diet low in fat, saturated fat, and cholesterol.
Choose a diet with plenty of vegetables, fruits, and grain products.
Use sugars only in moderation.
Use salt and sodium only in moderation. (USG)

That's why every diet that works is a duh diet. Face it: If you live on beer and bread and weenies, you'll get fat. If you live on tofu and kelp, you'll get pompous and self-righteous. But not plump. (TR)

HOW TO READ NUTRITION FACTS

Fat

You look like Oscar Meyer, but you want a body by Louis Rich. Between 3 and 5 percent of the fat in your body is called essential fat. It's the stuff in your nerves, spinal cord, and other organs. Think about this: Even your brain needs fat. Plus, it's what you might call the bare bones of padding, Nature's own version of packing peanuts. Alas, most guys' bodies are made up of something between 7 and 25 percent body fat. Average: 15. More than 25 is obese.

Fat watch. Looking at your percentage of body fat will tell you a lot more about your health than looking at your weight.

Sugar

Sugar is the Elvis of nutrients. It's *everywhere.* Look for terms such as "sucrose," "fructose," "maltose," "lactose," "honey," "syrup," "corn syrup," "high-fructose corn syrup," "molasses," or "fruit juice concentrate" in the ingredient list. If one of these terms appears first, or if several are listed, the food is likely to be high in added sugars. (USG)

Naked calories. If you want to see what calories look like naked, take a gander at a whiskey sour. Alcohol and sugar—a miracle food. What better way to get fat and stupid at the same time?

- **From a breathalyzer's point of view,** a drink is the standard measurement of liquid idiot. Here's what's equal to one drink:
- *A twelve-ounce can of beer.*
- *A glass of wine.*
- *A shot—one and a half ounces—of liquor.*
- **Lite beers have fewer calories than regular beer,** but they'll get you just as drunk just as quick. Wine coolers and so-called light wines have less alcohol and fewer calories than regular wine. (TRE)

Fiber

There'll come a time in your life, my dear chaps, when being regular will mean more to you than sex. The marketing department calls this "a Grape Nuts experience." But you know what we call it. Whole-grain breads, oatmeal, popcorn, and brown rice are the Mussolinis of the colon. (HG, TRE)

- *Fake fiber.* Some "wheat" breads have the same dark coloring as whole-wheat breads. But they're fakes. Sometimes caramel is used to give the bread that right color of brown, but there's not enough fiber in a loaf of the stuff to weave a sitcom plot. (HG)
- *Fake fat fiber.* The newly approved phony fat used as a dietary supplement in junk food—potato chips and the like—is really a kind of fat-as-fiber, since it can't be broken down by your digestive system. (TRE)

How to Eat and Drive Junk All at the Same Time

Sometimes, the great currents of civilization meet and produce what historians call a turning point. Take, for example, the development of the automobile and the sudden emergence of junk food. Conflate these two cultural gestures and you've got a mile-a-minute cheeseburger with fries. That's fast food.

It's also junk, of course. There are times, however, when a man just has to eat fake food. How to do that and still keep an eye on your fitness meter is why we're here with our customized, highly personalized, extremely low-tech Man's Life Fast Food Fat and Calorie Counter.

Here's how it works: You pick the franchise and we pick the menu. Our aim: To get you back out on the highway carrying as light a load as possible.

Talk junk talk: When the little talking box says, "Howdy," here's what you need to know before you say anything:

There are about eight to ten calories per gram of fat, and fast food has more fat than any other nutrient.

The condiments in a fast-food sandwich are diet busters, so get it plain.

All fast-food fish sandwiches are monsters from the deep-fat fryer, chock full of calories and grease. So forget the pseudo-sanctimoniousness of seafood.

Even the smallest order of fries—McDonald's portion—has more than 200 calories, half from fat.

Now, here's your order:

TACO BELL

Taco Bell's entire Border Lights menu is fast food's all-time nutritional champ, combining low-fat, low-calorie chow with great taste. You can't go wrong, but the best bets:

1. **Light Chicken Burrito:** 290 calories, with only 15 of them from fat (6 grams).
2. **Light Taco Salad without chips:** 330 calories, with 80 calories from fat (25 grams).
3. **Light Taco Supreme:** 160 calories, less than a third of which are from fat (5 grams).

JACK-IN-THE-BOX

The Jack's menu is a minefield of fat bombs, frequent ingestion of which will land you in a box even bigger than Jack's. The only reasonable choice:

- **Chicken Fajita Pita, hold the guac:** 300 calories, with (70 calories) from fat (8 grams).

Feeling suicidal? Jack's Colossus Burger will give you 1,100 calories—760 of them from fat (84 grams)—you get a bonus 1,510 mg of sodium at no extra charge! The good news? The Colossus also gives you 2 percent of your daily requirement of vitamin C. Eat fifty of these babies every day, and you'll never catch a cold.

KENTUCKY FRIED CHICKEN

Fat-o-Rama! If you're looking to add pounds as you roll, you can't go wrong at the Colonel's. Some golden-fried rules of thumb:

- *The Extra Crispy is extra fatty,* with extra calories to boot.
- *The biscuits can be eaten in one 235-calories bite,* including 11.7 grams of fat.

  But if you just have to be polite:
- **Chicken Little's Sandwich:** 169 calories, with 10 grams of fat.
- **Original Recipe center breast:** 283 calories, with 15.3 grams of fat.

WENDY'S

Wendy's burgers are square and ugly, but not as ugly as most other franchised restaurants.

- **Wendy's Jr. Hamburger:** 270 calories, with only 8 grams of fat.
- **Chili:** A find! The small bowl has a mere 190 calories, with 6 grams of

fat. The large one has another 100 calories and another 3 grams of fat. But caution: Skip the cheese.

- **Grilled chicken salad:** 200 calories, with 8 grams of fat. The reduced-fat Italian dressing adds another 40 calories and 3 more grams of fat.
- **A plain baked potato:** 310 fat-free calories, and 60 percent of your RDA of vitamin C.

BURGER KING

You might as well drive across the street to KFC and do your calories right. Everything on the BK menu comes loaded with calories and fat, with two notable, if predictable, exceptions:

- **Broiled chicken salad:** 200 calories, with 10 grams of fat. Add 5 calories if you choose low-fat Italian dressing.
- **BK Broiler:** 260 calories, with 6 grams of fat.

CARL'S JR.

You want to know where all the fat Californians are? Check the drive-thru lane at Carl's, where even your basic chicken sandwich packs 530 fat-laden calories. Every Carl's Jr. has a stack of gurneys in the back room for the use of regular customers. Cardiac care extra. The slimmest pickings:

- **Plain hamburger:** The best fast-food burger, with only 200 calories and 8 grams of fat.
- **Chicken salad:** 260 calories, with 9 grams of fat. Fat-free Italian adds 15 calories, but fat-free French adds 70! *Zut!*

MCDONALD'S

Say so long to the McLean Deluxe, a burger that contained about the same amount of bad news as a standard Mac cheeseburger two-thirds its size (340 calories, 12 grams of fat, versus 320 calories, 13 grams of fat). But say hello to:

- **McGrilled Chicken:** 250 calories, with 3 grams of fat. But watch it! Some lunatics toss on a slab of cheese for effect.
- **Chef salad:** 210 calories, with 11 grams of fat. Lite Vinaigrette, McDonald's diet dressing, contains an ugly 50 calories, with 2 grams of fat.
- **Vanilla low-fat yogurt cone:** 120 calories, with half a gram of fat.

By the way, a Big Mac has 510 calories and 26 grams of belt-busting fat. (GS)

How to Grow a Huge, Disgusting Ball-shaped Belly

Eat a lot just before going to bed. Instant gut. If you eat most of your calories early in the day, you'll stimulate your body's ability to use energy, according to experts. Studies have shown that overweight people consume 75 percent or more of their calories in the evening, when their bodies are slowing down and are more likely to store fat. Eating large late is also a primary cause of potbellies, even among otherwise trim guys. (AMcLL)

How to Eat Your Way Past a Bad Biopsy

The top-ten cancer-fighting foods, according to doctors and dietitians:
1. *Broccoli*
2. *Tomatoes*
3. *Spinach*
4. *Oranges*
5. *Garlic*
6. *Apples*
7. *Soybeans*
8. *Carrots*
9. *Hot red peppers*
10. *Green tea.* (PQ)

How to Make Lunch

Dozens of cookbooks for men have been published in the last ten years. This is, gents, a bad sign. For while we have known for a century or more that the greatest chefs were almost all men, the best cooks have always been women. That this should suddenly change is both a matter of concern and sadness. But it's also an opportunity—a chance to not only eat like men, but cook like men, too. Stand back.

HOW TO EAT BEER THREE TIMES A DAY

A beer drinker's work is never done. In fact, if you think about it, *brewing* beer is cooking. So, as long as you're in the kitchen with lots of cooking and lots of beer, here's a way to make it through a typical day with a case of beer to spare.

But first, a note about beer: Never use old, flat, or deteriorating beer. And don't use too much; if you do, you can get an unpleasant "hoppy" flavor. Don't bother with lager. The best cooking beer is ale. It's also the best drinking beer. You can also wash your hair with it. Horses will drink ale. Ale is also a medicinal drink.

BREAKFAST: SWEET POTATO BUBBLE-AND-SQUEAK

You'll need:
   ¼ pound Brussels sprouts
   1 medium, red-skinned, sweet yam
   1 large spud
   1 medium-sized onion
   ¼ teaspoon freshly-ground black pepper
   Some salt
   ½ pint ale
   ½ pound corned beef

1. Wash, peel, and chop the Brussels sprouts, and boil them for 15 minutes.
2. Peel and slice the yam, the potato, and the onion. Dice everything and boil the whole works for 15 or 20 minutes—or until the potato is soft. Not mushy. Just soft.
3. Mash it all up in a large bowl. Add some salt and pepper.
4. Stir in the beer.
5. Fry the vegetable mixture in butter, lightly browning it in a skillet. Don't rush. This might take 10 minutes or so. Turn it over and brown the other side for another 10 minutes.
6. Form the thing into several individual portions and serve them hot, topped with a couple of poached eggs.

If you add ½ pound of cooked corned beef, you'll have a fantastic hash. The sweet potato contributes significantly to the taste and blends well with the ale. Serve this dish for breakfast, and you won't have to eat again until lunchtime.

LUNCH: CHEDDAR CHEESE, SAUSAGE, AND ALE SOUP

Everything a man needs in one bowl. The beer character comes through superbly; it genuinely contributes to the blend of flavors and gives it balance. Plus, it leaves you with five bottles out of a six-pack to wash it all down.

You'll need:

4 teaspoons butter
1 pound fresh, lightly herbed sausage
2 cups chopped onion
2 cups diced carrots
1 cup thinly sliced celery
⅓ cup flour
Some roux
12-ounce bottle of ale
3 cups rich chicken stock—genuine stock, if possible
2 cups diced potatoes
2 cups milk
3 cups sharp cheddar cheese, grated
1 tablespoon dried thyme or 2 tablespoons fresh thyme
2 teaspoons Worcestershire sauce
2 teaspoons sweet Hungarian paprika
2 teaspoons tomato paste
Some salt
Some freshly ground black pepper
Tabasco
1¼ cups sliced green spring onion

1. In a large heavy pot, melt the butter over medium heat.
2. Fry the sausage, stirring occasionally, for 5 minutes or until it's brown, then cut the sausages into ¾-inch pieces.
3. Add the onions, carrots, and celery. Stir well and cook the mixture over a very gentle heat for 15 minutes.
4. Stir in the flour and coat the vegetables with roux.
5. Whisk in the beer and the stock and bring the soup to a boil.
6. Lower the heat, and simmer the soup until it thickens slightly. Should take 3–4 minutes.
7. Add the potatoes and cook them until tender—another 15 minutes or so.
8. Stir in the milk, the grated cheese, the thyme, the Worcestershire sauce, the

paprika, and the tomato paste. Keep stirring until the cheese is melted and the soup is smooth.

9. Add salt, pepper, and lots of Tabasco.

The green onions are what faux-chefs call your basic garnish. What you really need to balance out the five bottles of beer is a big chunk of bread—or, if you're dieting, some bread sticks.

DINNER: BOILED TROUT IN BASS ALE

How ironic can you get? You spend all morning and all afternoon eating beer and fishing for trout, and you end the whole thing with Bass. Goes to show that when it comes to the timeless battle for the hearts of men between beer and fish, the beer always wins.

Anyway, here's what you need:

4 big trout. (Either catch and clean your own, or snag some down at the Safeway. Four large trout fillets will also do.)

1 bottle Bass

1 cup vinegar

1 cup white wine. (This is optional, but women love seeing guys cook with wine. They think it's damned *continental.* If the wine makes you feel testosteronally challenged, add ½ cup of sliced horseradish root. In fact, add the horseradish no matter what.)

1 teaspoon thyme

1 teaspoon pounded ginger

Some grated lemon peel

1 tablespoon brown sugar

Some salt

Some freshly ground black pepper

The juice of half a lemon

1. Place the trout in a deep pan. Pour in the beer, the vinegar, and the wine.
2. Bring the liquid to a boil.
3. Add all of the remaining ingredients—except the lemon peel.
4. Lower the heat, and simmer the fish for no more than 10–12 minutes— until the trout is just cooked through. Don't overcook it.

The lemon peel is the garnish. Allow the fish to cool a bit—or eat it cold. A great way to end the day. (AWS)

HOW TO WOK LIKE A MAN

Inscrutably satisfying, incredibly easy.

- *The first step.* Use a wok made of carbon steel. Nothing else will do, because nothing else stands up and walks the wok walk when the going gets really hot.
- *Size it up.* Woks come in different sizes. Fourteen inches is standard: It will provide enough food for two gluttons, four adults, or six Zen ascetics.
- *Season it* before you cook in it by following these steps:
  1. *Wash the wok* with warm, soapy water, then dry it.
  2. *Wipe it* with vegetable oil—or, better, peanut oil.
  3. *Slowly heat* it for fifteen minutes, remove it from the heat, and wipe the inside of the wok with a clean towel. Repeat the procedure until you can wipe the inside of the wok with a clean cloth and the cloth remains clean.
- *Keep it steady.* The round-bottom wok comes with a ring stand. Among woks, a round bottom is better than a flat bottom. (This observation is considered to be universally true.) The ring is larger on one side than on the other, allowing you to get the wok closer to the heat source—especially important if you cook on an electric stove.

  Caution: Some people set the wok—filled with hot oil—right on the burner of a gas stove. They are fewer each year.
- *Choose your oil.* Be careful when you select a cooking oil for use in a wok. Peanut oil is best because it reaches the highest temperature before smoking. Although any vegetable oil will work, corn oil smokes at a relatively low temperature and olive oil might be too flavorful for oriental cuisine.

  Don't use animal fat, or you will smoke up, then stink up, and finally burn down your home.
- *Fire it up.* Turn the heat up as high as possible. When the bottom of the wok *looks* hot, add the oil, and when the oil ripples, the wok's hot.

Wok Virtues

The best thing about a wok is that it stir-fries better than anything else. A wok generally is sold with a bunch of utensils and is a kind of little oriental kitchen by itself. But since you have a big occidental kitchen, you should keep the spatula handy. The bottom third of the wok is where the stir-frying should be done, where the heat is most intense. Don't try to cook too much at one time: A pound of meat, for example, is the absolute outside limit. If you're going to deep-fry anything, two inches or so of oil is as much as you want to use. Since the wok cooks so quickly, it can be loaded several times without messing up the timing for dinner.

Our correspondent writes, "While deep-frying is the preferred method of cooking some dishes, I like stir-frying with the wok best. I like the noise, the steam, the smell, the intuitive feeling achieved with the wok—quick and intense—and the endless possibilities it provides for showboating. For example, I've worked out a way—a personal intuition aid, if you like—to tell when things have cooked: The time to cook most things on a wok is equal to the amount of time I spend thinking about a Zen poem. An exception is squid [see below], where the time is equal to the amount of time it takes me to say a Zen poem. Here's one I use:

> *Stars are floating.*
> *A winter shower*
> *Ripples the pond.*

"Another exception is when you are wok-cooking for a crowd not conversant with, or even interested in, Zen poetry. Such a crowd might possibly be found at a private dinner party in a public park. I once tried to prepare Rice in a Lotus Leaf at such a party, and I was unsuccessful, despite the fact that my companions held college degrees, some terminal. I don't remember the poem I used, but I remember having the feeling of a cherry blossom in a wind storm. One adjusts. Next game, I adopted my Kubalai attitude: Tailgaters can resemble a bunch of unhorsed Mongols. The recipe was one I called 'Thank God for Football, Regular Beer, Red Peppers, Garlic, and Shrimp Shrimp' [see below]." (SW)

After the steam, sizzle, and anarchy of preparing the wok, things calm down, and if you're doing your cooking in front of a mixed group, at some point that "what now?" moment arrives. Here's what to do next:

How to Stir-Fry Squid
- *To prepare squid for a wok* or for any other kind of cooking, pull off the head and cut away and conserve the tentacles. Discard the head and the viscera attached to it.
- *Next, peel off the squid's speckled skin.* Then stick your finger in the tube that makes up the squid's body and pull out the cuttlebone. It is transparent, one of those beautiful examples of design in nature, and a

wonderful conversational gambit in some circles. While discussing the cuttlebone, slice the tube crossways into little circles.

- *Marinate the squid* in equal parts soy sauce and sherry and with a little shredded ginger as you chop a bunch of green onions, mash a garlic clove and a stalk of celery, and put together a little chicken broth.
- *Prepare the wok.* Add a tablespoon of oil to the wok; remember, the wok does its job with a lot less oil than most recipes call for. When the oil ripples, the wok is hot enough for cooking.
- *Now cook.* Drop in the mashed garlic. Stir. Remove the garlic, and add the onions and celery. Stir. Add the squid. Stir. Add the marinade and a little chicken broth. Stir. Say the poem (see above).
- **Serve.**

A note of warning: Don't try to cook a squid big enough to stir Jules Verne's imagination. If the body of the squid is longer than six inches, it belongs in the sea, not in your wok. (SW)

How to Cook "Thank God for Football, Regular Beer, Red Peppers, Garlic, and Shrimp Shrimp" in a Wok on a Tailgate in a Parking Lot

This is a recipe that doubles as a prayer if one says "amen" after the first "shrimp." The recipe works at a tailgate party because everyone gets to play— it's chaotic, loud, steamy, smelly, and tastes great.

For tailgating, you need a hibachi to heat the wok. When the oil is hot, add a mashed garlic clove and a couple of chopped, dried red peppers. Remove everything after about twenty seconds. Or, if the crowd is particularly uncouth, leave them in. Then ask everyone to give thanks for Football and Harvest by pouring a small sip of beer into the wok; you might want to bring along a bottle of real beer in case your group is overloaded with lite types. When the beer boils, add a pound of shrimp. Boil the shrimp until they turn pink. Repeat this process with a pound of shrimp at a time until your companions are glazed with gluttony. (SW)

How to Stir-Fry "End of the Tailgate Party Wonton Cookies"

If you have a true understanding of the wok as the analogue of long preparation for one intense moment, here you are. Imagine, all the women standing around your sizzling wok, glassy-eyed with boredom—this is still the tailgate party—and low blood sugar as you make "End of the Party Wonton Cookies." They're good, they're easy, and you'll be the only object of romance on the entire parking lot. Have each lady pay you with a poem as you shake cinnamon and sugar on her cookie from your Winnie-the-Pooh shaker. Here's how to kick off:

- **Pick up a pack of wonton wrappers** and a yellow plastic Winnie-the-Pooh sugar and cinnamon shaker at your local gourmet shoppe.
- **Try folding and cutting the wonton skins** into interesting shapes at home so that you'll have it right at the party.

  The traditional butterfly shape is obtained as follows: Cut the square wonton skin diagonally, making two triangles. Cut a slit in the triangles, then pull the two acute angles through the slits. You may find something more interesting.
- **Fry the wontons.** Pour one inch to one and a half inches of oil in the wok. When the oil is hot, fry cookies three at a time until golden. Drain on a paper towel. Add sugar and cinnamon. (SW)

HOW TO MAKE APPLE CIDER

Making apple cider the civilized way—with a cider press—is nothing. You cut up a bunch of apples, grind 'em up, smash 'em down, and pour off the juice. No problem.

A problem arises when you want fresh cider and have nothing useful at hand, save some apples, some fat cousins, and a few of your brother-in-law's garage tools. Then what?

- **Sweet or sour.** First, decide how tart you like your cider. A box of Coxes or some Granny Smiths will add a jolt to a batch of sweet apples. Avoid Delicious and many other eating apples, since they're low on juice.
- **Box it in.** Take a couple of planks about a yard long. Drill some holes in one and add a lip around the edge—a cut-up two-by-four will do nicely. You've just made a small trough.
- **Add the apples.** Put the trough in a clean bathtub or in a scrubbed-out kid's plastic pool or someplace where you can catch the juice. Fill the trough with fresh apples. Then grab your garden rake, a maul, a hoe, a shovel—whatever's handy and dangerous—and pulverize the apples. Mash 'em up good.
- **Hold the press.** Take the other plank and put it on top of the apples. Then grab a bunch of the cousins and make them stand on the board. No living relatives? No problem: Take a handful of large C-clamps and tighten the plank down onto the apples. Lift the trough out of the tub, ladle out the juice, and pour it through a strainer into jugs. Let this stuff sit around too long, and it turns into apple jack, which will make you drunk and give you a hangover the size of Kong, all at once. (RMcE)

HOW TO BAKE A GREAT BROWNIE

- *First rule:* Do it yourself.
- *Second rule:* Do it the way your mom did.
- *Third rule:* Keep it simple. As men, if we're going to do the cooking, we have to keep it simple, because women refuse to listen to directions and cooking is a very precise science. Ask your wife how to bake a brownie, and she'll say things like, "Oh, you can do it basically at 350 or 400 degrees," and we always say, "I don't know, I think it's got to be one or the other."

So do it the way your mother did. Buy Betty Crocker and follow the instructions on the box. That's it. But you can add walnuts. (TA)

HOW TO COOK YOUR GOOSE

- *How to buy a goose.* We will assume, as you must also, that if you are going to buy a goose, you are not going to cook a wild one, for wild geese are chased by well-armed enthusiasts, not frozen and sold in supermarkets. So, to buy a goose, go to the frozen meat section of a quality supermarket and pick out the goose you want. Go home and cook it.

    For something so pregnant with an unsung liturgy, you might wish selecting a goose would be a more mysterious process, or that at least there would be more of the fresh kind around to select. But fresh goose is only available during the holiday season, and even many of those are probably thawed geese.
- *A goose is a low-demand item.* No diner sells hot-goose sandwiches; there are no goose franks, no goose salad sandwiches. So geese are a rarity, comparatively speaking. With the quick-freezing methods used today, a goose from a good supermarket is going to be your best bet.
- *Size.* The biggest you're likely to find will be around ten pounds—goose enough for four to six people. (SW)

    Before we consider how to properly cook the goose you buy, see below. First, though:

A Somewhat Atavistic Digression

Wild goose: A wild Canada goose brings the wonder of the primeval into a mundane life more than any other creature you can imagine. To hear the honking and to watch a gaggle of wild geese landing amid the shadows and the golden stubble of a cornfield on East Neck Island, along the Chester River around four-thirty on a cold November afternoon is to drop back through the memories of childhood to a feeling that lurks in the base of the spine.

A minor hypocrisy, one with which most of us can live easily: Most men who eat goose have never shot one, and it's very probable that they never will. It's nothing against hunting or hunters, although many of us would rather fish, personally. But *for a wild goose to be good to eat, it has to be a young goose,* a first-trip goose, so to speak. The meat will be richer and much leaner than the meat of a domestic goose, with a darker taste. A hearty wine will wash down a wild goose; domestic geese float best on white wine.

How to tell the age of a goose: Now, if you *should* happen to shoot a wild goose—that is, should your shotgun accidentally discharge as a wild goose is flying overhead—and if it should happen to be an old goose—and, while there's no telling the age of a wild goose until Fido drops the bird in the mud at your feet, the chances are that the goose will be an elderly one, indeed—you have to cook it using a traditional West Baltimore family method:

- *Put the goose in a pot* of water with an anvil.
- *Boil* until the anvil is tender.
- *Throw the goose out* and serve the anvil *au jus.*

For most of us, that's a waste of our time, and the goose's, too. *A wild goose that dresses out at more than four or five pounds is too geriatric* to be much use.

Your chances of finding a good eating goose are better down at the superette. Of course, domestic geese from the frozen food case don't honk and don't stir the soul. But you don't have to stand around for hours in a wet hole in the middle of November waiting for a frozen, plastic-wrapped goose to happen by, and at least you can see what you're getting *before* the dog drags it back.

How to Roast a Christmas Goose from the Local Grocery

- *Thaw the goose.* Follow the packer's directions for thawing. Careful, don't let any sort of poultry thaw carelessly, since it goes bad so easily.
- *Clean and rub the body cavity* with salt, pepper, and lemon juice.
- *Stuff the goose* loosely—both the cavity and the crop. Geese are greasy; stuffing helps. Close the openings with skewers.
- *Lace twine around the skewers* and tie tightly; imagine the goose is a high-top Nike. Truss the goose and put it on a rack in a roasting pan.
- *Preheat the oven* to 400 degrees and roast the bird for forty-five minutes.

- *Reduce the heat to 350 degrees.*
- *Roast the goose* at this temperature until it's done.
- *How to tell if your goose is cooked:* Your goose is cooked if the company has arrived and has stood around for a couple of hours, polishing off all the mulled cider and growing both boisterous and ravenous in the process, pretending the unguarded salad is finger food, while your mother and every other freeloading kibitzer says the bird will be tough as Billy-be-damned if you don't get it right. Some will counsel an immediate evacuation of the goose from the oven; others will advise patience to an oriental level. But if you want precision, see if the leg moves easily, see if the flesh is soft, and see if the meat thermometer you stuck in the large thigh muscle reads 180 degrees. Figure about twenty minutes per pound.
- *Remove the goose* to a carving platter. Let the goose cool one drink before attempting to carve it. (SW)

How to Roast a Wild Goose

You can simply follow the preceding instructions—with two important differences:

- *The roasting time will be much shorter* because the goose better be a *whole* lot smaller, if you plan on being able to actually eat it.
- *Cover the breast of the goose with a layer of fat;* doing the continent every year while people shoot at them keeps wild geese trim and almost fat-free. If the fatback at your grocery is too expensive, get a pound of the cheapest bacon you can buy. Check the bird as it cooks to make sure it isn't becoming too dry. If it is, baste the bird or put some fresh bacon on the breast.

Add a Simple Stuffing

- *Mix* about three cups of bread crumbs with a cup of dried apricots, two cups each of tart apples, celery, cooked and dried prunes—all chopped fine.
- *Add* a large onion, chopped and sautéed.
- *Add* some chopped parsley, a little thyme, and some salt. (SW)

HOW TO CARVE A TURKEY

You mix men, knives, and animals, and you've got all you need to make an authentic, super-ritualistic, sacrificial holiday thing, something the wife will appreciate and the kids will enjoy. Like a Thanksgiving turkey. Here are the complete rubrics for the carving ceremony.

- *Cooling-off period.* Before you begin to demonstrate your complete domination of the bird, allow a fifteen- or twenty-minute cooling-off period. Why? Three reasons: The cutting will be easier. The turkey'll be juicier. You'll have time for deep breathing. A win-win-win.
- *Clear a deck.* You'll want to do your slicing and dicing on a big platter, something with room for the bird's body parts and a little left over for a parsley garnish and maybe one of those radish rosette things.
- *Scalpel!* Get your tools lined up. You'll need a very sharp knife and one of those huge forks. Some guys use electric carving knives, which are nothing more than a kid-sized chain saw. Real men use muscle.
- *Pin it.* Make the bird assume the position: Breast up, back down, legs to the right (unless you're a southpaw, in which case modify). You're going to do this by halves. Ready? Okay, now, raising the fork high over your head, bring it down deep into the fleshy part of the drumstick.
- *Cut it.* Hold down the bird with the fork while you probe for the joint between the leg and the thigh with the tip of the knife. When you find the spot, slice it, amputating the leg, which you may then pass around to members of the family, or place to one side of the platter. Next, amputate the thigh using the same stab-and-slice methodology you used to sever the leg. If you're subduing a big bird—or, what the heck, The Big Bird—you might want to just slice off pieces of the thigh. Finally, hack off the wings.
- *Slice it.* The juicy white flesh of the breast should be sliced off the bird by removing thin layers from the bottom of the breast and working your way up. Make your cuts parallel to the bird's weak and cowardly spine, using the fork to keep the carcass from scooting off the platter and onto the floor.
- *Eat it.* Don't forget grace. (LL)

THE ART OF SHOP-COOKERY

One of the nicer things about being a man is our ability to be informal both in the kitchen and in the workshop. An even nicer thing happens when you combine workshop and kitchen. For one thing, food improvement is really what cooking's all about. For another, the tools are always handy.

- *Turkey baster.* Try using a paintbrush. Nylon bristles are best, though, since if they fall out of the brush while you're basting, they're easier to find than the others.
- *Meat tenderizer.* That's a hammer's job. You can use a hammer to do a lot of stuff in the kitchen. You can crack crab and nuts, of course, and in

an emergency, the claw can be used with a screwdriver to make the following tool:

- **Can opener.** Poke holes around the perimeter of the can's top by hammering the screwdriver into the lid. Give it twenty pokes around the perimeter, and then make one big slit by hammering in the screwdriver maybe five to seven times in one small area. Then stick one tong of the hammer into this big slit and pull up on it. The top should lift off along the perforations.
- **Chicken shears.** Tin snips. Clean them up after each use, though, or they'll rust.
- **Bread knife.** A new hacksaw blade works like a charm.
- **Coffee warmer.** Wipe off the tip of your soldering gun, plug it in, and slip it into the mug.
- **Chili for a crowd.** A clean wheelbarrow parked over a hibachi makes a wonderful chili pot—big enough for easy self-service, too.
- **Veg-a-Matic.** Use your hand plane to grate food. Thick or thin, the adjustment's an easy one. Use your vise if you need an extra hand to hold an awkward 'tater.
- **Rolling pin.** PVC with part of a broomstick through the middle. Easy to clean.
- **Dog grill.** Any long drill bit and a handheld propane torch. You can cook shish kebabs this way, too.
- **Salad bowl.** Hubcaps off almost any pre-1970 American automobile. These also make nice soup bowls. (DSa)

7. Brains

Mental health and mental fitness—what a dual drag. Ask most guys about their least favorite training technique, and they scratch a long-neglected muscle.

Why do we hate working hard to get smart? Well, there are two things wrong with smart. First off, it hurts your head. Heads are products of their times, and these aren't the brightest of days. You think too much with a modern head, and you can blow the sucker right up. A hundred years ago, when kids had to know Latin just to get into high school, heads were made of cast iron. Today, we get a polyresin job, and that's if we're lucky. Lots of guys just get mush with a plate on it.

Second off, smart doesn't just happen to you. For example, you can't just go to the beach, look at butts, eat sno-cones, and come back home smarter than when you left. To get smart, you have to get out there and catch it, make it happen, and stick it behind your eyes so you can find it later, in case you need it.

How to Lift Heavy Thoughts Without Hurting Yourself

Work your way into it, bit by bit, starting with the basics.

STUFF TO THINK ABOUT

Most of us could use a good thought now and then. For instance, here's a list of all the things every man ought to know:

- How to run a chain saw.
- When to buy a stock index option.
- The difference between a brook and a brown trout.
- The current value of his 401(k).
- The meaning of life.
- How to start an outboard.
- The difference between a beef and a dairy cow on sight.
- How to change the oil.
- What a woman wants.
- What time the game starts.

From this small list we can see there's a difference between industrial-strength cogitating and simple common knowledge. It's not as if you have to think your way through an oil change. If you don't know *exactly* how to change the oil, the guy next door does, and he'll tell you. In fact, all this stuff is the substance of comfortable masculine chat, the conversational topics that have instant and undeniable appeal because they are things that we know we ought to know, even if we don't. All of them, that is, except that "meaning of life" thing, which is something we talk about with others guys about as often as we swap tales of religious conviction or really helpful masturbatory techniques. "What's the meaning of life?" is one of those questions that's so big and so important, the only time it ever comes up is when it's the punchline of a joke. It's not that we don't care, of course; it's just that we don't even know how to think about it. This is America, after all, where the closest most of us want to get to a philosopher is watching Andy Rooney complain about shoes on Sunday nights, and where every public discussion of things like "spiritual values" turns quickly, in the hands of our dumbed-out media, into something resembling a Gabor family séance.

TIME TO GET MENTALLY FIT

Certainly, we all know that our mission as postmodern men is to fight flab wherever we find it. We know that the longer we put off a workout the harder it becomes, and that you can only ignore the obvious symptoms of laziness for so long. Fitness is fitness, so maybe what we need is a way to hone our philosophical fitness, really work the stiffness out of our ethical joints and moral muscles. The object of the game ought to be to come up with a personal philosophy of some kind, a Nautilus for the noggin. It ought to be something a guy can really use, a contraption perched on a solid base, with lots of room for weighty considerations, and all held together by some durable, highly polished principles. It ought to be the kind of thing which, if constructed carefully, can help a chap stay in shape for a lifetime. Your head is where you put the thing together, and where you use it until your brain hurts.

And then what good is it? Well, use it or lose it.

THREE FOOLPROOF WAYS YOU CAN START THINKING OLYMPIC-SIZED THOUGHTS FAST

1. *Avoid light thinking.* Modern thought is like modern water. There's a lot of it around, but most of it's unsuitable for human consumption. Besides, most of what resembles thought is really the kind of stuff you'd like to keep out of a place devoted to do-it-yourself philosophizing. Philosophies are built on large, complex thoughts, the kind of thing you will never see, for example, on the tail end of a car, where people are most likely to confuse what they feel with what they think. "Another Mother for Peace" has one 100 percent of the minimum daily adult requirement for feel-good sentiment. It also contains almost no useful thought, which, as you know, is the fiber of a good philosophy.

2. *Work out in silence.* Our culture is chock full of talking devices. Everybody wants to talk; everybody wants to be heard, whether or not they have anything to say. A century ago, formal discourse was considered an art practiced by the likes of Oscar Wilde and George Bernard Shaw, and good conversation came dear. Now we get Barbara Walters and Pat Buchanan, and talk is cheap, mostly because there's so much of it around. Because talking is not the same as thinking, there are two obvious things to keep out of a good home think-gym: a TV set and a phone. One thing to install: a decent bookshelf. (See the section "How to Build a Bookshelf" in chapter 1.) Before you accept anybody's idle

chatter as a bona fide idea, do what any sensible man would do: get it in writing.

3. ***Increase resistance gradually but consistently.*** Of course, a stick-built philosophy is only worth whatever you put into it. Since, as a rule, philosophies are designed to answer tough questions, it helps to know which ones to ask. Happily, life is supply-side crazy when it comes to providing thoughtful questions with built-in gradations of difficulty. Forget the big, huge philosophical questions like "What is love?" and "What is beauty?" Instead, start with some smaller, entry-level questions that are kind of open-ended.

  For example, "What am I doing here?"—the self-directed variant on "Hey! What're you doing here?"—is a superb question, one in which the difficulty of the answer can be ratcheted up in infinitely small increments, like a conceptual Soloflex. It's a take-anywhere question you can ask yourself any time in any circumstance, and it will always have an immediate effect: It'll help you define yourself, and it'll help you get philosophically fit fast. It might also save you a lot of trouble. For example, at lunch, Cheryl, the Madonna of marketing, notices a tiny speck of ratatouille on your cheek, and reaches over, pressing her perfect breasts hard against you, and carefully, *seductively,* wipes it away with one hand, while resting her other hand high on your thigh, dreadfully close to the lap devil, the blind idiot, the muscle that knows no morality. Just as you catch her hand in yours, you ask, "What am I doing here?" and bingo! the dogs of divorce are banished into the night. Asking the same question when you're alone in your home think-o-drome can also bring unexpected results.

• ***Caution:*** Beginners beware. If you experience pain or discomfort, lighten up. Do what I do: Stretch a little by asking yourself a slightly smaller question, like, "Wonder what's for dinner?"

Pretty soon you'll be ready for an iron-man thinkathon. Read on.

How to Get Brain Buff

Wise up! According to experts, the world's a dumber place than ever. The evidence of growing stupidity is everywhere. Test scores are tumbling. Blissful ignorance is on the rise. Schoolkids can't read or write. If stupid hurt, the whole planet would be a world of pain.

Hello and good-bye to the Nuckelhead Nineties. But wait! If you think about it, it's also a time of unparalleled opportunity. There's a bundle to be made outsmarting other guys—plus, women really like men with a little head-meat to go with those perfect abs.

So get to know your noggin. Be smart! And if you can't do that, at least *look* smart! Buy glasses! Wear tweed! Memorize tapes! Figure out how much you really need to know, *minimum*. Like the magazines say, get fit fast! But get smarter faster!

By the way, our trusty correspondents here are the guys at *Men's Health*, and especially our friend Dave. The *Men's Health* chaps are simply *rolling* in info. They probably had seven, eight million useful tips on how to get real smart lickety-split. But they only gave us fifty or so. They're not *stupid*, you know.

HOW TO THINK FAST
Concepts! Incoming!

Keep on Running
Senator Strom Thurmond is ninety-three, and a member of the Senate Judiciary Committee, which means he's smart enough to sit around and talk about Clarence Thomas's sex life with guys like Joe Biden and Ted Kennedy. Want smarter? Here's smart with a spritz of stamina: Thurmond has been running for the Senate every six years since 1954, and he's won every race. That's brain endurance all the way. How does he do it? Exercise, of course. He says:

- *To keep your brain working well, you have to exercise* to keep the arteries that take blood to the brain clear for nutrients, and to help push the blood there with your muscles. I swim a half mile twice a week and I do 10 minutes of stretching, 20 minutes of calisthenics, and 20 minutes of stationary cycling every morning. If you can do all that, there aren't many things you won't be able to do. (ST)
- *Other smart guys agree.* One study in California found that people who exercise routinely actually think better, remember more, and react more quickly than people who don't exercise at all. And an Illinois study found that subjects who exercised scored 30 percent higher on auditory and visual tests than sedentary subjects.

Feed Your Head
Your brain is as selective as the bouncer at a chic New York nightclub. When you eat, your body devours the protein, carbohydrates, fats, vitamins, and minerals

in the chow, then converts them into membranes and chemicals your brain will use to learn, think, feel, and remember. However, if one particular amino acid isn't up front and noticed, chances are that nutrient will be ignored and left standing at the door. And just like the nightclub scene, who gains entrance sets the mood for the rest of the night. Here's what you need to get in:

- **Bees.** The buzz in brain functioning comes from the B vitamins—especially B_6—found in oats, tuna, chicken, whole wheat, and bananas. Smart researchers in Holland figured this out by giving a bunch of healthy seventy-year-old guys twenty milligrams of B_6 every day for twelve weeks. They found that the B_6 men did better on tests of long-term memory than a control group who had been given a placebo.

  Other B vitamins (specifically numbers 1, 2, 3, and 12) boost mental energy, too. Vitamin B_{12}, in fact, actually helps in the manufacture and repair of brain tissues—a big help to guys who ride Harleys without helmets. Here's the optimum amount of each of the B vitamins:

VITAMIN	DAILY MINIMUM	OPTIMUM
B_6 (pyridoxine)	2 mcg	20 mcg
B_{12}	6 mcg	100 mcg
Biotin	—	200 mcg
Folate	400 mcg	1 mg
Niacin (B_3)	20 mg	250 mg
Pantothenate	10 mg	20 mg
Riboflavin (B_2)	1.7 mg	10 mg
Thiamine (B_1)	1.5 mg	20 mg

- **Hold back on carbohydrates.** Carbohydrates are what you need to eat if you're a guy who wants to lift heavy objects. Carbohydrates are what you need to avoid, however, if you want to be the guy smart enough to decide which heavy objects the carbo eaters ought to lift. A meal that's loaded with carbohydrates equals trouble for the brain.

  Here's the science: Carbohydrates contain the amino acid *tryptophan,* which competes with another crucial amino acid, *tyrosine,* to enter the brain, and you need tyrosine to be a smart guy.

- **Tyrosine** is crucial to quick thinking, fast reactions, and feelings of alertness, which pretty much describes how smart guys feel most of the time, especially when they're talking to beautiful tyrosine women who can use their tongues to pronounce foreign words, such as *zeitgeist* and *cul-de-sac.*

- ***Tryptophan*** slows reaction time, impairs concentration, makes you sleepy, and reduces the need to be in control. Tryptophan is the drug of choice for morons. Comes free with Whoppers.
- ***How to stay smart all the way through lunch.*** Eat the protein food *before* you eat the carbo food. And make sure that your ratio of carbohydrates to protein isn't more than three to one. Four ounces of tuna and two slices of bread, or a chicken breast and baked potato will do the trick.
- ***Eat less, think more.*** Graze, don't feast. Feasting causes a drop in energy because it shunts blood to the digestive tract—instead of your brain. Try to eat several small, witty, clever meals a day, instead of three big, stupid ones.

HOW TO THINK CLEARLY

Watch the Clock

If you want to use your smarts, use them while they're hot. For most of us, that means midmorning meetings and early lunches. Every day, you wake up dumb, then get smarter and smarter until around noon. Then it's downhill to dumb again, which strikes most of us sometime in the late afternoon. Then you make a slight intellectual recovery. But around ten or so, you're on the slippery slope of idiocy again, until you slide into the nightly coma, the end of the ride.

Use Your Head

Might as well. It's there, sticking out of the top of your shirt, holding open your collar, making sense of your ears. You might as well use it. Besides, your brain is like the other use-it-or-lose-it organ. If you neglect it, it gets permanently soft. Smart guys solve crosswords, read theology, analyze DH choke stats, or talk to their wives about money just to give the old noodle a workout. Hard thinking causes neural circuits to flash into action. Suddenly, capillaries expand, neurotransmitters zip back and forth, and blood flow increases. The result? A brain that stays younger longer. And your ability to handle complex issues—things that involve both reasoning and remembering—will remain strong five or ten years longer than those who aren't mentally active.

- ***Hung like Einstein's dendrites:*** Curious researchers at UCLA's Brain Research Institute, examining the brains of twenty dead adults, found that gray matter from college grads who remained mentally challenged throughout life had up to 40 percent longer *dendrites*—the branchlike parts of nerve cells that bring in information and help promote sophisticated processing—than the brains of people who had less than a high-school education and whose idea of advanced problem solving was trying to figure out what to watch on TV. Dumb people had dendrites so short you could sink a fifty-yard putt in their brainpan. Longer dendrites mean a greater surface for synaptic connections. The longer your dendrites, the better your noggin. Also with longer dendrites, you get free! bonus! *glial cells,* which nourish and support neurons and are known to increase in number with learning and experience. Smart guys can make their noggins into big, buff, lush, wet, glial plantations—with dendrites like wild capellini—by doing something they've never done before, brainwise, like learning Portuguese or figuring out what women want. The brain is a muscle. If you exercise it, it gets bigger and stronger. Like that other eyeless, one-track, brief-bound brain of yours. The number-one dendrite fertilizer? Hanging out with people smarter than you are.

And get this: In the early 1980s, UC Berkeley researchers, looking into the egghead of well-known thinkperson Albert Einstein, discovered the goofy-haired genius had longer dendrites in his brain than normal, less relativistic guys. In other words, *the inside of Einstein's head looked exactly like the outside!*

HOW TO REMEMBER WHAT YOU LEARN
Simply relaxing can significantly enhance your ability to learn something.

Be Blissfully Bright
In a Stanford study of thirty-nine people between the ages sixty-two and eighty-three, members of one group were taught to relax every muscle in their body from head to toe, whereas those in the other groups got a lecture about how to improve their attitude toward aging. The findings: ***The group that had practiced consciously relaxing their body before a three-hour memory-training course was able to remember 25 percent more*** than the groups that had not relaxed. Remember that.

Forget the Face
But remember the name. Sometimes when you meet people, you're so busy trying to impress them or struggling to keep the conversational rolling that the name breezes right by you and never enters your conscious mind. The key to remembering a name?
- ***Concentrate*** on the person you're meeting.
- ***Play around with the name*** for a moment or two in your mind.
- ***Say it*** at least once to yourself.

What you need is to rehearse the name in what scientists call a distributed fashion. To do this, repeat the name to yourself a few times, waiting an extra second each time you repeat it, until there are four or five seconds between sayings of the name. Example: You're introduced to your new boss, Jim Bozo. Say "Bozo, Bozo, Bozo" softly to yourself until you think you've got it.

Remember Important Events

Memories aren't always carbon copies of events. In fact, your mind is in a constant editing mode, changing the original memory so that it reflects newly acquired facts. Stuff that happens after an important event can significantly alter your recollection of the event.

To ensure you remember something exactly as it happened, to recall a business meeting or the negotiating terms of a major contract, write it down in detail *immediately afterward*. Then review it—aloud, if necessary. This records the memory while it's fresh, reinforces the memory by freezing it in place, and provides you with an opportunity to review what really happened so the original memory doesn't fade or get distorted.

Remember What You Read

Remember the last time you read a book? No, no. Not this one. The *last* one. Remember? Okay. Remember how, five minutes after you put it down, you couldn't remember anything in it? You've got a recall problem bigger than GM's biggest nightmare. Here are three ways to retain what you read:

1. *Get the big picture.* Use the table of contents to map the book and quickly find what you want to read. Skim through the index and look for things you already know a little something about, and flip to the parts of the book where they're discussed. Read the introduction or preface.
2. *Skip it.* Feel perfectly comfortable skipping the parts that don't really look interesting. Your interest is dictated by what you need to know. If it doesn't intrigue you, you don't need to learn it.
3. *Reduce the book or article to about six key terms.* Try to visualize the key players and events, and analyze the relationships between them. Ask yourself questions about what's in the article. In a novel, such as *Moll Flanders,* imagine yourself in the scene as one of the characters, dealing with the problems before him.

HOW TO ACE ANY TEST

How do you ace a test the next time an employer or professor pushes one under your nose?

Wrong.

See, *you shouldn't go with your first answer.* Most tests are designed to see if you can focus on the important information. If you don't ignore the *unimportant* stuff, you're likely to get the answer wrong. Conventional test-taking wisdom holds that as soon as you see the answer to a problem in a list of possible solutions, you should check it off and move on. But the obvious answer isn't usually the right answer. It just looks right because it's *close.*

Final Stress?

Nothing like a make-or-break end-of-your-life exam to really wake you up to some of life's other possibilities. However, if you want to actually pass all those grueling quizzes, get your pencils ready—and do some jumping jacks. Exercise will lower your anxiety level and improve your overall performance in any stressful circumstance. (AMcLL)

Ask the Right Questions

Smart people, like pollsters, know how to rephrase things to get the answers they want (e.g., "Do you believe the president of the United States or the politician who wants his job?"). If you want to effect an answer, learn how to change the question around until it suggests a completely different answer than the one you first thought you were most likely to get. For example: Ask a group of doctors how many would try therapy X, which gives the patient a 95 percent chance of survival. Then ask the same group how many would try therapy Y, which gives the patients a 5 percent chance of dying. Studies show that you'll get two very different answers, although the therapies have the same success and failure rate.

HOW TO LEARN TO DO TWO THINGS AT ONCE

Tune in: There is no Jerry Ford clinic. If there were, though, it would be devoted to helping guys do two things at once. One of the easiest ways to learn how to do so without dividing your attention is to put two TVs next to each other, tune them to different channels, and try to listen to both at once. See how much information you can absorb from each and try not to miss a thing. Once you're able to do this well, you can use the TVs to learn how to resist distractions. This time, instead of trying to take in everything from both

TVs, concentrate on one program and ignore the other. It'll be hard at first, but stay with it. When you think you've mastered it, try lowering the volume on the set you're watching and raising it on the one you're not. If it doesn't drive you crazy first, this technique is guaranteed to teach you how to pay attention effectively. (DH)

- *Downside:* You have two TV sets going, and nothing worth watching on either one.

HOW TO SPD RD

Fourstepstoreadingfasterthanabullet:

1. *Preview what you're going to read first.* Look at the titles, subheads, pull-quotes, or anything that's in *italics* or **boldfaced.** The author wants you to pick up on facts, concepts, and other important information.
2. *Use your hand as a pacer to underline what you're reading* and keep you moving rapidly through the material. The primary benefit? It's a concentration tool that keeps you focused on what you're reading. If you're focused, you'll retain more.
3. *Read groups of words.* Words are meant to trigger thoughts. Hearing everything in your head—as opposed to just seeing it—can actually slow your thinking. Start reading words in groups of twos and threes, and increase the number as your skill improves.
4. *Read vertically.* Left-to-right eye movement wastes a lot of time and causes you to read *everything,* most of which isn't all that important. If you keep your left-to-right eye movement at a minimum as you go down the page, your eye can take in swaths of up to 3,500 words a minute. (KJ)

HOW TO FINISH A BORING BOOK

No sleep, boring book—but you gotta read it! What to do? According to a virtually sleepless, somnambulatory *Today* show host:

- *Slap yourself* a lot and keep drinking a lot of cold water.
- *Try to find something you're interested in,* something you like in a book. If you have a problem with the prose, look for little facts you didn't know, things that you can get from the book and use. Or find a character you can relate to and try to feel what he's going through. (BG)

HOW TO ACT ON A GOOD IDEA

Sometimes, you have to coax an idea into reality. That takes a lot of time. How much? As much as you've got.

A blinding flash of light doesn't hit you and you just sit down and do great stuff. You have to take your idea and distill it. That takes time. Maybe you'll interrupt yourself a hundred times a day to eat, clip your toenails, and pick your teeth.

If things aren't working, put off your project for another day: It's amazing how much easier things are the next morning. (DBa)

HOW TO BUILD A GOOD EDUCATION

If you want to prove yourself invaluable, try to become an expert on something. Keep it in the ballpark, though. If you're working in shipping, don't try to study microbiology at home in your spare time.

- *A little expertise is a cool thing.* People who excel—whether it's in sports, or business, or the professions—spend a lot of time studying, even if they don't like to admit it. So do your homework. Spend a half hour going over some aspect of your job—or, if you're angling for a move, someone else's. It takes very little effort to get a leg up on other guys who don't take the time to increase their value.
- *Home school.* You can give yourself a tremendously wide liberal arts education by focusing on the one thing that interests you most—say, sex or canoeing—and slowly but tirelessly learning everything there is to know about the subject. The history of the world can be told in canoes or in fellatio. One thing leads to another, and if you programmatically follow each and every lead, pretty soon you'll know all there is to know.

No short cuts to smart. Once you get a good grasp, knowledge builds. What you already know helps you take the next step. At the foundation, the main areas must be history, English, math, and science. Once you understand them pretty well, everything builds on itself and comes together. (EDH)

HOW TO STAVE OFF FOGEYDOM

Everybody's cultural life petrifies the minute they leave school. If you left college in 1977 or '78, Springsteen's *Born to Run* is what pop music sounds like, *Star Wars* is what great movies look like, and Sol Lewitt is your idea of a crazy modern artist. Your wardrobe is likely to have frozen in time, too—not that you're still wearing bell-bottoms, but you don't dress the way this year's crop of grads dresses, either. And that, at least, is good.

But nothing tattoos your inability to adapt and learn as much as a time-capsule mentality toward American culture, which, after all, just keeps right on truckin'—as somebody used to say. Here's how to go with the flow:

- *Music.* Give music videos or the local college FM station an hour a week. If you really don't understand what you're looking at or listening to, take along a guide: Go out to a newsstand and buy a rock mag—not *Rolling Stone,* which is, after all, for guys *your* age. But something you think a reasonably bright twenty-year-old might read. If you've not been paying attention to pop music for the last decade or two, you'll be amused to see that what used to be bad protest poetry is now rap, what used to be bad club punk is now rock, what used to be rock is now country-and-western, and what used to be country is now folk music.
- *Film.* The introduction of cheap video cameras pretty much put an end to what used to be called "experimental" cinema. Once, a 16-mm camera was almost beyond all but the most ambitious film students. Now any kid with a job at Burger King can afford to moonlight as a "video artist." Pile an NEA windfall on top of that, and you've got a video professional. So the real creative action has shifted to areas such as computer-assisted animation, where genuine skill is still required before anything intelligible may be displayed.
- *Clothes.* This is where guys over the age of, say, thirty get in hot water, since clothing is the one aspect of popular culture that is readily available and fairly easy to identify: Just dress like the boy next door. But that's exactly how dumb guys go wrong: They don't understand the difference between *understanding* youth culture and actually wearing it. Remember in the 1960s, how squirrely fifty-year-old guys in love beads and tie-dies looked? Well, those guys are all goners now. Don't let it happen to you.

HOW TO IMPERSONATE A SMART PERSON

In the end, of course, there will always be limits to how smart anybody can be. If you feel like your cranium is running at redline and you just can't get any smarter, then punt. *Fake it.* Imitation smart, with the look and feel of the real thing, isn't the same as dumb, after all. Here's how to pretend:

How to Look Smart

Once you strip away professional considerations, it's much easier to look intelligent than you might think. According to a recent study conducted by a German university, people will think you're intelligent if:

- You are attractive.
- You are reasonably fit.
- You seem friendly and self-assured.

- You dress conservatively.
- You wear your hair in a stylish fashion.

You'll be perceived as less than smart if you "look unrefined," dress unstylishly or informally, or appear to be out of shape.

In addition, people with round faces look, to those surveyed, dumber than people with long or oval faces.

However, these factors all faded in significance once verbal expression was factored in. People who were ultimately rated highest in intelligence demonstrated high levels of verbal skills, which include

- Clear articulation of ideas.
- A pleasant voice.
- A lack of halting or confused speech.

Psychologists no longer rely exclusively on the standard IQ test as a sole indicator of intelligence. Researchers have, until recently, not paid much attention to how people perceive intelligence in others.

How to Look Smart in Your Field

The signs and cues people use to determine how smart you are—an important measure of success—depend largely on your occupation. To seem intelligent to others in your field, all you have to do is meet their expectations of what constitutes "intelligence." For example:

REALISTIC OCCUPATIONS
If you're a:
- *Mechanic*
- *Engineer*
- *Carpenter*
- *Police officer*
  Do this:
- Make few mistakes and solve problems on your own without asking others for help.
- Develop a reputation as somebody to whom others can turn for help in resolving dilemmas.

INVESTIGATIVE OCCUPATIONS
If you're a:
- *Biologist*
- *Researcher*

- *Physicist*
- *Mathematician*

Do this:
- Use a stilted and jargon-loaded vocabulary.
- Mock "laymen" who ask dumb questions.
- Offer opinions on very obscure topics.

If you risk being easily understood, you also risk being thought to be unintelligent.

ARTISTIC OCCUPATIONS

If you're a:
- *Painter*
- *Entertainer*
- *Musician*
- *Writer*

Do this:
- Come up with anything unusual, regardless of its intrinsic value.
- Ridicule any accepted wisdom.
- Put esoteric, obtuse theories ahead of conventional practice.

Practicality is not an issue when it comes to defining an artistic person as "smart." In fact, the more impractical the device or design, the smarter you'll seem to your peers.

SOCIAL OCCUPATIONS

If you're a:
- *Teacher*
- *Social worker*
- *Nurse*
- *Psychologist*
- *Doctor*
- *Counselor*

Do this:
- Come up with an especially acute analysis of another person's problems, the more intensely personal, the better.
- Don't worry if your analysis leads to a solution of the problem or not.
- Go heavy on the jargon.

The *perception* of perceptiveness is critical here for convincing others you are smart, so an extensive, unnecessarily vague vocabulary is a definite plus here.

ENTERPRISING OCCUPATIONS

If you're a:

- *Lawyer*
- *Politician*
- *Salesman*
- *Stockbroker*

Do this:

- Subordinate common sense to manipulation and persuasion.
- Define all contests on your own terms.
- Stick to a strategy.
- Above all, nurture your credibility.

CONVENTIONAL OCCUPATIONS

If you're an:

- *Accountant*
- *Motor vehicles clerk*
- *Computer programmer*
- *Tax auditor*

Do this:

- Allow for few variations to accepted rules.
- Cite regulations whenever possible—the more obscure, the better.
- Foster an air of aloofness, removed from petty human emotions.
  Nobody goes to an accountant for emotional support. (RH)
  More on ersatz bril:

HOW TO BE VAGUE

The smarter you are, the greater your ability to be specific and to articulate your thoughts with precision. *Really* smart people can operate at such a refined level of erudition that to mere mortals, they sound like Zen wind chimes. This is good for dumb but wily guys, since they know it means that if they can successfully mimic the inscrutability of a genuinely smart person, those around them may also assume that they're a genuinely smart guy, too.

For example, Employer X, in his own ethereal manner, would sometimes be overheard by others in the office saying to a subordinate, "When they zig, you zag," or, "I don't know what I don't know." Of course, genuinely smart people know that this kind of meaningless noise is to real thought what, say, Roseanne is to sex. But if you're concerned with the appearance of smart and not the *reality* of smart, this is a good tactic. Tonally pleasing gibberish can also lubricate a guy out of a tight spot. (RT)

HOW TO BE ESOTERIC

Better than vague, more colorful than smart, esoteric really works at pushing a brainy persona. Why? Because since almost everybody graduating from college these days has a vocational training and not a fundamental education, it's pretty easy to enhance your smart-guy image by simply leap-frogging a lot of dead Greeks and other white, male Euro-types, and going straight for the obscure and arcane. If you read five books about, say, Tibetan Buddhism, you'll know more about the subject than almost anybody in America. You may know nothing about Plato, Aristotle, medieval mysticism, Himalayan geography, or classical theology, but who cares? It's like being a scholar without having to bother with the tiresome, tedious business of actual scholarship. In no time at all, you'll be on your way to some oddball theosophical dead end, and if anybody asks you about it, you'll be able to shrug him off with some doubletalk about *devas, chakras,* and warps. People will talk to you and think to themselves, "Sure, he doesn't know the capital of Uruguay or whose side we were on in World War I, but he *must* be smart because he knows the fax number of the Dalai Lama." See? The more esoteric your knowledge and the more obscure the jargon you use to discuss your odd interest, the smarter people will assume you are.

Caution: Because you lack a fundamental understanding of the largest possible context of your esoteric interest, the more you read, the dumber you'll get. A metaphysical paradox, no? (RSA)

HOW TO GET BRAINS BY MAIL

Let's just say you've tried *everything*—the *TV Guide* crossword, *Wheel of Fortune, Classics Illustrated,* but you still just can't quite get from a dumb here to a smart there. As a last-ditch measure, try this:

- Pick up the phone.
- Dial an 800 number.
- Have your credit card ready.
- Collect your new, improved brains from UPS, along with the book light you ordered from Sharper Image.

Here's a basic catalog of stuff you can learn from U-VCR or from Professor Walkman:

Learn to Count!

Math Made Easy offers a series of videotapes on everything from arithmetic to calculus to statistics and other numerate stuff. Get a catalog by calling (800) USA-MATH.

- *How it works:* MME gives step-by-step instructions illustrating complex mathematical concepts. For example, let's say you want to learn about maximum and minimum heights, who knows why. In the calculus course, MME shows a football being thrown in the air, freezes the image, and overlays it with cool rotating graphics, grids, charts, and other stuff Sister O'Hagan couldn't do in her *prayers*.
- *The pitch:* "Most teachers aren't artists," says a spokesperson. "They aren't able to visually show a theory or a formula. We take information that's hard to utilize and apply a visual to it. We make it easier to comprehend by putting it in a visual format for you—and then providing segments of how it applies to real-life situations."

Learn to Talk!

Verbal Advantage is a $299 series of eighteen audiotapes all designed to help you build a totally awesome vocabulary.

- *How it works:* VA's learning philosophy is borrowed from an old North Korean torture formula based on—ready, vocab-freaks?—*repetition.* That means repeating something over and over and over and over and over again and again and again until you get it. VA's take is that the best way to learn is to listen to the word, hear it in context, and then use it in practice. Repetition, repetition, repetition. Over and over. Again and again. Repetition. Verbal Advantage gives you a word, defines the word for you, spells it, uses it in context, over and over. Call (800) 766-1960. That's (800) 766-1960.

Learn to Read!

Hooked on Phonics will take you from finger paints all the way to twelfth grade on the winged back of phonics.

- *How it works:* Hooked on Phonics—or, as new clients spell it, "Hukd on Fonix"—shows you how to take basic sounds (two- to three-letter phonemes) and combine them, albeit slowly, through to complete sentences. You learn to read by decoding the words into familiar, small chunks. For example, they teach you "ph" or "ch" and then combine them with other words. Note: You have to use flashcards, workbooks, and other

aids, so you're not going to be able to do this while commuting to Manhattan or stir-frying. Philosophy: Breaking down a word, sounding it out
with each syllable, phonetically, is the most successful way to improve
reading. Thirteen tapes cost $229.95. Call (800) ABC-DEFG.

Learn Big Words You Can't Spell!

We the People. Build your English and vocabulary skills in the context of a
history lesson.

- *How it works:* You get $130 worth of American history from the Revolu-
  tionary War through Lincoln's inauguration on sixteen different tapes, nar-
  rated by Martin Sheen. When Sheen gets to a really hard word—like
  "tumultuous," for example—the sound effects guys go to work and you
  get a head full of thunder, lightning, and a raging sea, which is sort of
  what "tumultuous" means. Wait until you hear the sound of "inalienable"
  and "manifest destiny"! Call (800) ABC-DEFG.

Learn How to Remember the Alamo!

American Memory Institute. AMI claims it will improve your memory by 500
percent—not 150 percent, not 425 percent, but a full, flat-out, recall-humping
500 percent—if you remember to listen to its fourteen hours of audiocassettes
and watch its video. Price? $139.95.

- *How it works:* We all have photographic memories. It's just remembering stuff that's the problem. On that memorable, but somewhat puzzling premise, the AMI's Kevin Trudeau has designed a program called
  MegaMemory to help you remember more. Techniques include such
  things as visualization—Forget your name? Try visualizing your face—
  and "pegging," where you are taught to remember things in manageable
  groups. So if you have to remember one hundred things, with pegging
  you'd learn them in groups of ten. Let's say you have to remember details
  about three Trudeaus—or *Trudeaux*, as the French say. You've got Kevin,
  the memory guy, and Garry, the cartoon guy, and Pierre, the Canadian
  guy. Now, one of these guys had a wife who ran around with the Rolling
  Stones. Was it Jane Pauley? Forget about it. No way. Then who was it? If
  you just can't remember, call (800) 562-MEGA. (DZ/MH)

How to Tell Whether You Have Any Common Sense

Elementary subtraction: If your investment portfolio is delivering 10 percent per and your Citibank Visa card is running at its limit and you're paying 18 percent per annum, you have no common sense. (RES)

How to Get Free Public Education in the Post-Education Era

By the time we reach adulthood, most of us are as intelligent and as educated as we're ever going to get. But many of us, while conceding that we're never going to get any smarter, would like to figure out a way to at least *seem* smarter. Here are a few time-proven tricks to achieve this, all free:

1. *Borrow audiocassettes* of the 100 Greatest Books Ever Written from the public library and listen to them while driving to work. If you sat down to read *The Wealth of Nations,* even if you were a fast reader, it would take at least a week. With a cassette, you can absorb all of its wisdom while suffering through a traffic jam. Hint: You don't need to borrow all one hundred books; ten will do. Cost: $0.00.

2. *Read the last page of* **Forbes** magazine while lounging around your newsstand. The last page of this biweekly magazine is a compendium of useful quotes, citing everyone from Cicero to Ghandi. What's more, the quotes are organized by theme, making it easy to figure out what they're about. Nothing impresses dinner companions more than the ability to quote from people like Alexis de Toqueville and Miguel de Cervantes. Cost: $0.00.

3. *Read the liner notes* on the backs of classical records. Why plow through one of those gargantuan histories of Western music when you can learn all you need to know about Mozart's love affairs, Beethoven's deafness, and Franz Schubert's hacking cough simply by perusing the liner notes on the backs of CDs? And you don't even have to buy them. Cost: $0.00.

4. *Read the first two chapters* of important books, but nothing more. It is widely known in the publishing industry that book reviewers, who do not get paid much, read only the first two chapters of works they review. As a

result, editors always encourage writers to put all the good stuff up front in the first two chapters. Everything you could possibly need to know will be right there. Cost: $0.00.

5. ***Do a crash course in world history*** by reading children's books. Everything important that Hernando Cortés, Napoleon Bonaparte, Abraham Lincoln, or Martin Luther King, Jr., ever did can be found in inexpensive books, aimed at seven- to ten-year olds, that sell for between $1.95 and $3.95. What's more, they take only about ten minutes to read, so you can devour them while browsing at the local bookstore. Cost: $0.00. (JQ)

How to Be Tolerable

You can win lots of friends and influence lots of people in the time it takes to have a simple conversation:

- ***When someone is talking, suspend your judgments*** until that guy has had his say.
- ***Lean forward slightly,*** nod, make eye contact, and ask clarifying questions.
- ***Don't take up all the airtime.*** Even if it's your program, give the other guy a chance to ventilate. (GW)
- ***Develop the art of mirroring.*** This is almost totally craven, but it works like a charm. What you do is try to imitate in subtle ways the person you want to like you. Human beings crave being with people who seem to be like themselves. This means if someone is talking to you and leaning forward at forty-five degrees, you do the same. If someone you're with crosses his legs, you do the same. If the other guy loosens his tie—well, you get the picture. To everybody else, you'll look like a couple of loose Rockettes. But to the person who matters, these small gestures will subconsciously make your acquaintance feel as if you're some kind of kindred soul, and, chances are, he'll like you for it. (MM)

How to Make Friends You Can Count On

Sometimes, friends die. Sometimes, friendships die. Either way, it's a painful deal. Ugly truth: Holding on to friends is tough. Uglier question: At any given moment, how many friends do you think you have? We're talking friends, here, not acquaintances, employees, or hangers-on, but honest-to-goodness, post-your-bail, ignore-your-buck-naked-wife friends. How many? Two? Four? One? Most men have a couple. Nobody ever has more than five genuine, true-blue friends at any one time.

What accounts for this lifelong shortfall of compadres, amigos? It's the difficulty of the rules. Friendship is a game so complex that only sheer luck allows you to bump into somebody else who plays the game just the way you do, who does unto you as you do unto, who behaves just the way you'd behave in a friendship. If you think your friends are people who can help you, or people who adore you, or people who will make you feel swell about yourself, you've got no friends at all. The recognition of your own values in somebody else is usually all it takes to put the good-pal seal of approval on an acquaintanceship. Most of these rules are vague and unwritten; they can only be intuited. But there are some things all friends can agree on:

MAINTENANCE IS OPTIONAL

One very nice thing about a friend is that you can take important aspects of his friendship for granted. This is important because most men's lives become more complex as they approach midlife. You spend your first thirty, forty years getting a life. Then all of a sudden, you have too much of one. As your responsibilities grow, your career and your family claim increasing amounts of time—and when you do get a free minute, it usually goes to some immediately accessible source of amusement, like golf-ball abuse or fish slaughter.

Here's the real-life priority list for most modern men:
1. Your family.
2. Your friends.
3. Your job.

For most men, it's a tight race between one and two, but generally it's three that demands the most attention. Still, this is the batting order, and if your priorities are different, you're in bad shape. However, real friends won't make you rock the boat with numbers one or three just to massage number two. For instance, friends don't need to see your face every day to know whether you're still a friend. Most men assume the quality of their friendship is sturdy, rustproof, and low-maintenance. Friends know their friends will be their friends until further notice, and that's really all they need to know. (GK)

TIME IS NOT OF THE ESSENCE

Lonely, friendless people claim that friendships must stand the test of time. They are incorrect. Friendships that must be tested by time (or by anything else, for that matter) generally fail the test. Your best pal may be somebody you've known for less time than it takes to run a pennant race, or it may be somebody your grandmother knew as a child.

FRIENDSHIPS ARE MUTUAL

For a friendship to flourish, there must be equal opportunity for friendship on both sides. If you have a chum who never asks for anything, ever, it's impossible to treat him like a friend. Then you have to decide if it's possible to be friends with somebody who won't let you be friendly. (LOP)

DUTY CALLS

Here's where the vinyl siding peels off a friendship: Friends must be defended when they're wrong, explained when they're irrational, respected when they're defiled. Friendship carries with it certain unpleasant duties. Ideally, they are rarely, if ever, required. But when duty calls, you can't dodge the draft.

Note: Defending your friend when he's wrong is one thing. You also have a duty to tell your friend when he's wrong, even as you defend him. He also has a duty not to put you in ridiculous situations for the sake of a friendship. (AC)

ALL SUCCESSES ARE SHARED

Well, this is true up to a point. You don't have a right to expect your friend to exploit his hard-won success by giving you its benefits. But you're bound by the rules of friendship to be genuinely glad for your friend's successes. You can also be envious, of course. You can even consider the success ill-deserved. But when a friend hits a homer, you have to cheer, even if you're batting zip.

NOT ALL FRIENDSHIPS TRAVEL WELL

Almost two centuries ago, the poet Shelley wrote that "when a man marries, dies, or turns Hindoo, his best friends hear no more of him." Often, when your life changes significantly, one of the biggest changes is in your roster of chums. This is especially true when you cross large cultural watersheds and suddenly see yourself living a different life. For example, the five best friends you have as a single man will be reduced by 40 percent if you get married. Why? Because the guys who live in the world of bachelors have different customs and very different interests than the guys who live in the world of wives, and at least two of your five best friends will start relating to you as if you were a foreigner. The real break comes when you have kids. Suddenly, to your single-life pals, it's as if you had become a Samoan transsexual. Shelley's right: For unattached men leading lives of supreme simplicity, married men with kids are like math majors or Moonies. They become guys with complications completely incomprehensible to men who have no responsibility other than to themselves and their abs. So if you're very, very lucky, of the five best friends you had at your wedding, only one will still be around when your youngest kid graduates from high school—and he probably won't be your best friend by then.

SOME WOMEN ARE NICE GUYS

There are a lot of places we forget to look when it comes time to find a friend. Like in the gynecologist's office. Despite the idiotic mythology of *When Harry Met Sally*—in which we were told men and women couldn't be friends, only lovers—women make great pals. They're as trustworthy, loyal, entertaining, and wise as any man, plus they're usually more scenic. Oddly, many of the women who make good friends are deeply critical of other women. Weird, no?

ANOTHER SECRET SOURCE

You can always pluck friends off the family tree. The upside of these kinds of related friends is that they know you intimately and their affection for you is virtually without qualification. Alas, the upside is also the downside: Most men just don't need to be that well-known nor that completely understood. Sometimes, in fact, you just want to reinvent your life on the fly as you go, and dragging around a lot of conflicting views and contradictory evidence can be a great deal of trouble.

A personal observation: When I was teaching, I once passed myself off as a guy named Biff—I actually said, "Call me Biff"—to a batch of kids in my freshman comp class. I wore aviator shades and a motorcycle jacket. Showed up with a girlfriend's rottweiler once. Why? I just wanted to check out my rugged, craggy, weathered, high-speed, no-hands, no-helmet inner self. I only did it for a semester. The next term, I became my old pale, wheezing, sensitive poet of a man, again. I don't think I could have pulled it off if Mom and Dad were in the class.

How to Improve Your Self-esteem

You're one helluva guy, even if you don't think so. Want proof? Okay:

HEY, YOU'VE GOT TO BE BETTER THAN SOMEBODY

Beijing bunters: In the summer of 1978, John Lowenstein, a left fielder for the Baltimore Orioles, came to bat in a late inning with the game on the line. He bunted. The ball floated high into the air, then lazily descended into the glove of the needlessly alert pitcher. There was a soft puff, then a thousand groans filled the night. Later, in the locker room, sportswriters surrounded Lowenstein wanting to know what had gone wrong, but, in the manner of good newsmen, afraid to tackle the subject head-on for fear of hurting an athlete's feelings. "That was a terrible bunt, John," one of them finally said. His colleagues murmured nervously.

"You know," said Lowenstein, apparently uninjured, "every time I bunt like that I think of China."

"China?" asked the writer. "How come China?"

"Because," said Lowenstein gravely, "there are a billion Chinese. And I'm a better bunter than all of them."

There's a corollary to this little law:

YOU'RE LUCKIER THAN YOU KNOW

Sure, not everything breaks for you. The schmuck in the next cubicle got his promotion the lucky way, while you actually had to work for yours. And it's quite true that if you had been in the right place at the right time your entire life would be completely different than it is today. But, in fact, it might be worse. True story: In 1982 in Yugoslavia, a farmer was walking along a road when suddenly a storm blew up: rain, thunder, and lightning, lots of lightning, a bolt of which hit our man and killed him. Bad luck, you say? There's more: This was, it turned out, the second time this guy had been struck by lightning. Plus, when he passed away, he joined his two brothers, his father, his aunt, two uncles, and his maternal grandfather in bad-break hell. Seriously. They had all been killed by lightning strikes.

You're luckier than dead people, and don't you forget it. At least you're alive! Feel the wind in your hair! Feel the rain on your face! Hear the thunder! See the lightning! Stand tall! Reach up to the heavens with that metal-tipped umbrella of yours! You're alive! (RE)

YOU CAN ALWAYS ATTRACT WOMEN

All you have to do is work on your material. Now, for women, that means plastic surgery, since men are relentlessly superficial. It's a horrible, irrevocable truth that most men don't care quite so much about what a woman says, but they care a lot about the way she looks saying it. In fact, for women, McLuhan was dead right.

For men, on the other hand, looks don't matter. Sex scientists have discovered that if you're an interesting guy, charming and confident, the kind of fellow who can tell great jokes about ducks while discussing Rabelais, women will go stone blind around you. You open your mouth and turn into Brad Pitt, while the woman you're talking to turns into Stevie Wonder. It's a miracle! And it's also what keeps the gene pool in a muddy uproar.

Money has a similar effect on some—but not all—women, so if you don't have good material, you should always let your wallet do the talking. (HS)

YOU'VE STILL GOT YOUR SENSE OF HUMOR

High self-esteem is often accompanied by a healthy sense of humor. Check out Dan Quayle. What a cutup. Cracked up the whole country, including himself, and it didn't bother him a bit. When you realize that the joke's funny, even though the joke's on you, you've got heavy self-esteem.

YOU'VE STILL GOT YOUR JOB

Beats begging: The reason the chairman of the board is happier about his work than the guy in the mail room has only a little to do with money, and a lot to do with power. Just think how much happier the mail room guy would be if he knew that on a really, really bad day, he might not be able to demand any more money, but if he felt like it, he could always pop up to the eighth floor and fire the clown in the corner office. He knows, you know, we all know there's a direct correlation between the amount of self-esteem you have and the amount of power you wield in your job. So if it's self-esteem you want, forget the money thing and go to work on the power thing. There are several rules at play here:

- *Perma-power.* Once you get power, your self-esteem will stay close to the surface no matter what. Clarence Thomas, for instance, got a public humiliation as part of his job interview. But he got the job, and a powerful job it is. Therefore his self-esteem is solid for the foreseeable.

- *Claiming responsibility is the same as claiming power.* Look at Janet Reno, one of the guys, at least for our purposes. Think she has a self-esteem problem? Think again. She sent tanks in against women, kids, and religious nuts, slaughtered them all, and she felt fine about it, because she knows the unbreakable subrule of bureaucratic self-esteem: *Responsibility is power, and power blinds everyone to your failings.* If you're a bureaucrat, nothing makes you feel better about yourself than having a standing army at your disposal. But only by decking herself out in the gaudy mantle of self-esteem could Janet Reno make all of us lose track of the difference between Waco, Texas, and Kent State.

- *Esteem may be earned.* If, on the other hand, you're just the guy driving the tank, you can get a certain amount of satisfaction from simply doing your job well. The rule here is that a lot of power in a narrow context gives more self-esteem than tiny power in a larger context. This can also be seen in one highly estimable hint: Performing your job at a level markedly higher than the level at which your superior performs his job is a wonderful source of self-esteem. Provided your boss knows it, it's also a terrific way to ensure job security—a kind of power—but only if you keep it to yourself.

- *Now. Use what you've learned.* Compared to many men, you're a witty, accomplished, lucky Don Juan, laughing your way through a life that, by any reckoning, is better than a couple of other guys' lives. Still a nonbeliever? If this were an article in a women's magazine, we'd give you a little quiz to help reveal the phenomenal worth of the you you really are. But we're men here, healthy men, so no matter what you scored, you'd be on the brink of an esteem breakthrough. Think about it: You're a helluva guy. We love you, you love you, we're all as happy as can be. In fact, forget us. Let's talk about you. You're marvelous, you big lug, you. You're wonderful. But, hey, you already know that. (FER)

8. Money

The symptoms of financial failure are, for many men, the stuff of modern fable. It usually works like this: Postmodern guy walking down life's road meets a beautiful woman with a big wardrobe and three children and marries her. He needs a larger home, of course, so he buys one. The kids need braces, the wife needs cars. The complications of his life soon form a mountain of paper on his desk—invoices, demands, threats. Now he's not sleeping well, so he moves to the couch at night. This eventually angers his wife, who moves in with the guy who cleans the *pool*, leaving our friend with the charming children and a bed all to himself. The children soon become adolescents, and one of them of course gets arrested. To make bail, the guy has to take out another lien on the house. It becomes impossible to pay alimony, so the court starts hounding him. He loses the house and moves into an apartment. This embarrasses the kids; one runs away, the other two become violent. One thing leads to another until finally his boss calls him on the carpet and asks why he's missing work and why the courthouse is calling the personnel office and why he's always so damned irritable. The guy certainly knows what's wrong: He has hit the black ice of poverty and skidded out of control. He's broke and getting broker. But it's all too embarrassing. Since he doesn't know what to say, he skips all the symptoms and goes straight for the cure: He asks for a raise. That's when his boss fires him.

Now the pitiable subject of our little lecture may be forgiven for his inability to discuss money once. After all, when he met the woman who became the instrument of his undoing, he should have simply asked, "Nice, but how much?" But maybe he didn't want to look at lust with jaded eyes. Or maybe he was just worried that he couldn't afford the woman and the excess baggage of her life. Whichever, he signed on and paid the price in long, painful installments. Long before he was fired, a friend asked him why he didn't go to his boss, tell the tale, and try to work something out. After all, the guy was a newspaper reporter, the class of humans most prone to personal catastrophe. His editor was an old-timer, and almost certainly would have been used to seeing sniveling, impoverished men weep across his desk. But our man said no. "I could never do that," he said. "I hate talking money with people."

So he never did—until it came time to come clean, and he started talking money when he should have been talking contrition.

So. There's a fable that should be a lesson.

Why Talk Ain't Cheap

Why can a man talk prostate, talk infidelity, talk atrocity and theft, yet still not be able to talk turkey?

- *Men and money.* First off, men do not understand what money is for. For many men, money is God's yardstick. It is the immutable measure, the absolute dimension of a man's worth, and to talk about it is to open a discussion about lots of important things—like power, self-esteem, conflict, humiliation, or generosity. Hence, for lots of guys, money can be an end in itself, since it is, in some ways, at least, the measure of one's own self.
- *Women and money.* Women have lives considerably more complex than most men's, so they tend to see money much more clearly. To a normal woman, money isn't some complicated scoring device in the full-body contact sport of life. To women, money is what you use to buy stuff.

  This is not to say women object to men making lots of money. In fact, women *love* men who make lots of money. Back in the 1960s and 1970s, would-be rock stars used to stuff a sock in their pants to make a mighty love-muscle. But they missed the point, if you follow, because most women weren't looking at love Lugers so much as they were checking out the *other* bulge—the money bulge, the one a wallet makes, the one that counts.
- *Conversational moolah 101.* Because men confuse money with every other estimable virtue—intelligence, muscle, power, whatever—money is a volatile subject for men, one that can catapult any civil conversation right into the oblivion of confrontation and resentment. After all, when money's the topic between two men, conflict is in the air. The guy who has the money hates the other guy for trying to get some of it, because money is the source of his strength and power. The guy who wants the money hates the other guy for making him ask for it. He figures it should be offered to him because it's so obvious that he's skilled, or talented, or a nice guy, or a brother-in-law. Consequently, all men—and especially men who dislike even the mildest confrontation—never discuss money. Instead, they stew about it in silence.

So now we know what we need to know:

How to Talk About Money

First, you have to get comfortable with the stuff. Try these relaxation techniques:

- *Demystify it.* A pile of money sitting in a room with nobody around has no mojo. To paraphrase our friend P. J. O'Rourke, you can't smoke it, you can't eat it, you can't f*** it, so what good is it? Look at a sawbuck closely. Meditate on it. Get to know it. Think difficult thoughts: Why should it take *twenty* George Washingtons to make one lousy Andy Jackson? How does this impact your life?
- *Don't measure yourself with it.* It's true that money can make up for many critical, personal shortcomings. But they're shortcomings you really don't want to admit having. For instance, a dollar bill is six and one-eighth inches long. The average length of an erect penis is five and a half inches. (CDA)
- *Do something stupid with it.* Demonstrate its worthlessness to yourself. Buy yourself a snowmobile or donate a big bunch of it to the people who make "Wage Peace" bumper stickers. Feed it to dolphins or overtip your way into the life of a cocktail waitress at a bowling alley. (MF)

DUAL CURRENCY

There are only two kinds of money: There's yours and there's theirs. The distinction between the two is usually not subtle, but there are some differences worth noting. For example, to you, your money is American money. You comprehend its worth almost intuitively: It has a familiar feel, a comfortable texture. A stack of it has an overupholstered exuberance, a sort of decadent resiliency that, when placed in your pocket in a thick roll, puts a spring in your step and a smile on your face. A huge, fat wad of bills in your hand is what immortality feels like.

Their money is foreign currency. When somebody starts talking to you about money that isn't your own (even though, perhaps, it ought to be), it's as if they were quoting hog belly futures in zlotys. You can't possibly understand the worth of somebody else's money because, for one thing, you don't know how much of it he has. If Mother Teresa gave you a C-note, it would seem like an awful lot of money. If Bill Gates gave you the same hundred, you'd think it was chump change. All you can know for sure about their money is that it exerts a gravitational pull on you. And that's what can help you determine exactly how much of it you need to have. (SP)

The Law of Money Migration, or, The Route of All Evil

There are physics involved here, actually, a little electromagnetic thing called the Law of Money Migration. Goes like this: The strength of the gravitational pull you sense about somebody else's bankroll is directly proportional to your conviction that it *rightly* belongs to you.

For example, let's say you walk into the boss's office looking for a bonus. You know what you've done to earn it, and so does he. You have a dollar figure in mind, and so does he. (And, believe it or not, these two figures will be phenomenally close almost every time.) You can feel the tug of his money; it's flopping and yanking like a bass at the end of a line. His job is to devibe the situation, to get that money of his to behave and stop trying to wiggle out of his pocket and into yours. Your job is to stand up for your conviction that you are offering that money its rightful place, that, to all those bills struggling to be free, your pocket is the promised land. (MF)

Power Talk

Ultimately, of course, **when you're talking money, you're talking power,** and power is the big Harley of life, the one that rides you unless you learn to ride it. Power is best seen in the Jacobean sense of being something God doles out to a lucky few just to impose a little order on an uncivilized world. So if you have power, you can be Ivan the Terrible or Æthelred the Unready or Richard the Lion-Hearted, since what you do with power is a better measure of a man than the half foot of a dollar bill.

So if you have power, play the benevolent despot, firm but caring, but above all, fair. And if you are a petitioner, make fairness your own talking point, since no deal is a good deal unless it's a good deal on both sides. But above all, as our friend learned too late, remember that if you're going to talk money, make sure money's the topic of conversation. (MF, Anon.)

How to Do Tricks with Money

- *You can double it.* Here's a formula to use if you want to double your money. It's called the rule of seventy-two and here's how it works: To double your money in any investment, divide seventy-two by the number of years you're willing to wait to reach your goal. The resulting number will tell you what percentage rate you must get on your money today to double your money in that many years.

  Example: You loan one thousand dollars to your cousin so he can invest in a wig factory, and you want to charge him sufficient interest that

What to Do with Too Much Money: Start by making that big triangular shape, then fold it into a box. Then put wings on it. The rest even Warren Buffet could figure out.

your investment will double in five years. The interest rate you'll have to charge is 14.4 percent.

The depressing part: Most credit card companies charge more interest than that. (GFa)

• *You can fold it up* so it makes a little swan.

• *You can make it grow* slowly but steadily: Municipal bonds, some mutual funds, and some blue chip stocks offer safe and productive investment potential, provided you have lots of time, lots of patience, and a visceral dislike of even moderate risk. (KHG)

If you want a little more excitement than that, you're looking for a different game.

How to Invest Your Money in a Treacherous World

The following guidelines used to be called "investment strategies." Now they're called "survival tips," since strategy implies you actually have a chance of winning.

• *Buy low and sell high.* Sure, but these days, you have to be willing to spend time in a federal pen for insider trading to make any use of this well-worn insight. If the newspaper is full of stories about people buying gold or Netscape stock and getting rich, you have already missed the boat on that investment. (TSh)

• *Don't buy anything you don't understand.* That means avoid complicated investment schemes that boggle your mind even though they seem to make perfect sense to your uncle or neighbor or the broker who is telling you about them. It also means you should avoid buying real estate in areas unknown to you. It also means avoid buying stock in companies that do things that are beyond your comprehension: You can't safely invest in particle accelerator manufacturers. (BV)

- *Keep your eye on the long term,* and base investment decisions on logic instead of emotion. People who lost lots of money after the stock market crash of 1987 only lost money because they panicked and sold right away. Had they waited, their investments would have enjoyed the benefit of a now-booming stock market.

- *Have a strategy* before you buy. No matter how good a stock is, for instance, it may not be good for you. If you want to make a big return quick, you don't want a stock that will appreciate slowly and solidly over time.

- *Diversify* your mix of investments for safety. A good rule of thumb is to put one-third of your investment money into stocks, one-third into income-producing real estate, and one-third into other things like a money market fund, an annuity, or precious metals.

- *If you are conservative,* invest about 30 percent of your portfolio into domestic growth funds, 10 percent into international growth funds, and 60 percent into safe, fixed-rate investments.

- *If you are a maverick,* invest 45 percent into domestic growth funds, 15 percent into international growth funds, 5 percent into international bond funds, and 35 percent into safe, fixed-rate investments.

- *Your age should be a major factor* in how you invest. First of all, if you are seventy-five, you don't want to invest in something that pays off over thirty years. Second, at seventy-five you probably can't afford to lose what you've got, so you're smart to invest conservatively. On the other hand, if you are thirty, you can afford to take greater risks in the hope of getting a greater return because even if you blow every cent you've got, you've still got plenty of time to make more.

- *Watch the clock.* Some investments, like real estate and the stock market, can be extremely time-consuming. Real estate needs to be managed—or else you have to pay someone to do it for you, which eats into the profits. To play the stock market well, you have to read voluminous amounts of newspapers, magazines, and newsletters. On the other hand, if you want to be a silent partner in your investment portfolio, annuities and mutual funds are the way to go. Once you do your initial research and decide where you will put your money, in most cases you can walk away and let it grow on its own. (GRE, TSh)

See below for mutual funds, stocks and bonds, and real estate.

How to Bet on a Sure Thing

The 9 percent rule: Everyone always wants to make a lot of money fast and easy. However, when potential returns are high—say in the 20 percent-plus range—so are the risks, no matter what anyone tells you to the contrary. Therefore, consider this: Any time you have the opportunity to earn a fixed 9 percent on a relatively safe investment, you should take it. Sure, it sounds unglamorous and it's no fun to chart on a day-to-day basis—and even less fun to brag about at parties—but the truth is, 9 percent is about what most common-stock investors make when they average out their winnings and losses over time. Yet they have to put a lot of time and effort into their portfolio and run the risk of making a lot less. But with a little homework, you can write one check and be reasonably assured of your 9 percent return for the life of the investment. (TSh)

How to Get Rich Quick

Broke, need money fast, but just too busy watching TV to actually go out and find work? Try this: Glue small, unmarked bills to your pillow. Then put the pillow inside a conventional pillowcase. Next, put the pillow and case on your bed, near the headboard. Lie down on the bed and gently place your head on the pillow. Turn off the lights. Dream. (KGK)

Retirement Accounts

HOW TO CALCULATE YOUR IRA

How much of your IRA contribution will be tax deductible depends on your adjusted gross income. For example, at press time:

    If you're single:
- *With adjusted gross income under $25,000,* your IRA contribution is fully deductible.
- *With adjusted gross income of $25,000–35,000,* your IRA contribution will be partially deductible; see an accountant, banker, or broker for more information.
- *With adjusted gross income over $35,000,* your IRA contribution will not be deductible.

If you're married:

- *With adjusted gross joint income under $40,000,* your IRA contribution is fully deductible.
- *With adjusted gross joint income of $40,000–$50,000,* your IRA contribution will be partially deductible; see an accountant, banker, or broker for more information.
- *With adjusted gross joint income over $50,000,* your IRA contribution will not be deductible. (GS)

HOW TO KEEP AN EMPLOYEE PENSION PLAN SIMPLE

Check a SEP: SEP stands for simplified employee pension. It lets an employer make contributions toward his own and his employees' (if he has any) retirement plans, without getting embroiled in something as complicated as a Keogh. Here's how it works:

- *Go to the bank or to a broker* and ask to open a SEP-IRA. You can invest the money in stocks or mutual funds or money market funds or even just a savings-account type of account. So far, it's an IRA. But here's the corner: With a regular IRA, you can only contribute $2,000 per year, which is the same as saying you can only reduce your taxable gross by $2,000 per year. But with a SEP-IRA, you can contribute as much as *15 percent of your gross* or $30,000, whichever is less. This also means you can reduce your gross income by as much as 15 percent or $30,000 before calculating your taxes. The limits are slightly lower for self-employed people.
- *If you are an employer,* you open the SEP-IRA and your employees choose whether they want to contribute to it from their own paychecks.

Just like an IRA, though, you have to pay the taxes when you withdraw the money, and most of the other rules and limitations of a regular IRA also apply. (GS, NMN)

HOW TO SET UP A 401(K) ACCOUNT

A 401(k) is a employee-funded retirement savings plan. The name refers to the section of the IRS code where it can be found.

- *How it works:* The IRS says that with a 401(k), an employee can contribute up to a certain amount of his salary to a retirement account, and that the employer can match it with a certain percentage of that contribution, up to a maximum amount.

An example: An employee contributes up to 7 percent of his annual gross salary to the plan. The company, meanwhile, matches half that contribution. Between the employee and the employer, the total contribution to the plan is 10.5 percent of the employee's salary.

- *Impact on taxes:* You can make all or part of your contribution to the plan from pretax (gross) income. The benefit here is that it reduces the amount of tax you pay from your paychecks because your tax is now calculated based on the reduced gross figure. However, you are only deferring the tax: You do have to pay it when you finally withdraw funds from the plan. In most cases, you can start withdrawing from a 401(k) plan at age fifty-nine and a half.
- *Limits to contributions:* Currently, up to 15 percent of your paycheck can be withheld for contribution to a 401(k), which also means that you can defer up to 15 percent of your taxes as well. The IRS also limits the total amount that one can contribute to a 401(k), but that's an ever-changing number, so it's best to check with the IRS or the personnel department of your company for details.

Advantages
- *Your contributions are being matched* so you immediately have more in your retirement account than you yourself contributed.
- *Contributing to the plan decreases* the amount of tax you pay now.
- *Over twenty or thirty years,* the combined contributions from you and your employer to the account will grow dramatically.

Disadvantages
- *You're tying up as much of 15 percent of your income* automatically.
- *If you ever need that money, you're going to pay stiff penalties* to the IRS for using it before you reach fifty-nine and a half. The IRS will allow you to borrow from it for certain hardship reasons, for buying a home, or for paying education costs. Ironically, if you borrow money from your 401(k), the IRS requires that you pay yourself back—with interest—on a regular payment schedule. You can also withdraw from your 401(k), but you have to then pay all the taxes on the money you withdraw as well as a 10 percent penalty.

What Happens If You Leave the Job
A 401(k) plan is a company-administered plan. If you change jobs (or lose your job), your savings may be affected. Because every company deals with this differently, you should check with your employee benefits department.

Here are a few ways a company might handle the contributions of a former employee:

- *Some companies will allow you to leave your savings* in the plan until you reach the age at which you are eligible to begin withdrawals.
- *Other companies will require you to take your contributions* when you leave. However, it is not necessarily true that your new company will let you "roll over" the money from your old plan into their plan. In this case, you might have to take the contributions from the old plan and put them into some kind of IRA. (GS, DF)

How to Figure Out How to Achieve Financial Independence

Financial independence is life in a hammock—a sweet, blissful state of near-Nirvana, in which you have enough assets to support a reasonable standard of living, whether or not you actually have a job.

The rule of thumb for a forty-year-old guy who has no pension plan, no investment portfolio, and no long-term assets: If he wants to retire in twenty-five years on 75 percent of his current income, he needs to save approximately 25 percent of his income from now until age sixty-five. (DKA)

How to Pick a Mutual Fund

A mutual fund is a one-stop shopping approach to creating a diverse investment portfolio. Mutual funds are professionally managed, and the investments—stocks, bonds, certificates, whatever—are owned by many different people.

FIRST, GET TO KNOW THEM

- *Investment strategy:* Every fund has an investment objective and investment plan that govern which stocks or bonds are considered appropriate for the fund. For instance, a fund may only buy communications stocks, or investments from Third World nations, or only stocks that have a long history of paying dividends. In 1993, there were about four thousand mutual funds on the market, making about $1.6 trillion in investments, and each one followed a different investment strategy.

- *What you get:* When you buy into a mutual fund, here's what you are really buying:
  1. *Professional skill.* The talents of a particular group of investment professionals are key to the success of the fund. Ultimately, what separates one mutual fund from all the others on the market are the people who are making the decisions about what to buy and sell.
  2. *Tactical power.* Unless you are a big-time player, you can't afford to spend the money to research hundreds of companies before you buy. A good mutual fund can, and does. Meanwhile, once it is ready to buy, it buys in such volume that the cost of buying is much less than it would be for you.
  3. *Diversification.* A good mutual fund may own holdings in hundreds of different companies, so if one goes belly up it doesn't break you. Meanwhile, a good mutual fund has the manpower to continue monitoring all those different companies so as to know when to sell or when to buy more.
- *Types of funds:* There are two types of funds:
  1. *Open-end funds.* Most funds fall into this category. For a fund to be open-ended, it must sell as many shares as there are buyers to take them. The size of the fund at any given moment is determined by whether there are more people buying or selling shares at that time. But note that managers of a fund can decide to close a fund if interest swells and the fund grows too large to manage. When a fund closes in this way, new shareholders are not allowed to buy in, although current shareholders can continue to invest.
  2. *Closed-end fund.* This type of fund resembles a stock. There are a set number of shares that can be issued and sold and resold on the market, and the issuers only raise money with the initial offering. While the value of an open-end fund is generally dependent on the value of a fund's holdings alone, the value of a closed-end fund generally depends on both the fund's holdings and investor demand for the fund's shares. (DF, MN, LO)

THE MOVING PARTS

- *Sources of money:* There are three ways to make money from mutual funds:
  1. **Profit.** The market value of your shares increases and you sell.
  2. **Dividends.** The holdings of your mutual fund pay dividends or interest, and your mutual fund distributes these income distributions according

to a predetermined schedule. Many funds allow you the option of reinvesting your income distributions back into the fund.

3. **Capital gains.** These are distributed according to a predetermined schedule. Many funds allow you the option of reinvesting capital gains distributions back into the fund.

- *Commissions and fees:* Three sisters—two ugly, one beautiful: "load," "no-load," and "back-end load" fees.

  1. **A load** is a commission you pay up front when you buy a mutual fund. The disadvantage here is that this part of your investment dollar will never earn a return.

  2. **A no-load fund** is one that charges fees, but no commission, ever.

  3. **A back-end load** is a commission you pay when you sell. The disadvantage is that if the value of the fund increases wildly, the buyer ends up paying a much higher commission than he or she would have paid if the commission had been collected on the initial investment.

  Funds charge other fees as well, including an annual management fee for the administration of the fund and a distribution fee that covers things like marketing efforts and employee bonuses.

- *Taxation:* Both income distributions and capital gains distributions are taxable in the year they are distributed, whether the holder takes the distribution in cash or reinvests it. On the other hand, if your fund loses money in a particular year, the loss is offset against future gains and distributions are not taxable until profits exceed the accumulated losses, even while the market value of shares may already reflect increased value.

What It Takes to Make It to the Bigs

NYSE

To qualify to be traded on the New York Stock Exchange, a company must have the following:

- Pretax earnings of at least $2.5 million.
- At least 1.1 million shares of common stock outstanding, with a market value of at least $18 million.

Types of companies found: The biggest and the best-known companies in the United States, like American Express, Federal Express, and Coca-Cola.

Number of stocks listed: 2,089.

AMEX

To qualify to be traded on the American Stock Exchange, a company must have either of the following:

- Pretax earnings of at least $750,000.
- At least 500,000 shares of common stock outstanding, with a market value of at least $3 million.
  Or:
- Pretax earnings of at least $750,000.
- At least 250,000 shares of common stock outstanding, with a market value of at least $2.5 million.

Types of companies found: Midsize or growth-oriented companies, like TWA, Viacom, and Greyhound.

Number of stocks listed: 841.

NASDAQ

To qualify to be traded on NASDAQ, a company must have the following:

- Pretax earnings of $750,000.
- A market value of all shares totaling at least $1 million.
- At least 400 shareholders.
- Net assets of at least $4 million.

Types of companies found: Growth-oriented companies of all sizes, like Gymboree, Starbucks coffee, and technology companies.

Number of stocks listed: 4,700.

OTC

The OTC has no restrictions. There are 28,000 stocks listed on the OTC, most of which are high-risk, low-cost stocks. (GS)

How to Buy Downtown

Your kind of town: When you buy a municipal bond, you're helping to provide the capital needed to keep your town, city, and/or state supplied with new roads, schools, airports, and ballparks. In exchange for providing that capital, the IRS (and usually your state) doesn't make you pay any tax on the interest you earn on your money. It's a pretty good deal for everybody. After all, if you didn't lend the money to your city to build that new sewer system, your state or the feds would have to. Conventional stocks and bonds, by contrast, have a tax liability attached.

Here's the tricky part, though: If you could buy, say, $10,000 worth of bonds for the AAA-rated Widget America for five years at an annual return of 6 percent or buy $10,000 of tax-free munis from your AAA-rated city fathers for the same rate, you'd want to buy the muni bonds, right? After all, you'd not only get the stated 6 percent return on your money, you'd also be saving on the tax that you would be paying on the 6 percent you earned from Widget America. Thus, you'd think the return from the munis would be higher.

Unfortunately, it's never this simple, or everyone would buy munis and no one would buy bonds for private corporations. In reality, there is always a "spread" between the higher rate a corporate bond pays and the lower rate a comparable muni bond pays. Obviously, the smaller the spread between corporate bond and muni, the better deal the munis become.

Better for some: Actually, muni bonds are better deals for some people than others. High-income investors, it turns out, make out better on these than anyone else. Why? Because they pay the highest taxes on each dollar of income they earn, and that is money they are saving with tax-free bonds. In other words, the investor who is in a 30 percent tax bracket earns the stated percent return of the muni bond—*plus* up to 30 percent of that amount in tax not paid, depending on whether or not local taxes also come into play. By comparison, an investor in a 25 percent tax bracket saves only 25 percent above the stated percent return of the muni bond. (GG)

Let's see how it works with real numbers. Let's say you're in a 30 percent tax bracket and your brother is in a 25 percent tax bracket. You both buy the same tax-free muni for $10,000 at 5 percent. At the end of the year, you both have earned $500 in interest. Now, had this been a corporate bond, you would have paid $150 in taxes. Your bro would have paid $125 in taxes. Because you aren't paying *any* tax on your earnings, you have to add these savings into the annual yield to be able to compare the income-earning potential of these bonds with the potential of equivalent corporate bonds.

When you do that, it becomes obvious that the muni bond was a better deal for you than for your brother. His adjusted return for the year was $625, while yours was $650. That's why he doesn't like you. (GS, DWT, GG)

How to Bet on Red or Black

The dumb-luck investment of the end-of-the-millennium is called a "derivative"—technically, a transaction that does not constitute ownership but merely is a promise to convey ownership at some time in the future.

For some institutions, derivatives are life. Banks, for example, deal in promises all the time. They make swaps today with tomorrow's interest rates, next week's currency, or next month's options on futures. The problem is, sometimes when one bank comes around to square up with another bank, it finds that the other bank has literally disappeared.

Now, if the bank that disappeared was a really big bank, with a whole lot of casual derivative transactions outstanding, then a whole lot of other banks run the risk of going under as well. After all, without the funds they are owed from the big bank, they are now unable to meet their own derivative obligations to other banks, and a domino effect is unleashed.

Stock-index options are a more familiar form of derivative. You can simply bet—by buying an index option—whether or not the market will go up or down over the term of the option. It's a fifty-fifty ride. The only advantage these so-called investments have over other high-risk investments, such as commodity deals, is that with a stock-index option, you can never lose more than you invest. With a commodity option for, say, hog bellies, you can lose the whole pig farm, no problem. (GS, RET)

How to Lend Money to Friends

Tired of investing in boring derivatives? Here's a real clever way to develop an ulcer to replace that awkward stock portfolio: Lend money to friends.

For some guys, *the litmus test of friendship* is how quickly you reach for your wallet when a friend hits you up for a loan. If you grab your billfold or checkbook without a second thought, standing before you is a guy you've never had second thoughts about before, even in the deepest recesses of your psychological being, and you probably never will. If the request for a loan causes you to pause for a even moment and ask yourself how to get out of the situation with all your cash in one piece, the friendship itself may need reexamination at some later date. (HES)

Money lending between friends can take many forms, including the "tide-me-over" loan, the "get-me-out-of-trouble" loan, and the "I-need-it-to-start-a-new-business" loan.

THE TIDE-ME-OVER LOAN

is generally casual in nature and small in amount. Unless you seriously question the character of the guy in front of you, a tide-me-over loan should be made without question. In fact, if you're lucky, you have a few good pals with whom you can always be lending to and borrowing from at a moment's notice so no one is ever caught short—which is the same thing that Bank of America, Exxon, and Chrysler do.

THE GET-ME-OUT-OF-TROUBLE LOAN

is a little more serious, both in circumstance and in the sum required. For one thing, the very thing that got your friend into trouble may get him into trouble with you and your money, too. Should you lend money to a friend who has a drug problem, a spending problem, or a mistress problem? Only if you are comfortable with the idea that by doing so you are probably helping to perpetuate these problems and that, eventually, he will end up in trouble with you, too. In other words, you probably won't be helping at all, and you will probably lose both a friend and your money in the process. If a situation like this causes you to pause before reaching for your wallet, trust your instincts and cry poverty—this is one friend who can really benefit from a little white lie and some tough love. On the other hand, if your friend has a sick wife or child and needs cash, how can you say no? In this circumstance, it's best to expect never to see your money again and only make the loan if you accept that as the probable outcome. You can always be pleasantly surprised if repayment comes at some future date. If you can't afford to make the loan, just say so without any hemming and hawing. He's already got enough problems without having the false hope that you'll cough up cash for him when in reality you just didn't have the chops to tell him that you won't or you can't.

THE I-NEED-IT-TO-START-A-NEW-BUSINESS LOAN

is very similar to the I-need-it-for-the-down-payment-on-a-house loan. Don't ever consider one of these to be a loan between friends. This is a business arrangement and should be treated as such. *You should only lend money to a friend under these circumstances if the deal is a good one for you.* After all, if you don't tie up your money here, you can put it to work somewhere else and have it earn interest or income for you. Here's what to look for before lending a friend money for a business or house:

- *How will the loan be secured?* If your friend doesn't have something of value to put up as collateral, think long and hard about making the loan.
- *What are the terms of the loan?* Make sure he understands that if he does not repay you as specified in the written loan document he is signing, you will foreclose on his house or whatever else he has posted as collateral.

- *Is he willing to a pay the going rate in interest?* Again, if you can get 6 percent at the bank and your friend can pay only 3 percent, he's asking you to make a handout, not a loan. (HES)
- *Will you be involved in the business?* A little control is worth a lot. (GS)

  A dissent: Any loan made between friends is the price of the friendship. (JY)

  Another: Sometimes, a friend's offer to participate in a business can be exactly what it ought to be—a friendly gesture. Friends should offer friends good deals. (HES)

How to Start a Small Business

In most cases, success is determined long before the computer is bought, the phones are installed, the letterhead ordered, the lease is signed, or the first sale is rung up.

If you want to start your own business, start by doing some planning:

- *Ponder the concept of supply and demand.* There are two obvious and basic ingredients to every successful business.

  1. A product or service to sell
  2. People who are willing to pay for it

  One without the other does you no good. The first step in any marketing research is to define your product and find out who, if anyone, would want it. And be careful when defining what it is you plan to sell— sometimes it's not what you think it is. For instance, MailBoxesEtc. may have set out to sell postal supplies, but what they ended up selling was convenience. America OnLine may have initially seen itself as a provider of on-line information and entertainment, but for many people, it's simply an e-mail provider—with, of course, a lousy web browser attached.

- *Do the numbers.* Hear about the guy who had a great idea for a product, manufactured several million, sold every one—and then went bankrupt? It's not enough to have a great product or service that people are buying. You've also got to know what to charge for it.

  What is your cost of doing business? What are your manufacturing costs, packaging costs, shipping costs, the cost of sales, the cost of marketing, the cost of printing up those fancy reports you like so well? Factor in every cost imaginable that is associated with your business and then divide by the number or products you expect to sell in the first year. You've got your cost of doing business per unit. Now, how does the wholesale price of the item compare to the cost of manufacturing it? Every industry has a different rule of thumb, but if you aren't selling your product for at least twice what it costs you to make it, you may be in big trouble down the road. (GG, ERD)

- *Make a plan.* The phrase "business plan" scares people because they envision something that only an accountant can understand.

How to Make a Business Plan Less Intimidating

Write yours on a napkin while having lunch at your local greasy spoon. If you do it right and have all the information at hand, it shouldn't take you longer than a burger, fries, and Coke.

- *Here's why you need one:* Without a plan, running your business will be like driving down a dark highway at night with your headlights off: You'll never know where you are or when you're headed off a cliff.

THE PLAN TRUTH

Here's what you need to include in your business plan:

- *Start-up capital.* It takes money to make money. Where is yours going to come from? And how will you use it to get the maximum benefit from it? Make sure you have enough money in the bank to run your business for at least six months with no or minimal sales.
- *Projected monthly expenses,* for a year. Include everything you can think of for the year, and don't forget to pay yourself, either—at least in your projections.
- *Projected monthly income,* for a year. Forget about pie-in-the-sky stuff. How many widgets do you really think you can sell in a year? If you tell a lie here, you're only lying to yourself. Once you come up with a monthly figure with which you're comfortable, break it down into a daily sales figure, then an hourly sales figure. Still look doable?
- *Cash flow chart.* You can be making more sales than you ever dreamed possible and still go out of business if your cash flow is out of whack. Think about it: Unless you have a cash business, you've always got to have extra money lying around with which to pay the bills—until your clients pay you off. If your clients have thirty days to send you a check,

how will you survive in the meantime? And what will you do for money when some of them take sixty days or longer to make good? Success takes more than just healthy sales. It also requires that you have healthy cash flow. (GG, ERD)

- *Profit projection for year one.* Who's better off: The guy who makes a million in sales in the first year and has nothing to show for it because he had a million dollars of expenses, or the guy who had half a million in sales and only $250,000 in expenses? Sales alone don't mean anything. What is important is profit, which can only be determined by comparing your sales with your expenses. (ERD)

LET THE RUBBER MEET THE ROAD

If you're satisfied with your projections, it's time to hit the streets.

- *Location.* If you're in the market for space to open a store or restaurant or shop, remember the first rule of retail. The more people that already frequent and shop in the area, the better chance you have of succeeding. Before you sign a lease, ask the business tenants of the adjacent shops and stores about the neighborhood. Do you get a lot of foot traffic? Auto traffic? Any parking? What kind of people frequent the area? Are they the kind of people who are likely to be interested in what you have to offer? What happened to the previous tenants?

- *Atmosphere.* If you need office space, your needs will be determined by whether you will be meeting with clients or other business associates in your office. If yes, you may need to pay more for some fancy surroundings. If the office is just for you and your employees or partners, forgo the fancy and pay as little rent as possible in the beginning.

- *Infrastructure.* If you need manufacturing space, consider such things as floor load levels, elevator size and weight capacity, zoning laws, as well as access to highways for shipping.

Once you have all these ducks in a row, you're ready for duck soup. (GG, ERD, HTF, GS)

How to Go Broke Feeding the Hungry

People will tell you that opening a restaurant is the riskiest business decision you can make. Actually, restaurants come in a close fourth, right after clothing stores, furniture stores, and camera stores. Nevertheless:

WHY MOST RESTAURANTS FAIL

- *You run out of money* before the public discovers you. You'll need somewhere between $100,000 and $500,000 before you even open the doors.
- *Awful food.* Your chef's résumé tastes better than what he cooks in the kitchen.
- *Your employees steal you blind,* either by pocketing the money or just giving away too much free food and drink, usually to friends or in an attempt to buy a big tip. Happens all the time.
- *Your employees are rude,* and people never come back.
- *The wrong crowd* adopts your restaurant as a hangout. For instance, all the local kids come to your place because you've done such a fine job of decorating it, but they scare off all the people in town who have money. Kids equals zero money. You lose.
- *Ugly.* Your restaurant isn't appealing from outside. It's appalling inside.
- *Location.* See previous section.
- *Bad pricing.* Your prices are not high enough to cover your costs. (MN)

A RESTAURANT IS NOT A STORE

A simple fact, but one eatery-rookies forget.

- *When you own a restaurant,* you're not just selling prepared food. You're also selling what restaurant-weenies call "an experience." For this reason, you attach a lot more importance to the behavior of a waiter than you do the behavior of a clothing salesman. Meanwhile, when you go to a traditional pizza shop, part of what you are looking for is dark wood, a pool table, jukebox, and video games. (MN)
- *Inventory.* A store has a fixed set of inventory. A camera store, for example, buys a certain number of cameras and film and equipment and sells these items; the amount of inventory can always be quantified. Not so with a restaurant. Food and beverages are bought in raw form, in bulk. They are then parceled out in small quantities, and two or more ingredients are often mixed together. For this reason, inventory becomes a bit intangible. It is harder to keep track of inventory, sales, and distribution of raw materials. For instance, one cook may make three-egg omelets, and one may make four-egg omelets unless an official policy is set in advance. Seems insignificant—unless you sell three hundred omelets a day and you have set the price based on the cost of three eggs.
- *Cleanliness.* You can be a lot more tolerant of "odd features" and a lack of cleanliness in a shop than in a restaurant. After all, you won't eat the furniture you buy; you'll only sit on it. If a shop wants to keep its extra

inventory in the bathroom, what do you care? If a restaurant keeps the extra potatoes there, you probably won't go back.

- *Intangibles.* What you buy in a restaurant is almost intangible, while what you buy in a shop may last you a long time. For that reason, consumers have a completely different set of criteria for where they eat than they do for where they shop. This boils down to a lot of intangible things that make one restaurant successful and another a failure, and few of these intangibles have anything to do with the price or taste of the food. They may, however, include the way the waiters treat the customers, the location of the restaurant, the ambiance of the dining room, and public perception of the restaurant. (TWa)

Ultimately, it is this group of intangibles that makes starting and owning a successful restaurant so difficult because intangibles are, well, intangible and the best you can do is hope that your instincts are steering you in the right direction.

In lieu of puzzling over the intangibles, why not devote yourself to working on things that are within your control and understanding.

GUIDELINES FOR SUCCESS

- *Make sure you find a location that is suitable* for the type of restaurant you are opening. For instance, you don't want to open a hamburger stand in an area where you get no foot or auto traffic. On the other hand, you don't want to open a fancy French restaurant in a strip mall. People will drive out of their way for a well-prepared French meal, but most likely a hamburger stand will get most of its business from people who are already in the area. (JER)
- *Take care in preparing your menu.* Start by identifying your potential customer. Then consider the cost and availability of certain ingredients. Finally, create a well-balanced menu that has something for everyone—a little chicken, a little beef, a little vegetarian, a little plain, a little saucy, a little baked, and a little fried.
- *Generate goodwill.* If people come to your restaurant only once, you've got a big problem. Your goal is to make your restaurant a favorite of all who visit. How do you do that? Treat them well from the moment they walk in the door, make them feel comfortable in the environment, serve them food that is well prepared, tasty, and attractively presented, and be prompt and attentive with all service when fulfilling all requests. (TWa)
- *Manage your personnel well.* Treat them with respect, and they will, in turn, treat your customers with respect.

- *Advertise.* Start with a good, easy-to-read sign. Consider advertising in the local daily or weekly newspaper or try including a coupon in a coupon mailer. In smaller communities, billboards and radio can also be effective.

- *Become a public relations pro.* Join the local chamber of commerce and offer to throw a mixer at your restaurant or offer to cater an event. Sponsor a Little League baseball team. Find a niche and fill it; for instance, make your restaurant a center for wine connoisseurs. Invite a local service organization to use your restaurant as its regular meeting place.

- *Create an ironclad inventory system.* When a jewelry store gets a new shipment of diamonds, it has a system for handling them that ensures that none will be lost, stolen, or priced incorrectly. You should be equally diligent about your food and liquor shipments. Not only do you have to worry about theft (particularly of liquor), but you also have to ensure that you will have enough food and staples on hand at all times to prepare all of the items on the menu.

- *Be a good shopper.* Make sure the quality of food you are paying for is truly the quality you are receiving—particularly when buying meats. When you are buying food in bulk, make sure quantities are exact instead of rounded off. Don't ever buy *products.* You will pay for increased refrigeration and decrease the storage space you have for other items. Never discourage salespeople from making sales calls; it's the best way to find out if you are overpaying for some or all of your food items.

- *Manage your money.* One great appeal to owning a restaurant is that it is a cash business. Great for some, the beginning of the end for others. Create a system for dealing with cash, checks, and credit card vouchers, and stick with it. Make sure it is a system that keeps you and your money protected, but also protects innocent employees from the risk of being accused of wrongdoing. For instance, if you have the head waiter toss the night's receipts into a bag of potatoes every night before locking up, you are putting him in a dangerous position: Not only are you putting him in a tempting spot, you're making it easy for someone else to steal the money (in one fell swoop or a little bit at a time) while making it look as if the head waiter did it.

- *Maintain the plant.* No one likes to eat in a restaurant that looks run-down. In fact, no one likes to even stop at a restaurant that looks run-down. Keep the outside and inside of your restaurant looking new and clean to keep your clients coming back year after year. (MN, TWa)

How to Know When to Hold and When to Fold

Here's how to know when to give up the entrepreneurial ghost:

- *Wait* until you've been in business one full year (TSB) . . . or five years (JG). This seems like a critical distinction, no? The variation can be explained, though: Some businesses do require more time to fail or succeed than others. If you open a pop stand and nobody shows up during the first year, they won't show up during the second or third years, either. But if you're manufacturing widgets, it may take a couple of years just to get your product in the marketplace. Figure it out.
- *Calculate* the value of all receivables, add the value of *10 percent* of all reasonable prospective sales for the next ninety days. Mark that figure "Sum A." Add the total of all payables, plus the total of all overhead costs extrapolated forward ninety days. Don't forget your own salary. That's "Sum B." Subtract B from A.
- *If the result is a wash or worse, fold.*

Another measure: You're bored with the whole thing and don't care whether you make it or not.

Think of every new business you start as if it were a hand of poker. The earlier you fold because you realize the odds don't favor your success, the better off you'll be for the next deal. Eventually, fate will deal you a boat. (TSB, MN)

How to RSVP the IRS

Good form: In a small village somewhere dwells a man and his wife whose lives are pleasant but unremarkable in every respect save one: Alone among all working Americans, they file their taxes on time. For everybody else, it's a mad race to the post office by midnight, April 15. If you have only one form to file, and it's not a 1040, make it this one: Form 4868. It's used to apply for an extension of the filing deadline. You still have to pony up your estimated tax, and you have to file the 4868 by April 15, but you get another ninety days to do the paperwork. (DBa)

How to Get Out of Town

HOW TO IDENTIFY A COUNTRY HOME

There are **two basic types** of country homes:

1. *Cabin on a creek:* One is a cabin or bungalow or some other cute little contrivance situated on a handful of acres and surrounded by other pretty country houses, a trickle of water, and some trees. This is country living at its most restful, where there is no smelly agricultural work, and where most of your neighbors are either city immigrants, too, or old-time residents who are making a killing off newcomers and tourists by selling them quilts and honey. While this may represent country living to some, most objective observers would claim this is suburban living, except the front yards are real big.

2. *Agri-hut:* The other kind of country place is a farm. *Farms mean work.* Most of the people who move to the country on purpose are, at the most, part-time farmers. In fact, most people who have *always* lived in the country are part-time farmers, since to make a living at farming today is very difficult. Successful farms—as opposed to small, family farms—are little different from other large-scale industrial operations. There are ways to specialize and chance making a living, but many of these specialties are so time-consuming as to make living in the country no pleasure, business-wise or otherwise. The last turkey farm in the Baltimore-Washington area closed after the holiday season of 1990. It had been in the same family for two or three centuries, but the family got tired of the never-ending work and worry. One of the brothers commented that the only thing more stupid than a turkey was someone who raised turkeys. (PJN)

Somebody Else's Pigs

People have tried everything from worms to chinchillas, and many of them have ended up with nothing. One successful method is to raise something for one of the large food conglomerates. On the Delmarva Peninsula, for example, a family can earn a good income raising chickens for a company like Perdue. Some agri-corps are out building huge sheds for those people who just need to have a thousand or so hogs hanging out on the other side of the driveway. But you quickly find that selling chickens to Perdue makes you little more than a chicken-sitter, buying everything from the supplier and selling the grown chickens back. You have to be there all the time, but you do have a lot of your own time while you're there.

Remember, this is only an example: Before you invest in a hog farm, for instance, it would be wise to visit one, and to take several deep breaths while you are there. (EWi, FAC)

HOW TO FIND THE RIGHT PAGE ON THE MAP

This is a big planet, and, believe it or not, more than 95 percent of it is rural. If you wake up one morning and say to yourself, "Think I'll move to the country," start by asking yourself *which* country, and narrow it down from there.

Go to What You Know

Watch the movie in your mind: Lots of people have a fairly cinematic version of what life in the country should look like. To some, it's a purple sagebrush kind of thing, with earth-tone highlights. To others, it's a log house in a backwoods, down-East boondock. But if you've never even been to say, New Mexico or to Maine, don't pack up your kids, your VCR, and your Burpee catalog and try to make a new life for yourself in a strange corner of the world. It's more likely that your idea of moving to the country involves moving to the country near the city in which you now live. Don't hurry; plot your move with military precision.

Boonie Companions

Everyone can recall friends of their parents who moved somewhere that was hard to reach and only semicivilized. When you were a kid, going to these exotic, agrarian places was an all-day adventure on narrow roads and rusty bridges. Now that little cottage overlooking the river is five minutes off an interstate, twenty minutes from the city, and worth a half million, easy. Well, you have to think like those people did thirty years ago—and not like your parents who *didn't* move because they didn't want to commute, or because they didn't want to take you away from the neighborhood school, or because they liked living in the city just fine, thanks.

How to Get Started

You can, of course, start by saying, "I want to live within X hours of Y metro area," but remember, you cannot draw a circle on the map with a radius of one hundred miles and make that your target area. Two hours on an eight-lane expressway could leave you a half hour into the ocean, while two hours on a two-lane blacktop might put you in an expensive suburb. So merely specifying a time boundary may not work well. (PL)

- *Start with a little common sense:* Choose a direction, any direction. Let's say you live in Tri-Metro. And let's say that to the north and the south is more urban sprawl, but to the west are mountains and to the east is the sea. If we assume that you hate the ocean, your decision is easy: It's mountains for you. (PJN)

Which Old House?

- *Are you an old-house buff?* The chances of finding an eighteenth-century house are growing less each year. There are still a few left, although the areas where they can be found at an affordable price are hard to find. Too often the only ones left seem to be near the most important crossroads in the town and right across the street from a gas station. Sometimes, it seems the federal government routes interstates across the front yards of the nation's most beautiful farm homes.
- *Would you be willing to settle* for a mid-nineteenth-century farmhouse instead? These old brick or wood-frame structures are generally a good bit more comfortable than the ancient houses. They're also a great deal easier to find, and you don't feel you are destroying a part of our American heritage when you knock down a wall or put a skylight in the kitchen.
- *What kinds of repair and maintenance work* are you willing or able to do around the house? Self-reliance is one of the central virtues in traditional American rural culture. If it is not a virtue for you, you will do well to address this issue before you buy the stone house that needs the north wall rebuilt. (SS, EWi)

You Must Remember This and This and This

Nothing flies from memory faster than the details of a house, especially if it's one you find attractive. While you're being mesmerized by the arboreal setting of the quaint old dairy shed, your common sense is taking a nap, and details about the most important structure on a farm—the farmhouse—become mere annoyances. Make yourself a checklist, one easy enough to complete even in a semihypnotic state, which will provide you with some eye-opening information once you get on the on-ramp to the real world. Be sure to include your comments on the following items:

- *The structural integrity of the house and any outbuildings.*
- *The electrical supply.*
- *The plumbing.*
- *The kitchen.*

- *The basement.*
- *The heating plant.*
- *The condition of the insulation.*
- *The flooring.*
- *The windows and doors.*
- *The all-important roof.*
- *The fireplace and flues.*
- *The walls and ceilings.*
- *The toxic potential.* Get *everything* tested—radon, lead, cooties in the well—*everything* before you close the deal. And make the owners put it in writing that they've not buried toxic junk on the premises. And, finally,
- *The neighbors.*

Take note of these things and you can safely skip the rest of the stuff. (CAC)

9. Work

Lucky women. They are what they are. But men? We're nothing more than what we do.

How to Find a Job

The best way to meet really charming and beautiful women is to get married. Ten minutes after your wedding ceremony, all the women you sought during your miserable bachelor sex-drought will be at your feet.

Same thing with jobs. When you don't need them, they're a dime a dozen. The best advice? Ease the pressure by turning up the income. Take a job, *any job.* Take a job at a beach resort as a lifeguard. Take a job as a car salesman. Take a job doing something you know is going nowhere. Wait until you get two or three checks under your belt. Then pursue your job search in a pleasant and leisurely fashion. Bosses are like women—often, bosses are women—and if they think you're desperate, the kind of man nobody wants, they're not going to want you either.

Four more ways to a regular payday:

1. *Don't whine.* Tell anybody who asks that you *like* the job you have. Even if the guy who asks is the personnel director at Acme Incorporated, and even if the job you have is busing tables at IHOP. But, of course, you can add that you'd obviously like to be doing something more interesting.

2. *Don't shortchange yourself.* Trading time and effort for money is as basic a barter as any man makes, and if you're going to be successful in any kind of horse trade, you have to know what your horse is worth. If you can't be realistic about your marketable skills, ask a friend to help you set a fair price.

3. *See the moves.* If you have to choose between a good job in an industry in which you have no interest, and a lousy job in an industry you find fascinating, take the lousy job. In other words, when you look around for a job, deal with the industry as a whole. You may have to take a job in the mail room, but if you're smart and good and work hard, it's not the job you'll have in five, seven, ten years. You have to see the whole road. If you don't know where you're going, you'll never get anyplace. (GF)

4. *Hide your ambivalence.* Every job has a downside, but no job has a downside as big as the downside to having no job at all. Opportunity is sometimes a moving target; don't hesitate to take your best shot. (SI)

HOW TO DECIDE ON A JOB

Of all the questions asked by suffering correspondents looking for cheap advice about jobs, the question "What should I do next?" is asked more often than any other one.

Well, here's the answer no job-searching man wants, but at least it's the truth: *It doesn't matter.*

A personal observation—and a big **Main Thing:** *Any time you have to make a decision, remember that any decision is better than none. Here's how I came by this cheap insight: I was riding with my grandfather, Claude Boyles, in his huge, old Chrysler just outside nowhere, Kansas, when a jackrabbit jumped out in the middle of the road. "Now, watch," he said. The car kept a constant speed. The rabbit feinted left, feinted right, then left again, then right, then, at the last minute, just as the car was right on top of him, left again, and right under the tires, flat. I was upset. Claude Boyles said, "The problem was he couldn't make up his mind. It wouldn't have mattered either way."*

A good lesson; animals have died for less. The problem with not making a decision is that if you don't, events—those big Chryslers on the thoroughfare of woe—will make the decision for you. People spend years responding to crises and reacting to events, and feel miserable because they have no control over their lives. Can't decide between Acme and Consolidated or between the army and college? No problem. Flip a coin: Heads, you join the army. Tails, you go back to college. It really doesn't matter, because everything else will work itself out. The only thing that matters is that you choose.

HOW TO SPOT A JOB TO AVOID

Here's another **Main Thing:** *Never take a managerial job in a family business if you aren't a member of the family.* You'll be cheated and mistreated, pushed from one side of the family to the other, and you'll never be loved. Instead, you'll be fired. (KM)

HOW TO TALK ABOUT WORK

The most important conversations about work are the ones you have with the chap driving the personnel desk. That first interview is the make-or-break chat, the one that says, "You're hired!"—unless you say otherwise. According to the president of a Dallas recruitment firm, here are the three deadliest mistakes an interviewee makes:

1. *Not listening.* Don't jump into the interviewer's question. Let him ask the question, make the comment, declare the obvious without help from you. The interviewer doesn't care what your agenda is. He wants to know that you understand *his.*

2. *Holding back.* Show a little interest when the interviewer tells you about

the nuances of Eastern European tractor production. One tip: Lean forward when you speak to create a sense of involvement and interest.

3. *Rambling.* Answer only the questions asked of you, not the ancillary question you wish you'd been asked. Remember, it's not you running the show. If the interviewer wants to dog the pace, slow up and shut up. (CGG)

How to Spot an Office Politician

Talk about your Halloween horror: Look in the next cubicle. That smilin' Jack with the curious collection of sharp knives is every working man's nightmare: the back-stabber.

Guys who smile at your face while they wait for you to turn your back are not just jerks. They're passive-aggressive jerks. Here are the signs of the basic model double-dealer:

- *Plays dumb to hide resentment.*
- *Weasels out of promises.*
- *Agrees with you* when you're face-to-face, but disses you to your boss or coworkers.
- *Keeps a low profile* while a tough project is under way, then emerges at the end to share the credit.

The solution? If the guy's your subordinate, face him down. If he's a coworker, cover your butt. If he's your boss, quit. (SWe)

How to Hook Up with a Mentor

When it comes to sailing the crazy sea of careers, mentors hold the wheel. Everybody needs one. So go out and get one. Then pay attention, because the next mentor may be you.

- *Browsing for a mentor isn't easy.* There are a million would-be mentors out there, guys with 800 numbers and camps in the woods where you can be mentored inside out. By and large, most mentors are modest men. They don't offer a course in miracles or a better way to love the inner you.
- *Mentors also aren't always your father.* Fathers are the working models we use to determine how we're doing as a man, how well we're measuring up to the big job. After all, fathers, either by their accomplish-

ments or by their lack thereof, show us what we need to do to meet a wide range of responsibilities and thereby acquire manly virtues. But the ability of any given dad to mentor is dependent entirely on the subject at hand. Sometimes, in fact, you want to be able to count on your father to duck out of the loop and hook you up with a good mentor when circumstance calls for it. Smart pops know that mentors are often given a more utilitarian role: They don't have enforcement powers of the papa police, and they don't have to worry about paying the bills for your misspent youth. They are instead expected to combine a relatively small sphere of practical advice within a useful moral framework.

For instance, the first mentor—named, conveniently, Mentor—was the aged, trusted adviser with whom Odysseus left his son, Telemachus, when he went off to fight the Trojan War. He made that decision not based on Mentor's baby-sitting abilities. Instead, Odysseus figured Mentor would be able to give Telemachus enough useful information—both applied and theoretical—that, given the example of manly virtues he had set for his son, he could reasonably expect the boy to someday meet or exceed his own expectations for himself. Odysseus knew that a mentor can help you succeed in life sufficiently that you can eventually meet your old man on somewhat equal terms.

Mentors have several well-defined characteristics:

- *They have "mentor" written in large letters across their foreheads.* You'll recognize your mentor because not only will he walk your walk, he'll talk your talk. In fact, he'll speak your language, metaphorically, better than you do. He'll articulate your concerns and ideas much more clearly and perceptively than you can and at a much higher level. He'll assume your values are much the same as his, and he'll be quite right.
- *They are often a professional pal.* When you sign up your mentor, you gain an intellectual friend. If your mentor is engaged in something other than your own occupation, you'll get plenty of philosophical underpinning and a pretty decent moral spine. But none of that will protect you when your boss looks for somebody to lay off. However, if your mentor is one of the guys in the office, you'll have the added advantage of making yourself a protégé. When you become a protégé, you get the lease on the catbird seat. When you become your mentor's protégé, your power is his power, your success is his success. You wear the same armor he wears, you wield the same weapons. If you goof up, not only will he cover for you, he'll deep-six anybody who threatens you, since he knows that your invin-

cibility is the measure of his own corporate *cojones*. There is a downside, of course: Protégés are protégés because their mentors believe that by making them protégés, they will increase their own stock. If making you a protégé becomes less than cost-efficient, you're outta there pronto. It's all business, after all. Mentors unrelated to your profession operate at a slightly more altruistic level.

- *Mentors have great eyesight.* They see through the shuck and jive of a cluttered, confused life—yours, mine—to what is really important for our happiness. Consequently, mentors—even the ones you find on the job— are often not vocational counselors. If all you want to do is feed your blind ambitions, you don't need a mentor. After all, if you want to get ahead in most corporate climes, all you have to do is find the butt one rung up the ladder from where you're standing and give it a big, wet smooch. A good mentor, however, will help you acquire sufficient probity to understand that there is a profound distinction between sincere gestures of affection and kissing ass. Plus, as every brownnoser eventually discovers, nothing's worse than kissing the boss's ass and having it kiss you back.

- *It's an appointed position.* You can't nominate yourself as a mentor. It's like joining the Elks: Somebody else has to put you up. You can, however, make yourself available to be some guy's mentor by hooking up with organizations that link *potential* mentors with *potential* mentees. Unwanted mentors, by the way, are called "pests." It's a thin line.

- *Mentors can decline the job.* Just as you can't jump out of life's thick scrub, grab a truant by the collar, and tell him you're his mentor, a chap looking for a mentor also can't automatically assume that the mentor he has chosen is willing to take on the job. It's a pretty thankless task, after all, and awfully time-consuming to nudge, cajole, and prod a recalcitrant, knuckleheaded, lazy, occasionally self-destructive no-goodnik like me along a career path that also happens to be the moral high road.

- *Mentors have gravitas.* There is no English translation for this word. Yiddish speakers come close with *mensch,* however. *Gravitas* encompasses the complete ensemble of qualities essential to those who would successfully give advice to those who need it. *Gravitas* is what Colin Powell will wear everywhere he goes until the day he reveals himself to be a politician, at which time his own cloak of *gravitas* will be magically transformed into a polyblend leisure suit, something in a nice pastel. Lots of guys wear a fake-*gravitas,* as if it were fake fur. On television, you can imitate a guy with *gravitas* by having swell hair and a sincere visage. Tom

Brokaw and Peter Jennings are the examples that probably come to mind. But people know *gravitas* when they see it. It's like art that way.

- *Mentors are not banks.* Unlike your old man, mentors should not be seen as financial resources. It's very unwise of a mentee—especially a protégé mentee—to hit up his mentor for lunch money, since it gives the mentor a fully warranted opportunity to turn from mentoring to lecturing, or worse. Once, when I was in college, I put the touch on my mentor. He lent me five bucks and then he didn't talk to me for a year.

- *Mentors know their limits.* Ever notice the way fathers—like politicians, car salesmen, and some magazine writers—just go on and on, well past the point at which their point has been made? Ever notice how that can irritate and annoy? Another way in which mentors differ from fathers is that mentors know when to stop. They know precisely when to bring the curtain down. They know exactly when that magic moment of glad welcome has expired. Ever notice how they sense, intuitively, when to stop moving their mouths and making those noises? A good mentor always knows when you want them to *please* shut up. Did you ever notice that? Did you?

How to Buy and Sell Anything

In these disputatious, fractious, ill-spirited times, we know there are a million ways of dividing the planet in two. There's the North-South thing, just for starters. There are haves and have-nots, men and women, owners and players, First World and Third World. Finally, you've got what we can call the OPEC duality: buyers and sellers. And that's where life on earth gets tricky—and expensive. We're buyers some of the time. We're sellers some of the time. And a man needs to be mindful which is which.

Virtually every meeting between a buyer and a seller leaves behind a residue of resentment. Who knows why. It's not that sellers are carnivores in a world of vegan buyers, or that those with money have bludgeoned those with goods. The real problem is that very few people know how to sell anything, and too many people are ready to buy anything. That's why unscrupulous sellers are called "sharks," and why nitwit buyers are called "fish." Which brings us to this useful aphorism:

The angling angle: Everything a good salesman needs to know he can learn by figuring out how to catch a fish. (NS)

THE PARTS OF A SALE

When salesmen go to sales school, they learn that every sale has just four ingredients:

1. *Discovery.* When you listen to what the customer wants.
2. *Presentation.* When you offer to supply what the guy says he needs.
3. *Close.* When you shake on it.
4. *Follow-through.* When you call the next week to see how everything's going.

When we want to sell something, most of us have almost no interest in the discovery and follow-through parts, because we know what we want to sell, and we don't particularly care how it works out later. But we go crazy on the presentation and the close. Watch some chap in full courtship mode. He meets a woman, says hello, but can barely bring himself to listen to her name before he starts playing the endless tape of his life. The presentation part of his sale goes on forever. He's thinking that if he can just pitch the product the right way, the closer will take care of itself. Follow-through? Yeah. Sure. He'll call in the morning. Most of us sell cars, houses, garage junk all the same way.

EARS ARE A SALESMAN'S BEST TOOL

Ever notice how some guys can sell anything? We like to think that guys who can sell anything do their work by talking fast and slick. But that's not how it works at all. **Guys who are great salesmen use their ears, not their jaws,** because they know that of all four parts of a sale, it's the listening part that counts most. A good salesman listens to as much as the seller wants to tell him. For example, let's say you're the manager of your local hardware emporium and some suburban gentleman walks in looking for a snowblower. If you're any good, you'll spend the first few minutes listening, maybe asking a few questions: Gas or electric? Hilly lot or level? Macadam driveway or gravel? Because you know if you sell the guy the new General Dynamics Desert Storm snowblower, when what he really needs is the McDonnell Douglas turbo-charged Sno-Sluice Deluxe, you'll have made an enemy. Buyers want guidance and help, not shortcuts.

Besides, *there are added benefits to listening.* Two to be exact: *First, it makes the buyer want you to succeed* in selling him, since you seem to be on the same side, and everybody loves a good listener. *Second, it makes the buyer do the heavy-lifting part of the sale.* Get the buyer to talk to you long enough, and he'll tell you what he needs, why he needs it, and how much. You, the salesman, just have to sit back and write up the order. (A *side tip:* To get a compulsive talker to clam up, start talking about yourself. Works every time, usually within three minutes.) (DB)

HOW TO BE A BUYER

There are no schools for buyers as there are for sellers. But if there were, they'd teach the same routine, starting with the importance of listening. If you listen to the salesman, you'll better understand what he's selling and why, and you can make a better deal. Some principles:

- *Find out what's in it for him.* The more the salesman needs the sale, the more likely he'll give you a better price. When you go into a car dealership, you'll know you're in the right place when you see the sales chart showing your salesman is only one sale away from beating out all the other salesmen. The lesson? Go on the last day of the selling period—and that usually means the last day of the month. (SF)

- *Be ready to walk.* If the salesman has really listened to you talk about what you want, why you want it, and how you plan to use it, he knows whether or not he's got a sale. It's what happens next that counts. Some salesmen won't try to sell you something you've already said you don't need. But most will. The chance that you'll leave angry is one many salesmen are willing to take. After all, once you're out the door, what difference does it make? Car dealerships, especially, often see a sale in terms of conflict rather than cooperation. Look for a salesman who's willing to work with you, instead of against you; he's the kind of guy who sees his customers as long-term investments, rather than short-term pony-shots. (BB)

- *Listen to yourself.* If you expect the salesman to listen to you, you ought to expect the same from yourself. If what you hear is a slight murmur of ambivalence, duck out of the deal until you've had time to think it over. By the way, if a salesman tries to tell you the deal is now-or-never, it's always never. Always.

- *Make the salesman talk.* Just as the salesman gains an edge by listening, the buyer can gain an edge by refusing to talk. Zen-inspired salesmen call this the "Trick of Silence," in which you don't volunteer information, you don't explain conflicting data, you just follow the sort of admonition once given by the smartest man in the world, the late rare-book expert George Leinwall, to a rookie bibliophile attending his first book auction: "Keep your hands in your pockets and your mouth shut."

Now, that doesn't mean you lie, exactly. It just means that you make the seller come to you.

You say, "How much?"

The salesman says, "Twelve-fifty."

And you say nothing. Eventually, the salesman will either say, "Twelve," or say, "So long."

The Trick of Silence works because, just as nature abhors a vacuum, so do natural-born talkers feel compelled to fill any silence. The result is that you get to listen to a lot more than the salesman really intended to tell you. Another example: You say, "How's that car running?" The salesman says, "Fine." You say nothing. Eventually he'll say, "There was a minor accident, but don't you worry. We've repaired the crack in the frame." Keep not talking and eventually you'll learn about the bubble in the tires, the rust on the muffler, and the stains on the backseat. Then, price is up to you. (JH)

- **Don't buy the salesman.** Most people instinctively like a good listener. Good salesmen are very good listeners. If a salesman does listen, it's only for purposes of obtaining information. It doesn't mean he likes you. (SF)

  This is also how men find themselves in alliances with women who are often much smarter than they are. Remember our small scenario, in which some guy is letting the hot air out of the gaseous epic of his life while the woman he's with waits patiently, occasionally counting ceiling tiles? Do you know which party is doing the selling in that situation? The one talking? Or the one listening?

How to Get a Career Back on Track

- **You're worth exactly what you say you're worth.** Don't allow yourself to be treated with disrespect or rudeness. Don't get angry, get blunt: Often a career gets sidetracked because your superiors think you're too wishy-washy to command respect. So command it by demanding it. (TR)
- **Corollary: Get ahead by confronting your enemies.** Everybody hates confrontation, but some are much better at it than others. The secret? Control. Never, ever lose your temper. (JG)

  The reason some guys get angry during a plain-talk confrontation is fear. Before you walk into a dispute, ask yourself what's the worst that can happen. If the worst that can happen is something you can't afford to have happen, duck the confrontation. Otherwise, go for broke, but play it cool. (FED)

You can break up a career logjam by threatening to walk out. But remember: If you threaten it, you have to be ready to carry through with it. Think of it as high-stakes poker, no folds allowed. (Anon.)

- *Take a chance.* If you're stagnating in your present job, yet you're sure you're reasonably employable, take a leap. Do something that, if it works out, will be truly remarkable. After all, what difference does it make if you don't succeed? You're out of there, anyhow. But you may get points from other potential employers for having taken a chance on something brash, creative, or innovative. (EKH)
- *Change directions.* If you've reached a dead end on your current path, choose a new direction. But don't do a 180: Jump to a profession or industry ancillary to the one you were in before, and start up again. You'll be able to transfer a great deal of your experience and credibility, and you'll have none of the old obstacles to try to overcome. Instead, you'll have new ones. (PDS)

How to Be an Expert

The **Main Thing** about experts is they cure us of all our insecurities. For example, who has a lock on being a good parent? Nobody. As a result, every parent is an insecure parent, fretting over every single decision and worrying whether or not it's the right one. Eventually, this kind of anxiety can wear a pair of folks out; they reach a point where they just want to know what to do. Since they've squandered their own credibility by second-guessing themselves for fifteen years, by the time the kid hits adolescence, Mom and Pop see themselves as rank amateurs. Worried about whether or not it's normal for your teenage daughter to have motorcycles parked in her bedroom? Call an expert and ask. Why go with your own instincts when for a few grand you can call up somebody else and go with theirs?

HOW TO RECOGNIZE AN EXPERT ON SIGHT

There are some traits held in common by all experts:

- *They don't speak English.* Experts self-define themselves by mastering the regional dialect spoken by their profession. Jargon is generally the only thing separating an expert from a know-it-all; as a rule, the more obvious the field of expertise, the richer the jargon. Want to put your collection of birthday-party videos onto a laser disc? An expert will be happy to discuss repurposing with you, and may even suggest a few custom aplets—maybe a calc or an uploadable link. There's also a very strong correlation between the impenetrability of the language and the bill at the end of the road. Even a muffler repairman can verbally complicate the job sufficiently—"Might need to remount these baffle-bearings"—to make you completely unsure of what you're buying.

One other thing: Their invoices are as complicated as the language they speak.

- **They belong to institutes.** Institutes are great, if you're an expert. You join an institute, and you get a bulletin, semiannual conferences, regional seminars, and enough certificates to paper the john. You also get the annual convention, where you get to see a bunch of experts drink like amateurs.
- **They are very sensitive.** You corner an expert willfully violating the laws of common sense, and you've got yourself one hell of a catfight, buddy. Apparently, an expert is to his expertise what a virgin is to her virtue: There are some things a gentleman just doesn't question.
- **They flourish in an atmosphere of failure.** Obviously, unwillingness to assume responsibility is a serious symptom of failure, and so it's not surprising that when an institution, business, or organization puts its future in the hands of experts, failure always follows. If you need proof, look at American public education, a social institution dominated entirely by a self-perpetuating class of education experts, each generation of which is dimmer than the last. The inevitable result: Kids even dumber than the experts who supervise their education. (JDa)

HOW TO BE YOUR OWN EXPERT

Obviously, being an expert is something within easy grasp. Here's how to take control:

- **Make decisions quickly.** Experts hide their ambivalence from their clients. Hide yours from yourself.
- **Don't be afraid to make a mistake.** Do you think soybean experts go to bed at night worrying that maybe they were wrong about that tofu thing? If you go wrong, fix it later.
- **Dispense advice freely.** This is the key to being an expert. If somebody asks you a question, answer forthrightly and with confidence. If you actu-

ally know the correct answer, fine. If you don't know the correct answer, that's fine, too, since when somebody's looking for an expert, he's just looking for an answer. If it's also the correct answer—bonus!

- *Try anything once.* Look, real expertise is a thin sheet of experience welded to a solid chassis of common sense. By the time you do something the third time—not counting marriage—you'll be an expert, practically. (JDa, SP)

And even if you screw up, what's the worst thing that could happen to you? See below.

How to Join the French Foreign Legion

Good career moves have a way of sneaking up on you. For example, let's say that after a six-year engagement, you're finally marrying the daughter of the man who has not only been like a father to you for the past six years, but, more important, has also been the man who owns the large corporation that has employed you for the last six years, the man who has tearfully anointed you his heir and successor-designate.

But—*darn!*—there's that brief misbehavior in Thailand you forgot to tell your beloved about. It just never came up, that's all, until the day before the wedding when a certain Mr. Martinez, Esq., calls and says he's coming over with Billy Fong, your eight-year-old Amerasian son. Billy's mother, Suzy—you *do* remember Suzy, don't you?—wanted you to have Billy should anything ever happen to her. Not to worry, says Mr. Martinez, Esq., Suzy told him just before she died that the kid didn't need much maintenance, growing up by himself the way he did on the streets of the Tai Do district of Bangkok. Billy is, by all reports, says Mr. Martinez, Esq., a *superb kick-boxer.* Now, says Mr. Martinez, Esq., coming to the point, will you come pick Billy up, or *should he just drive Billy over to your future father-in-law's house so he can participate in the wedding?*

1. *Call the French Embassy.* The number, in Washington, D.C., is (202) 944-6000. Ask for the telephone number and address of Fort de Nogent, the busiest of the sixteen French foreign legion recruiting centers in France, and the one nearest the airport in Paris. Call Fort de Nogent and try to find out something about the enlistment procedure. No information

will be forthcoming—*particulièrement* if you don't speak French. Don't worry about this; it's the legion's subtle way of telling you that the only way to find out how to enlist is to show up and enlist.

2. ***Call Air France.*** Fly to Paris, France. Try to get a bulkhead seat. Get drunk on the airplane. When you arrive in Paris, check into a grotesquely overpriced hotel—the Ritz, maybe—and book a table at the Colombe d'Or. Order the quail, drink *two* eighty-year-old Armagnacs after dinner. The tab will come to $1,092 for one. Don't bother paying. And, say, why bother paying your hotel bill, either? All will be forgiven after you spend five years—the minimum enlistment term—in the legion.

3. ***Present yourself at Fort de Nogent.*** Sign up. You can enlist under an assumed name, so choose something wonderful. The legion will take away all your possessions, including your passport, your traveler's checks, and all your identification. You'll be sent to the legion's HQ at Aubagne, just outside Marseilles, where, for the next three weeks, you'll be put through a battery of vigorous medical exams and highly detailed security checks. Then you'll be bused to Castelnaudary, located conveniently off the A61 between Carcasonne and Toulouse, where you'll join the training regiment. You'll be taught the graceful French language in a terrifically effective linguistic program employing force and the avoidance of pain as motivation. For the fifteen weeks of basic training, you'll be paid 6,816 francs—about $1,300. After basic, you may be sent to paratrooper school at the Citadel of Clavi on Corsica. If you try to desert, the legion will hunt you down and kill you, no kidding.

4. ***See the world.*** After training, you'll be shipped out to serve France, maybe in Djibouti. Question: Where is Djibouti? Answer: It's the capital of the French territory of the Afars and the Issas. But you knew that. Question two: Do you know what they do in Djibouti? They make *salt*.

5. ***Get paid.*** Every month, you'll get 1,700 francs ($325) for the first few months, a little less than you made in basic. After three years, you'll get 2,091 francs ($400) per month, unless you're a paratrooper, in which case, you'll get 3,115 francs ($595) per month. After five years, you can get married, which is where you came in; after fifteen years, you'll be eligible for a small pension; after twenty years, you'll receive a larger one. The legion will take care of you until you die at a home for old soldiers at St. Maximin in the south of France, less than an hour from a beach where the girls wear bikinis without tops *or* bottoms.

Trivia: Get to know your foreign legion:

- **There are eight thousand legionnaires,** but fewer than 1 percent of the legion are American. Forty percent are French, followed by Germans, Eastern Europeans, Brits, and Spaniards.
- **The legion most recently saw action** in the civil war in Chad.
- **The legion was founded in 1831** by King Louis Philippe as a means of ridding France of political troublemakers.
- **Cole Porter was a legionnaire.** So was Ali Khan. So was Alan Seeger.
- **After you've served your time,** you can get French citizenship.
- **If you're over forty, forget it.** Tell Mr. Martinez, Esq., to pick up a tie for the kid on the way over. (WB)

10. Trouble

Most men avoid trouble assiduously only if it comes in unattractive packaging. Put a load of trouble under the hood of a red sports car or in a tight, black dress, though, and trouble becomes our collective middle name. Then we go blind. Why? Because even if it walks like trouble, talks like trouble, and looks like trouble, it looks like fun to us.

Alas, the line between fun and self-destruction isn't even a fine one. It's a four-foot-wide stripe painted in tears, whatever those are.

How to Get in Touch with Your Feelings

For two decades and more, woman have been trying to reduce men to tears, and for just as long, men have wondered why. The answer is here, in this small lesson on the folly of *tearfulness*, the wildly popular, socially approved barometer of men's sensitivity.

TACTICAL TEARS

The ugly truth is that crying, for men, is the faked orgasm of emotional coupling, the one thing that convinces women we really do feel something from time to time. The **Main-Thing problem,** as you already know, is that *most of us just aren't big weepers.* That sad but inescapable fact belly-slams against conventional wisdom, which, for a long time now, has held that women like sensitive guys, men who aren't afraid to cry. Since most us want only to do whatever will make us look better to women, lots of us have been massaging our duct muscles, working up a big wail of woe. It's a reasonable ploy. Crying is no more odious than the other goofy, ill-advised scams we use to persuade women to do the senseless, clothesless, irresponsible things we most wish them to do. If it works, hey.

But it never does. And that's the crying shame. For, as it happens, tears will gain us nothing, lads, save a small sinus inflammation.

For a full explanation of why, we need to acquaint ourselves with *two basic rules:*

RULE 1. THERE'S A DIFFERENCE BETWEEN WHO WE ARE AND WHO WOMEN THINK THEY WANT US TO BE

Women prefer men who cry at times women think appropriate, like maybe at sunsets, or in heartfelt moments of sharing, or in movies about relationships. In the real world, men who cry about this stuff are neurotic. Only two kinds of men are good for instant tears. Crazy guys are one. When a guy cries over an episode of *Sisters*, he's really crying out for a mood-leveling drug. Actors are the other: Ask an actor to cry, and he'll do so by summoning a memory of the worst thing that ever happened to him in his life, like that time he was ignored.

So that leaves all the rest of us, a planet full of dry-eyed regular guys, wondering how to express ourselves in emotionally approved ways, such as:

How to Cry at a Screening of *Fried Green Tomatoes*
- ***Reach your hand into the tub of popcorn.*** Eat the popcorn, but don't lick your fingertips.
- ***Next, give a little shudder,*** and touch your salt-encrusted fingertips to your eyes.

Stand back! you big tear jerk, you. Great gush. You figure, hey! a little of this and she's going to think I'm a raw, fleshy pillar of throbbing sensitivity, and she may want to tame the wild poet inside me, and comfort me, possibly horizontally.

If you're caught at this, however, you're dead, because women are tremendous believers in feelings. We've all been taught that women are much more sensitive than we are, but this turns out to be only half true: Women are no more sensitive to the feelings of others than men are. What women are more sensitive to is their *own* feelings. And they attach great significance to those feelings, and they wish we would, too. Which brings us to:

RULE 2. THERE'S A DIFFERENCE BETWEEN WHO WOMEN THINK THEY WANT US TO BE AND WHO THEY REALLY WANT US TO BE

When it comes to the stuff that counts, even women know crying won't cut it. You can stare right into the eyes of an IRS auditor, for example, and you can cry your heart out, but it won't make your golf pro into a tax-deductible charity. So crying around a woman you care about is really destructive behavior. It's like crying at a job interview; in fact, when it comes to real courtship—in which the prize is a wife-for-life—the whole adventure is a kind of job interview. Women, quite rightly, want to know what you're good for. *They do not necessarily want to know how you feel.* Especially all the time. Put a crying man in a romantic relationship and, guaranteed, the whole thing will end in tears, since most women know that a guy who shuffles around sniffling is kind of useless for doing real work, like running a rototiller or engineering a public offering. Women know, albeit only instinctively, that Kleenex makes man-sized tissues for big snot problems, not for big cosmic problems. Here are a few no-fear, no-tears **Main Things** over which women think *no* man ought to cry:
- His career.
- His finances.
- Another woman.
- Physical pain.
- His spiritual health. (TJM)

In other words, if you want a woman to admire your sensitivity to sensibility, *don't cry about the stuff that really matters.* Women see crying over real problems as a sign of weakness, and, trust me, men, the women you want despise weak guys.

BUMMED, BUT NOT TEARFULLY

There are lots of things you can feel plenty bad about without pushing the envelope to include crying. For instance, a guy goes sappy whenever he thinks about the incredibly beautiful woman who accosted him at a party, volunteered to perform a certain genetic experiment with him, but was turned away when he couldn't face the prospect of adultery. "It may never happen to me again," he says, his voice cracking with emotion, and of course he's right on that one. Other guys get worked up over Wall Street crashes. Others weep over NFL fumbles. These are all the tragedies of real lives. But they are, technically, only "disappointments," and nothing to cry over.

THE REAL THING

On the other hand, we all know that **there are times when tears will sneak up on you** and flood the basement of your soul with emotional debris and spiritual mud. These have nothing to do with the fashionable politics of sex. They are simply the moments when a man has to cry, no matter how sensitive he isn't. You can't plan for these, you never know when they'll get you, but when they do, you'll want to hide your head and cry like a baby—in fact, maybe like a baby girl.

- *Rent a man's movie. Nell* and *The Piano* don't get your ducts in a row? Then try renting *Pride of the Yankees.* You don't need to be a baseball nut to see what happens when Lou Gehrig tells the crowd he's the luckiest-luckiest man-man on the face of the earth. Or *The Natural,* when Robert Redford sits up in bed and says, "God! I love baseball!" Because baseball movies trade on the mythic idealization of what the game ought to be—as opposed to the squalid, boring reality of what it actually is—the baseball you get on video is much better than the baseball you get at Dodger Stadium. In fact, Hollywood baseball is so much better than the real thing that many men would be willing to skip the whole inter-leagued, wild-carded, postseasoned season altogether in favor of an all-star baseball movie season on HBO.

- *Get religion.* It's easy (and acceptable, too) to get all teary once in a while about the vastness of creation and your puny place in it. Your basic church or synagogue will do the trick here. A Jewish high holiday or an Eastern Orthodox Divine Liturgy will provide an extra dimension of exciting special effects, if these are required for tear inducement.

- **Go to a funeral.** In particular, attend the funeral of a fireman, where a bagpiper plays "Amazing Grace." We mean nothing cynical here, chaps. Men and women who end their lives courageously well deserve a few of our tears, and, as a rule, these flow unbidden whenever we confront the memory of those who have done a great good for us all. There are a number of variants on this theme. One well-recommended venue: The Memorial Day ceremony like the one at the cemetery in Burr Oak, Kansas, especially when the vets play taps while the living heroes of one war, men like our uncles and our fathers, pay tribute to the dead heroes of another war, like our grandfathers. While guys like us just watch. (DB)
- **A personal observation.** *Another guaranteed gusher:* **Be with your wife when she has a baby.** *The first blush of that little, matted noggin pulls the trigger on most guys. I've had three daughters, and all three times their mother, the doc, and the nurses have been busy patching things up, while the only people crying in the delivery room were me and the new kid. Pathetic, no?*

How to Cure a Hangover

- **Use science.** You thought it was the booze. Wrong. It was the chemistry: That mixed cocktail of misbehavior dehydrated your body, nauseated your stomach, and beat you up alongside the head. So fight chemistry with chemistry: Drink plenty of—do we have to say it? *nonalcoholic*—liquids, eat something savory to help retain water, and give your body a good dose of protein. One man's prescription: double cheeseburger, large fries, huge cola with ice. And that's for *breakfast,* chum.
- **Eat a dry cracker with honey on it** if you feel bad when you wake up. (VSDa)
- **Take one thousand milligrams of vitamin C,** drink salted cucumber juice, eat raw fish marinated in hot sauce, and take ginseng or willow bark. (EL)
- **Eat tomatoes,** drink V-8 and coffee, and take a cold shower.
- **Drink lots of water** and ginger root tea.
- **Exercise.** (GH)

How to Prevent a Hangover

If you ate cheeseburgers for breakfast every day for a week, you're ready for these handy hints, for curing a hangover is what you must do when you fail to prevent one. To do that:

- **Drink an eight-ounce glass of water** for *every* drink you drank just before you go to bed—and don't cheat.
- **Then pack some carbohydrates** to take along on Slumberland's Tilt-a-Whirl. Bread works.

  Neither of these are easy things to do when you're stumbling around the kitchen drunk, but doing both is a lot easier than waking up with a hangover.
- **Try fifty milligrams of vitamin B,** eat a piece of bread, and drink two big glasses of water before you go to sleep. (GH)
- **Take two or three aspirin,** acetaminophen, or ibuprofen with a couple of glasses of water before you go to sleep. (PA)

How to Make Swigging Water and Eating Bread in the Middle of the Night a Really Meaningful Experience

Outbreaks of genital warts occur more than twice as frequently in people who drink five drinks a week than in nondrinkers. That's the bad news. The good news: Regular drinking promotes nosebleeds. (PA)

How to Excuse an Occasional Gutter-Sweeping Binge

Let's say you've been faithfully doing your exercises *all year long.* But let's say a gang of strawberry daiquiris grabs you in a bar, throws you on a table, and forces you to eat an even cord of cheese logs. Will you insta-morph into the fat person imprisoned inside your trim, well-toned body?

No.

The **Main Thing** about exercise is that if you do it regularly and with aerobic enthusiasm, your body will automatically turn up the burners to incinerate those extra calories at a faster clip. Indolent bingers? They just get fat.

How to Keep a New Year's Resolution

Now. You finally ready? First, cut yourself some slack. By bachelor law, you get the whole month of January to really fine-tune your resolution. This gives guys without wives time to make sure the resolution is a good one, one that's designed to resolve you right up and onto a whole new level of better you. Let's say you're going to swear off alcohol. Granted, some research says moderate drinkers have a better record in the cardiac department, and some research shows drinkers live longer than nondrinkers. But you resolve that you're not going to drink. Fine. That's your end-of-January New Year's resolution. To make sure you keep it, here's what you do:

- *Tell everybody.* Make it a matter of personal honor.
- *Write it down* and post the note where you'll see it.
- *Bet your bartender*—or another close, personal friend—a C-note you can keep your resolution a whole man-year, which is eleven months. (Anon.)
- *Tell your father.* (Anon.)

How to Ditch an Annoying, Month-Old Resolution

For some obscure reason, until the recent lounge movement, people under, say, thirty just didn't appreciate the virtue of a well-made martini—unless they'd drunk a dozen. Now a cold martini is a hot item. Here's how to be the Bond of the bar:

- *Cold start.* Keep your ingredients on ice or in a freezer until you're ready. One option: Mix your martini in a pitcher or large flower vase and chill the thing.
- *To make one from scratch,* pour two fingers—that's four ounces—of gin or vodka in a chilled martini glass. Add just enough vermouth to cover

the bottom of the vermouth bottle's cap. Stir gently. Add a couple of olives. If you add those little cocktail onions, your martini becomes a Gibson. If you add a dash of bitters instead of onions, you can call it a Nigroni. Drink six or seven of them, and not only will you not care what they're called, you'll be well on your way to developing a high-concept resolution idea for next year. (CSW)

How to Swallow a Sword

First, you have to swallow a guiding tube, which is generally seventeen to nineteen inches long and less than an inch wide and made of thin metal. This tube will protect your throat from the sword's sharp edges.

So, the real question is: How do you swallow a sword-guiding tube?

- *Start with something small,* a spoon perhaps, to overcome the gag reflex. The greatest danger here, believe it or not, is getting so comfortable with a spoon thrust down your throat that you drop it and—ouch! And ouch, again!
- *Open wide, tilt back, and align the spoon* with your pharynx. That's about five inches down. Now it's time to move up to something a bit longer—a chopstick, perhaps. Past the pharynx easily, and into the esophagus (ten to eleven inches). The idea here is to make a straight line from your mouth to your stomach.
- *Now use the guiding tube as a practice instrument.* The last door to pass through is the distended stomach. When you get there, you're ready for a real sword. (DSA) See also "How to Find a Wife" in Chapter 11.

How to Hire a Private Eye

Look in the yellow pages under "Investigators." Then ask these questions before you sign:

- *Are you licensed?*
- *Are you bonded?*
- *Do you offer an initial consultation* for free?
- *Can I get your rates* in writing?
- *What do you mean* by "reasonable expenses"?

Remember this: When you hire a private investigator to investigate something or someone, part of what he'll be investigating is *you*. Do you really want someone opening that can of worms? (Anon.)

How to Organize a Friendly, Little Poker Game

What we have here is your basic euphemistic oxymoron, since there is no such thing as a "friendly" poker game. There may exist a poker game played by people all of whom are friends. But poker is quiet war; it's tidy bloodlust; it's ripping the guts out of the guy next to you and tossing them back in his face with a pair of aces. Unless, of course, you let women play and use wild cards. In which case poker is a card game.

Regularly-scheduled poker nights have something slightly institutional about them; they acquire traditions and eccentricities that somehow make them different from all other poker games. Partly, that's personnel; partly that's

- *Location:* Probably one player's home. It's best not to rotate the venue; situating the game more or less permanently in one place reinforces the notion that the game is a regular, unchanging thing.
- *Primarily poker:* The venue should be dedicated to poker for the night. Mixing poker with your wife's Tupperware party somehow denigrates the intrinsic importance of The Game.
- *Facilities and materials:* Good lighting, enough chairs, a practically proportioned table, plenty of ashtrays, a mess of red, blue, and white chips, and four decks of cards—two red, two blue—are standard.
- *Refreshments:* There are two ways to share food duty: Either one person is *always* responsible, or the winner is responsible for bringing food the following week. If you choose the former option, rake a buck from each pot until the tab is paid.

    A limited supply of beer is okay, but avoid hard stuff. Poker is best played with a straight face.
- *Players:* Seven is ideal; five or six will do. Never play a four-handed game. The best way to ensure a steady supply of players is to find five or six regulars, leaving one or two chairs open for guests. That way, if a regular becomes irregular, he can be demoted to guest, and a guest can be elevated to regular. Boot chronic no-shows.

Try and exercise some demographic sense in picking your players: If your group includes three guys on student loans and three neurosurgeons, odds are you'll have a short and uninteresting game.

- *Stakes:* The stakes and limits are probably the most important elements in a regular game. The stakes should be high enough to mean something—ever try and bluff your way into an eighty-cent pot?—but not so high that some guy's kids won't be able to eat. A quarter or a half-dollar seems to work pretty well for most people, especially if you limit raises to three.

- *House rules:* House or game rules should be sensible and easy to remember, and they should be made clear to everyone before the very first hand of the very first game is played. Newcomers should always have house rules explained to them. Remember that the object of house rules is to ensure fair play in a congenial atmosphere.

Here's a decent list of house rules:

> *Maximum three-dollar initial bet* with a three-raise, three-dollar-per-raise maximum.
>
> *No check-and-raise betting.*
>
> *Ties split the pot.*
>
> *No wild cards,* and no games that require more cards than the table can supply (i.e., in a seven-man game, no eight-card games).
>
> *A card laid is a card played.*
>
> *Hoyle's* Rules of Poker *is the judge.*

- *Games:* Stick with games everyone knows. Esoteric games with lots of blind flips, wild cards, extra buys, and passes are social games, not poker games, and usually find favor only when the game is thoroughly co-ed. For a good, smooth game, stick to draw and stud games and their variants. Adding high-low splits can liven up a game.

- *Duration:* Set a quitting time and *stick to it.* If you have a midweek game that starts at seven, call for a last deal around the table at, say, midnight.

- *Clean up:* Either everybody pitches in, or the winners clean up and the losers are excused. But never ask your girlfriend or wife to do janitor duty, since if you do, there's a very good chance your first poker game will be your last.

- *If you're invited* to someone else's game, learn the house rules, try and gain at least a superficial acquaintance with the other players, and stay until the end. Ask the person inviting you what the stakes are; if they're too high for you, don't go. (RS)

- *Know the odds:*

POKER HAND	ODDS
A pair	1 per 2.4 hands
Two pair	1 in 21 hands
Three of a kind	1 in 47 hands
A straight	1 in 255 hands
A flush	1 in 509 hands
A full house	1 in 693 hands
Four of a kind	1 in 4,164 hands
A straight flush	1 in 72,192 hands
A royal flush	1 in 649,739 hands (GS)

HOW TO INJECT PURE FEAR INTO A FRIENDLY, LITTLE POKER GAME

*A **personal observation:** A Mr. F. W. of Los Angeles wrote to me asking about weird poker games: "Is there one particular card game that's more exciting than any others? I'm looking for something to really shake up my regular group." That's an odd question to ask from L.A. Just call for a quick round of earthquakes.*

If you're looking for a scary card game, there's a certain charming terror in any poker game in which you are the regular loser. In fact, I used to be part of a weekly poker game in Hollywood in which I played just that role. The other regulars—agents, writers, actors—were all rich, and I did what I could to help them stay that way. I played every Wednesday for five years, and I lost the equivalent of a new Toyota every year. I was actually pretty fair at conventional games—stud, draw, all those. The economic stimulus I gave the nation was from a brutal, barbaric game without a name, but based on one much more civilized called "Bourée," a word which in French means, "Your money or your wife."

Here's how you make it hurt:
- *Ante a buck.*
- *Deal four cards facedown to everyone.*
- *Turn up one card from somewhere in the middle of the deck. That's your trump suit; aces are high. Bury that card and shuffle.*
- *One betting round. Here's what you're betting: You're betting that you can take at least one trick of the four tricks that will be played.*
- *Then the first declaration: Play or fold?*
- *If you play, you can replace any number of cards for a dollar each.*

- *If you fold, you're not only out of the hand but out of the game.*
- *Another betting round.*
- *Second declaration: Play or fold?*
- *If you play and manage to take just one, little, lousy trick, all you have to do to stay in for the next round is ante another buck.*
- *If two players tie at two tricks each, they each ante a buck.*
- *If you take all the tricks, you take the pot.*
- *But—and, really, this is the unpleasant part—if you take no tricks, you match the pot.*

This ugly exercise continues, round after round, until every player but one folds. At a table of seven players, I'm willing to bet your hands will shake so hard you won't be able to hold your cards during the last round. This monstrosity is the spinal tap and root canal of all poker games. Give it a name and let me know what you decide. "Testicular Cancer" might work.

How to Spot a Cold Dealer

There is such a thing as a cold dealer in twenty-one. When you spot one, make sure you sit down and get in the game. Here's what he looks like:

Watch the hands he deals himself. If he shows a 2, 3, 4, 5, or 6 in five out of ten hands, make him a friend for life—or at least until the cards change.

Here's why: If he's got a 2 to 6 showing, odds are he's got a high card underneath. Since he has to hit anything under 17, the odds are still in favor of him getting another high card, thus going bust.

Keep in mind that the rule may also be true for you: If you get a 2, 3, 4, 5, or 6 in five hands out of ten, it might be time for you to get out of the game. (JR)

More gambling wisdom:

- **Believe in streaks.** They can be proven statistically. Therefore, stay when you're on a good one, split when you're not. (RS)
- **Pick the right game.** At a casino, the game with the best odds in your favor (if you know what you're doing) is blackjack. The worst odds are the slots.
- **Don't play the state lottery.** But if you must, play in Virginia, where the odds are the best. (JR)

How to Post Bail

First, you have to qualify. If the judge thinks your crime is too awful or that you seem likely to try to escape the court's jurisdiction, you may be sent to jail to wait for your trial.

But *if the judge feels that you are trustworthy enough* to be let free until your trial, he will require that you put some money up front to assure you won't fly the coop before the trial is over. The money will be returned to you when you show up as promised. (RHWa)

- *If the money is more than you keep lying around,* you'll have to go to a bail bondsman. How to find one? Don't worry: Their cards and signs will be everywhere around you. In exchange for collateral or a fee that will begin at about 10 percent, the bail bondsman will pay your fee to the court. The amount of the collateral or fee will vary according to how likely the bail bondsman feels you are to jump bail or disappear before your trial is over.

- *If you fail to appear* in court as ordered after having your bail posted, you will have compounded whatever problems you were already having. The court will file charges against you for jumping bail; you will lose whatever fee you paid or collateral you posted to the bondsman. And what's worse, you will have an angry bondsman on your tail. Chances are, given his line of work, he's got all kinds of friends who know how to take care of guys like you. (Anon.)

How to Negotiate a Late-Night Re-entry

Circumstances: Out late misbehaving. Wife home in bed.

- *Objective:* Silent re-entry.
- *Obstacles:* Unexpected objects on floor, creaking floorboards, squeaky hinges.
- *Solution:* Unlock the door making as much noise as you wish. Run inside, turn on the TV. When your wife comes downstairs to ask what's up, tell her you fell asleep in front of the TV and thought you heard a racket at the door.
- *Alternate:* Take off your clothes, unlock the door, run inside, pile clothes next to sofa, claim you decided to sleep on the sofa because she had taken

all the blankets—never pass up a chance for guilt manipulation—but that you were awakened by a racket at the door.

- *Caution:* The alternate plan is so outrageous that it usually works. There is a slight risk, however, in the doorstep strip, so plan carefully in case you have to dive into the shrubbery. (FZ)

And if your wife or girlfriend is sitting quietly reading by the fire when you rush in, naked, and pop on the TV?

- *Watch out for crafty women:* The danger is with all that stuff they make and over-decorate the house with. For example, baskets of pine cones on the floor, cluttered-up bathroom fixtures, arrangements of dried leaves—these things are all distant early-warning devices designed to catch an unwary prodigal spouse. (JAC)

How to Move a Bee Nest

- *First, pick the right day*—a warm sunny one—when the bees are already in a good mood.
- Next, *rent a smoke-blowing unit* and use it to encourage the bees to leave the hive. The smoke makes them bee-drunk and passive.
- *Wear light-colored clothing* with a smooth finish—like polished cotton or khaki—and protect your face and neck with a bee veil.
- *Wear boots* and loose-fitting gloves that seal well around the wrists and your shirt collar.
- *Tie your trousers* shut at the leg.

Once you have the nest in hand, move slowly and confidently. Exhibit no fear or nervousness. The bees will sense it. (HJT)

How to Survive a Towering Inferno

- *Go to the door* of your room and feel it with your hand—but don't open it! If it is hot, leave it closed. If it is cool, open it and see how much smoke is in the hallway.
- *Check for smoke.* If there is little or none, leave your room and go to the emergency stairwell. Do not use the elevator.
- *Make sure you take your room key* with you. If the stairwell is filled with smoke or flames, you many need to retreat back to your room.

- **Block the door.** If the door of your room is hot or there is heavy smoke in the hallway, wet some towels and put them along the base of the door to keep the smoke out. Remember: Smoke kills most victims of fire, not flames.
- **Move to the window** or balcony with sheet in hand. If you have a balcony, close the door behind you. If you have a fear of heights, turn and face the wall.
- **If you can't get out, get air.** If the room has narrow windows you can't fit through, put a wet towel over your head and get low to suck in the fresh air coming in the window.
- **Wind direction.** If your room doesn't have a balcony, determining the direction of the wind is crucial: If the wind is blowing toward you, you can open the window as wide as you like. But if the wind is blowing away from you and you open the window, you will create a vacuum in the room and the fire and smoke may come rushing in to fill it. If the wind is blowing away from you, don't open the window any more than three inches. The same rules apply to windows that are sealed: If the wind is blowing toward you, break the window. If the wind is blowing away from you, do nothing.
- **One last tip.** Whether you are in a hotel or at home, it is always a good idea to sleep with your shoes at the side of the bed. Why? In the event of fire or earthquake or other disaster, window glass may break and fall on the floor, waiting to cut an unsuspecting and barefoot victim. Besides, you may have to do a little fire-walking to get away safely. (JYF)

How to Duck an IRS Audit

To successfully avoid an audit, you must first know the mind of the IRS. Here's the meld:

- **An audit is not an accusation** of wrongdoing. It's just an audit.
- **All returns are run through a computer,** which checks the math and flags returns with errors. At the same time, the computer also flags returns with high deductions at each income level. The higher your income, the more likely you are to be audited. Also, people who live in large cities are more likely to be audited.
- **Flagged returns are then examined by a human,** who decides whether an audit is warranted or not.

- Ergo, *the best (but not foolproof) way to avoid an audit* is to keep your deductions within the range that is considered "normal" for someone of your marital status and income level. However, don't get smug if you do this: A certain number of "normal" returns are randomly selected and audited each year.
- Meanwhile, *having an unusually high deduction doesn't guarantee that you will be audited,* either, so the best thing to do is to report your income and deductions honestly, and make sure you can document everything you are deducting.
- *Hold on to those slips of paper:* The IRS can audit you for any or all of the past three years. (RES)

How to Survive an IRS Audit

- *It's okay to be pleasant,* but don't try to be obsequious.
- *Don't try to* make the examiner like you.
- *When you feel like talking* to fill in the silences, don't.
- *Don't yammer.* Briefly, politely, and succinctly answer the question asked, nothing more.
- *Don't get angry* or complain or threaten to write your congressman— the examiner is only doing his job. Being pleasant may not hurt (and it could help), but getting angry certainly won't help.
- *Bring every piece of documentation* necessary to answer the examiner's queries. (RES)

How to Deal with Fear

Perhaps one of the most well-trod lines in American political speechmaking is FDR's claim that we have nothing to fear but fear itself. FDR is obviously not a man who ever skidded broadside across the width of the Pennsylvania Turnpike heading directly at the big, white underbelly of a gasoline truck.

The fears of a normal man. FDR, as it happens, wasn't talking fear at all, as any sensible fellow can attest. He was pitching a get-up-and-get-going, don't-worry-be-happy cheerfulness to the nation when it was in a state of severe depression. What Roosevelt meant by "fear" was really something a little closer to defeatism, a thing to be avoided, no doubt, but hardly the kind of thing that makes your hair stand on end. If FDR really wanted to take the fear out of fear, he should have at least been talking about the fears we all know and, well, fear. Here's a fearful little list:

1. *Fear of dropping the ball.* Literally. You're sitting with your kid in a box behind third, Rube fouls one off. The ball comes right at you, your kid yells, "Catch it, Dad!" and you feel your hands turn to mush. The problem, of course, is that most men wilt under too much carefully observed pressure. That's why public speaking is a big fear.

2. *Fear of dancing.* Lots of guys are afraid of dancing, because the moment they get out on the dance floor, they have an out-of-body experience, in which they see themselves as Al Gore frugging to "Don't Stop Thinking About Tomorrow," and nearly lose their will to live. Usually, guys who want to dance but fear the sight of themselves dancing have to drink so much to work up nerve enough to take a turn that when they stand to rumba, they fall over.

3. *Fear of beautiful women.* Most middle-aged women think men are terrified of smart, strong, independent women. That's nonsense, of course. Men love smart, ambitious women, since they're exactly the kind of women who will work hard enough to make sure we all get plenty of time for golf. No, men are terrified of beautiful, *young* women. There are a number of ways men mask this fear. The most common method is by cranking up their level of testosteronal boorishness and behaving rudely toward a good-looking woman, so that when her inevitable rebuff comes, these guys can attribute it to something other than their intrinsic undesirability. Men know beautiful women can be wooed only with an arsenal of wit, charm, civility, and, in distant fourth place, attractiveness—or, occasionally, their cash equivalents—and no man wants to admit he's lacking in these respects. As we all know, smart, strong, independent, not-so-great-looking women can be won with a combination of good hair and a lascivious smolder.

4. *Fear of asbestos in the basement.* It's a planet of radon out there, in which every day we find a new secret killer in our midst, a silent, insidious terror against which only really expensive experts can protect us. The experts, of course, tell us that there are invisible killers everywhere, spreading cancer and strep and HIV. Trouble is, they're right.

5. *Fear of changing the oil.* There are many, many things of which a man is capable but which he chooses not to do by simply saying, "I don't get it." Here's a short list: Taxes, fatherhood, engine maintenance, macroeconomics, nutrition, religion, and multiplication of fractions. Once we agree

that all these things are mastered by people of quite ordinary intellect, people even dumber than us, we have to admit that we, too, could do any or all of them, except *we don't want to.*

6. *Fear of dentistry.* This is the only fear that fits the dictionary definition of fear—as anxiety caused by the possibility of danger. Just *thinking* about a guy with a hangover drilling holes in your head is enough to give pause to the most fearless of stout hearts. In fact, as most dentists will tell you, it's the fear that gives their patients the willies, not the actual thing— excruciating pain—feared. Most people get in and out of dental chairs with no untoward incidents, other than the sheer misery of being there.

7. *Fear of Sam Bohn.* Sam Bohn represents the guy in your town who owns the local bank. Nice guy, a tennis nut, but you owe him a lot of money. That makes him your inspiration, for it's our incessant fear of creditors that keeps us on the run, workwise, because we're rightly afraid of what they'll do to us if we take a day off. No money means no control. *Boo!* Very scary.

So there they are, the magnificent seven of fear: Failure, ridicule, rejection, death, responsibility, pain, and powerlessness.

SITUATIONAL AND OTHER FEARS

You'll notice many phobias missing from the above list. Fear of flying, fear of drunks in trucks, fear of homicidal crossing guards—all these things are fears, real enough. But I don't think anybody not insane is really living in fear of these things. That is, you get scared of them when they're around, that's all. Otherwise, you never give them a thought.

Other fears are so big you can barely see them, let alone worry about them. Take the wrath of God, for example. It's there, like a tiny leak in a basement pipe. You know you should worry about it, but you get busy and forget it. Then one day you're face-to-face with a flooded basement. Damn!

HOW TO PACIFY YOUR OWN FEARS

Had FDR said, "We have nothing to fear but ridicule, rejection, pain, and death," the nation would *still* be down in the dumps. Ironically, Roosevelt was right about the cure, wrong about the fear. What FDR needed was a good spin on the Cyclone at Coney Island. It would have made all fears comprehensible to him.

Here's how you can cope with fear: Take the thing you're most afraid of—impoverishment, for example—and spend some time developing a whole scenario based on what could *conceivably* happen to you if, to use our example, joblessness came your way. Work out all the details—all the conversations with friends, all the snide remarks of enemies. Get it all down. Live it. Survive it. Then get back on your feet and try again. A little fear is a useful thing, so long as it's a know-it-and-love-it kind of deal. That's the very thing that makes roller coasters so attractive: You get to *almost* die. See? Roller coasters are to death what sex is to love. That's why roller coasters are so much more popular than actually dying. (DB)

And, on that cheerful subject, a poll taken several years ago reported that 2 percent of respondents were willing to take a 99 percent chance of dying for one million dollars. Scary, no?

HOW TO JUDGE A CIGAR BY ITS ORIGIN

IF IT'S FROM	IT HAS THIS TASTE:
Jamaica	*Mild*
Dominican Republic	*Mild to medium flavor*
Honduras	*Stronger, heavier*
Nicaragua	*Richer, more full-bodied*
Cuba	*Rich and creamy* (VCS)

A *dissent:* A fine Cuban cigar is a thing of the past. The cigar industry's been so badly mauled in Cuba that the cigars you get there are simply inferior to those from Central America. Cuban cigars are coasting on a reputation under continual assault by smokers' experience. Ironically, the final nail in the coffin of Cuban stogies will be the lifting of the embargo against them: When American smokers taste how awful the things are, they'll never smoke another Havana. (ESD)

HOW TO SIZE UP A CIGAR

The larger the diameter of the cigar—measured in cigar-ring sizes—the richer and fuller the taste. The longer the cigar, the cooler the taste. (VCS)

To see how the popular brands stack up, consult this handy table.

NAME	LENGTH	RING SIZE
Corona	5½	42
Double Corona	7¾	49
Churchill	7	47
Robusto	5	50
Panatela	5	50
Lonsdale	6½	42
Toro	6	50 (VCS)

HOW TO SPECIFY SPARE PARTS FOR A CIGAR OR A PIPE

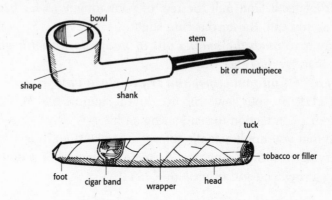

HOW TO PERFORM AN AUTOPSY ON A STOGIE

Know the parts:

- *Wrapper:* The outer tobacco wrapping, which ranges in color from light to very dark (called "oscuro").
- *Binders:* The layer of tobacco just beneath the wrapper. It's used to hold all the filler tobacco in the center together.
- *Filler:* The tobacco at the center of the cigar. This is the stuff you're really smoking. There are two kinds of filler:
  Long filler: Runs the length of the cigar
  Short filler: Comes from the trimmed edges of the long fillers. A high percentage of short filler is undesirable. (VCS, NR)

How to Blow a Smoke Ring

- *You don't need a weatherman.* If there's any wind at all, no ring.
- *Fill your mouth completely with smoke.* You need not a wisp, but a billow.
- *Slowly open your lips* to form a perfect "O." Not a pucker, and not a yawn. An "O." A perfect one. Bring those lips over those teeth. Come on. An "O." No other vowel will do. In Poland, smoke rings are an impossibility, owing to a linguistic shortfall in vowels. But in Hawaii, where vowels grow wild, there are smoke rings everywhere.

- **Push the tip of your tongue down** into the fleshy spot behind your lower front teeth, and pull the rest of your tongue as far back into your mouth as you can. Raise your chin slightly.
- One way is to **push the smoke out of your mouth with your tongue.** Try it. Okay, try the other way:
- **Keep that "O" on your lips, and try to close your mouth.** You'll feel a sort of click as your jaw tries to do the impossible. You'll create just enough of a contraction to send a ring aloft.

    Note that you don't actually "blow" a smoke ring. In fact, if you exhale while trying to blow a ring, you'll create too much of a draft. Instead of blowing a ring, you sort of *push* one. (STI)

How to Land a Big Rig

Say, frequent fliers, here's a trouble clip n' save for that next time you hear the dreaded announcement over the intercom: "Ladies and gentlemen, there's been an accident in the cockpit. Is there anybody on board who knows how to land a 747?"

Boeing 747s are wonderful airplanes. But they're real huge; the late, great Michael O'Donoghue once suggested making a matchbook advertising a study-at-home course called "Learn to Fly the Big Rigs." Well, this isn't the whole matchbook study plan, but it's the part that counts:

1. **First, admit you have a problem.** Grab the radio and tell anybody who'll listen that you're at the stick of a 747 and you aren't quite sure what to do. While you're waiting for acknowledgment and instructions, go on to step two.

2. **Engage a single channel of the autopilot**—you'll see three buttons marked "CMD." You want to light only one button. Point the heading indicator in the direction so you can keep the airplane straight and level. A 747 weighs a lot. The last thing you want to do is wrestle with it. Now you've got some time to get organized.

3. **Find the checklists.** The landing checklists and cards are always in the side pocket next to the pilot's and copilot's seats. The checklists will tell you if you're landing a 747-400 or another type of 747. If it turns out that you're bringing in a 747-400, you're in luck, since this model is equipped with an automatic landing system (ALS). If it turns out to be another type of 747, see below under "How to Land When There's No ALS."

4. **If you can't find the checklists,** use the three that follow. They're for a British Airways 747-136/236, checklist, and while other companies and types of 747s have different lists, these are better than no lists at all.

1. *Before descent checklist:*
   A. The EO's system check should be *completed*.
   B. Pressurization should be *set*.
   C. All a/c packs *on*. Set the airfield altitude so that the aircraft is depressurized on landing. (See below under "Find the Jeppeson.")
   D. Humidifier *off*. You'll still sweat, don't worry.
   E. Landing data and limits: *Checked and set*. This means you've reviewed the data for landing.
   F. HSIs: *Radio*. Switch the horizontal situation indicators to radio navigation mode.
   G. Approach briefing: *Understood*. Now here's where things can get confusing, since normally there would be a full and comprehensive briefing by the landing pilot, but since that's you, well, skip it.
   H. Auto brakes: *Set*. This optimistic step will turn on the automatic braking on touchdown.

2. *Approach checklist:*
   A. P.A. call ("Cabin crew fifteen minutes to landing"): *Done*.
   B. Cabin signs and exit lights: *On*.
   C. Ignition: *On*. This will switch on all engine igniters for landing.
   D. Fuel system: *Set for landing*.
   E. Fuel heat (only on 747-136 aircraft): *Check/off*, to prevent fuel icing.
   F. Q.N.H.: *Set*. This is for the altimeter barometric setting that will make the altimeters read the airfield altitude on touchdown.

3. *Landing checklist:*
   A. *Gear check: Down, in, green*. In other words, the gear handle is down, the gear handle is in, and the green gear-down lights are on.
   B. Speedbrake: *Armed*. Speedbrakes deploy on touchdown to reduce the lift on the wing and to keep the aircraft from bouncing down the runway.
   C. Hydraulics: *Checked*.
   D. Landing Flap: *Set*—probably at twenty-five degrees of flap, but thirty in a pinch.
   E. SCCM's report: *Received*. This tells you that the Senior Cabin Crew Member reports that the cabins are all secure for landing. (PF)

5. *Find the Jeppeson.* While you're running down the checklists, grab the Jeppeson charts. These are big notebook-shaped volumes. Inside are maps and landing approach diagrams for practically every airport in the world. Find the airport you're hoping to reach, and locate its radio frequency. Keep the Jeppeson handy. You'll need it again in a sec.

6. *Find the flight management system.* Look for buttons on the mode control panel—mounted on the glareshield—marked "LNAV" and "VNAV."

7. *Find the airport on the Jeppeson map.* If the crew had entered the arrival airport and approach information before being raptured, put the map on a one-hundred-mile scale using the EFIS control panel on the front instrument panel. When it is time to descend, there will be a yellow FMC MESSAGE message on the middle screen.

8. *Next, look down at the control display unit* mounted in the aisle stand between the pilots' seats. The bottom line will read "Reset MCP Altitude." That's telling you to lower the altitude on the mode control panel. Twist the knob in the direction that makes the little numbers go lower, and stop at about one hundred feet above the field elevation, as shown in the Jeppeson.

9. *Get the aircraft set to land.* Even though it's early, the LOC and G/S buttons on the MCP can be depressed to engage the autoland function. This should make all three autopilot CMD buttons light up. The system will *automatically* tune the appropriate ILS frequency. Cool or what?

10. *Turn on the autobrakes.* The autobrake panel location differs between airlines. Right about now, the airplane will have descended to intercept the radio-based landing beam. The autopilot will land the airplane. Forget trying to use thrust reversers. Let the autobrakes do the job. (DA)

HOW TO LAND WHEN THERE'S NO ALS

If the aircraft is a 747-100, -200, -300, or some other type, you won't have the use of an automatic landing system, and, frankly, that makes your chances for success somewhat remote. But what the hey—give it a shot.

Let's say you take the controls when the aircraft is flying along at a cruising speed of about 300 knots, somewhere around 37,000 feet above the ground. You're thinking it's time to land this thing when the control tower radios you: "Descend and maintain a position at 20,000 feet, at X point in space." Respond by saying that you don't know what they're talking about. That will get their attention, and they'll try to give you some advice. Take it.

1. *Retard the throttle.* Since you're a long way up and have a long way to go down, start your landing procedure by retarding the throttle. Actually, there are four throttles—one for each engine—and if you're sitting in the pilot's seat (the one on the left, facing the nose of the aircraft), they'll all be positioned at your right hand. To retard the throttle, pull the levers toward the back of the airplane.

2. *Lack of power means loss of altitude,* and decreasing altitude increases speed. When you retard the throttle, that causes the nose of the plane to drop. But that's not what you want. What you want is to glide down to earth nice and easy. To bring the nose back up, pull back gently on the yoke—the thing that looks like a steering wheel. Let the aircraft settle gently to 20,000, using a combination of reduced throttle and increased pitch. When you reach point X at 20,000 feet, bring the throttles back up and you'll still maintain your 300-plus knots. Sure, you decreased your throttle, but you also picked up a lot of speed compliments of gravity when you started flying down the hill.

3. *Changeover.* Next, the control tower will say: "Descend to 9,000 feet." In the United States, there's a "changeover" at 10,000 feet. You're not allowed to go below 10,000 feet with a speed of more than 250 knots. But you're cruising along at 300 knots. Therefore, not only do you have to drop to 9,000 feet, but when you pass 10,000 feet you also have to drop your speed by 50 knots. How? Retard the throttle again.

4. *At 11,000 feet, bring the nose back up but not the throttle.* Bringing the nose up increases the lift, which increases the drag, which decreases the speed. With a little finesse, you should be able to cruise at the proper speed.

5. *Traffic area.* From 9,000 feet, they're going to bring you into the traffic area. Center says: "Descend to 5,000 feet." Now is the time to start thinking about getting those flaps out. What you want to do is transform your sleek airliner into a big glider. You do that by using the flaps to increase the size of the wing. The best way we can explain is to compare a big, fat pelican to a superfast hawk. The pelican's slow because he has great big, thick wings. The hawk is fast, because he's got little thin wings. However, a pelican can carry a big fish in his mouth while he flies, but a hawk can only carry a little mouse. Strike it up to surface area. So, while we're jetting along in the cosmos, you want little teeny wings—just big enough to support the airplane's weight. When you're ready to swoop down to the ground, you want big, overgrown wings like parachutes that will let you drift slowly down from space. The retractable flaps of a 747 allow you to do both. The flaps retract into the wings when you're

cruising. When it's time to take off or land, they come out and dramatically increase the surface area of the wings.

6. ***Drop airspeed.*** The control tower will send you to down to 4,000 feet. Now, as you approach the airport, you're going to want to start slowing up and bring the throttles back. So bring the nose up a little bit more so the airspeed will start dropping off. Tell your copilot, "Flaps five"—as in five degrees—and the airspeed will come down. Ask for "Flaps 15," and airspeed will drop even more.

7. ***Wheels.*** At about 3,000 feet, you can put the gear down. Don't forget, every time you put something out like this, you're going to have to increase your power because you've just created a lot more drag. So give the aircraft just a tad more throttle.

8. ***Next, as you get on glide slope***—visually or mechanically—ease the power off and start a slow descent. As you start gliding toward the runway, ask for "Flaps 20," then "Flaps 30." That's the final flap setting used on a 747 under normal circumstances.

9. ***You're now at approach speed***—hold it all the way down. Relax for a minute. You're carrying power and your throttle is somewhere around 20 percent.

10. ***When you reach 50 feet,*** suddenly, the radar altimeter starts talking to you—"50," "30," "20," and "10." What it is telling you is the number of feet there are between the ground and the bottom of your wheels. You'll go from 50 feet to 10 about as fast as you just read it.

11. ***When you reach 30 feet,*** bring your throttles all the way to idle.

12. ***When you reach about 10 feet,*** start raising the nose to slow down and get closer and closer to stall speed—the speed at which the airplane ceases to fly. Stall's important—but you can't worry about that now because before you know it, your wheels will roll on the ground as airspeed decreases.

13. ***Easy does it.*** Slowly lower the nose down, bring the throttle reversers up over the gate and into reverse, apply the braking, and come to a stop. (JS, DBW)

How to Jump out of an Airplane

Give up on that 747? Practice your getaway move on something more modestly sized. There are three ways to make that first jump:

1. *Static line:* You go alone and—usually—your chute opens automatically just seconds after you leave the plane
2. *Accelerated free-fall:* You jump (or get pushed) out of the plane at 10,000 to 12,000 feet with two certified jumpmasters, both of whom keep a grip on you and help you get stable in the air, . . . monitor the altitude, and—after free-falling for about 50 seconds—pull the ripcord at about 4,000 feet.
3. *Tandem jump:* You and a tandem-master are strapped together for the duration of the jump. The tandem-master wears a really big chute, under which you both free-fall for thirty seconds, then float to the ground. (HFD) After flight, there's fight.

How to Fight

For a species whose chronicle is an annotated timeline connecting the dots of war, we are remarkably inept at arguing, confronting, fighting. When we do it as nations, we wreck the real estate and kill the kids. Amazingly, we're better at waging wars than we are at squabbling with the neighbors. Why? War is history. Arguing is rumor. Whole volumes have been written on how to fight a war, but there's nary a word in print about backyard battles or how to get even with the guy in the next cubicle or the yahoo down at the Texaco. We flap and shout at the wife, toss verbal grenades at the pool guy, and invite the elderly man in the right lane to pull over for a little fisticuffs, all without the slightest idea of what we hope to gain, and what kind of investment we'll have to make to obtain our goal. We're so bad at confrontation that some people go into a rage simply because they've been confronted.

That's going to change, right now, starting with the **Main Thing** to know before you go into battle:

YOU'VE GOT TO HAVE A PLAN, OR YOU CAN'T WIN A WAR.

This is where everybody goes dumb. When we fight with the guy next door or with the holy mother of our sacred children, half the time, we don't even know why we're fighting. We almost never know what we want to win. And we rarely go into battle with a plan. It doesn't work like that in the real world. When nations go to war, somebody makes a plan, because without a plan, you're a POW before you start. You didn't see the Allies doing this kind of thing on the beach at Normandy, did you? Do you think Eisenhower went into war with a note from FDR reading, "Dear Ike: When you get to France, please catch all the Nazis you can find and beat 'em up bad." No. Ike had a strategy, one that took into account not only what sort of victory he ultimately needed to win, but what kind of battles he'd have to fight along the way.

FIGHT TYPES

That's the way to go to war, packing a plan. The first thing you need to know is what kind of war you're going to fight. Here's a little martial pecking order of the battles most of us fight, along with a few notes on how to actually win some of them:

The Tiff

On a guess, let's say 73 percent of all fights have no specific cause. For example, you argue with your wife because it's just a bad day for you and a bad day for her. Or you got up too early, and a guy cut you off on the expressway on the way home. Or your feet hurt. Anything like that can set off what we all must recognize as the mildest form of personal warfare: the basic tiff.

- *A tiff has no specific form.* It has no object and it has no focus. It's like gray on a rainy day. Nobody wins tiffs, because there's no capital city to bomb, no flag to capture. What can you expect to get out of winning a tiff? The most you can hope for is an oral pronouncement by your opponent that you are a good person and he is not. That's why nobody takes tiffs seriously. Nothing's really at stake.
- *The solution:* Your best bet is to ignore a tiff. You can only emerge the victor by not becoming embroiled. But if you can't do that, up the tiff one notch to a grudge.

The Grudge

A grudge is the guerrilla war of personal confrontation. Here's how it works: Your neighbor puts his really tacky garden gnome right on the property line. You know it's right on the line, because in the middle of the night, you went outside with the property deed and paced off the yardage across the front lawn. You hate the gnome. But what you hate most is that the gnome's little elbow actually protrudes across the boundary and invades your air space. This makes you crazy, but not crazy enough to actually do anything about it. Instead, every time you talk to the guy next door, you satisfy yourself by making a little dig and smugly laugh that dry, bitter inner laugh. Trouble is, you're the one obsessing about the violating elbow. The neighbor doesn't even know about it. As far as he's concerned, he's done you a favor by decorating his front yard. Remember, some people actually like gnomes.

- *The solution:* To win at a grudge, personalize the conflict. You don't care about the gnome, I mean really. You just don't like the guy next door. If he was a nice guy and a sport with the brewskis, you'd think his gnome was cute. You'd buy a hula skirt for his gnome. You'd give it a name—maybe Ted Koppel. But hate the guy, hate his gnome. With this realization, you have three options: (1) You can forget the gnome, knowing that the gnome-monger next door is just one more drop in an ocean of people you really don't like. (2) You can turn down the heat by arguing with your neighbor about the gnome, thereby downgrading the grudge to a petty bicker. (3) You can upgrade the grudge to a full-fledged vendetta.

The Vendetta

A vendetta is a grudge grown to rich, ripe, full maturity. Vendettas are better than bickers and grudges because you can actually win a vendetta. Let's say your current business partner and ex-best friend, Lou, got a little tipsy on Saturday and made a pass at your wife and she said, "Fine with me." Then, on Sunday, she confessed everything and begged you for forgiveness. On Monday, and on every day after that, you have to go to work and face Lou, who of course feigns nonstop innocence. This is the stuff of which vendettas are traditionally made, because you never forget what your old pal did, ever, and the longer he delays begging for atonement, the more you despise him.

- *The solution:* The good news? A vendetta practically demands a strategy: You hatch a long-term, highly complex plan to repay Lou for his transgression. Your object: Lou's utter humiliation. Nothing less will do. You seem to accept his good-natured bantering, and you seem to gullibly swallow his protestations of palhood. Eventually, he tells you about his date with Marcia in sales. You pretend to be interested, and he spills the beans— *which you calmly gather and present to his wife and her lawyer.*

  The bad news? Well, it's a bad-news doubleheader. First off, you have to live with a vendetta every day. It's like bringing home a stupid dog, with bad breath, on purpose. Also, there's always the excellent chance that if Lou's six-four, two-fifty, and he gets wind of your plan, he'll come up to you one day in the employee cafeteria and toss you through the Coke machine. What do you do then? Instant upgrade to fistfight—a vendetta on fast-forward.

The Fistfight

Fistfights are the ugly details of war. Put a whole bunch of fistfights together, and you've got another Vietnam. Therefore, because a punch-out is a conflict with real limits—how much you can take, how much you can dish out— there's an opportunity here for more sophisticated strategizing than with a simple vendetta.

The solution: There's more than one. You can fake, flank, or flail. In fact, one good strategy for surviving a fistfight in which you really aren't the favorite: Feign insanity. Just go berserker. Before you make your strategy, though, take a quick measure of what's at stake. If it's just an embarrassment thing, in which you're worried your coworkers might think you're a wuss, then don't be stupid. Surrender. Retreat. Weep. Or start preaching the Bible's good news. However, if the guy you're fighting is a lunatic with a knife in the hallway, and the safety of your wife or children is on the line, then fight to win, hesitate at nothing, cheat, kick, gouge, fight like a rabid wolverine. Many assaults are abandoned by the bad guy when he realizes the price of victory is just too high.

KNOW YOUR ENEMY

Once you've got a sense of what kind of battle you're going to be fighting, size up your opponent. Every general knows that finding a perfect strategy depends not only on the fruit of his own sweet inspiration but also on determining the exact nature of his enemy. For example:

Your Wife

Nature of conflict: Temporary disruption of long-term alliance.

Strategic complexity: High.

Special problems: You can't fight to win, and you can't hit, and half the time you also have to figure out what she's mad about, and all the time you have to frame her argument in terms acceptable to masculine logic. Also, you have to sleep with her when the dust settles.

Best bet to win: Try to surrender. There's a fifty-fifty shot she won't let you.

Your Boss

Nature of conflict: Class struggle.

Strategic complexity: Varies.

Special problems: You can only fight as long as your boss says you can, since, any time he wishes, he can utter the two words that not only put a stop to the argument, but also say, "I win, you lose" in any language: "You're fired."

Best bet to win: Make the conflict revolve around issues affecting your boss's best interests, not yours.

A Coworker

Nature of conflict: Darwinian battle to determine who is fittest for corporate survival.

Strategic complexity: As high as you want to go.

Special problems: This is a classic struggle. You are everything that is good and true. The guy who ratted on you to the boss is the embodiment of all evil for all time. You are England, 1940. He is Germany, 1939.

Best bet to win: Surprise attack.

A Corporation

Nature of conflict: Jihad.

Strategic complexity: High.

Special problems: You can't really fight a fair fight with AT&T. It's like fighting with Iranians or bureaucrats. They don't care if you're right and they're wrong. Go ahead, they say, go to Sprint. We don't care. We're AT&T. You mean nothing to us, they say, even though you wrote all those letters trying to get them to admit they were wrong, and even though you sent them copies of the canceled checks, and never even got a reply. Does this sound personal yet?

Best bet to win: Bide your time and eventually you'll be able to capitalize on an opportunity to cost them more than they are costing you.

A Bill Collector

Nature of conflict: Frontal assault.

Strategic complexity: Low.

Special problems: You need to decide quickly what you want to win. So choose: The war? Or the battle? If you want to win the war, do whatever it takes to buy time. One way: Tell him you'll put your reason for not paying in writing. If you want to win the battle, however, pull out the ridicule howitzers and light up. Tell him that you don't know what you'll be doing tomorrow or next week or next year, but that you know what he'll be doing: He'll be on the telephone, talking to people who hate him, who despise everything he stands for. Also tell him that this is the best job he'll ever have. Then tell him this conversation is his professional high point. Then call the credit bureau, give the clerk your Social Security number, and yell, "Incoming!"

The Guy Next Door

Nature of conflict: Geopolitical.

Strategic complexity: Low.

Special problems: The great thing about fighting with the neighbors is you can do it as long as you want, with whatever intensity strikes you as amusing, and, unless you actually say something, nobody even knows you're fighting, including the neighbor. Best bet to win: Well, you could always get a dog.

Note: Neighbor-bashing is an especially effective way to bring your own family closer together. There's nothing quite like huddling alone in a neighborhood full of strangers alienated from each other by muted hatred to really pump some life into those tired family values.

KEEP A LID ON YOUR EMOTIONS

Despite the great pleasure it would give you to win the battle, you're better off winning the war. And you can't do that by blowing steam. According to a lawyer correspondent, you will lose every battle, no matter what, if you permit your temper to determine your course. The key to surviving conflict is to floor it along the road to confrontation without allowing your emotions to grab the steering wheel. That means the first fight you have to wage is against your own temper, the devilish author of your ultimate dishonor, and the thing that will make you forget that in every conflict, you're undone if you can't remember why you're right and the other guy's wrong. *If your anger starts to rise, keep your eye on the ball:* Focus on exactly what it is you wish to win. The lawyer's favorite temper suppressors? "Concentrate on keeping your voice as low as possible, forswear swearing, and suggest that some of your opponent's points are 'interesting,' even if they aren't. Makes 'em crazy when you do that." Deal with everything else—all the yelling, pushing, pouting—as simply factors. "Remember," the lawyer says, "all their accusations are just stuff. But the war is what you want to win. That's the only thing that isn't stuff. That's the whole game." (RHWa)

11. Women

We admit women are smarter than men, cuter than men, and more sensitive than men. In fact, we admit that women are superior beings in every way. There's only one thing we really want to know:

How to Become a Sex Object

You'd think, after all the careful scrutiny we have given to sex objects, we'd have a better idea how to be one ourselves, yes? No. Men are so convinced that they ought to be the sex subject of a sex object that they never give women a chance to objectify them. Alas, objectification is what separates friends from lovers.

Besides, sometimes our goals are not so lofty. Sometimes, all we want is to drive women insane with desire. Is that so much to ask? Not at all, not at all. The trick is to make the woman you love stop seeing you as a thinking, feeling, complex person with hopes and dreams and fears, and start seeing you as a sex object, a simple tool for doing a simple job.

Becoming a sex object is something within the grasp of Everyman. Here are five paths to objectification—along with more than a dozen object lessons—all of which will help you help others.

Caution: Each path is paved in peril. This is one more time when the end doesn't necessarily justify the means.

- **Path 1: The Path of Least Insistence**
- **Path 2: The Path of Most Insistence**
- **Path 3: The Path of Coexistence**
- **Path 4: The Path of Charitable Assistance**
- **Path 5: The Aisle.**

Five paths, one goal: To get what you want out of a bedroom, other than a good night's sleep. Now, that's an object worth striving for.

FIRST PATH: DON'T TRY SO HARD

According to modern psychologists, men are motivated strongly by two easy-to-confuse commodities: money and sex. It's easy to see how an average man can mix these up. Money, after all, has a wonderful look and feel all its own. It's great to get a lot of money whenever you want, plus no matter how much you have or how often you get it, somebody else's money always looks better than yours. Also, you fool around with too much of it, you could get in trouble. You don't know where it's been.

While sex shares most of these qualities, most men find it easy to tell sex from money because it's often easier to get rich than it is to get laid. The reason for this is simple, but exquisitely unjust. Most men have been taught, rightly, that if you work very hard to make money, you'll eventually get it. This lesson, unhappily, is nontransferable when applied to romance, for if you work very hard to get sex, you'll die a virgin.

Case Study: Mr. F

Take a friend of ours, Mr. F. F lives in a swank Southern metropolis. After fleeing California when a relationship turned unexpectedly serious, F drifted through a half-dozen Eastern cities, pausing once in New York where he enjoyed, he said, "a certain kind of relationship" with a beautiful artist in a car parked in an alley, and once in Baltimore, where he was found in a cocktail lounge unable to handle his alcohol because the two women between whom he was sandwiched wouldn't take his hands from their laps. When he arrived in Dixieville, he was, he said, "automatically given women when I crossed the city line." After a monumental swivefest, he finally had to take a breather because he clocked himself in the noggin on a side table while performing some libidinal legerdemain. "Now I'm thinking about buying a house," he said when he came to, "and filling it with a wife and kids." Alas, he added, "good women are too easy to find."

All women love Mr. F, and, as a consequence, Mr. F is having sex for all the rest of us. Why? F understands that women are immensely interested in men who are pleasant, charming, witty, and, above all, pleased to be in their company without any expectations. "I guess sex just never crosses my mind," F said. "But it's nice when it crosses theirs." By not making women into sex objects, F allows them the liberty of making him into one, and he hates to disappoint.

Lessons of the First Path

- *Love overpacks,* so courtship can come with a lot of extra baggage. You don't always have to do all the heavy lifting, however.
- In the cafeteria of love, *there is such a thing as a free lunch.*
- *You usually get more than you need* if you don't ask for anything at all.

The First Path Downside

Mr. F (the example used in our case study) is miserable because he's no closer to a stable relationship than he was the day he first said "Howdy" to his sex life.

"This makes a quarter century of living like this," says F. "Maybe it's time I grew up or something."

SECOND PATH: GIVE IT EVERYTHING YOU'VE GOT

There is another side to the argument presented by Mr. F (for those of you who have trod completely through the first path). It's the one that says, if it isn't worth begging for, it isn't worth having.

An explanation: In the rhetoric of professional sports, nothing quite says nothing like the pitcher or the quarterback who, when asked how he did what he did, says, "I just do my best, I give it all I got, I give it 100 percent, I'm just glad to be out there." That's understatement. What the fellow means is that he brings to his chore a focused wholeness of desire, a burning need to succeed, a gut-bottom, soul-selling, white-hot, do-or-die intensity to achieve, without which his life will cease to have meaning.

This can work. Sometimes women, like men, lead lives of homogenized predictability—stark, unadorned, unfurnished, one-bedroom existences that cry out for a little ornamentation. Suddenly, there's a voice in the hall, a knock at the door. She opens it, and it's a maniac interior decorator with Day-Glo spray cans in each hand. Next thing you know, her life looks like a Jimi Hendrix poster.

Case Study: El Coyote

A man whom we shall call the Coyote is a master of blitzkrieg lovecraft. Every encounter with a woman has a tactical dimension, every handshake lingers a little too long, every first glance is just a tad overfilled with nuance. Coyote sees an attractive woman, and he immediately thinks, "Road Runner." All of a sudden, huge, cast-iron safes full of romance are tumbling out of the sky, there are explosives everywhere, and, without being asked to, he's running off the edge of cliffs into thin air. Sometimes, a woman, bored with too much prime-time TV, sees this sort of behavior, says, "What the hell?" and is swept up into a pyrotechnical scene in which she realizes she's done all the things she swore she'd never do, including that Polaroid thing. So two weeks, two months later, she's saying, "Beep, beep," and vanishing into the landscape in a cloud of dust.

Mr. Coyote has winter wives and summer brides, but no relationship that stretches across more than two major holidays, for nothing can stand up to such an acute level of stress. That's why ball games last only nine innings. When it's over, it's over. But until then, the Coyote is 100 percent sex object and just glad to be out there.

Lessons of the Second Path

There are some things to be learned here, by the rocket's red glare:

- *If you're going to be a grizzly, be a bear.* There's no sense hoping some woman is going to grab you by the lapels of your sensitivity suit and rip your clothes off. Go naked.
- *Get rhythm.* If you want a romance to hip-hop, don't beat out a waltz.
- *Never sprint* if you're running a marathon.

The Second Path Downside

When it's over, it's over. But the problem, says the Coyote (of our case study), is that "every relationship I have is over, even before it's over, if you know what I mean."

Unfortunately, we know.

THIRD PATH: IF YOU CAN'T LICK 'EM, JOIN 'EM

We're surrounded by women, just "eat up in girls," as one writer put it. Their very ubiquity creates a certain demographic twist, in that most of the time, half the people we're with are the very people who can cause us greatest joy and profound anguish. It's the joy part you want.

So get to know them. Despite media-driven drivel, many women don't respond to overt empathy. In the real world, women and men like their partners to conform to comfortable stereotypes. But there are still plenty of women out there who are attracted to *hombres con mucho sensitivismo*, or weeping men who read their souls.

Case Study: Mr. Bill

Take, for our case study example, a chap of recent acquaintance whom we shall call Mr. Bill.

Mr. Bill isn't the most handsome guy, and while he can outwit his dinner, he's not a genius by any stretch. As a teenager, he was foiled in romance, just like the rest of us. Couldn't get to first base. But, in college in the 1960s, he learned that women, as dates, liked men who liked Women, as a movement. So he would take his dates to Germaine Greer lectures and feminist rallies. With the warm, cozy fires of the sexual revolution crackling in the background, he'd seek to raise the consciousness of his women friends, and when he heard women talking about how deeply moved they'd been by other women, he would feel the big wave of empathy smack him in the chops, and he'd weep, right out loud.

Women dug it. Mr. Bill was suddenly surrounded with women. Some of them looked a little on the earnest side, but some were pretty good looking, and some of them were also smarter than him—and capable of earning lots more money than he could—so he married one of those.

Mr. Bill is now a well-known man, and some women—total strangers, mind you—dream about him, nasty stuff, too. To them, he is a dreamboat, a sex object.

Lessons of the Third Path
- *Do whatever it takes,* so long as it's worth whatever you get.
- *Women who get serious* about sexual politics can also get serious about sex.
- *Even apparently humorless women* can take a joke for better or worse, for richer or poorer.

The Third Path Downside
You marry the woman, you marry the politics. When a third-path woman yells, "NOW!" you have to check whether she means the movement or the motion.

FOURTH PATH: LET WOMEN MAKE YOU A MAN
Men are often at odds with each other. Contentious from birth, men strive to vanquish one another, or, failing that, to find a quiet corner where other men will leave them alone. In commerce, this sort of thing is essential, since the game has been structured to be won, not to be tied. But in terms of the inner guy, where hope, self-esteem, and doubt all live in a troubled neighborhood, men wrestle with themselves, and women are the referees, the ones who decide who's a winner and who's a loser.

Case study: Q
Take, for instance, a stockbroker whom we'll call Q, because of his extraordinary skill at snooker, billiards, and pool. Q lived a life of limitless success, moneywise. Q had the helium touch: He was apparently forbidden by fate from choosing a stock that was capable of downward movement. He was also a reasonably handsome man. Yet, he was filled with doubts. He would ask his friends hideous questions: "Do I seem stupid?" or "What can I talk about to make me seem important?" His friends were mortified for him, and so, of course, were the women he dated, since he sought from them some creepy affirmation, and they were the one place where it wasn't available.

One day, he met a woman whom he thought unattainable. His friends agreed, since she was obviously smart and confident and scenic. Remarkably, and to the immense confusion of his friends, the beauty liked Q. Was it the money? We'll never know, for eventually, they married, and Q settled down with his wife and his new, confident, interesting, concerned self. His friends watched this transformation in fear, but the marriage was apparently sound. Eventually, several of Q's friends pinned him in the pinball corner of a barroom and asked him how he had done it. "I didn't," Q said. "She did. She would pick a fight with me whenever I asked those stupid questions, the ones that made me look so lame. The fight would be about something else, something that didn't have anything to do with my doubts. Then she'd let me win the argument."

Q's wife refused to let him slip into full-nelson dorkness. In his new, more masculine wardrobe, he's her sex object.

Lessons of the Fourth Path

- *Women's work:* Some women know that if they want a man made right, they'd better make him themselves.
- *It's one thing to be a man among men.* It's another to be a man among women.
- *A mojo is like money.* If you have to ask whether or not you've got mojo, you haven't got it.

The Fourth Path Downside

What a good woman builds, an angry woman can tear down. If you want to make yourself a man, make it a do-it-yourself project.

FIFTH PATH: COMMIT TO IT

For many women—especially the ones you'd most like to have treat you as a sex object—nothing greases the slip-n'-slide into the bedroom quite like a well-planned marriage ceremony. There's something in the cake that just makes a woman downright agreeable. If you need a case study to illuminate this timeless truth, your problems are bigger than any solution you'll find on the Web.

Not only that, but *the lessons of the Fifth Path* won't quite fit a list. They just show up every now and then over the course of a lifetime. One small lesson does recur, however: You may think you're strolling down paths one, two, three, or four, only to turn a corner and find yourself on five. Incredible.

The Downside

There's as much downside as you can fit in a lawyer's office. That's the bad news. But the good news is that there's always more upside than there is downside—even if you have to live through a pile of downside to get up.

You can reduce the downside of the Fifth Path by following simple numbers:

- *Fifty percent.* Cohabitation before marriage increases the chances of divorce by as much as 50 percent.

- *Eight years.* If you marry somebody, close your eyes, shut your mouth, and hang around for eight years. Statistically, marriages that last eight years have a terrific chance of lasting a lifetime.
- *One kid* is all it takes to make a couple into a family, and marriages with children have a higher success rate than childless marriages. (RMcEl)

How to Find Women

Marrying women, that's easy. It's finding them that's tough. Smarter than a grouse and much harder to track, women are everywhere except when you need one. In order to mate with women properly, thus furthering the species, is it not more productive to study their habits, to learn to observe and interact with them in their own natural settings? One outrageous correspondent thinks so.

With his help, we've assembled *The Women of North America: A Field Guide.* Taking a page from ancient Indian lore, from the *Boy Scout Handbook,* from the Mark Trail comic strip, from John Audubon, and, apparently, from our own correspondent's extensive experiences hunting ring-necked pheasants, we've determined that the North American female *Homo sapiens,* the most desirable of the species, is to be found in the following times, places, and incarnations.

CLASSIFICATION: GREAT SPOTTED OF SWARTHMORE
- *Habit:* Owl-like. Nocturnal/very difficult to flush during the day.
- *Plumage:* Cashmere cardigan with the sleeves pushed up, jeans, glasses, white T-shirt, sneakers, auburn hair.
- *Sighting:* Friday night, 9:30 P.M., the video store. She couldn't care less that she doesn't have a date. The last three guys who asked her out didn't have an opinion on Jane Alexander's first year as the head of the National Endowment for the Arts. She's renting *Jules and Jim.*
- *Rules of engagement:* The Pentium chip is in there somewhere, so you watch your butt. If you're man enough, grab a copy of *La Dolce Vita,* tell her you're embarrassed you've never seen it, but you'd like to know what she thinks of Mastroianni's role.

CLASSIFICATION: VALLEY KINGFISHER
- *Habit:* Diurnal/nocturnal when necessary.
- *Plumage:* Well-defined triceps, calves, and lats, frosted hair, gilt Rolex Oyster, pink-and-white "L.A. Style" aerobics shoes, Vuitton tote.

- *Spoor:* Sweat running down the back of her crisscrossed sport bra.
- *Consumes:* Evian water, antioxidants, stress complex, RU486.
- *Sighting:* The health club, Saturday morning, 10 A.M.
- *Rules of engagement:* Like bald eagles and other raptors, kingfishers—also known as "Trophy Wives"—know how to go on fishing expeditions to bring home the big salmon. That's what the killer workout is about. She could wipe the squash court with your carcass. But the fact is, unless you happen to be Ted Turner, Roone Arledge, or T. Boone Pickens, don't bother. You'd just be making her late for her tennis lunch at the other club to which she belongs, where the really big salmon frolic in the streams.

CLASSIFICATION: HOUSE MARTIN

- *Habit of movement:* Diurnal only/total exhaustion prevents nocturnal activity.
- *Sighting:* Saturday morning, 11 A.M., the supermarket checkout line.
- *Distinctive markings:* Anything she could find that is relatively clean. No time for makeup. Brown bags under eyes.
- *Vocal manner:* Shrill. Imperative.
- *Rules of engagement:* Whether or not she has a career in addition to this, she will be toting the kids around on Saturday morning to bring food into the larder. She will also be checking you out with a mixture of suspicion (you belong to the same vile subspecies that produced her husband) and curiosity (she'll be wondering how you'd hold up). Your job is to be real nice. Cede your place in line to her. Compliment her children. Women, no matter how long in this state, are always slightly upset at their own false impression that they're not fabulous, when, of course, they are. So flirt with her. The basic rule here is to show her compassion without making it look like outright pity. After all, she needs all the help she can get: Yes, she's smart; yes, she's very pretty. But she's also married to somebody a lot like you.

CLASSIFICATION: BROWN BRYN MAWR CREEPER

- *Habit:* Completely diurnal, with exceptions for Shawn Colvin concerts.
- *Plumage:* Shetland sweaters, white turtlenecks, corduroys, usually a good spread on the rear end, owing to lots of sedentary poring over dusty manuscripts, and lots of footwear ordering out of the L.L. Bean catalog.
- *Sightings:* Late afternoon, the bookstore.
- *Rules of engagement:* Fine words should strike terror in your heart—Bryn Mawr College Archaeology Department. How's your ancient Greek, dude?

CLASSIFICATION: WASHINGTON SNIPE

- *Habit:* Diurnal/nocturnal when husband wears black tie.
- *Sighting:* Saturday, 3 P.M., the farmers' market. She's buying organic mesclun for the dinner with Tony and his new wife tonight. Tony's doing that analysis of the former Soviet Union for Merrill Lynch.
- *Plumage:* Rolex, but not an aspiring Rolex (see Valley Kingfisher, 2 above). It will be a settled, satisfied, solid, happy Rolex. Missoni scarf. Ferragamo tote. Bulgari cuff.
- *Nesting characteristics:* Weekend nanny, silver Volvo 960, Gordon setter.
- *Rules of engagement:* Haven't you gotten your invitation from the Clintons to the Hilton Head Heritage weekend this year?

CLASSIFICATION: GROUPING CRANE

- *Habits:* Nocturnal, except when at Canyon Ranch.
- *Sighting:* Saturday, 10:30 P.M., Stanley and Kiki's annual bash.
- *Plumage:* One skintight and very short black miniskirt, sheer black stockings (garters visible), vertiginous heels.
- *Rules of engagement:* Stanley and Kiki know the damnedest people, which is of course why you go to these things. But make no mistake: This creature's emphasis on her legs is no joke. She is fleet. She differs from the kingfisher in that she is not interested in settling down. Anywhere. She has a little black book and can drop a dime and be out of here, in the passenger seat of a number of Ferraris, within minutes. Unless you happen to be the leader of a rock group with a current number one.

CLASSIFICATION: PROFESSIONAL PETREL

- *Habit:* Diurnal/clumsily nocturnal when trying to build nonexistent social life.
- *Plumage:* Anne Klein or Donna Karan suits, white collars, pearls.
- *Sighting:* Monday morning, 8:30 A.M., your lawyer's office. You stroll in expecting to be met by Chuck, your longtime barrister, carrying your files. Instead, she marches in, says she's taking over, and proceeds to ask you, point for point, why you haven't yet done what you were about to tell Chuck that you thought it was time to do.
- *Rules of engagement:* She's going to be more effective than three of sedate old Chuck could ever hope to be. And if you're going to go after this with anything but clean, crisp business intentions, get organized.

CLASSIFICATION: CALIFORNIA GULL

- *Habit:* Whatever.
- *Plumage:* Print dress, not too overt but not too covert, flats, a sweater draped over her chair.
- *Forage:* Cappuccino.
- *Sightings:* Wednesday, 2:45 P.M., upscale coffee bar, Westwood. Then 5:15 P.M., Pacific Coast Highway, Tracker, top down.
- *Speaks:* French or Italian.
- *Rules of engagement:* You are just going to have to get used to it; they are younger, faster, smarter, and take less crap off you than ever before. Their times are closing in the marathon, too. Ever get the sense that they just tolerate us? But true danger brings its own kind of bliss. She is going to be absolutely unafraid of pursuing her ends to get you, if that's what she decides she wants. She may, while sitting there waiting for you to come up with a line that isn't too lame, be planning some small child's education.

CLASSIFICATION: ROUGH-WINGED JERSEY SHORE SWALLOW

- *Habit:* Primarily diurnal/nocturnal when Springsteen or Southside Johnny is playing the local arena.
- *Sighting:* Tuesday, 11 A.M., the gas station, as she fills your Cherokee with 92-rated octane.
- *Plumage:* Timberland boots, brown pump-attendant/dead-basketball-coach pants. Maybe she even has one of those short-sleeved striped shirts with her name tag sewn on the left breast, and a little gold Shell patch on the other breast. Her brother killed a lot of deer last year, and some of the antlers are on the wall behind the register there.
- *Forage:* Tequila, jalapeños in her scrambled eggs, lots of sausage.
- *Rules of engagement:* Whoo-ee baby. Doesn't it feel, well, strangely good when she inserts the nozzle into your tank? Now you understand what Clinton was doing down in Arkansas all those years.

CLASSIFICATION: CURVE-BILLED SEATTLE THRASHER

- *Habit:* Exclusively nocturnal.
- *Plumage:* Logging boots, torn Lakers shirt, leather jacket, miniskirt, broken nails, nose ring.

- *Forage:* Black coffee, rare hamburgers with fried onions, strawberry milkshakes, Camel straights, vodka.
- *Rules of engagement:* Quick, what is Kurt Cobain's widow's band called? What charges did Snoop Doggy Dogg face? And while we're at it, when was the last time you got dressed to go out at 1 A.M.? (WB)

How to Tell if a Woman Likes You

Women's feelings of attraction to men are a little like the centrifugal clutch on a Subaru Justy: They start out just fast enough to get you going, catch up with you halfway down the stretch, and don't really hit top end until you're ready to stop. That means a woman's feelings toward you are manifested differently, according to where you are in the relationship.

- *It's a very straightforward deal:* She's attracted to you if she's still talking to you even though she doesn't have to. There are other symptoms of positive feminine response: Laughing at your lame jokes, touching your arm or leg when she talks to you, asking you about your incredibly dull job down at the gas works. We discuss at length, immediately below, the intrinsic meaning of extended, direct eye contact. If she does any of these things, you can safely ask her out for a first date.
- *Postdate reevaluation:* After you take her home, you have to reevaluate the deal. If you want to spend another four hours with her, and you think she wants to do the same with you, then call her up. You can figure a woman's attracted to you if she says she'd like to put herself through the whole thing again and go out to dinner next Saturday. (JSE)

Bear in mind, however: **This is the start of a trajectory toward nudity that may or may not be interrupted by a marriage ceremony.** The whole course of a courtship is a constant escalation of mutual superficial attraction. We say "superficial" because you never really know whether or not a woman's feelings toward you are situational and subject to change without notice. In order to tell if a woman's really attracted to you, wait until she has your second child. Then you can figure you've got her attention for good, more or less.

THE RULE OF DOUBLE EYE CONTACT ON A SINGLE OGLE

Sometimes, trying to figure a woman's unstated intention can require a bit more deliberate analysis. For example: What does it mean when you're ogling a woman and she catches you at it and instead of looking away, returns a direct stare, not once, but *twice*?

- **The elements** of this case are simple:

  Two guys.

  A mall.

  An escalator.

  Two women.

  One ogle.

  Two eye contacts.

- **The details:** A sunny day, but brisk. Two friends decide to meet for lunch at a downtown enclosed shopping mall. There's a quick dash into a Brooks Brothers outlet, where a suit is purchased within three minutes. Then there's lunch.

  The dining area at the mall is one of those American adaptations of a Euro-trough, the standard street café, where people sit and look at other people until they are caught, at which time they stare intently at their corned beef sandwiches. Next to the café is an escalator, and next to the descending half of the escalator is where our two chaps encamp for a quick bite. One guy is married, and he has his back to the escalator. He can't see anything, girl-wise. The other guy is single, and he can see everything. The escalator practically dumps shoppers at his feet.

  The conversation is a heavily fragmented one. The married man, his back to the scenery, is talking about media coverage of the deficit. The single guy is frequently distracted by the sudden appearance and descent of one or another metropolitan beauty. In the middle of a sentence, typically, the bachelor clams up, raises one eyebrow in a sullen smolder, and, frankly, *ogles*. He's been doing this for years, of course, and his scan is a well-practiced one. As a face man, he starts there. The face is his screening device. Bad face, back to the deficit. Good face, go directly to the shoes. He ogles like a bibliophile, like a man who knows exactly which details and nuances create desirability, and which ones are fatal flaws. The married guy waits patiently for the appraisal.

- **Let's digress for a moment to consider the narcissistic corollary:** Men ogle not to fantasize about women, but to see how they measure up as men.

  The mall ogler's pastime is not a gender-specific one, of course. Women ogle as much as the next guy. Usually, they ogle other women, although since their mission in ogling is essentially fact gathering—why did she wear that scarf? you call that eyeshadow? nice pumps—it may be demeaning to ogling to call it ogling. Women sometimes ogle men. That's ogling. Ogling is when you look at somebody in an effort not so much to evaluate the person being ogled, but to evaluate your own ogling self. For example, a man looks at a woman crossing the street. He ogles her. Generally—and there are certainly exceptions to this corollary—he is making a precise calculation that involves this equation: Beauty plus availability divided by self-image equals relative worth of ogler. There are many tiny variables that can nudge the ultimate solution one way or another. For instance, you might look at a beautiful passerby and find she is almost certainly out of range of your ability to attract women. Maybe the self-image part of the equation is just too low, or her beauty + availability number is just too high. But then you say to yourself, "Sure, that's now. But with a dash of Rogaine, a few years on Somali-Fast, and a Samsonite full of C-notes, she'd be at my feet." Suddenly, your projected self-image numbers rise, and you find it more and more likely not only that she could be yours (if you really wanted) but that maybe you wouldn't have time for her, what with all the other women around.

But back to the double eye-contact on a single ogle rule. When a normal guy is ogling, part of what he's actually doing is just thinking about what politely might be called a relationship. But sometimes in ogling, as in all relationships, things sort of sneak up on you. After a burger-and-fries worth of idle ogling, the single guy suddenly pales. "I got eye contact," he says tensely, almost grimly. "No, wait. That's it." His voice drops to a burdened whisper. "I got *double* eye contact."

Significance of Double Eye Contact on a Single Ogle

- *This response is a gesture of commitment* more meaningful than many marriages. When a woman returns an ogle with a mere single glance, it can mean anything. Might mean: What's-he-staring-at-is-there-toilet-paper-on-my-shoe? Might mean: Let's-see-what-kind-of-jerk-I'm-dredging-off-the-bottom-of-the-gene-pool-today. Might mean: Make-a-move-and-I-call-the-cops. Hence, most men disregard the single glance to an ogle response. Single glances used to mean something. But with the widespread availability of go-go dancers, all of whom are quite accomplished in the art of making prolonged single-gesture eye contacts with oglers in bulk, a glance doesn't carry much weight anymore. A double glance in response to an ogle, how-ever, is something else. Double eye contact on a single ogle means this: I know you're watching me, and I think you're sort of marginally inter-esting, and I think I'll see what you're made of, buster.

So. You ogle. She does a double take. Now what do you do? If you look away, too stunned or embarrassed to continue ogling, you're scrapple. A guy too cowardly to stand up for his own ogle isn't much of a man in most women's books. But if you continue to ogle in the face of a double glance, the ball's back in her court. If she looks away, no point. If she smiles, you can figure you've been asked to politely identify yourself, your motives, your marital standing. If your papers are in order, you get permission to cross the line, to go the next step. Whatever that is.

OTHER OGLING SCENARIOS
The Never-Fail Principle of Bad Timing

- *Women almost never return an ogle until your wife or girlfriend is looking*—first at the woman, wondering who she's smiling at, then at you, when she figures it out.
- Because men ogle as a means of taking stock of themselves, they know *there's nothing intrinsically threatening* to the whole activity. Men don't ogle, after all, because they want to. They ogle because they have to. It's horrible. Call it ogle burden. It's what we do, and sometimes a man's gotta do what a man's gotta do.

That's why different men ogle in different ways. Involved men out with the objects of their involvement do an indirect ogle. They look around the supermarket as if they'd never seen anything quite like it before. Look at those lighting fixtures! they seem to be saying. And how about those metal shelving units! Their necks are suddenly rubberized for such occasions, and the fact that a clearly ogleable woman just happens to be in their line of sight is pure coincidence. That way, if the woman responds to the ogle with a smile, the guy can always look at his ferocious wife and shrug. Men know they can ogle their brains out and never get so much as a notice until one fine, spring day when an ogling kind of guy and his principal sugar-pie are out for a stroll. He tosses off an inconsequential ogle and presto! He gets a double—no! a triple—take in return. Then he starts explaining.

Competitive Ogling by Guys in Packs

A woman walks down the street, and there's a wild pack of oglers staring at her. She nervously glances over to make sure they aren't armed oglers, and instantly every man claims eye contact. "She was looking at me, man," one of them says, while the others produce documentary evidence refuting the claim.

- *A single-man ogle is a serious thing.* Women know that. That's why they never seem to respond.

The Law of the Knowing Glance

- *Here, the situation is reversed:* The woman is the ogler, and you are the oglee. There are two basic ways of handling this. One involves ignoring the ogle, a decision made after the all-important first glance. She ogles. You glance. In a nanosecond, you have to process a great deal of information, all of it effervescently superficial and exactly the kind of information on which men make all important decisions, like whether or nor to look again.
- *If you take the second look,* you might be well-advised to invoke the law of the knowing glance, which says an ogle is always trumped by a leer. In other words, you slowly look up and meet her gaze, while on your face you wear an expression that says, "Was that good for you?"

This has the effect of ram-injecting the encounter and giving it a NASA-level rate of acceleration. Suddenly, you're not just two strangers exchanging a goggles for gapes. You're on intimate terms, and with you, Mr. Mojo, in the driver's seat. You saw her ogle and raised her an innuendo. You can't lose. If she looks away, give her five minutes, and she'll ogle again. If she smiles, you can figure your glance was good enough that you can roll over and go to sleep. Either way, you'll have this encounter in the bag, if you'll pardon the play on words.

The Obviated Ogle Injunction

- *An ogle is diminished by overshadowing eccentricities.*

Let's say you're sitting alone in a subway car when a gaggle of art school painters' models—women who have been ogled with aesthetic passion—gets in. They're young, they're beautiful, and they stare right at you. But you're wearing a Santa suit and darning your socks. All ogles are off. No return glances are scored, and your self-image numbers are expressed in negatives.

How to Make Small Talk with Your Server

Speaking of direct eye contact, one nice thing about waitresses is they all look right at you, at least once. For waitresses, in general, this is just another plus. As we said up top, in the real world there are many things that women do better than men. It's when you get specific you get in trouble. Maybe women make better dentists or neurosurgeons, and maybe they make better firefighters and better fighter pilots. Maybe they don't. Who cares? But one thing's for sure: **No man on Earth slings a burger better than a babe.**

Hold it. Can we please catch you in midrecoil? We mean to cast no aspersions here on men or burgers or women—or babes, for that matter. But men are often confused by women as waitresses, so we only want to say that when a great-looking woman comes at you with a handsome pile of food in each hand, you're forgiven for thinking you're as close to the goddess as you're ever likely to be: You're looking at man's version of protowoman, Eve with a side order of apple, Salome with that head, Mom with lunch.

After all, a wide variety of men may admire a wide variety of women for a wide variety of reasons. But all us fellers agree that *no other combination of primary elements so clearly comes close to the gratification of every man's principal desires as a beautiful woman bearing food.* For the ugly truth is, we're hounds for chow and slaves for sex, and we can skip the brains and soul part if we really, *really* have to, no sweat. In fact, it is in our early, formative encounters with waitresses that we first confuse nature and nurture—men who were breastfed as babies, for instance, almost always marry waitresses—and after that, it takes a lifetime of lunches to get it all straight.

WHAT WE SEE WHEN WE SEE A WAITRESS

On one level, of course, we see future bank vice presidents and telejournalists, embalmers and actresses. We see hardworking mothers with kids and patient ex-wives with deadbeat ex-husbands. We see nurses without needles and divorcées without lawyers. But on another, shamefully intuitive level, we also see **temporary wives who make perfect flapjacks,** serve 'em up hot and with a spicy little quip, then get out of the way. All across this great land of ours, men are wolfing down hash like so many turbaned pashas, surrounded by a seraglio of women who allow sports pages on the table and don't go on about the dishes.

But remember, *inside every waitress is a woman who wants very much to be served.* This unfulfilled dream accounts for almost every surly waitress on the planet, because instead of men in waiter's suits bustling around with bottles of expensive bubbly, there's a counter-full of joes like you and me, and we quite obviously don't know how to behave.

HOW TO MAKE THE WAITRESS'S WORLD A BETTER PLACE

Waitresses ask so little—just three small things, really:

- *Whatever it is you were going to say, don't, because she's already heard it a million times.* In the course of a forty-hour week, a good-looking waitress hears every conceivable variation on the are-you-on-the-menu-sweetheart? theme. The sad fact: Waitresses generally only talk to men because if they didn't they'd get the order wrong.

• *Don't confuse food with favors.* In the feverish first blush of satiation, men sometimes confuse the message with the messenger and think that because the turkey's mighty friendly to an empty stomach, the turkey toter will give a similar satisfaction. In reality, of course, waitresses don't care how hungry you are. Waitresses are simply paid members of the serving profession—which is a long rung above the caring professions. Members of the clergy *care*. Social workers *care*. Waitresses *serve*. When it comes to animal desires, most men prize good service above genuine concern. When a man is hungry, he wants pot roast, not a sympathetic analysis of the root causes of his condition.

• *Always overtip.* Think about what a waitress goes through. Every embarrassment our gender can muster is displayed before a waitress at work, where the daily special's an all-you-can-take bad manners buffet. For minimum wage, she has to put up with you and cousin Larry, the guy who *always* asks a waitress what kind of pie she has. For her, life at work is like being a professional pedestrian working a construction site. Why is she wearing that tight, white, little, semitransparent dress? Because she wants us to admire her incredible body and applaud her good taste in lingerie? Yeah, sure, maybe. But maybe she wears that dress because the owner, a guy named Nick, told her she has to.

All this—for minimum wage, no benefits.

Her side of this stupendous deal requires her to act in good faith toward all comers, to treat all men as though they were gentlemen, and to chuckle indulgently when they aren't. Plus, she's expected to be nice when some putz rounds-*down* to an eight percent tip.

WHAT WAITRESSES WANT

Here, culled from actual interviews with actual waitresses, is the list of their secret desires, the things every waitress hopes to find in a customer:

• A nice guy who tips big.
• A funny guy who tips big.
• A handsome guy who tips big

Notice the common thread here? Right. They're all guys. Waitresses are notoriously heterosexual, apparently.

WHAT WAITRESSES KNOW

You don't hang out in a hash house all day without learning something. If we men could only master a little waitress lore, we'd all be smarter diners. Here is just a little of what a waitress knows:

• *Avoid out-of-state food.* This seems to apply especially to franchise restaurants, where, for the sake of consistency, food is prepared in Kitchen Central someplace on the far side of the continent, then frozen and shipped to local kitchens, where microwave ovens do all the heavy work. As one waitress noted, "Everybody freezes everything these days," and, besides, even bachelors can operate a microwave.

• *Don't eat the kitchen flotsam.* Make sure the day's big deals aren't just 'fridge cleaners like tuna chili or hot Spam medley. "We get rid of all our left-overs that way," a certain Wendy told me. Meatloaf and other processed-chow platters are favorite blue-plate candidates, and most waitresses won't warn you off, since to do so can cost them their job.

• *Churlish charm.* Waitresses are savvy when it comes to service. They're more prone to insist on attention, and they also claim to be better tippers. Most of them say a good waitress is a sign of a good restaurant. As one server reasoned: "If the people working in a place seem happy and friendly, then the owners of the restaurant must know something, since nobody's going to be happy working in a bad place, with bad food, mad customers, and no tips."

• *Truckstops attract trucks.* Once, you could follow a Freightliner right to chicken-fried-steak heaven. No more: Truck drivers are no longer a sign of good chow. There are too many reasons other than good grits—cheap diesel, some fleet credit arrangement, a need for a fax and a shower—for truck drivers to frequent a truckstop, and besides many are now part of nationwide chains. The new wisdom among waitresses is that places filled with old-fashioned nuke families, with a high-tipping pop at the helm feeling guilty for causing so much ruckus, are likely to be better bets for providing good food at a reasonable price. The only sure thing you're likely to find in a truckstop, one vet said, "is a lot of truck drivers." Another good measure: local license plates in the lot.

A FINAL NOTE CONCERNING WAITRESS-COURTSHIP

Every waitress's dream date involves food served by someone other than herself. Follow the rules in the next section.

How to Pitch Woo

Valentine's Day comes only once a year, but the aftershock of forgetting it can shake a romance all year long. So do it right.

- *Femme faves:* Romantic dinners, two dozen roses (one in the morning, one at night), a pro massage, a diamond engagement ring, a puppy, a weekend escape to a surprise-and-no-tell destination.
- *What to skip:* Chocolates, sappy cards, books of sappy poems, vinyl nighties, drinks at Club Les Gals, you in a loincloth, a video of *Steel Magnolias.* (AMcLL)

How Not to Pitch Woo

Never mind about the way she walks, the way she looks, and the color of her hair. She's not there. Here are four recent "offenses" that have landed men in sexual-harassment hell:

1. The SEC was successfully sued for sexual harassment after a number of office romances bloomed. The plaintiff? A woman lawyer who wasn't involved with anybody, but claimed the affairs conducted by others offended her. She was given back pay and a promotion.
2. A woman received cash and free shrink service after it was discovered that her name appeared in some men's room graffiti.
3. A grad student at Nebraska was given a reprimand after a female coworker complained he was creating a hostile environment by posting a photo of his wife in a bathing suit in his office.
4. After sleeping with her attorney not once, but *two hundred times* over an eighteen-month period, during which marriage was discussed, a woman in Rhode Island sued, claiming the lawyer had taken advantage of a client-attorney relationship and had therefore "coerced" her. (AMcLL)

How to Avoid Marriage

If staying single is what you consider to be a worthwhile goal, here're the best ways to ensure you'll be successful:

- *Be especially careful* between now and your twenty-ninth birthday. By then, half of all men have been married at least once.

- ***Don't get too lax*** after your twenty-ninth birthday, either. Or at least contain yourself until you turn thirty-five. At that point, if you have never been married, the odds are ten to one that you never will be.
- ***Until you turn thirty-five,*** you might consider spending all of your free time in bars and clubs, since almost no one ever meets a prospective mate in places like that.
- ***Places to avoid:*** schools, churches, and offices. In organizations specializing in social services and physical therapy, women outnumber men two to one. (GRE)

How to Justify Marriage

The only justification for marrying is children. No kids in the plan? Then why marry? Hang out, commit, talk, walk, watch TV together. But don't get married without a family plan. (Anon.)

How to Find a Wife

A pre-marital Main Thing: What you need to know before you go out looking for a wife is that you don't know what you need to know.

Explanation: Before marriage, the stuff about women that seems to count involves technical aspects such as the ideal 1:1.7 waist-to-hip ratio, high-yield child-feeding apparatus, and the outcome of an objective income-to-investment analysis. The latter is especially important; more men than ever are marrying for money, since more women than ever are making lots of the stuff.

But after marriage, all the stuff you thought was important fades into insignificance. One day, about six months into the marriage, you realize you could make up a whole new list of things that are important to defining a good wife, and that none of them were things you would have ever thought about when you were a bachelor.

Here, from a variety of sources and from a deep well of experience, is why:

- ***Most men marry women based on looks*** and, to a lesser extent, on income. Other, less important characteristics also enter into the picture, of course: You got your personality thing and your brains thing. Some men go the extra yard before marriage and inquire of their potential soulmates whether or not they'd like to have children and how they feel about NASCAR. Sex looms large. Among all the things we know we ought to look for in a wife, sexual compatibility seems like it should be the most important. But no, no, no, dear lads. It's *personality*—that much-dissed hallmark of the prototypically plain blind date—which may be the most important, or at least more important than we think.

• ***The List:*** Since we go shopping for a wife blinded by bachelorhood, what would our sighted brothers advise us we should look for? Well, take C. We all have a friend like C, a guy like any of us who somehow bamboozled a very attractive, very smart woman into marriage. C of course realized that the woman he was marrying was smart and attractive. Attractive and smart are neon-sign qualities. But the really great thing about C's wife is this: She's *capable*. Not just competent, which is a sort of limbo-pole standard of minimum acceptability. No, C's wife is outright *capable*. She is the sleek, smooth, energy-efficient engine that makes the marriage hum; she educates the children, handles the moolah, books the vacation. In our imagination, we see marriage that way—as a satisfying, somewhat blissful condition, decorated with adoring children and plenty of good chow. Plop a very beautiful but completely incompetent woman in that picture, and you have a bad snapshot of a marriage carelessly made. Capability, after all, is an estimable virtue, something a smart guy wants in a plumber or a urologist. But it's a quality that isn't even on the chart for most men as they stalk the planet in search of wives. Too bad, as some fellows find out later.

• ***Here's a list of five other no-see-ums in the big woods of bachelorhood.*** When it comes to matrimony, these are the things you didn't even know you needed. To estimate how far beyond your over-the-horizon radar these virtues are, simply substitute the quality listed for the blank space in this sentence: "Sure, she's smart, she's rich, and she's incredibly good looking, but will you please just check out her [blank]?"

1 *Mutual fund portfolio.* When you're courting a woman, retirement is such a touchy subject. You wine her, you dine her, you bring Chinese carryout to her motel room and borrow her toothbrush, yet you just don't feel intimate enough with her to discuss your 401(k). If you did, you'd be surprised at what you'd find. Perfectly wonderful women doze off in the middle of the most colorful descriptions of tax-deferred annuities. Ditch 'em. You want somebody who knows that if she doesn't get your money-act together for you, she's going to have to carry you, drooling and whizzing, into a perma-care sunset. A woman who under-

stands you right down to your slot on an actuarial table is a woman in whom you can safely invest your future.

2. *Maternal instincts.* Maternal instincts are great. But you don't want a woman with maternal instincts who isn't, technically, maternal. Why? Because she'll mother you into disability. We all know men who are spoon-fed and spanked by a woman driven mad with maternal instincts, yet who is too self-absorbed to actually bother with having a real child. I say go for a woman who claims to have no mom-jones, since children come from the manufacturer with a full, lifetime supply of maternal instincts, which they instantly pass along to the proper authority.

A personal observation: *Allow me to give you a small vignette from my own IMAX-sized life. Like most men, I make important decisions about women based on blatant superficialities. My wife is blond and superbeautiful, which is why I married her. Also, she worked in the fashion business, so she looks pretty swell, plumagewise, too. Plus, she is funny and good company. But when we met she appeared to possess no domestic instinct. Once, returning late and hungry from a bacon hunt in Manhattan, I walked into the park-sized apartment in which we then lived, and said, "Hi, honey. What's for supper?" She said, "Popcorn." When we discussed children, she told me she had no maternal instincts. I said that made two of us, so we had a baby girl. On the way home from the hospital, I complained that her overindulgent labor (forty hours of demanding drugs and attention) had fatigued me, and I said that when I got home, I would need a small doze. We walked in the door, and she started itemizing her routine: "I have to feed the baby. Then I have to wash some clothes." Then she turned to me and said, "Then I have to put you down for a nap," which was just a tad more maternal instinct than was strictly necessary, as far as I was concerned.*

3. *Sisters, moms, and aunts.* If you want to see how your sporty new model is going to look once the odometer goes around a few times, visit the factory. Family reunions are especially useful in this regard, since older sisters, moms, girl-cousins, and aunts are all produced by much the same design team of hardworking, helix-twisting, DNA molecules.

4. *Driving habits.* Fair play, sense of duty, love of goofing around—these are all associated with traditional manly virtues because they are the traits that define for us the qualities we like in the friends we admire. Women who possess at least some of these typically masculine traits are also loved by us men because they understand us, which means they under-

stand how to adore us, how to amuse us, how to worship our early morning breath-musk. One surefire way to gauge a woman's guyability is to monitor her driving habits. Men and women drive differently. PC scientists claim the affection for flooring it on an empty interstate is learned masculine behavior, something we pick up from TV or Little League. But that's not true. Put a six-month-old boy behind the wheel of a Mercury Cougar on I-70 in the middle of Indiana, and he'll floor it, too. So what you want to do is check out your future bride as she drives you around town on a bar safari.

- **Is she a take-charge driver,** quick to anger over a breach of the rules of the game, such as getting cut off in traffic or being nosed out of a parking space?

- **Is she willing to follow a chump six blocks** while flashing her brights in his mirror because he turned left in front of her as soon as the light turned green?

Yes to either one? Then, bingo! That's man-driving. We like that. If she drives like a man, chances are she understands men, and if she understands men, she'll be everything you ever wanted in a woman. However, if she drives like a woman—sensible, *defensive,* slightly concerned—she'll be mad at you for driving like a man, and that's that.

5. *Shrink bill.* Don't marry anyone who is an outpatient for anything. Serious women often have serious problems; neurotic women go to shrinks because they can't take life's big joke. Since the analyst won't cure her, you'll inherit not only the cost of the treatment, but also its cause—acute humorlessness. The best-looking, most attractive attribute any woman can own is a decent sense of humor. Drape one of those suckers over any woman in the world, and she instantly goes gorgeous. One way to tell whether or not she's joke-dead? Show her this small list of handy hints.

HOW TO PICK A WOMAN FOR THE LONG HAUL

If you were going to be marooned on a desert island with only one woman, the woman to pick is the one with a boat. (DBa)

How to Buy a Rock

Engagements are expensive. Once you decide to put a woman on layaway, you'll have to come up with a deposit.

The priorities in setting the price of a diamond:
1. Color
2. Clarity
3. Cut
4. Carat weight.

The priorities in determining the beauty of a diamond:
1. Cut
2. Color
3. Clarity
4. Carat weight. (KL)

How to Get Married in Style

IN LAS VEGAS, NEVADA

- *No blood test* is required.
- *No waiting period* is required.
- *The marriage license* costs thirty-five dollars (*cash only*).
- *Both of you must make a brief appearance* at the Marriage License Bureau at 200 South Third Street, first floor. The hours: Monday–Thursday: 8 A.M. to midnight. But get this: Open continuously from 8 A.M. on Friday to midnight on Sunday. Open twenty-four hours on all legal Nevada holidays. For a good time, call (702) 455-4415.
- *Consent:* None required for adults. In Nevada, that means eighteen and over. Proof of age required through age twenty-one. For sixteen and seventeen-year-old children, Nevada requires the consent of one parent or guardian, who must appear in person when the license is applied for. Consent can also be furnished with a notarized affidavit containing the birthdate of the minor and the relationship of the minor and the person giving consent. A child under the age of sixteen must have the consent of a parent or guardian and the consent of the Nevada District Court.
- *One witness* is required. Some wedding mills will supply one for a fee.
- *If you are divorced,* the divorce must be final and you must actually know the date of the final decree and the city and state where the divorce was granted.

IN BOULDER COUNTY, COLORADO

- *No blood test* is required.
- *Both bride and groom must sign* the marriage license.
- *The signed license must be presented* to the marriage clerk by at least one of the two parties. If one party is not present, he or she must complete a notarized absentee affidavit.
- *Applicants don't have to be residents* of Colorado.
- *Restrictions:* Neither party may be married to another person. The two parties may not be ancestor and descendant, brother and sister, uncle and niece, aunt and nephew.
- *The license may be obtained during normal working hours,* 8 A.M. to 4:15 P.M., at the office of the county clerk. The license is valid for thirty-one days anywhere in the state of Colorado. The fee is twenty dollars.
- *Consent:* No parental consent is required if both bride and groom are over eighteen. The consent of both parents (or one parent with legal custody) is required for somebody sixteen or seventeen. Under sixteen? Go to Vegas.
- *Both parties must bring proof of identity* and birthdate—a driver's license, or a birth certificate with raised seal, or a passport. (GS)

How to Reform Health Care

Okay, honeymoon's over. Time to get down to married life and catch a bad cold. So bad you can't go to work. So bad you can barely see the TV. A bad cold, the kind of cold that makes a man sensitive to certain injustices and to shortcomings in others, yet not so bad a cold that he doesn't want to help. For most of us, that means helping our helpmate learn how to help us the best way she can. We're talking home care here, lads. And it's important to get it right.

WHAT'S AT STAKE

Mopping your brow might seem to be a small gesture of kindness, but it's part of a big problem because every relationship is in a constant state of tension to see who's going to end up taking care of whom. Women know this. After all, not long ago, marriage vows reflected an assumption of mutual disintegration—all that sickness and health stuff. Men go deaf at weddings, but women hear everything. Women disposed to think ill of even healthy men have apparently decided the sickness-health deal is only half right: They'll cherish us in health, okay, but in sickness, it's every man for himself. There's no mystery to their motive: For each of these women, to act otherwise is to entertain the notion that her man might not be able to care for *her*—in sickness or otherwise. So it's her job to keep you on your feet until she's frail enough to demand your full-time solicitude. Therefore, if you get sick early, you may be putting her long-term care at risk. In terms of who takes care of whom, nobody thinks of marriage as a partnership. It's a race to the Depends.

MEN AS BEASTS

Men are forever being pilloried as creatures who objectify women. It's all true, but that's just so we can have sex with them. If we want to actually get to know them, we talk to them. All the *real* objectifiers of this planet are women. A man looks at a woman and says to himself, "Hmm, how good are you?" But a woman looks at a man and says to herself, "Hmm, *what* good are you?" That's why beautiful women often stoop to marry unattractive but successful lawyers. This pragmatic approach to human sexual relations has been muffed by modern mainstream media. For instance, the *New York Times*, a regional newsletter aimed at single, white, urbanites with peculiar personal interests, has recently noticed the lack of hard scientific evidence justifying the existence of guys like us. In a piece published recently, "The Male of the Species: Why Is He Needed?" the *Times* just couldn't figure out why men had to be part of the human equation at all: "It doesn't look like a reasonable idea for a female to have anything to do with a male and his contaminated gametes," said one of the *Times*'s sources—obviously a scientist with no experience paying alimony, relocating the refrigerator, or keeping the IRA up to date.

MEN AS MACHINES

In a weird way, the *Times* was close to the truth—though only by accident, of course. In fact, women have a hard time understanding why they have anything to do with males and their contaminated gametes when they (the males, not the gametes) are—at least temporarily—no good, out of order, *busted.* **When men are sick, women suddenly realize they aren't good for *anything*,** and, as we all know by now, women hate broken machines. Name even one unattached woman whom you know, personally, who has a 1974 four-door Chevy Nova up on blocks in her front yard. Name just one single woman who keeps a garage full of broken lawn mowers because throwing away a *potentially* good small engine is a violation of manly mechanical values. The defense rests. If men lived in bachelor suburbs, maybe there'd be no lawn jockeys and no garden trolls, but there'd be a handsome Briggs &

Stratton on every front porch. To us, machines are beautiful objects, and we adore them even if they don't run. Furthermore, we feel the same way about the women we love. If they go on the fritz, we don't toss them out. Some civilizing part of our psyche tells us that even when women don't have full functionality—a broken leg, maybe a case of *pneumonia*—there's that cute factor. Even when they've hacking up phlegm, they're still nice to look at.

So, to sum up the problem: **Women lack imagination when it comes to new and better ways to make us feel better about ourselves,** especially when we're most vulnerable. What can we do to help them?

HOW TO HELP YOUR WOMAN HELP YOU

- *Make her strong.* Women sometimes find themselves helplessly sliding down the slippery slope of self-pity, thus making it more difficult for them to perceive your pain. A woman who has just had a child, for example, will resist any effort to equate the throbbing pain of your migrainesque headache with her labor-room discomfort, even though her drugs were better—and even though she gave you the throbbing noggin by *shouting right in your ear* during delivery. The rule? Don't mention pain in connection with your ailment. Women *hate* weak men, and a man who feels pain is on the brink of weakness. Instead, stress your emotional state. If you come down with a bad back, for instance, don't talk about how much it hurts. Rather, discuss the crazy cycle of your depression, your feelings of powerlessness, your fear for the future. Women love solving problems of esteem and anxiety—their own, of course, if possible, but yours in a pinch.

- *Make her a saint.* According to a lawyer specializing in environmental law, we err when we forget to rely on women's traditional strengths. "Women respond differently," he said, adding that no man ever went unloved by appealing to women's instinctive sense of compassion and their sensitivity to the fundamental injustices of life. A woman who cares is a woman at her best. In this regard, as in many others, women really are superior beings, and we should not let that blessing go unpunished. After all, there's a reason why there's a Mother Teresa, but no Papa Teresa.

- *Make yourself a saint.* Remember how, in really good war movies, the wounded corporal, the kid from Kansas, would say to his buddies, "I'll . . . I'll be okay. You guys go on without me?" Were those the words of a dying mensch or what? According to a married man from Manhattan, here's how to replay that scene on the domestic front: "If . . . if you can just help me get to the kitchen, I think I'm well enough to whip up a bouillabaisse." If you are convincing, it's as good as if you'd actually made the dinner you're apologizing for not being able to make—plus, she'll whip up the bouillabaisse for you, and not only will she feel good doing it, she'll insist you eat lots of it. This tragically sacrificial gambit is almost foolproof, by the way, although you should try to observe logical limits. For instance, "Honey, if you'll just wheel my gurney out to the garage, I think I can change the oil in your Mazda" might send her running down to Jiffy-Lube. But, "Sweetheart, if you can just tighten this bandage to stop the bleeding, I think I can paint the house" might not get you that new coat of Sherwin-Williams you so richly deserve.

- *Make caring attractive.* Shave. Slick back your hair. Don't leave soggy tissues in the bed. Even if you really are sick, you don't want to look it. Dress the way Howard Hughes did when he was hiding out in Honduran hotels: Get a nice pair of pj's, some expensive slippers, and a decent robe, preferably not one made of terry. Make yourself look as Hefneresque as possible, as if illness were just a convenient accessory to a suave informality, the kind that comes with a certain lascivious payoff. Some women like fooling around with guys in various stages of acute gastric or respiratory distress. Kind of kinky. Kind of weird. But kind of caring.

- *Provide real-world incentives.* This idea, offered by a correspondent of the arc-welding persuasion, is almost quaint in its old-fashioned directness. Offer her money. "If you want good help," said the welder, "why shouldn't you pay for it?" Good question. But how much? Discussing wages with wives can sometimes be awkward, so set your rate in a manner you know to be fair. Suggestion: Call the local home nursing agency and ask them how much they want for one nurse, eight hours. Then multiply that figure times point seven five, because you have to reckon your wife's lack of training will reduce her effectiveness by, say, 35 to 40 percent, but there's a 10 percent offset because of the possibility of sex, and, besides, you have to be fair to yourself. (There's no need to go into these details, though, when you get to talking numbers.)

If you do manage to get your wife to do the long-term housecall, remember that your recovery may be a slow and sometimes painful process—two steps forward, one step back, and all that. Don't make a headlong rush to wellness. Time is the great healer, don't forget, and you shouldn't push your luck because you fear taking advantage of the woman who loves and cares for you. After all, what good would you be to her if you weren't any good to yourself? (DB, WB)

How to Make Love

TURN-ONS

Try smearing pumpkin pies and Twizzlers behind your wife's ears. The smell of pumpkin pie and other pleasurable foods, such as doughnuts and black licorice, are sexual turn-ons for men. In tests, men who were exposed to these scents experienced increased blood flow to the penis. (STT)

CLITORAL VERSUS VAGINAL ORGASMS

This distinction speaks to the heart of the disagreement between men and women. For us, any release at all is a sweet surprise, not only something we believe we may not deserve, but also something our wives often think we don't deserve, either. For women, any emotional stimulation at all must be subjected to instant and prolonged analysis. And if the emotional stimulation comes with a little physical stimulation, that's just more meat for the sausage, more grist for the mill, more sit for the com.

• *Here's what the lab boys report:* A clitoral orgasm is an orgasm that is the result of clitoral stimulation. A vaginal orgasm is an orgasm that is the result of vaginal stimulation. Nobody ever said sex was rocket science—although a quasi-clinical approach can be brought to the enterprise by trying to put your finger on that vaginal Brigadoon, the G-spot.

• *Clitoral orgasms are more intense* and peak rapidly, leaving in their wake a shaken woman and a clitoris that is often too tender to touch. A vaginal orgasm is more *oceanlike,* to use a nonmasculine analogy. A vaginal orgasm is a kind of organic orgasm.

The two different orgasms may be felt in the same place or different places by a woman, but where the orgasm is felt by a woman is immaterial to this discussion, which is sort of ironic.

The **Main Thing** about orgasms is that in the context of a relationship, they're the paradigm of charity, in that until you learn to truly give, you'll never really be able to receive. (EWS)

• *The question* most men ask without proper reflection is whether or not there's life after orgasm.

CYCLE CHICKS

If you don't want to use birth control and you don't want to be a proud papa just yet, you can try the cycle God gave you. Here's how:

HOW TO TALK DIRTY AT VICTORIA'S SECRET

Top row: baby doll, body stocking

Second row: bustier with a bikini, camisole and tap pants, chemise. The last two look good on big women. The first one, the bustier, doesn't.

Third row: Garter belt, G-string, high-cut panty. Big-hip alert here.

baby doll
(not for skinny women)

body stocking
(not for fat ones)

bustier with a bikini

camisole and tap pants

chemise

garter belt

G-string

high-cut panty

- *Figure out what day* of the month your wife is going to ovulate.
- *Count back five days.* And then:
- *Stay away* from her for a week from that day.

   The tech sheet: For your wife to conceive, there's got to be a healthy egg and a healthy sperm. What we're really talking about here is keeping the sperm away from the egg, so let's look at the life span of each: An egg almost never lives longer than twelve hours after ovulation. Our award-winning sperm, on the other hand, no, the other hand, can live as long as five days

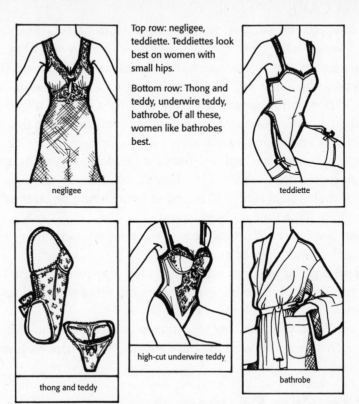

Top row: negligee, teddiette. Teddiettes look best on women with small hips.

Bottom row: Thong and teddy, underwire teddy, bathrobe. Of all these, women like bathrobes best.

negligee

teddiette

thong and teddy

high-cut underwire teddy

bathrobe

inside a woman's body. Therefore, if you have an idea of when your wife is due to ovulate—some women need to chart this with a thermometer; others can pinpoint the exact *second* ovulation takes place just by *feel*—you can count back five days and forward one day to determine the span of time when it is most important to use restraint.

• ***Determining when your wife will ovulate is a tricky subject.*** As noted, to be accurate, it requires that your girl chart certain changes in her body on a daily basis to become aware of what those changes mean in relationship to her menstrual cycle. In other words, just counting the days of her cycle and hoping that she will ovulate at the same time every month is not a reliable method. But if used properly, this method—the basis of what is called "natural family planning"—is as reliable as any other. For details, contact any Roman Catholic church. (DW, LI)

If your sex life's already too imprecise for you, there's always the over-hyped alternative:

CONDOM CARE

The FDA does periodic site-test checks of all condom manufacturers. One test it does is a water leakage test to make sure the condoms don't have holes in them. If more than four out of one hundred leak, the FDA makes the manufacturer destroy the entire lot. In theory, only 2 to 5 percent of all condoms made should tear during normal use. That combines to offer a 94 to 91 percent effectiveness rate. But unwise use of a condom can lower that considerably. Hence, this tutorial in condom care:

- *There is an inside and an outside to a condom.* If you put it on inside out, you reduce the chances of its effectiveness. How to tell what is inside out and what is right side in? The roll of latex should be on the outside of the condom, like a little rubber band.
- *Roll out the barrel.* If, in the heat of the moment, you don't unroll it all the way, the condom loses its effectiveness.
- *Just a pinch.* You've got to leave a half inch of space at the tip. Therefore, when you put a condom on, *gently* pinch the tip of the condom between two fingers while you roll the condom down.
- *Hold on.* When you withdraw after orgasm, you've got to hold the condom in place. That thing gets loose too early, anything might happen. (Anon., LRE)

How to Say Sayonara

There are few moments as illuminating as the moment you first realize that not only are you not with the one you love, you can't even love the one you're with. This split second of clarity comes with the intensity of a welder's arc. Most men simply look away for a second, then open their eyes again when the moment passes.

But what do you do when the light's always in your eyes? What do you do when your leg is in the trap and the only way you can see getting out is to gnaw it off at the knee? What do you do when you're the one who realizes the household stench is from rotting love? How do you get out and let a little air in?

- *Here's the situation:* You meet a woman, you fall in love. Then it's love, love, love for a few months. Then it's not. Suddenly, you're the impacted molar in the jaw of romance, and you face, head-on, the gruesome realization that the extraction of a man from love gone bad is long, painful, and leaves behind a remorseless throb. What's a man to do? You know you have to end it, but how? How do you tell somebody you were just kidding about that love thing?

How do you get out of a relationship that has you in the genital compactor? How, after all that time and effort spent getting in, are you going to get out?

• *We have the answers,* assuming you have the right problem. Here's what works for those involved in a less-than-marital kind of hogpen. However, please note: If your problem also involves something like a wedding vow, you might need to do a little more research.

TWO WAYS TO LEAVE YOUR LOVER

Basically, and Paul Simon's advice notwithstanding, *there are only two ways to leave your lover:* There's the easy way, and there's the hard way.

Slip out the Back, Jack

The easy way seems so easy it's hard to imagine why anybody would do it the hard way. Think of the relationship as a machine with only one moving part—you. One day you're there, the next day you're not, like the guy who says to his wife and five kids, "Hey, everybody, I'll be right back, just going out for a newspaper," and the next thing they know, he's living in Seattle with a cocktail waitress he met at a bowling alley in Tucson.

In every logical way, this is how love should end: "I'll be right back," then you're gone. No fuss, no muss, no crying and carrying on.

Is there a catch? You bet. Several, in fact:

• *You have to hear the fat lady sing.* Resolution counts, especially in a complex relationship. She'll want the whole thing resolved right away so she can get on with her life. You won't want to give her that, naturally, because it will be uncomfortable for you. But someplace down the line, you may want a little resolution, too—especially if this sort of exit turns into a routine. Lonely guys sometimes wonder how they ever got so lonely. Their ex-girlfriends could tell them, no problem.

• *You have to pay your debts.* If some woman is willing put up with the incredibleness of you, you owe her the dignity of making a decorous exit—and you owe it to yourself to make the last gesture of the relationship the one that invests the romance with a little meaning. Why? Charity aside, you have to remember that it's not just her relationship that's ending, it's yours, too. You invested your share of time and trauma.

• *You might want to look back.* It's one thing to burn a bridge. It's quite another to blow up the dam, too. Slipping out the back leaves such an indelible stain of resentment behind that if you ever want to pass that way again, it'll be impossible. Not only will she detest you forever, but so will her family and friends, and so will some of yours, since few men admire men who have no honor.

- *It's unrealistic.* This is the real reason you can't just steal away in the night: People are too complicated for that sort of thing. There will be things you want to say that she won't want to hear, and things she'll say you won't like much, either. As a rule, people never simply walk away from affairs unless they never took the affairs seriously to begin with.

The Hard Way

Before you say anything, before you shut the door forever, sit still a minute and *think about what's happening.* Most men, when it comes to break-up time, are looking only about ten minutes down the road. They see the front door and the bright light outside. They see the big so-long, then they see a five-hundred-yard straightaway. But there are curves in that road, and one of them might be just sharp enough to throw you into the ditch of despair.

- *Count your losses.* When you say "adios," it'll be the last rational word you'll speak or hear. Know where you're going once you leave. Figure out if what you're going to get is better or just different. Do a quality check on your present household model: Trustworthy? Loyal? Helpful? Courteous? Kind? Obedient? Cheerful? Thrifty? Clean? Reverent? Good-looking when naked? One guy, a Pennsylvania-based pilot, abruptly left a woman he'd been with for four years to go to another woman who threw him out after two weeks. His analysis: "Bad move."

- *You or her?* Be honest with your own self-serving self for a sec. Which one of you two has the problems in this deal?

    Here's one way to find out: Tell yourself the story of your relationship as if it were a movie. Okay, okay, not a great movie, maybe, but a movie nonetheless. Who's the hero? Who's the villain? Once you have your tale down pat, run it past a good friend. Let him ask questions. Let him decide who the villain is. Don't be alarmed if a relatively objective rewrite gives your little drama a surprise ending.

If it's her, no sweat. You get the moral edge and she gets a free education.

If it's you, you get to do this over and over again until you figure out how to put the blame where it belongs.

EXTRACTION STRATEGIES

Once you figure out exactly what's wrong, you've got to do the heavy lifting required to get yourself out of that quagmire you're in. Here are some field-tested romance breakers.

Make a Fight

Pick a fight, make it a whopper, get plenty of yelling and screaming going, say what you want, do what you want short of violence, but just make sure it's about the Big Issue—the one thing that really is your last straw. This can be anything from squeezing the toothpaste tube the wrong way to squeezing the postman the right way, but keep your main peeve in the foreground. "The thing that cracked it for me was how she'd blow up whenever we fought," said Tim, a Pittsburgh artist. "Didn't matter what it was about, she'd start throwing things—bottles, food, anything. Once, she threw a hammer at me. So I said I was fed up with that crap, I was leaving . . . then, she really went ballistic."

Upside: Not only will you have spelled out your grievance clearly, you'll also have enough anger built up to actually carry you out the door. "I had to leave, or die."

Downside: Screaming out loud is usually a poor way to engage in analytical discourse. "She called three days later," Tim recalled, "and said she couldn't remember what we had been fighting about. Is that crazy crap or what?"

Make a Mess

One surefire way to spell breakup is to have your honey walk into the bedroom while you're lying in bed sandwiched between two steaming Samoan stewardesses. Gene, a hotel worker from Las Vegas, said that one of the reasons he moved to Nevada was the "extremely high numbers of women between the ages of twenty-eight and thirty-four who are great looking, employed, and single." Gene says he makes his segues "extremely seamlessly, where I just get the next woman to move in before the last one moves out. This," he adds gravely, "always seems to work."

Upside: Gene's right. It works.

Downside: The $625,000 lawsuit Gene got hit with last August from his last girlfriend came on the heels of a previous settlement that cost him his house. "She owns the place now," he said. Gene was toying with an idea recently about rekindling his romance with the new owner of his house, "but she's still pissed." Some women are never happy.

Make a Stand

Compose a statement of belief, something comprehensive, clean, forthright, and unambiguous. Think it through carefully and thoroughly. Couch it in the terms normally used to express deeply held convictions: "I cannot respect someone who eats kippered herring in bed." Clearly spell out the reasons you have for wanting to call it quits, and try to keep your emotions in check while you do it. Be compassionate and considerate, but not patronizing. Leave no question unanswered, and make certain you are on firm moral ground by tying everything to an ethical point of view. Allow for a certain amount of vituperation, and offer to continue the conversation later if she becomes airborne. Show no anger. Mention love; use words like "care" and "profound." Never allow a hint of ambivalence.

Upside: You will have given her the chance to keep her dignity by guarding your own.

Downside: Disappointment. It must be noted that this approach is nearly impossible. As a rule, it's the way most men start out, but they get distracted by shouts, screams, knives, something that changes the direction or the tenor of the conversation. "I tried to tell her sort of politely," said Tim, "but she just wouldn't have it that way." There are no soft spurns, apparently.

Make a Deal

This strategy is one tailor-made for the man who wants out of the relationship he's in and wants to build a new relationship—but with the same woman. Here's the angle: **Figure out what it is she is doing that you just can't stand.** Then tell her you might be back if she'll fix whatever it is that's broke. To use a real-life but awesomely downmarket example, let's say you're like Bill, a native of Nebraska, and the thing that is driving you away is her constant nagging about the dead fish you keep bringing in and tossing in the sink with the dishes. "That's just me," asserts Bill. "That's who I am. I love to fish, she doesn't—and she doesn't like anything about fishing, either." Trivial? Perhaps to you, and obviously unimportant to Bill's girlfriend. But not to Bill. Fishing, to Bill, is like golf to aging yuppies, or like God to Baptists. "Fishing's the end-all, as far as I'm concerned. I don't need to do nothing else." Nor, presumably, anyone else, either. Anyway, let's say your beef is with the fish you catch and that she won't clean. That's the thing that's wrong. So you say, "What's so bad about cleaning a fish every now and then?" And she says, "They stink. You kill 'em, you clean 'em and get 'em off the Limoges." Now you lay out your nonnegotiable blueprint: You work out a recovery plan for her. You say, "Look, honey, it's a two-step thing: First, get your china out of the sink, and, second step, clean fish when I catch them, otherwise [as Bill put it] color me gone." She may decline, but at least you've established some means by which she can, if she so desires, retrieve you.

Upside: Humane, and holds out the possibility of redemption, always nice. After all, if she's willing to change whatever it is that's bothering you, assuming that's the real issue, how could you do better? In fact, like all these tactics we've listed here, this one simply involves isolating the problem, then deciding whether it can be solved. Some problems can't be. But for those that can, this strategy provides a means for the solution.

Downside: You might have to learn to clean fish.

HOW TO LIVE THROUGH DIVORCE

For something so life-altering, it's amazing how many men wander through a divorce like a kid lost in an IGA. So: Someone say "Divorce"? Pay attention. You may learn something valuable.

• ***How to guarantee that you will have an unpleasant divorce:*** Don't do your homework! A better idea: before you do anything, even call an attorney, stake out the divorce section of your local library and read every current book you can on the subject. Buy copies of the ones that are most useful so you can mark up the parts that are most useful.

• ***Plan:*** Getting a divorce is like anything else in life: The more you plan and the better the strategy you cook up, the smoother it will go. Even if it doesn't go as planned, you will already know what to do when things go wrong, and most problems won't take you by surprise because you will have at least considered them in your planning.

Consider the three possible outcomes:

1. Uncontested divorce.
2. A controlled, contested divorce settlement.
3. All-out warfare.

Now, ask yourself which of the following you would prefer:

1. Dealing with your wife in a calm, reasonable fashion.
2. Having an attorney deal with your spouse and her attorney in a calm, reasonable fashion.
3. Bitterness, acrimony, the hope of revenge with great pain inflicted upon your spouse and children—and the risk of suffering great pain, as well.

Ask your wife (in person, by phone, by fax, by mail) which of the three she would prefer. (VF)

Uncontested Divorce

If you both agree that you would prefer to settle the matter of your marriage in a calm, reasonable way, you can file for an **uncontested divorce.** One of you files all of the paperwork asking for what you want from the dissolved marriage and the other party. Since you are able to talk to one another about the divorce, there should be no surprises. Legal help should be minimal, unless you find you need an attorney or mediator to help you resolve a point or points on which you're having a hard time coming to terms. You'll each need an attorney or paralegal to review the final documents to make sure what you have agreed to in the divorce is accurately represented in the settlement, as written. In addition, some states won't permit couples with children to file for an uncontested divorce. That doesn't mean you must be enemies. It just means that a finding must be obtained, mostly to facilitate the legalities of custody and support.

Divorce Handled by Outside Parties

Here, your goal should be to keep the divorce under control even though the two of you are not able to communicate on the subject directly. **You can keep your costs down by educating yourself about divorce** and giving your attorney direction, and knowing what questions to ask, instead of dumping a huge box of papers on his desk and sobbing in his office while you tell him your whole sad story. At $150 an hour, it's best to keep economy in mind with this guy, hire the kids next door to do your filing, and unburden yourself to a bartender who will be thrilled to listen if you leave him a fifty-cent tip every time he brings you a drink. How to get the most out of your attorney for the least amount of money? Make a plan before you go see him. Know what you want. Prepare the evidence to prove that what you want is fair. Anticipate what she will want. Prepare the evidence to prove that what she wants is unfair. Don't do anything nasty or mean-spirited that she could use against you in court—especially if there is a child custody battle involved. Don't say anything to anyone about her that could later be used against you. Play smart, and play to win. (VF, Anon.)

A Divorce Without Forethought and with Malice Intended

This kind of divorce will cost you a fortune, both financially and emotionally, and no one will win because everyone involved will come out of it burned and angry and bitter. Don't do it. The best revenge you can get on your soon-to-be ex-wife is to live a happy, successful, and healthy life. (Anon.)

Kids Pay the Price

Remember that in every divorce in which children are involved, **the children will pay more for the destruction of the family than either of the grown-ups** who caused the destruction. Therefore, any small thing you add to that toxic mess you've made—any obvious animosity, any manipulation of the children to get at your soon-to-be ex-wife, any depressed-to-death hysteria—won't help you, but will cause grave harm to your children. Be a man for them, old chap.

The Universal Fifty-State Divorce Guide

Here's how it works, coast-to-coast.

- *The petition.* One of you files a petition with the court. The petition contains information about the date of the marriage, the date of separation, information on children and property, and an account of any debts. The petitioner also states what he wants out of the divorce with respect to custody, money, pets, and all that.

- *Temporary orders.* One of you will want to ask the court for temporary orders, which are a kind of freeze in the action. They specify who, for the time being, will remain in the house and who will have custody of the kids while the divorce process is in motion. Temporary orders also require leaving your children and spouse on health insurance policies and prohibit things like the sale of real property.

- *The response.* The person who *didn't* file must file a response within a set time period. In this document, the respondent can agree or disagree with anything in the petition. If the respondent doesn't bother, a default will be taken out and the respondent will forever lose the chance to tell his side, thus granting the petitioner everything that is asked for in the petition.

- *Discovery.* The whole point here is for each side to find whatever information it needs to make its case in divorce court. A discovery can be quite informal and inexpensive—say, you give her a list of questions, and she gives you a list of questions and you each answer the questions as honestly as possible. Or you can do it the difficult and expensive way—every lawyer's preferred method—which is to be uncooperative and have attorneys get the same information through lots of interrogatories and disclosure statements. In either case, both parties will end up with the same information, but the second way the lawyers also end up with a lot of money.

- *Settlement conference.* You attend this conference to see if the two of you can come to terms about money, kids, the house, and all that without going before a judge. Unless you have a very good reason for wanting to go to trial, do your level best to let this all end here. Be polite, cooperative, even supportive. In the long run, you'll win if you do, because you'll be saved the time, expense, and paralytic turmoil of airing your entire life and failed marriage in front of a judge and a room full of strangers.

- **The settlement.** Once a negotiated settlement is reached that is agreeable to you, accept it and follow it to the letter—and to the spirit. (JTF, NO)

How to File Your Taxes After a Divorce

You know who *really* cares about the pain and anguish brought on by your divorce? The Internal Revenue Service. While you're crying on your auditor's shoulder, here's what he's thinking:

- **Alimony.** If you pay it, you deduct it. Here's the good news: Your ex-wife must report it as income. If your divorce decree requires you to make payments to your ex-wife for things like medical expenses, rent, and tuition, they are only deductible if they qualify as alimony. Ditto house payments, if she's living in it. If you continue to own the home jointly, and if she lives in the house and you continue to make the full payments, you can deduct half the payments as alimony. Meanwhile, the other half is treated as a regular mortgage payment, since you still own half the house. Therefore, there might be another deduction for you. (LW)

  Note: The rules on this change often, though, so you might want to call the IRS and double-check.
- **Did she take your house?** She'll have to pay capital gains taxes when the house is sold at a later date.
- **Your child support payments** are not tax deductible. They also don't count as taxable income for your ex-.
- **Filing status.** Most people, after divorcing, file as a single taxpayer. However, if your child lives with you most of the year, and if you provide most of his support, you may be able to file as head-of-household, which is more advantageous, taxwise. (STo, LW)

How to Come Clean After a Divorce

Good-bye Rosie! When you put her name on your chest, you'd been in love with her for five solid hours, and you thought it would last a lifetime. It did—the tattoo, that is. Rosie was history the next morning.

Now the tattoo may be a thing of the past, too. Using a technique called "infrared coagulation," a dermatologist gives the tattoo a second-long blast with a handheld wand. A week or so later, the tattoo vanishes, leaving behind a small scar. Cost: $250 or so for a little tattoo. To get a scarless tattoo removal, figure three times the cost. (AMcLL)

12. Family Life

Single people, childless couples, couples with one kid, line up on this side. Everybody else—including you, there, with your teeming masses—line up on the other.

If you're a married man, there are only two people in the world who can take your life and fill it with almost unmanageable complexity. One of them is your secretary; an affair in the office is the Western equivalent of an Oriental tea ceremony with a suicide chaser. The only other person capable of complicating a well-organized life? Your *second* child.

How to Know Where You're Going

For many men, family life is the unexplored exit off the Jersey Turnpike—a place they not only never thought about visiting, but never even knew existed. Who could guess that one minute you're turning around the wrong way in a barroom in Baltimore, to see for the very first time the girl of your dreams— and when you come to, you're trying to squeeze three car seats on the back bench of a station wagon?

GET THE LAY OF THE LAND

There are some obvious landmarks out there, and if you squint you can see most of them from where you're standing. There's the Great Falls of Love, the Mountains of Marriage, the Plains of Poverty, the mighty River of Reproduction, the trackless Dunes of Divorce. And someplace way, way off in the purple haze are the fabulous Fields of Fulfillment.

You can tell where you are in relation to any of these landmarks by simply paying attention to the figurative flora, fauna, and topographic oddities around you. For example, if last month you were buying lunch for all your unemployed friends, and this month people who can't pronounce your last name are calling you at home at 7:30 A.M. to ask where the payment is, chances are pretty good that you're in some sort of income-to-debt-ratio-type-thing, or, to be blunt, you got lost on the way to the bank.

MARK YOUR TRAIL

One well-trod path to self-location is to **keep a journal.** No, no, no, not some weepy account of field trips you've taken with your inner child. Just a straightforward accounting, on a daily basis, of where you were, whom you saw, what they said, what you paid, and how much it rained. There's no right or wrong way to keep a journal: Make your entries as stark as you please. If you don't feel like a florid kind of guy on, say, March 21, just get down the facts: Ate, worked, ate, TV, sleep, rain. If, however, the very next day the sex fairy leaves a prize for you under your pillow, and you suddenly feel compelled to drop your feelings a little line, go ahead and do it— although by May 12 you'll look back at that fateful day with some interest. Journals, kept faithfully for a year, will cause two things to happen. First, your life will magically focus itself, so that decisions will come easier and self-evaluations will increase in accuracy. Second, you'll become a better writer. (DE)

Dyslexic? Lazy? That's what Polaroids are for. **A snap a day keeps confusion away.** It doesn't really matter what you take pictures of. If you limit yourself to one a day, eventually some sort of prioritizing spirit will capture the enterprise and you'll end up with a big snapshot of a year. Note, however, that as easy as taking pictures is, especially compared to keeping a journal, a photo account lacks some important therapeutic values, not least of which is focus. Also, remember what we all learned from Woody Allen, and keep those pictures to yourself. (Anon.)

• *Another way out of the woods* is to ignore the passing trees. What I mean here is that many of the things that were important to you when you were, oh, twenty-seven aren't the same things that are important when you're forty. So one reason you may suddenly wake up one morning and feel lost is that you went to sleep as an entirely different person. The stuff that was important to you when you dozed off disappeared in the dark and was replaced in the morning's first light by a different set of priorities. Bingo. Lost.

• *What's happening here is obvious:* The world is passing you by, as if you were doing a psychic moonwalk. Prescription? Turn off the TV, open a hard-to-read book—Henry James, *Moby Dick, Madame Bovary*—and listen to some smart chap provide a little perspective on life. Or check out Aquinas or Maimonides. This kind of activity will also make you a rarity among men, in that intellectual reflection—as opposed to semipsychological analysis—is something almost nobody does these days. Most of us would much rather carry a heavy object up two flights than carry a heavy thought through to a resolution. (LF, Anon.)

KNOW WHERE YOU WANT TO GO

This is the hard part. *Maps are useless unless you know two things: Where you are and where you want to go.* Let's just say, for example, that you're living in a motel in Baltimore and spending your days at the racetrack, and you have no wish to squeeze three child-restraint chairs onto the back seat of a station wagon. Suddenly, the phone rings. It's a bud asking you to go out for a brew. What do you do?

Answer: Check your map. If you want to play the ponies, *don't answer the phone.*

How to Change a Diaper with One Hand Tied Behind Your Back

Every now and then, a man has to do what a man has to do—namely, demonstrate with a terrible effectiveness that compared to his life, his job, all other lives, all other jobs are a snap.

This is an especially useful thing to demonstrate just before begging off dinner with your wife so you can play poker with the happy chappies. And what better object for a demonstration than the wee tyke bellowing in the corner for a new disposable die-pee?

- **Fill one hand.** You need to keep one hand busy with something distinctly adult in order to heighten the contrast with what you'll be doing with the other hand, namely, changing a diaper. Find something that suits your mood. Feeling debonair? A full martini glass is terribly dramatic. Expressing your normalcy? A handful of the sports section will work, too. The whole key to this is carrying it off as if you didn't even realize you were doing it.
- **Floor the kid,** faceup. Gently, now. On a thick carpet, or on the sofa.
- **Pop the tapes.** The old diaper will practically fall off. Turn the kid over so his heinie's up. Take a diaper wipe and do a quick butt-buff. Then stand him up, give him a tiny giddy-up swat, and let him run a lap. This airing out of the skin is a good thing, but you'll want to softly say a prayer for protection against spontaneous urination—his.
- **While he's running,** you grab a clean diaper and spread it out on the floor, business side up. Open up those little tape tabs.
- **Catch the tad** as he sprints by and lay him on the diaper so his rear end is in place. Holding both feet up in the air will temporarily immobilIze him and allow you the element of surprise for the next daring step.
- **Quick, let go of his feet,** grab the diaper by the right-hand front corner, and in one upward motion, pull it up between his legs and in place on his left hip. Snare the tape part and stick it in place. Don't worry about precision. Just get the kid sealed. Now, repeat with the other side.

In rodeos, when the cowpoke has finished tying the steer, he gives a slap with his hat and a shout to the crowd. You won't have to bother—although you may wish to reflect on the fact that only several generations ago, the equivalent of this trick was to roll a cigarette with one hand while chasing cattle across Wyoming with the other. What have men come to? (RHW)

How to Hang Out with Your Old Man

Let's say it's a quiet Sunday afternoon in Pleasantville. The kids are in the yard, the dog's sleeping on the porch. A neighbor is playing some Beethoven ditty, and the music passes through the kitchen, where a pie is baking. You're half awake, thumbing through a catalog from Black and Decker, she's upstairs organizing her lingerie file, while outside the window, a bee does the wild thing with a pansy.

Suddenly, there's a knock at the door. In our little scenario, that's the bad news. The good news is, you get to choose who's there. But the other bad news is, whoever it is, he's going to stay for the weekend. So choose. Is it

1. A modern poet?
2. An aluminum siding salesman?
3. The lady from the local NOW chapter?
4. Your old man?

The problem here is that for many of us, figuring out how to hang out with the old man is a knack learned relatively late in life, one of those things you finally get a handle on just about when you don't much need it. If knowing how to spend easy time with Pop were part of an adolescent's survival packet, much of our domestic life would have been better for everyone in the house, yes? Imagine, you and old Dad, strumming Stratocasters together out in the garage, ripping the air filter out of Mom's Chevy, and cruising the A & W on Saturday night. Would that be bitchin' or what?

Never happened, of course. Instead, dealing with Dad is just part of the background noise of everybody's life.

That brings us to the very shank of the dad dilemma: *Fathers aren't guys.* The hardware store guy is a guy. Cops and robbers can be guys. Cousins are guys all the way. Anybody you feel comfortable calling by his first name is a guy. But dads are guys the way Pope John Paul II is a guy. Between you and your dad is this odd curtain of impenetrable angst and expectation. Respect and solicitude don't work, and neither do subservience or condescension. The fact of the matter is, you can't hang out with Dad unless you first can make him into one of the guys. Alas, the best part of hanging out with the guys is the sheer democratic excess of it all, and, until we're of a certain age, making Dad into a guy involves just a tad too much egalitarianism for most of us.

The Main Thing: *Life's short, and there comes a time when you just have to figure out how to hang out with Dad, because not knowing how is more trouble than it's worth.* And, like it or not, the only way to do that is to do a complete guy conversion on the old feller. Nothing else will enhance his overall hangoutability.

Here's how you rig it:

LOOK FOR HIS SECRET LIFE

• *Fathers have an existence that parallels the one we see*—sort of the same way dogs and houseplants have secret lives. It is there, in that hidden world, where pops all live life like guys. Every dad's guy-world is different, so you sort of have to test for it, the same way you do for allergies. Now, lots of repro-men shed their father follicles in the presence of strange women. Put a pop in a room with an attractive woman of a certain age, and he goes guy right away, reaches down deep, and comes up with great lines and funny war anecdotes, instead of his usual advice on how to straighten out your IRA. Different dads have different triggers—dragsters, particle colliders, ten-point bucks—but they all have the same effect: They make a dad stop being a dad, even in the presence of his progeny, and turn into a normal guy.

• *Sometimes, you have to settle for the symptoms of hidden-life guyness,* instead of the real thing. For example, you stop by the old homestead one Sunday, and there's a dark-haired stranger inhabiting your father's body. Turns out, according to Mom, he went out and OD'd on Grecian Formula. Other dads send the bags under their eyes out to get pressed, others put their jowls in storage. When you see your dad struggling to look just like you, take no comfort in it, for you're next. But check it out for its guyesque qualities. Dads with late-life vanity are practically pure guy. (TC)

ADOPT YOUR DAD

• *Everybody's dad is just another guy to everybody else.* So adopt him. Pretend he's somebody else's pop, and a pretty nice guy, to boot. (JER)

GET HIS JOKES

• *The first sign of anybody's nice-guy congeniality is usually his sense of humor.* As the commissar of Law and Order in the household gulag, dads often don't engender big belly laughs in sons. That doesn't mean he wasn't cracking wise. It only means you weren't getting the jokes. You thought he was dour and humorless. He thought you were mind-numbingly intense. One correspondent, a Mr. F, Jr., found himself at his mom and dad's house for a weekend. Short on good ideas, and desperate for distraction, he volunteered to accompany his old man to the golf course. Junior F teed off on a ball and sent it at a right angle deep into the rough. Senior F lined one down the fairway. As they were walking away from the tee, F the Elder said, "If you can't hit it as far as the ladies' tee, son, you ought to drop your pants and walk that little thing right through the course naked." The neo-F almost seized up. Why? First, because he'd never heard his old man make a ribald wisecrack before, and his knee-jerk reaction was that it was unseemly. Second, the last guy in the world you want to make small penis talk with is Pops, who, assuming a certain sexual orthodoxy on your part, is the only other guy on the planet who knows your equipment almost as well as you do. Third, it was, for the time and place, "a really funny thing to say," according to small F. By the time they were on the back nine, Junior F had figured out that his old man was actually a pretty funny guy, and by the time he broke one hundred, young F was telling jokes of his own. Some of them were funny—one or two of them even funny enough to make the old F laugh. (FS)

PLAY HIS GAME

The story of F also illuminates another essential ingredient in the guy mix: *Play your old man's game.* On the most superficial level, this can mean that you can always kill a weekend afternoon on the links, if that's your father's game. It gives him plenty of opportunity to do what dads love doing most of all: instructing their young. In fact, if you're already a pretty good golfer, and you want to finally reel in that big tuna of papa-approval, go out to the local club and throw a game his way. Let him tell you how to do everything. Then do it almost right. He'll feel like a million bucks, and you'll feel like a philanthropist.

Remember, every dad's favorite sentence starts with the phrase, "Here, let me show you . . ." That means that no matter what you do—balancing your checkbook, rewiring a table lamp, rotating the tires—you'll have ample opportunity to turn it into a dad-kid project. In fact, if you really want to lock it down, you can simply pronounce every son's least-favorite phrase: "Hey, dad, what do you think of . . . ?"

TALK HIS TALK

On another level, *playing Dad's game means hanging out on Dad's terms,* instead of yours. Maybe you've got a cosmic bone to pick with the old man, and you think the best way to tackle it is to sit and talk, man-to-man. That might be what you want, but that's the kind of thing that makes most men's skin crawl. Almost all guys like to talk to each other while they're doing some-thing else, so if you want your dad to talk to you, find out what he likes doing, and do it. He'll talk. It may be about the horses at the track or the old spark plugs he's changing or the pictures in the museum, but talk's talk, and eventually it'll turn into guy talk, and, given enough time, it'll also turn into the conversation you want.

Warning: If you feel like the conversation has to be wrenched around to get to what you want to talk about, you're missing the point here. If you want to know the real story on why Pop left you and Mom and the farm and ran off with the preacher's wife, you stand a much better chance of finding out by talking about agriculture and religion than you do trying to meet the subject head-on. Men talk around important subjects. Just pay attention, and you'll get what you came for.

WALK HIS WALK

Lately, dad bashing has become a booming Boomer industry. Every man jack worth an ounce of self-absorption will chatter on endlessly about how little he got from his old man, how badly Dad screwed up, and how much more involved he himself is as a father. What that really means is that our dads never sat around the kitchen table talking about how much they loved everybody. Instead, all they did was work, work, work, while Mom stayed home and mopped up. Today, we know better, and to demonstrate our deep involvement, we pick up Junior from day care on Mondays, Wednesdays, and Fridays and tell him we love him all the way to his mother and stepfather's house, where we drop him off until the next alternating weekend. *What also makes it tough for us to fill Pop's boots is that by almost any measure, the world is a dumber, more hostile, more dangerous, less civilized place today than it was on the old man's watch.* We make less and know less and spend more and talk lots more, mostly about ourselves. All this makes it difficult for us to enjoy good hang time with Dad, as there's always the chance he'll say, "Idiot. I told you so." Fortunately, most dads are nice guys and keep all this to themselves. You gotta like a guy like that.

LET BYGONES BE BYGONES

If much of your life is devoted to conducting a private Nuremberg for your old man, you're the one making the big mistakes in life, not him. One chap bristles every time his father innocently asks whether it's time for a haircut, because, he says, he "still remembers the time he dragged me to his barber and made him cut off my Beatle bangs." Now, of course, he cuts his hair just like dad's.

Dads get a worse deal than air pirates. Armed fanatics on a 747 do what all dads do—they instill fear and discipline in their charges. But by the time the highjacking is over, most of the hostages love their keepers. So think of your adolescence as an unscheduled trip to Havana, and give the guy a break. Besides, you've got jets of your own to highjack.

LET HIM HELP OUT

This guy-conversion project may seem a bit daunting, but once you get into it, it gets progressively easier. Besides, your old man will chip in and do half the work, once he sees what you're up to. First of all, to him, sons aren't guys either. And second, he's already been through all this once with the guy he called Pop. (DB)

How to Spend the Holidays with Your Family

Relax. 'Tis the season to be jolly, dammit.

NAIL THE HOLIDAYS YOU LIKE

The problem: too many holidays. Look at your calendar. See all that joy, all that glee, all those days marked in red? Now look at your life. See? Flag Day. Secretaries' Week. Come *on*. Nobody needs that many holidays. Plus, there are thousands of boutique holidays for everyone from Shiites to the Gaza crowd. For Orthodox guys like me, for instance, *every* day's a holiday, each more, well, more Byzantine than the last, from the near-melancholy of Cheese Fare to the literally lamentable Commemoration of the twenty thousand Martyrs of Nicomedia. With so many people observing days marking so many heroes, memorials, observances, and birthdays, the whole year is like some extravagant street fair with lots of ethnic booths serving all that's bad for a man's heart.

There's just so much holiday spirit a man can stand. With this much diversity, from a purely secular point of view, it only makes sense to select the holidays you want to actually celebrate, and ignore the rest.

Figure, for purposes of maximum celebratory enjoyment, you can only handle two big deals, one for summer and the other for winter. Let's say you choose Arbor Day and, mostly to make your family happy, Christmas. So now you got your two major holidays. By limiting your annual festivities to just two big days, you keep your focus. On Arbor Day, you're a tree nut, hugging them, planting them, chasing doggies away from them. When somebody calls, your wife says, "He can't come to the phone right now. He's treeing." Then, after a sufficient passage of time, Christmas rolls around, and you're happy to be a fat bozo in a red suit. This is what balance is all about.

BE TOLERANT OF OTHER HOLIDAYS

Of course, other people choose other holidays, and, because holidays seem to require festivities, and because festivities are disappointing when performed alone, **you have to be a part of the larger picture.** This also teaches tolerance, the new virtue. If Uncle Bill is an Easter-and-New-Year's man, you have to do your part: In the spring, show up with a chocolate bunny in a basket and a smoked ham under your arm, then roll around eight months later with a lampshade on your head. *Just don't try to make Uncle Bill's holidays your holidays.* By removing any expectations you might have about their potential to deliver personal fulfillment, you lighten the load. If you get caught in a holiday you really hate, you can just nod and smile and be polite and get out before the dishes leave the table. (Anon.)

WARM-WEATHER HOLIDAYS

For purposes of instruction here, we'll dispose of the postspringtime, warm-weather holidays right away. First off, most of them suffer from a uniform lack of good holiday motifs: You got your holiday for working guys and your holiday for dead guys and that's it. In fact, there's really only one summer-time holiday, and it's got everything a man needs—explosives, beer in kegs, boats, plenty of chances for misbehavior and injury. *All guys are Fourth of July guys.* (DB)

COLD-WEATHER HOLIDAYS

It's the cold-weather follies that confuse and dismay. Plus, the timing's bad: These things always come at the end of the year, and just when you think things can't get much worse, an entire nation, the whole poor and huddled mass, reaches out its hand to you and asks for presents. Most people like getting goods and services free, so maybe it's understandable that Hanukkah and Christmas are big faves. As Yulophiles well know, it's not the season to be cheap. When December shows up, there's nothing for it but to get a grip, open that checkbook, and go with the cash flow.

Gift-Giving Tips

- *Think infantile.* Impose a strict "toys only" policy on the gifts you're willing to receive. Just make it a clear, firm rule that if potential donors can't buy you something fun to play with, they should just skip the whole deal. In fact, one good reason to send Christmas cards out before Christmas is to give friends and relatives ample warning that if they try to ply you with socks and underwear, they're off your list forever. (RHWa)

- *Give 'til it hurts.* For most men, the painful part comes during the actual shopping procedure. No wonder: Check out last year's Jolly List, and you'll see that every freeloading nephew and every braid-chewing niece made out like vandals. The cousin end of these little lists is especially terrifying, since cousins are, for most of us, a personal demonstration of the consequences of unbridled, exponential population growth in a mighty shallow gene pool.

    It's easy to see what good sense mandates: *Choose one, possibly two blood relations and shower them with excess.* Buy them Lincoln Town Cars. For everybody else, buy ornamental soap. The following year, change the names, but keep the principle. This means that two or three times in a lifetime, some ne'er-do-well twig on the family tree will be broken under the weight of your largesse—and will remember that gift, even after years and years of Cracker Jack booty.

- *Think packaging.* The cheaper the present, the more expensive the wrap. This is America, where appearance becomes reality. If you wrap junk like jewelry, everybody'll be happy with junk. (Anon.)

- *Be careful when buying gifts for household members.* Unlike Uncle Milt and Cousin Shep, who have little opportunity to seek revenge for gift-giving slights, the relatives who live in your house can kill you in your sleep. Therefore, it pays to give a little thought to gifts given to intimate family members.

- *When it comes to kids, tear your list in half.* Children really want only half of what you give them, and it really doesn't matter which half it is. Rookie dads know that the first year they buy presents for the new kid, they have to yell at her to get her to open the fifty-fifth one and the fifty-sixth one. Little ingrates. Kids rather like it when they can actually recall with some clarity exactly what it is they have been given. The old burlesque adage has a special appeal here: Leave 'em wanting more. (ND)

- *When it comes to wives, double your list.* If you're like most men, your impulse will be to buy thoughtful gifts that show you're thinking on your feet: Useful stuff of the garage-door-opener variety that you needed to pick up anyway. Wives have almost no appreciation of this sort of practical application for the holidays. So you have to compensate for your innate good sense by matching every small kitchen appliance and tool with something appropriately mawkish and sentimental. Examples: A set of Revere Ware equals an eighteen-inch string of pearls. One new garbage disposal equals five pounds of lingerie-negligee medley, plus costume trinkets. A catfish-gutting kit equals a Princess Cruise. (KL)

- *Make one big gift to somebody you don't know.* Send a Moulinex to Václav Havel or donate a turkey (not a live one) to the local orphans. Pack off some expensive, playful gifts to a magazine columnist or send Winnie Mandela one of those Nintendo power gloves. By giving altruistically, without any expectation of acknowledgment or gain, you gain a special sense of what a holiday is supposed to be about.

- *Think leverage.* Sometimes, it's helpful to have a barometer to help measure gift pressure. You can easily build one yourself by simply using your own birthday as a standard against which you measure what you have received and what you will, consequently, give in return when the winter holidays roll around. This is also a morally appropriate way to handle present exchanges, of course, since it helps others see that if they wish to be done unto handsomely, they will first do unto you what's right.

- *Corollary: Give the gift that keeps on giving.* By choosing something flamboyantly thoughtful, you ratchet up the manipulative potential of the gift-giving process, resulting in a sure-to-fail attempt by the recipient to regain the moral edge by trying to match your ingenuity and generosity. Smart guys buy their boss's little whatnot with this rule firmly in mind.

Go Back to Basics
If all else fails, get religion. Ever notice how so many of these Yule holidays have some hidden, obscure spiritual meaning?

What to Do If Gifts Give You Hives
If you don't like gifts, concentrate on holidays that are essentially food festivals. Then set about making the holiday as nice for you as possible. For instance, when invited to somebody else's house for Thanksgiving, always volunteer to bring the condiments. Nothing on the festal menu is quite so vague as the condiment part. So, if you're rushed and bothered, smear peanut butter on some celery stalks and call it "condiments." If you hope for a reprise invita-

tion the following year, however, you may want to go a bit beyond celery to something more exotic, like ripe olives. Or a bottle of Baker's. (AH)

THE MAIN THING TO REMEMBER

The point of holidays is to make people happy. So the best advice may be to do what you can to make yourself the jolliest, most jovial of holiday celebrants. Good cheer, when it isn't liquored up and downright revolting, can be quite contagious, and once you get in the swing of things, even gift giving can be charming and downright self-redeeming, especially if kids are around.

It's a cinch to forgot that part, the part about why this is all worth it. Family holidays generate their own kind of warmth. Seen in the light of charity and affection, they provide a cozy corner in a crazy, cold world. So try to get past the humbug. By entering into the spirit of the holidays, you'll add your voice to the sacred, universal carol, the one about comfort and joy, about sweet children's dreams, and peace on Earth.

How to Teach Your Kid to Drive

There are six simple rules governing the way in which fathers pass knowledge down to their children, and they all come into play when you're teaching your teenage kid how to drive a car.

1. *Stop the clock.* It really doesn't matter how long it takes for a kid to learn to do, say, a three-point turn. Make a driving lesson an open-ended affair, with no set goals and no fixed schedule.

2. *You're just along for the ride.* The whole point of driver's ed, homeschool style, is to spend time with the boy. Make your demonstrations incidental to companionship, and your pedagogy supplemental to respect.

3. *Acknowledge your superiority.* The kid knows you know he's not a great driver. Don't insult him by trying to pretend he's Dale Earnhart. If you both start with the same assumptions, you'll both travel together more easily.

4. *Don't hector. Don't lecture.* Say what you need to say once. Unless there's a clear opportunity for danger, don't repeat it, unless you're certain you have been misunderstood. You can't make something happen by talking it to tears, so speak your piece, then sit on your hands.

5. *Do as little as possible, but as much as necessary.* Don't let the kid get in hot water simply because you were too reticent or too lazy to offer

advice and correction. If he doesn't know how to parallel park, don't let him push bumpers as some sort of punishment. He knows he doesn't know how to parallel park. He knows you know it, too. So help out.

6. ***Don't damn with excessive praise.*** Did he do it right? Then a simple "Nice job" will do. (KCA)

How Not to Educate Boys

Some expert words of caution on sending boys off to public reeducation centers:

Sons and Daughters: A few years ago, the AAUW reported a decline in the self-esteem of teenage girls and told of their battle against institutional prejudice. Every network, every newspaper, and every national magazine has repeated the same terrible story ever since: Teachers consistently show favoritism to boys, girls are suffering a crisis of self-esteem, and the hopes and dreams of girls are regularly shattered by the discriminatory treatment they receive in the public schools. Legislation was passed to address the problem. Millions of dollars were spent studying ways to improve girls' self-esteem. And the Ms. Foundation launched its Take Your Daughters to Work Day. The girls-at-work day became such a publicity and fund-raising success that the Foundation filed trademark protection for the name "Take Your Daughters to Work."

A Big Main Thing: The trouble is, *nothing in the study was true.* The study was designed to produce the desired politically correct result. The media has perpetuated the study's findings until they have become accepted as fact. Yet the real story—arguably the biggest, most under-reported educational story of our time—has been the successful conquest of American education by girls and women. Those who claim gender bias in the schools purposefully ignore the remarkable changes that have taken place in just one generation of women.

But, worse, they also ignore the dangerous plight of boys and young men. Here's a reality checklist:

• ***Collegiate success.*** In 1970, women accounted for only 41 percent of college enrollment in the U.S. Fewer than 10 percent of degrees in law and medicine were awarded to women. Only 14 percent of all doctoral degrees went to women. What's happened since?

Women now constitute the majority of all graduate and professional students in American higher education.

Fifty-five percent of all collegiate undergraduates are women.

Women are 59 percent of all masters' degree candidates.

Women account for nearly half the enrollment in law and medical schools.

Thirty-nine percent of all doctoral degrees will go to women.

- *Boys are falling behind,* and this may have critical social consequences.

- *Higher hopes.* Surveys conducted by the U.S. Department of Education—and by independent researchers—agree that women and girls have higher aspirations than their male counterparts. Items:

Eighth-grade girls are twice as likely as boys to aspire to a professional, business, or managerial career.

Twelfth-grade girls are more likely to aspire to a college or graduate degree than boys—and more likely to have their dreams come true.

In elementary and high schools, girls have higher scores on national tests than boys in reading and writing and equal or only marginally lower scores than boys in math and science.

In fact, since 1980, young men have been *less* likely than young women to go to college.

- *Boys lose.* Some of the most disturbing trends in our schools concern not girls, but boys. Contrary to the prevailing myth, boys are not pampered beings. Witness:

Eighth-grade boys are 50 percent more likely to be held back a grade than girls.

In high school, *two-thirds of the special-ed students are boys.*

In 1990, among fifteen- to twenty-four-year-olds, *young men were four times more likely to be victims of a homicide* than young women.

The same study found that *fifteen- to twenty-four-year-old young men were five times more likely to kill themselves* than young women (the homicide rate is highest for black males; the suicide rate is highest for white males).

Is there any more profound indicator of low self-esteem than the decision by a young man to end his life?

Why are young men killing themselves and each other in such unprecedented numbers? Except for occasional attention given to the problem of African-American males, no one—and certainly not the women running the Ms. Foundation—has given much thought or attention to the escalating despair of young American men of all races. (DR)

How to Take Control of Your Public School Board

There are a million dad duties, but none quite so pressing as making sure the kids can read and write. Once upon a time, this was a do-it-yourself chore (see next section). But these days, we frequently send the kids out to get their wrinkled brains neatly pressed and starched. The problem starts there, because for many parents, once the kid's at school, their involvement with education ends. With an abundance of two-income and single-parent families, too many grown-ups just don't have the time to get involved in local school problems. Instead, parents look to education experts to take charge. The result of that abdication of responsibility is predictable: **After a century of education reform, kids have been reformed right to the brink of stupidity.** Perhaps as a consequence, the latest generation of education reformers actively discourages parental involvement at the local level. If you think your local schools aren't doing their job, nobody's going to pay much attention to your complaint—unless you happen to be on the school board. Running for such a thankless public office can be hard work, and, for most of us, it's really the last option. But if you have no choice, here are the steps you need to follow to regain control of your local schools:

- *Try proper channels first.* Try working with the local PTA. Attend town meetings. Talk to administrators. Make sure your candidacy is the result of having tried everything else first.

- *Be skeptical of the status quo.* Most educators will tell you nothing can be done to solve local school problems. Don't believe them. Think through the problems for yourself so you'll have a clear grasp of the issues.

- *Start small.* To get a grass-roots movement going, put together a small group—say, less than a half dozen—to meet with regularly. Write letters to the editor of the local paper, organize appearances on radio call-in shows, and spread the word about the most pressing issues.

- *Thicken your skin.* Once you start making an impression as a possible threat to the sitting board, they'll unload on you with both barrels. Don't take it personally. It's only politics. Be honest and straightforward in your replies. Stick to the facts and the issues.

- *Borrow experience.* Make an ally out of somebody who has run for public office before. He'll be the person who'll help you figure out how to file and when, and how to meet some of the more obscure candidacy requirements.

- **Raise money.** This is the worst part of the entire process. Take the campaign a week at a time so spending doesn't run out of control. Volunteers are essential cost cutters. A carefully run campaign for local office can be mounted for less than one thousand dollars, but if the field's crowded or the district's large, it can easily cost more.

   A *good, lowball rule of thumb* is a dollar a voter.

- **Knock and talk.** Going door-to-door is the most effective form of advertising, but also the most difficult. Look for ways to address groups of people—clubs, church affairs, that sort of thing. Put together a press kit, including a black-and-white photo, a résumé, and a printed handout giving your view of the issues. Get to know the local newspaper editor.

- **Use the postal service.** Often, the most effective campaign tool is the direct-mail piece you send to all the voters in your school district.

- **Watch it happen.** On election day, make sure you have local faces at the polling places. Monitor voting carefully, and, if possible, watch the count take place. (KM)

How to Get into Home School

If your public schools just aren't working, and you don't have the time or inclination to fight the system, there is another option: Do it yourself.

You may think home schooling is the wild frontier of education, dominated by fringe dwellers with survivalist or religious paranoias. But you're wrong. Where, only ten years ago, there were fewer than twenty thousand home schoolers, today some estimates put the number of home-schooling families as high as a half million—most of whom are mainstream, middle-class parents (including a surprising number of schoolteachers and administrators) concerned with the obvious shortcomings of the nation's public education system. The results are often worth it: *Home-schooled children typically perform well above national educational standards.*

However, opting to home-school a child is a major decision, one not to be taken lightly. In fact, home schools, like all good schools, ought to have an admissions test of some sort, asking not the kids but the parents some tough questions that require thoughtful, honest answers. If such a test existed, it might look something like this:

1. ***Can you afford it?*** Home schooling usually requires that one parent stay home. In families where both parents work outside, home schooling is difficult.

2. ***A related question: What are your personal goals?*** What will you be giving up to home-school?

3. ***Do you enjoy spending time with your children?*** Or do you prefer to spend part of your day on your own?

    A rule of thumb: On average, it takes three hours a day for a home school to do what it takes a public school all day to do.

4. ***Are you willing to be different?*** Many people—maybe even your own parents—will be uncomfortable with your decision.

5. ***Are you willing to commit your best effort to it for at least a year?*** That's about how long it takes to know if you *really* want to home-school.

6. ***Can you make your kids behave?*** Remember, as the principal-teacher-dean of students of a home school, you have to make them do schoolwork they'd rather not do. Plus, you'll need more help from them on household chores. Figure that at least once a day, they'll have to do something *just because you asked them to.*

7. ***Are you willing to study along with your children?*** Whether you are spontaneous or well organized is less important than your willingness to learn along with the kids.

8. ***Are you willing to admit mistakes and learn from them?*** Nothing else is more crucial to home-schooling success.

9. ***Are you will ing to develop your children on their own path, rather than to a school standard?***

10. ***If you were honest in answering questions one through nine, do you still want to learn more?*** If so, here's what to do next:

Home-school yourself about home-schooling. Try *You Can Teach Your Children Successfully* by Ruth Beechick. Or get in touch with your local home-schooling support group. Everybody knows somebody who knows somebody who's home-schooling his kids. Home-school support groups provide the regular social interaction and group activities that complement out-of-school programs. If you need more information on support groups, send a SASE to one of the national clearinghouses, such as the Moore Foundation, Box 1, Camas, WA 98607, or Growing Without Schooling, 2269 Massachusetts Avenue, Cambridge, MA 02142. (CF)

13. Manners and Morals

Here's a commonplace situation: You're out on a Saturday, shopping for a bargain-basement epiphany, some cheap, discount-model insight upon which you can hang the skeletal framework of life's small lessons. Usually, this kind of search requires a lot of rack sifting and shelf scouring. But let's say you get handed one the easy way on your way into Wal-Mart. You hold open the door for an overdressed, angry woman obviously from out-of-town, which, for most of us means from some big, Eastern city. As she brushes by she gives you a scowl: "What the hell are you?" she asks. "A Boy Scout?"

Now, as it happens, my dear lads, many of us have indeed served in this country's unarmed forces. We have been soldiers of virtue. We have pitched the good tent and dug the deep hole. Many of us have long since retired from active duty. But once you've been through a camporee or two, it's hard to forget all that Webelo drill you learned in basic. Like how you're supposed to hold the door open for girls, women, ladies, and even stray babes, like the metropolitan harpy at the budget store. It's an instinct thing.

So hers is a good question. Most of us like the idea that some part of us is still an old-lady-walkin', merit-badge-totin', two-sticks-rubbin' Boy Scout. But some other part of us recoils at the very thought of walking all day just to go camping in a pair of shorts. Scout? Non-Scout? Many of us are in the same boat, lost on the big, dark lake of modern mayhem looking in the deep for some sadly misplaced virtues.

How to Be a Good Scout

To find out whether you're still a good Scout, you have to get out your old handbook. You'll find what you're looking for in the part of the book that talks about the Boy Scout "Law," a collection of straightforward statements— "a Scout is trustworthy, a Scout is loyal," and all that. Who doesn't like the idea of a Scout Law? Like Moses', the Scout Law seems pretty elementary. You read down the list, and if all the shoes fit, then you must be a Scout. But that's also where it can turn a little ugly. You end up doing the only thing you can do to tell whether you've still got your Cub *cojones*—asking yourself a bunch of earnest, cornball questions.

ARE YOU TRUSTWORTHY?

Most of us see this one coming out of the gate, and think, hell, there go *all* the politicians, most of the journalists, and half the academics. But wait! you think. There I go, too! How trustworthy am I? Most men have a few overdue library books sitting around, maybe next to that late notice from Sears. The librarian and Sears both trusted us. We let them down. Bad Scouts. But we didn't mean to. And we were going to drop off the books on our way to the post office, and send Sears a check right away. Good Scouts. So we find ourselves yanked between the poles of probity. You too? Want to know if you're trustworthy? Here's the four-point checklist:
1. ***Visa and the bank are both after you to borrow money,*** and the guy down at Chevy Central will sell you a new Caprice with no money down (but see also "Are You Thrifty?").
2. ***You wouldn't cheat on your wife or girlfriend*** even if the chances of getting caught were less than 5 percent.
3. ***You refrain from blaming God*** for all your problems.
4. ***You keep a big secret*** even though revealing it would directly profit you.
    If you said, "yeah, yeah" to all the above, or even to two or three of them, you can trust yourself.

ARE YOU LOYAL?

Hmm. **Loyalty, naked, is nowhere.** Blind loyalty is blind to other moral considerations. Want to know if you're loyal? Go out in the backyard, grab that mutt of yours, look him square in the eyes, and see if you can say, in all honesty, "Feeling's mutual." But you whip that dog, he'll gnaw at your throat someday. Even dogs know better than to let their loyalty run around loose.

ARE YOU HELPFUL?

Here, **they must mean a nonreciprocating kind of helpfulness.** Strictly speaking, it's not being helpful if you're simply trading favors with the guy in the next cubicle, in which you cover his heinie and he covers yours. The ultimate test of helpfulness is when you do something that directly benefits somebody else, yet has no benefit to you. *An example:* Your brother-in-law decides to move next door, and you show up to tote some boxes. In this instance, you have been a help to him, even though you have perhaps been a hindrance to yourself.

ARE YOU FRIENDLY?

Yow. **"Friendliness" has really taken some hits lately,** especially since the public differences between Nicole and her friend O. J. and Selena and her friend the fan-club lady. In fact, there are almost no "friendly" role models, except possibly Fred Rogers and Cal Ripken. Friendly people in sitcoms and in public life are seen as weak losers. Also, friendly people are not taken seriously. Success and power are more closely allied to sullen rudeness than genuine friendliness. It takes a heap o' confidence to be a friendly sort these days. If you can be consistently friendly to those who work under your sufferance, you are a fine Scout of a man.

ARE YOU COURTEOUS?

You did hold the door for the crazy woman. You did. Would you do it again— same woman, same door—if you knew that all you'd get for your trouble was an ersatz insult?

The rules of etiquette are timeless; they are objective behavioral truths, and we can't let the bastards change them. "Courtesy," as a virtue, is apparently a curious anachronism. Supermarkets give you "Courtesy Cards," entitling you to a small measure of courtesy from the help. That's nice. If you're a woman, here's how to use a courtesy card efficiently: You stand at the front door of the supermarket with your arms full of grocery bags waiting for the box boy to give you a hand. When he doesn't show, you drop your groceries all over the floor, rummage through your bag, and produce your courtesy card. You wave it wildly over your head and shout, "*Courtesy!* I've got a card here and I'll use it!" Then, while you pick up your peanut butter and Spam, the box boy comes running and holds open the door for you. In this case, if you're the box boy, you're also a Scout-flop.

ARE YOU KIND?

Since "generous" and "compassionate" aren't on the Scout Law list, **"kind" has to encompass more than just being nonviolent.** Maybe this is what is meant by "tolerant," another word not on the list, but one much on the lips of those who wish for kindness in exchange for noisy, rude self-righteousness. Bumper stickers urge us on to new heights of kindness: "Commit Random Acts of Kindness." Sensible men say if you kick no poodles you are kind enough.

ARE YOU OBEDIENT?

While we can all agree that obedience, like loyalty, must have reasonable limits imposed by common sense, we might also all agree that of all the Scoutish qualities, **"obedience" is the one least likely to succeed at this end of the millennium.** Why? Because, first off, it implies a filial relationship with a set of parents, and many parents don't come in sets anymore. In fact, many parents are invisible, and obedience to something not seen is similar to *faith,* and faith is very much despised, because faith is obedience to moral conviction, and obedience to moral conviction gives the same people who demand "tolerance" acute willies.

A suggested replacement might be "responsible." Being "responsible" is recently something people love to talk about. It is the single most commonly lamented lost virtue, and we all figure that if we talk about how much we need responsibility long enough, somebody will come along and do something about the lack of it. Maybe the government could help more here.

ARE YOU CHEERFUL?

Ha! Like, someday we'll all look back on these ebola outbreaks and ozone holes and laugh about them. But until then, try to keep smiling through. Maybe **this doesn't mean you have to go through life laughing insanely.** Maybe it's enough to be simply optimistic. A simple optimism test: Take a ten-dollar bill to the bank and get two fives. Send the principal author of this book one. Now look at your five. Do you see a half of your old ten-spot and feel bitterly cheated? Or do you see a full Lincoln and a happy stranger? Be optimistic, for this kind of optimism is contagious: If you're able to generate spontaneous optimism so easily, imagine how optimistic that will make the recipient of your banknote.

ARE YOU THRIFTY?

Here's how to tell whether or not thrift is even possible for you to obtain: Down the left side of a piece of yellow legal pad, list all the things contributing to your inability to manage money. Now, down the right-hand side, list all the things you could do to rectify the situation. If even one of the items on the right-hand side is something you have to go out and buy—like a PowerMac, with that cool, new version of "Quicken" to help you see exactly where your budgetary shortfall is—then you're dead meat, moneywise.

ARE YOU BRAVE?

In the Scouts, bravery meant you'd run into a burning building to rescue the hamster. Now we realize that kind of bravery doesn't really count. We all know guys who drove tanks through Vietnam and across the Iraqi desert, but who are just a little afraid of commitment. **When you pass age thirty-two, bravery means something completely different.** There are many men out there who are brave simply because they don't divorce their harridan wives. Any passerby can rescue the drowning kid. A real act of bravery is when you stand up at a school board meeting in an effort to rescue dumbed-down kids.

ARE YOU CLEAN?

Of course, this is a Scouting euphemism for avoidance of masturbation. Baden-Powell, the proto-Scout, was, like all Englishmen of his day, virulently antiwhack. You may choose to interpret this literally, however, and so bathe daily. Do you need to be told how to check your own hygiene levels? No. All you have to do is ask the guy next to you on the bus. No, wait. You don't even have to do that. If there's nobody next to you on the bus, your question has already been answered.

ARE YOU REVERENT?

This is tough. The Scouts used to make reverence a focal point of every campfire singalong and every walk in the woods. That was good, since when you started feeling a little uncomfortable about your relationship with your Creator, you could always distract yourself by admiring His creation. **For grown men, thinking about God can cause acute headaches.** But kids? They don't care. They want to know all about heaven the first time a goldfish goes belly-up, so reverence is something forced upon fathers. It gets easier all the time, and for good reason: Like it or not, fathers are the patriarch in their own family-tribe. Therefore, not only are they reverent, they are also revered.

Other circumstances can also summon a contemplation of the divine. For instance, hospitals are full of religious nuts. So get sick and get reverent.

Thus, the question posed by that unfriendly, irreverent, discourteous, unkind, no doubt unclean woman was a pretty good one. Now, obviously, she's no Scout. But what about the rest of us demobbed fire starters? The "Law" of the Boy Scouts is, as my Scout manual points out, unique in that there are no injunctions in it—no itemization of things thou shalt not do. There's just that list of stuff you ought to be. It should be noted that many of the qualities we're now told women most demand in a man are not on the Scout's list. A more politically correct Scout would perhaps be sensitive, caring, sharing, feeling, giving, serious, prudent, and prim. He would also not piss in the woods, for the bears have to live there, too. The Scout Law doesn't seem to fit into modern sensibilities about what a young man should be. After all, when women ask if you're some kind of Boy Scout, they think they're being insulting.

The virtues demanded by the Scouts are more difficult to achieve than the qualities some women might demand. For instance, any yahoo with the price of a drink can get sensitive. But it's *hard* to be brave, thrifty, friendly, and courteous. So you have to go down the list, try to remember what those little laws meant, and see how you come out. It's like the driver's test: You miss one and you flunk. "By doing your best to live up to the Scout Law," says the old BSA manual, "you are a Scout. If you should willfully break the Scout Law you are not a Scout. It is as simple as that." Even if you get all the way down the list to "reverent" before you wash out, you may be one hell of a guy, but, hey, you're no Scout. There is a certain theological purity at work here—the formulation used by the Scouts to determine who's in and who's out is the same as the formulation used by the Roman Catholic and Orthodox churches to determine whether sinners have excommunicated themselves. But there's not a lot of guidance in this approach, since really, nobody is, say, kind and clean *all* the time. *Most* of the time ought to do.

So **the answer to whether you're a Scout is in how you read the facts.** Maybe you need something like one of those old mechanical oil pressure gauges, in which the needle floats between high and low, good and bad. Wire it up to each of the Scout categories and read the result. A Scout is cheerful. Are you cheerful? Sure, sometimes. If the gauge reads more than halfway to "cheerful," you pass. If it's drifting more to bummed, you don't. In fact, there used to be a car with gauges just like those. You could take it anywhere—over hill, over dale. It was, of course, called a Scout.

Meanwhile, other virtues, unlisted by the Scouts, show up elsewhere. For instance: Are you polite?

How to Be Polite Under Virtually Any Circumstance

These may not be the best of times, and these may not be the worst of times, but for sheer rudeness, these times beat the dickens out of most other times. Why? Because where once we got the laws of bourgeois etiquette from Emily Post and Amy Vanderbilt, now we get pop-etiquette from Beavis and Butthead, Ren and Stimpy, and Homer Simpson's little boy. **More than at any time in recent memory, crude is cool.** Rude is the mood to sell food, jeans, music, cars, politics, and feminine hygiene products. From Howard Stern's morning howdy to Greg Kinnear's last later, misbehavior's in the air.

   The bad part about all this is that not knowing good manners from bad can make you an unhappy boy—sullen, mean, stressed like the metal on an old Boeing wing. The plain fact is that even in a brave, bad new world, most guys just want to know what the rules are for decent deportment in the real world—not which fork to use with shrimp or how to bow, but the real nerve wrackers: How to decline a date with the boss or what to send your broker's wife when they take him off to jail. We know that if we get the rules right, we can pull off anything with cool calmness.

   We all have questions about the uncharted waters of life and which rules apply and when. Some of these questions are ones you may have asked yourself. We thought it would be rude to not reply.

MONEY MANNERS

Money is dirty. Filthy. Essential. It's also inherently mannerless and the root of all bad manners. Some people will sell their friendships, their moms, and their souls if the price is right; these guys love money dearly and are never offended by it. On the other hand, the very existence of money on the same physical plane can be an affront to a polite guy. The result is that whenever you're dealing with money, you're working outside the envelope of etiquette, like a spacewalk, where special protective measures are required for survival. (RMcE)

How to Ask for a Raise

In a polite world, it would never be necessary to ask for a raise. It would be politely offered. The boss would knock softly on your cubicle frame and say, "Sorry, Withers. Do you have a sec? The chairman of the board wondered if it would be inconvenient if we slipped a few extra grand into your pay packet. I mean, if that's okay. If it's no trouble." And you would nod, say, "Yes, of course, Mr. Murdoch, very kind," and there would be no further discussion about something so utterly distasteful. But since we live on Rude World, a man's got to ask. The rules of politely begging for money are these:

- **Be reasonable.** Know what you're worth. A raise is not a right; it's not something granted as a matter of course every few months or years. In fact, you're rude if you ask for a raise simply because nobody's got around to firing you; seniority may be either a mark of your competence or a testament to your employer's humanity. But if you know what you contribute, and you know what that contribution's worth, and if that's not what you're getting, say so in as straightforward a manner as possible. The perfectly phrased raise request comes disguised as an astute observation: "You know, chief, last year I saved the firm three mill, yet I'm getting ten grand less than the other kids. I figure I'm worth more than those guys, and a lot more than what I'm getting now."

- **Be sensible.** You must time a raise request with an awareness of what's going on around you. If the firm has just lost its biggest client, laid off half the force, or had its assets seized by the feds, your request for a raise may strike your boss as being a trifle insensitive, and he may wish to politely trash your behind. The best time to ask for a raise is soon after you or your department has obviously earned it by making a visible and obvious contribution to the company's good fortunes. (WM)

- **Be prepared.** There's a good chance any sensible, reasonable request for additional salary might be declined. Refusing to give a man a raise when he's clearly entitled to one and when circumstances obviously permit it is an unambiguous statement from management about one of two things. It means the boss is greedy. Or that you're despised. Either way, the sign you should be looking for reads "Exit." Accept this calmly and politely, and the next day, start a well-planned, deliberate, and overtly civil search for somebody else you can ask for a raise.

How to Deny a Raise

- **Say more than no.** Saying no is the most difficult feat of mannerly legerdemain, since a simple no is generally not understood as a simple statement. Let's say the shoe's on the other foot, and you're the one who has to deny a subordinate's request—for more money or for anything else, for that matter. Don't waffle. Just say no. And explain why, perhaps also tempering your directness with a good-natured shrug. Your explanation may be factual or not, depending. But it's rude to respond to a yes-or-no question with a maybe, unless that's clearly the only proper response. If a weaselly, overpaid underling comes whinging around with his hand out, and you really can't see your way clear to grant him his wish, say so. You should also add your reasons for saying no—but only if you wish your denial not to be misunderstood as a larger gesture, such as telling the worthless whiner to go find another job. If you really want the guy to get lost, an uninterested, uninflected "No" should do the trick. (TRW, BAS)

What to Do When the Waiter Comes back to the Table and Says, "Sorry, Your Card's Been Denied"

This is a telling example of the **Main Thing** about etiquette:

> The rules of etiquette exist not to make boors out of those who don't know them, but to make sure everybody feels as comfortable as possible in as many situations as possible.

- *Consider the comfort of your dinner partner.* Don't make the credit card problem a big deal, because it isn't one. It's nothing personal between you and the waiter, and it's nothing you can rectify on the spot. Don't feign outrage and indignation, and don't abuse the messenger. Simply acknowledge what has happened as an awkward situation—you're apparently over the limit imposed by the credit card issuer—and ask the waiter for a suggestion about other means of satisfying the bill, say, paying by personal check or with a charge card (which, unlike a credit card, has no fixed limit).
- *Consider the comfort of your waiter.* If none of the above means of payment is acceptable and you volunteer to run around the corner to an ATM for cash, it is proper manners to leave something behind of obvious value—your driver's license, for example, or your dinner companion.
- *Make a stink with your banker.* Having said the above, we should also say that it's awfully bad manners to impose a limit on a chap's credit, since it presumes his inability or unwillingness to repay the debt. This is a personal insult, of course, and one you may wish to bring up later, when you call the bank. (Anon.)

SOCIAL MANNERS

What to Do if You Cut One

Speaking of bringing something up: If the waiter's news comes as such as shock to you that you actually pass gas, you have a new but somehow related problem. What to do in case of flagrant fragrance?

- *If it's a silent poof, ignore it.* S**t happens, as they say.
- *But if the foghorn in your shorts screams, "Fart alert! Dive! Dive!"* you have to acknowledge its existence in the world. The best way: Deal with it as if it were an unexpected burp. Just say, "Yow. Sorry." Make even less of this than you did about the credit card, even though both situations stink. (TRW)

How to Propose a Formal Toast

Some guys make it look so easy. But standing up in a room full of strangers and talking to a wineglass can be the first step to social oblivion, unless you plan ahead.

- *Don't extemporize.* Reduce what you want to say down to three, maybe four sentences. Then be still.
- *You're funny enough.* Unless you're Billy Crystal, you're going to have to get by on your charm, not your wit. Make your toast friendly and pleasant, not pretentious and not forced.
- *Timing is* everything. So wait until everybody's on hand, and hold off until all the chairs have been pulled in. The principal toast to a guest of honor should come just after everybody has been seated. A toast saying thanks should precede dessert.
- *Speak up.* Clink your fork on your wineglass—softly. Then say what you have to say loud enough for everybody to hear it.
- *Drink up.* Don't dribble. (AMcLL)

How to Know Who Pays on a Dinner Date

The one who pays is the one who tendered the invitation. Period. Or, rather, semicolon; the exception is when the two of you are simply workmates out for grub, in which case you:

- *Split the check down the middle.* It is sometimes shocking to modern men's delicate sense of newfound sensitivity and old-fashioned decorum to watch two or more women hunched over a table, figuring to the penny the amount each of them owes. Men customarily take the total, add the tip, and divide by the number of diners—done.
- *But don't abuse the equal-split rule.* When dividing the tab equally, polite guys avoid ordering the eighteen-dollar lobster-and-truffle appetizer, or if they simply must have it, offer to pay extra for it. Nobody likes the boor who polishes off every expensive, oddball dish on the menu, tops it off with a twenty-dollar glass of brandy, then is the first to say, "Shall we

just divide this four ways?" when the bill arrives. Also, if you're out with your buddies, you have to pay for the drinks you spill. (RL)

FRIENDLY MANNERS

What a wide word is "friendship." Once used sparingly to describe a relationship built on a complex of love and concern, modern friendship runs the gamut from mutual tolerance to mutual devotion, and can be said to exist anywhere in the absence of outright hatred and betrayal.

But just because modern friends aren't what they used to be doesn't mean we expect any less from them—nor they from us.

How to Answer a Friend Who Asks for a Loan

There's no reason money and friendship can't be mixed, provided you observe the rules of friendship, especially in making or requesting a loan. Here's what that means, bottom line: You know your friend, you know how he ticks, you know how he feels about money, women, stocks, baseball. You know he doesn't feel the same way about all these things as you do. But you also know, as a matter of respect, that you're not going to impose your values on him or be able to change his behavior in any big way. So when it comes time to lend or borrow money, you have to evaluate two things: One, how the loan is structured. Two, the dollar value of the friendship. It's not polite to borrow from or lend money to a friend until you do those things first. So,

- *Set the ground rules.* If your pal is an organized guy, normally solvent, temporarily short on cash, but otherwise careful in managing the details of his life, he's probably a guy who sees a loan as a relatively mundane business matter. That means you should both be able to make the loan contingent on a mutually agreed payback date or sequence of payments, including interest if you think that makes sense, and to put it all in writing.
- *Or at least be aware of what you're risking.* If your friend is crazy-wild with women and debts, but that's part of the reason you like him, make the loan with an assumption that you may never see your money again. The friendship, after all, is the only collateral you have, and if your buddy reneges, it's the only thing you can repo.

In both cases, it's as rude to lend more than you can afford to risk as it is to borrow more than you can possibly repay. (GSD)

See also "How to lend Money to Friends" in Chapter 8.

What to Do if You've Been Left Off a Party List

Last year you got invited to the Party of the Century. This year, you didn't. What do you do? That's easy. You assume it's not a mistake and that she's not your friend anymore, and you forget it. Don't call, don't seek revenge, don't whine to all her friends. **Nothing's more impolite than belaboring the obvious.** (Anon.)

How to Confront People Who Are Bad-mouthing You

Hmm. That brings us to **Main Thing** number two of modern etiquette: When the only polite thing to do in response to rude behavior is itself rude, do it with relish.

• *Tell it like it is.* While it would normally be rude to confront somebody with evidence of his misdeeds, in this case the thing to do is seek to alleviate the discomfort you have obviously caused someone. The way to do that is to ask the guy to his face why he said what he said behind your back. Simple enough, no? Then you can ask what he suggests you do to make him feel better. Do it like this: "I understand you think I pilfer pocket change out of the March of Dimes box at the reception desk." The chump will hem and haw and probably deny it. Don't let it slide; force it out into the open. Ask straight out, "What would make you feel that way?" When the guy says it's because he saw you with your arm up to your elbow in the money jar, you can tell him you were just making change or whatever, but the important thing is you'll have diffused the situation on your own terms. Not only is this direct approach polite, it feels good, too.

• *But don't sabotage your informant.* One caution: This confrontation must not be made at the expense of a third party, so if challenging the miscreant reveals that another friend has shared a confidence or is otherwise tattling, let it go until you get it from at least one other source. Meanwhile, you can take solace in this: Nobody is so thoroughly reviled as a coward, and since bad-mouthing is usually done to obtain favor, it will comfort you to know that it actually has the opposite effect. Therefore, by the time you can seek redress, the gossip has already paid the price of his wickedness. (HDO)

How to Patch a Friendship You've Damaged by Neglect

You haven't returned five phone calls and two letters? Simply call and suggest a specific date for lunch or a round of miniature golf. Any rapprochement is polite. But agree on a precise time and place to get together. None of this, "Let's get together sometime" stuff. (HDO)

MANNERS AT WORK

Work is where manners assume really huge dimensions of hypocrisy, simply because a failure to be polite at a critical moment can spell the difference between continuing to spend your days at your place of employment and spending them in your basement rec room.

How to Be Nice to Your Boss Without Appearing to Kiss His Ass

It all depends on how honest you are with yourself. If you really do want to brownnose, get an adjustable ball cap with a toilet-paper dispenser mounted on the bill. There's no proper etiquette for brownnosing, but nothing anybody says will stop you. On the other hand, if you think simply being nice, honest, a hard worker, and so forth, will be mistaken for brownnosing, you're making a rude mistake. **Be as nice to the boss as he is to you,** and you'll be golden, etiquettewise. (SS)

How to Work for Somebody Who Was Once Your Subordinate

You can't, and to try to do so only puts an impolite burden on your new honcho. Some management decisions carry such an unmistakable subtext that only a desperate fool will ignore the message. Do we have to spell it out? Your name is mud in this company. That said, **this is a situation in which simple rules of good manners will stand you in good stead.** Go to your new boss and tell her you wish her well, that you'll be leaving in a month or so, and that you want to do everything you can before you skedaddle to make sure everything goes smoothly for her. Then do what you said you'd do, *especially including the skedaddle part.* You'll at least leave with a nice reference and a friend, where you could have left an enemy. (Anon.)

How to Deal with a Backstabbing Coworker

Biz-betrayal is everywhere. Let's say you had a brilliant idea, shared it with the guy in the next cubicle, and now's he's getting a raise on the strength of it. What do you do?

   Sometimes the rules of etiquette exist not to make others feel at ease, but to make sure we don't hurt ourselves. This is such a scenario. So,

- *Don't make a big, embarrassing fuss.* The rude route, when you discover that you've been looted, is to write a memo outlining your claims, send it to your boss, who has already gone out on a limb for your rival, and ask him to see that justice is done. It's not going to happen, first of all, and second, you'll probably be asked rudely to leave.

- *Since you can't lick 'em, join 'em.* The polite thing to do is also the sensible thing to do: Go to your idea-grubbing competitor, whom you rightly despise, and sign on to help him make the idea work as well as possible. Be his biggest supporter and his right-hand man. Be loyal and trustworthy, especially trustworthy. One of two things eventually will happen: Since he's operating at a creative level higher than that to which he could rightfully aspire, there's a good chance smoke will eventually spew from his engines, oil will streak along his wings, and he'll crash and burn, at which time you should politely stand aside so as not to be struck by flying debris. That's one thing that might happen. The other thing is that you'll come up with another brilliant idea, and this time you'll guard it wisely and well and with polite persistence until you can implement it to your own credit. (Anon.)

SEX, SEDUCTION, AND RELATIONSHIP MANNERS

Why lump these three things together? Because this illustrates how two apparently rude and mannerless enterprises can eventually lead to a situation in which manners are everything. Goes to show that good etiquette resembles a food chain, in which swinging occupies the bottom link, and marriage occupies the top, and divorce lawyers represent rabid mutants with bolt cutters.

How to Work with Women Without Becoming Paranoid

What with the current political climate, lots of guys are worried about being sent up to the Big House for sexual harassment.

- *Don't worry. Be happy. And be polite.* Look, you can't run your life according to your fears. If you are cordial and friendly and—above all—polite to the women in your office, nobody's going to be able to nail you on a bum charge of sexual harassment. Obeying the rules of etiquette are critical here, since that's what will keep you on the good-guy side of a bad-guy–good-guy conflict. Not only that, but times are a-changin', at last, and the personnel police are catching on to the excesses at large in this area. Angry women with attitudes used to be able to destroy a man's career on a whim. No more. Now they need witnesses and proof of a pattern of bad behavior before they can send you packing. So demonstrate instead a pattern of mannerly behavior, and not only will you be safe and sound, you'll also be wildly popular among most women, who are suckers for a well-polished dude who can hold open the door and tip his hat on cue. (DSD)

How to Meet a Beautiful Woman

The operative principle is that even though a woman is beautiful, she merits consideration as a human being. This platitude comes courtesy of a woman who is a looker and tells us that she is sick of men who assume the best way to make her acquaintance is to insult her. "Why," she asked, "can't men just say 'Hello'?"

The answer, of course, is that "Hello" has no hook. It's not what we call a sell line. And for men, seduction is nothing more than salesmanship with a higher-than-average commission at stake.

Therefore, the polite thing to do is remove all that goal-oriented effluvia from the implications of a simple introduction. The rules of a introduction are simple:

- *If a mutual friend is making the introductions, a man is always presented to a woman.* "Trixie? I'd like you to meet my buddy, Ralph, Ralph Cooper. Coop, Trixie Rockefeller."
- *If you're introducing yourself, mention your name before asking for hers.* "Hello, I'm Van. Van Boutons." Then make a subtle gesture as if to stick out your hand for a quick shake, but don't go through with it until she offers hers. The rules say that a man must wait until a woman first offers her hand for a handshake. Otherwise, no hands are shaken. A side benefit: By holding back in this way, you can avoid the embarrassment of standing there with an unshook hand. If she doesn't reply with her own name, you know two things: (1) she's rude, and (2) nothing, no matter how witty and inventive, will be sufficient to induce her into a conversation, since she's already completely aware that a casual conversation may well be the first step along a slippery slope that can ultimately lead to a situation such as that addressed in the following instruction. (RTS)

What to Say if You Can't Quite Get it Up

- *Don't whine.* The rude response is to apologize abjectly and claim that you don't understand because it's never happened before, ever. This type of apology only makes her responsible for what is clearly your problem, and the lie serves only to suggest that your partner is so hideous that she takes the fairy dust right out of your wand.
- *Take it like a man.* The polite response is to express mild disappointment, "Gee, too bad." Then you can get on to other things, since flaccidity need not stand between you and your partner's pleasure. (Anon.)

What to Say When Your Wife or Girlfriend Asks, "Honey, Do I Look Fat?"

Later in this chapter, we'll discuss how to lie. Here, let's focus on the rules governing the telling of "little white lies."

• *Lie if the truth would cause unnecessary pain.* For example, lie if she's fat.

• *Lie if the truth doesn't suggest an alternative or an easy remedy.* Again, let's say she's fat. Are you doing anything about it? No. Can you do anything about it? No. So keep your lips zipped.

• *Lie if the question hits the line between truth and fiction.* She's not *exactly* slender as a twig, but neither is she Orca. You like her just the way she is, which is to say, a little broad in the beam. She's asking you to tell her she looks fantastic. And, come to think of it, telling her that is no lie.

Which brings us to another **Main Thing**: Don't dignify a rhetorical question with an answer.

How can you tell a rhetorical question from an honest question? It's rhetorical if your partner asks, "Where were you last night?" when, in fact, you were sleeping on the other side of the bed. In such a case, she doesn't need an answer to that question. She needs to ask herself some new questions, instead, such as, "Why am I insanely jealous?"

Maybe you can ask yourself some of the same questions and figure out what—if anything—you're doing to cause such anguish. Try these:

• *Have you been punctual and reliable* in the performance of standard sex duty?

• *Have you been staring intently at waitresses' breasts* while asking for the fifth time what kinds of salad dressing are on the menu?

• *Have you been working late a lot?*

• *Have you been stumbling in drunk* wearing lingerie not your own?

Aside from provoking illogical fits of jealousy, these kinds of things constitute a sort of rudeness in and of themselves. And besides, "Where were you last night?" is not a rhetorical question if, instead of sleeping next to your wife, you were rudely occupied at the local Motel Six. (PP)

How to Handle a Jealous Lover

• *If you weren't at Motel Six,* but really were out of gas on the interstate, then politely explain to your wife the rudeness of assuming infidelity. Jealousy is a fine and mannerly barometer of affection. But unrestrained suspicion is the symptom of a larger problem, and the best thing to do is stop what you're doing and get it straightened out. Don't neglect your own possible culpability, either. Is there something you're doing—or not doing—that might warrant her suspicions?

• *If you were at Motel Six,* no polite explanation will wash away the indelible rudeness of your behavior. You are then faced with two rude alternatives: Confess all. Or deny all. Either way, there's a real good chance you'll soon have an opportunity to discover the etiquette of alimony. (DV) Which brings us to:

How to Handle an Angry Ex-Lover

The final **Main Thing** etiquette is this: In an embarrassing or awkward situation in which all other remedies have failed, do one thing: *Disappear.*

That doesn't mean you should move to Rio and change your name. It does mean you should forward your alimony or child support payments through the mail, and make any other contact as formal and brief as possible.

What you learn from all this is that it pays to learn marital manners on the honeymoon, and to never forget them. Why? Because divorce, as those who have been there already know, is the institutional, legal response to bad behavior, in which she was rude to you, and you to her, until you both needed lawyers to spell out all the rules of postmatrimonial etiquette. And that can be a rude awakening, indeed. (HGE)

How to Lie

Here, check out this trusty, old, yellowed Bible, the one with the hole clear through it from the time it stopped an assassin's bullet. Thumb through its singed pages, still covered with ash from when it gave protection from the great fire. Someplace in the Book is a piece of suitable moral armor, just the right size for everybody: We call these the rules of the game, but theologians call them the Ten Commandments. Most of them contain pretty good advice—no fooling around with the matron next door, no cussing allowed, and please don't kill anybody. But what about this one: "Thou shalt not bear false witness against thy neighbor"?

This one, of course, may well be a lie. You *have* to bear a little false witness every now and then, or you're dead meat, socially speaking. The reason you know that is because you lie all the time. You gotta. After all, there are plenty of good reasons for bearing false witness, while there are only a few good reasons not to. Thus, this small lesson in what we must call Survival Lying.

THE MERITS OF CHEAP FABRICATION

Here's a small list of circumstances in which, generally speaking, lying is essential to survival.

- *Deception against your enemies.* Lying is more than just making stuff up, of course. It's also a matter of not telling the truth when you know it. Sometimes, whole armies lie at once because if they didn't, they'd be truly dead. Stormin' Norman didn't tell Saddam the whole truth in the days leading up to Desert Storm, just as Ike didn't fess up to Hitler that Omaha Beach looked like a nice place for an on-shore, D-Day assault. (VS)

- *Lying for medicinal purposes.* The tangled relationship between a doctor and his patient can become a tightly woven lace of lies if the doctor determines that the patient's possession of the truth would be hazardous to his health. Likewise, we all lie to doctors and—especially—dentists all the time. In revenge they lie right back: "This won't hurt a bit," he said, pushing a Black and Decker right through an upper molar and into your cranium. It should be noted, though, that sometimes the lie of the patient has as much effect on the outcome of an illness as the lie of the doctor; sometimes, only the will of the patient to believe he will live—despite verifiable evidence to the contrary—is all he has to pull him through. When this happens, doctors say, "It's a miracle," while patients say, "I told you so."

  Alas, sometimes patients also say "I told you so" after complaining to a doctor they were sick, only to have the doctor assume they were lying—until just after the funeral, when the body goes in and the truth comes out.

- *Lies of social lubrication.* When people ask you how you're doing, they are fervently praying for you to lie, unless you're doing fine, thanks. People ask men on their *deathbeds* how they're doin', and all they want to hear is, "Pretty damned good, considering," or something similar. Here's a scene replayed frequently: The emergency crew shows up to wrestle most of a guy out of a squashed car, and the first thing they ask him is always, "How you doin'?" There's a fifty-fifty chance the guy'll say, "Uh, hanging on," just before he dies, the lie still on his lips. (GK)

- *Lies of self-flattery.* Telling ourselves lies is an important ingredient in building self-esteem. There are a number of ways of doing this, but dressing for it is the easiest way. As some of you lads may already know, beneath every cashmere sweater lies the double possibility of a well-upholstered lie. Lies have long been a staple of fashion, of course: The whole business of clothiers is to make us look better than we, in fact, do. But nothing screams "Fiction!" with quite the sincerity of a WonderBra. This may seem trivial, but it's not. If we can't trust our eyes, whom or what can we trust? Only this modest book, alas.

- *Lies forced on us by divine will.* Despite the abundance of deceitful propaganda to the contrary, men are the sex possessing the greatest virtue. For the most part, we work hard, play by the rules, treat women fair and square, and despise rogue males who sully our reputation. But we also love sex, and so we are vulnerable to women who often *strip* of us our honor, *use* us as sexual toys, then *abandon* us to our moral failure. A small example: Your wife shows up at home one day with a haircut like Andre Agassi's, a black ninja-clown suit, and a face from Disney and says, "It's the new me! Do you like it, honey?" Suddenly, you are robbed of your moral armor, stripped of your virtue, cheated out of sinlessness, because your alternative to telling a huge lie—"You look *marvelous!*"—is to fast from the flesh forever. This ultimately defeats the life-giving desire of Nature and therefore is a slap at God. So lie or burn. (Anon.)

- *Lies of labor.* Many men find employment because of their awesome ability to lie. The PR business is rich in accomplished deceivers; the same guys who represented the Kuwaitis to America—remember those hospital slaughters later found to be fakes?—next represented the Bosnians. We used to trust our newspapers not only to tell the truth but to manufacture our wars. But now, nobody in their right mind believes what they read or hear in the media.

But in a larger sense, we are all hired contingent on our willingness to tell a lie when our employer wishes the lie to be the truth. *Telling the truth to your employer is just as difficult as telling the truth to your wife,* even though every boss on the planet says he wants employees who aren't afraid to tell the truth. They all say, "I hate yes men." And their employees all rise as one to say, "Me, too, boss!"

THE WHOLE TRUTH—FAST AND LOOSE

There is a modern conceit in the air that suggests that the truth is a relative thing—that what you see as true is only true for you, and that it may be false for others. This is tolerant enough, but it's also ridiculous, since the truth is one of those things—like bad checks or foam falsies—that are subject to eventual verification.

An example: Women who on the telephone have absolutely fabulous voices. (FS)

Understanding that truth is a real thing is critical to understanding a lie. Hell, you can't even lie if there is no objective truth. It's pretty squirrely that we all agree on what constitutes a lie—"I didn't inhale"—easier than we agree on what constitutes the truth—is the guy a pothead? But one's as good as the other when you come right down to it.

This counts, because *lies require heavy maintenance.* You can't just tell a lie and walk away from it. You have to nurture it, prune it, water it, keep looking after it, making sure it doesn't get choked out by the weeds of truth, which is the cosmic volunteer and the ultimate victor. Therefore, when you lie, make sure you know the truth. Otherwise, not only will you add confusion to your already complex life, but you'll never know when you're lying. For examples, consider:

THE DARK SIDE OF LYING

This is the kind of stuff that gives lying a bad name. With these abuses of the truth, harm is done to others, no matter how thoroughly you have worked out your own self-justification.

- *Ideological lies.* The ultimate result of trivializing the truth and making it relative is that the truth is often subordinated in favor of superior virtues. When politicians, bureaucrats, and special-interest pleaders want to achieve a goal—say, the right to a free education by all mammals—they crank out reports, surveys, "findings," and other spurious research designed to create a smooth, synthetic truth suggesting that beavers flourish when exposed to Russian literature or that whales are fine painters, despite the fact that none of it is objectively true. After all, the goal isn't to reveal the truth, but to achieve virtue. It doesn't matter to either the politicians or the media that the virtuous end is a false one, since everybody knows the truth is often far less compelling than self-righteousness.

- *Lies of optimism.* We all tell these teeny whopperettes all the time. Here's how they work: Somebody will ask you to meet him at the corner of State and Main, thirty miles from your house, at noon. According to you, you live five minutes from State and Main. It's right *there,* around that corner and down that road and hang a left. Okay, seven minutes, tops. According to the laws of physics and the Department of Motor Vehicles, however, you live at least thirty minutes away. Nevertheless, even in the face of overwhelming scientific evidence that one cannot drive a conventional automobile the 240 MPH required to actually reach State and Main from your house in the 7 minutes you invariably allot yourself, you remain optimistic that it can be done. So you are always twenty-three minutes late. This causes others distress.

- **Lies of blinding stupidity.** These are the lies we most regret telling—lies that gain us nothing, yet bind us forever to the lie we've told. Entire Presidential administrations have been shaped by lies of this variety.

- **Lies of aspiration.** These are the lies you tell because you think by telling them, the lie will become the truth. For instance, you make fifty yards per, even though you know that you're really worth a lot more—say a hundred grand. And when somebody asks what you make, you ignore the fundamental impoliteness of the question and admit to making a hundred grand a year, since that comes a lot closer to the truth to which you aspire than the truth to which you must submit. The IRS really grooves on aspirational liars and gives them the greatest respect and understanding.

- **Lies of sales and seduction.** Salespeople often find that they have unwittingly told a lie by simply casting the truth in the most promising light. This does not alarm them. Here's how it goes: A woman asks you if you're married. You say, "Married? You know, I think it's sad how little commitment means to people these days. I think commitment is crucial to a society's health and sanity. How can we expect strangers to respect us if they have no respect for those they say they love?" Then you ask her if *she's* married, and the next thing you know, you're lying to your wife's lawyer.

Besides, you know you're on the wrong side of the moral tracks, even before you tell a lie. For instance, your wife asks a simple question: "Where have you been?" If you were at the hardware store, you don't even see the possibility of a saving falsehood. On the other hand, you don't have to wait to hear your gaseous attempt at self-exoneration to know the misdeed you committed down at Motel Six is going to look mighty ugly under the clear light of truth, which has, alas, been left on for you. (Anon., MF)

How to Keep Guests

The instructions here vary, according to whether you mean from the guest's point of view or the host's. So we'll cover both bases.

If you're a guest, shop around among your friends until you find guest quarters with these nonnegotiable features:

- *Privacy.* A sofa in the living room is not a guest room.
- *Plumbing.* You want instant and, if possible, private access to that which flushes in the night.
- *Clean sheet,* solid pillows, warm blankets, and fresh towels.
- *A bathrobe.* What the hey.
- *A selection of basic toiletries,* including a new toothbrush, still in the box.
- *A radio* or, better, a TV.
- *A reading chair* and lamp.
- *A small desk* for writing or working.
- *A decent view.* A private entrance is good.

Some optional features: lots of groceries, a good-cookin' woman, and plenty of hunting, fishing, and golf nearby. A wet bar is nice, too.

If you're the host, things change a bit. A wise host typically feels that a guest room such as that described above is like welfare for transients, and that it ought to be reformed. It's just too comfy, it strips away the initiative to move on in a day or two, and it encourages dependency on the host, his wife, and their refrigerator. So a host's dream guest room looks like this:

- *Cement floor,* permanently damp.
- *100 percent pure cinder block construction.* No windows.
- *One bare light bulb* hanging from the plywood ceiling.
- *A narrow, steel-frame bed* with a quaint and interesting antique "mattress."
- *A sheet made of synthetic fibers,* nonfunctioning electric blanket to match.
- *Chair* with one badly wounded leg.
- *Nice picture of Joe Stalin* on the wall.

Extra touch: a couple of wadded-up pieces of toilet tissue in the corner, just to stimulate a certain kind of apprehension. (SA)

How to Choose a Perfect Gift

There are two kinds of presents. One kind goes to all your buddies, your coworkers, your relatives. The other kind goes to your wife or girlfriend.

- *Type one:* The rule to giving a memorable gift is thoughtfulness. That ramshackle cliché requires explanation: Your gift has to suggest that you thought about it, not that you're actually a thoughtful person. So go for ambiguity: Skip the fruitcakes and soap collections, for instance, and pick up something at the local junk emporium or antique shop. Some weird, old artifact—an ancient egg poacher, a deco toaster—will set you back a sawbuck tops, but it'll seem to say something more personal, something more meaningful, but nobody'll know exactly what. (JGY)

- *Type two:* Your wife or girlfriend has already told you *exactly* what she wants. So don't try to outwit her by selecting something she hasn't even thought of. If she hasn't thought of it, she doesn't want it. Instead, take her suggestion, add some money to it and upgrade to the next-best model. Unless, that is, she's asked for a weekend in Mazatlán with you. (AMcLL)

How to Make Business Trips with Women

Pack the right assumptions: Here are some observations on mobile manners you might want to take along next time you hit the road on business, coed-style.

- *It's just business, stupid.* It's not a date. When men and women travel on business together, you can avoid any discomfort or misunderstandings by assuming she will always pay her own way—in the same way that you would expect a man you were traveling with would. Let's face it, an expense account knows no gender.

- *Professional protocol takes precedence.* Offering to pay all the time, as you would in a social situation, is wrong in the company's point of view—plus it puts you both in an awkward position professionally; it's awkward if she is your superior, because it transfers a form of control to you when you should be deferring all such control to her, and if you are her superior it creates a situation that, we're sorry to say, could lead her to feel that she "owes" you, and that, we're even sorrier to say, could lead to things like charges of sexual harassment. In other words, unless you have something in mind other than business, let her pay her own way.

- *Polite porterage?* Some guys say you should let her carry her own bags. If that represents progress for women, so be it. Maybe that's just the way things are nowadays. But there are obvious limits. If your hands are free, help her out. On the other hand, on a business trip, there is no reason for her to stand at the curb waiting as you make two or three trips with things piled up in your arms to load up the car. In that case, she should help you carry things.

Three rules of thumb:

1. If something needs to be lifted that is heavy or large, you do it regardless of who's bag or parcel it is.
2. Take her cue. If she seems to be saying "I'll do it and if you try to help me I'll give you a black eye," then by all means, let her tote it.
3. Let courtesy and common sense dictate what you do in any given situation.

• *Be politely sociable.* When you are traveling with a woman on business, you should invite her along with you on recreational outings—golf, a workout in the hotel's gym, a run—just as you would invite another guy if you were traveling with him. You may well hope she won't join you, but you should invite her anyway to avoid an uncomfortable situation. *This is especially true when there are two men and a woman traveling together.* It would be very impolite for two men go off together and leave a woman behind, unless it was her choice to stay behind.

• *Be careful.* Romance is everywhere, like the common cold germ. When you travel on business with a woman, you have to remember a couple of things: First, you may have no interest in her romantically, but that doesn't mean she feels the same way. And second, if a misunderstanding arises and gets blown out of proportion, public sentiment and the law are on her side, and any accusation of sexual misconduct or harassment by her about you—true or not—will be taken as the gospel. Unlike any other aspect of legal life, accusations of sexual misconduct of any kind are sufficient to convict in the court that matters—your own life. By just being at the other end of a pointed finger, you can suffer severe consequences, including a ruined career and a broken marriage. In fact, any time you're alone with a woman coworker, no matter how well you know her, you need to think of your situation the same way a woman looks at walking down a dark, deserted street late at night: *You're at risk, and you'd better be able to protect yourself.*

When traveling with a woman, keep your wits about you. Although most women would never dream of making an unwarranted claim of sexual harassment, you don't really know if the one you're with is one of the few who would. The world's full of lunatics, and some of them are pretty good looking. Keeping your wits about you means controlling circumstances that can spiral out of control easily: For instance, when you have a meeting with a woman colleague in a hotel room, make sure you are appropriately dressed—and if she is not, do not enter until she is. Also, avoid booze; once you reach a certain point, it gets harder to gauge the impact of the things you say and how they will be taken. (GS, JRL, Anon.)

How to Be Polite in a Gym

Hey, remember that in a gym, there are plenty of guys around who can enforce the rules of etiquette, no sweat.

- *Don't delay.* It may look like a lounge, but it's really a bench, so do your set and get on with the rest of your program. If you want to read or daydream, get over to the stationary bike department. And if you want conversation, do your talking away from the machinery.
- *Consider the environment.* If you want to dress grunge, do it on purpose. Dirty clothing and rotten pits suck. Nothing—well, almost nothing—smells worse than clothes-crud. And, while we're at it, wipe your sweat off the equipment when you're finished.
- *Remember the next guy* isn't your mom, so put stuff back where it's supposed to be. (GS)

How to Make a Nice First Impression

You can't make everything in your life complex, so start the uncluttering here, as you meet somebody for the first time.

Making a good first impression—putting your best foot forward, to use your old man's terminology—is an almost overwhelming preoccupation for anyone with a normal dose of sensitivity. Worrying about it is what keeps our teeth brushed, our hair combed, and our briefs off our heads. But believe it or not, your part of this equation—the part that has to do with how you come off—is not nearly as complex as the other part—that is, how somebody else comes off to you.

In fact, we worry this kind of thing to death. *Everybody* wants to look good to everybody else. But, ironically, nobody is sure *exactly* how they look to others. That uncertainty is what causes all the problems. Take your own cool self, for example. You've been hanging around in that body of yours for a lifetime, talking that talk and walking that walk, and you still aren't terribly sure what other people think when you walk into a room. Want the truth? They don't think anything. When two strangers meet, it's every man for himself, since nobody's thinking about the other guy. What with their own insecurities and concerns, nobody cares about somebody they don't know. If we cared about strangers, we'd have the world's poor living in our attics.

Here's the **Main Thing** about good impressions: We're interested in ourselves, in how we look, not in somebody else.

THE IMPORTANCE OF LOOKS

You have good reason to fret about your looks. The last time you knew with any degree of precision exactly how you looked to others was when you were in high school, when everybody looked like everybody else. Once you reach your twenties, your appearance is at the mercy of your judgment and taste, so anything can happen. You may think you look swell, and perhaps you do. But if you don't, nobody will ever let on. Twenty, thirty years into a marriage a woman turns to her husband and says, "You look stupid in bolo ties," and the guy's flabbergasted—not at her tactlessness, but at the fact that he's been a bolo man for three decades and never knew he looked like a feed sack tied at the top.

- *The way you look is largely out of your control.* You can scream for attention, of course. You can mousse that receding hairline into something more meaningfully Krameresque, or you can flash those thousand-dollar shades and that matching money clip. But you'll only strike an impression other than the one you wish to make. For most men, the best bet is reverting to adolescent methodology. Wear a suit like everybody else's and a tie like your boss's. You'll make a great impression, of course, since everybody you meet will see in you validation for their own bland taste in suits and ties.

- *Men are invariably impressed by looks.* Most of us are first attracted to our wives, cars, houses, dogs, and shoes not by their intrinsic value but by how they look—or, more precisely, how we think these things make us look. But most men distrust other men who rely on looks, and most women find men who look *too* good a little creepy. So what's a guy to do?

FOCUS ON BEHAVIOR

- *Be normal.* "Normal" is a word recently outlawed for use by writers in the *Los Angeles Times,* an abnormal newspaper if ever there was one, presumably because it makes oddballs feel bad about themselves, and in Los Angeles, that can be a problem. But you and I know what "normal" means. For our purpose here, it means not trying to make a good impression at the expense of the person you're meeting. You can ask several people how to make a great first impression, and they'll all say what you already know: A terrifically effective way of demonstrating personal power, self-confidence, *savoir-faire,* and charisma is to appear to be genuinely interested in making a stranger's acquaintance. When you're introduced to somebody, look in his eyes, listen carefully to his name, smile, and do any one of the following three things:

1. *Ask the new guy a question* about his work or his hometown.
2. *Ask his opinion* about some value-neutral guy-thing: his car, his Zippo, his favorite ball team.
3. *Remark on whatever crazy thing* has caused the two of you to be brought together in the same room. Unless it's the men's room.

Just don't go overboard. If some guy says, "Pleased to meet you," stay normal. Don't come back with "Oh, God, no, no, no. I'm pleased to meet *you,* to make the acquaintance of somebody who's life is bound up inextricably with my own in this crazy cosmic farce we call life. Meeting you makes me feel a little less *alone.* May I kiss you full on the lips?" Too much emotion puts some guys off. Most of us aren't in touch with our feelings for a good reason, and we have almost no interest in being put in touch with somebody else's. (WC)

- *Don't tease.* Don't make a wisecrack about the person you're meeting. You might think teasing is a great way to show affection, but most people are so anxious about introductions, it only pisses them off. (WPB)

- *Keep your life to yourself.* When you meet somebody, try to save the really good stuff about your incredible life—your rich parents, maybe, or maybe your extraordinary job as Imperial Wazoo, or maybe your phenom undergrad career at Harvard—for a second or third meeting. Unless specifically asked, don't read your résumé to strangers. (Anon.)

- *Be bland.* If you've got one of those crazy, bizarre, kind of *wacky* senses of humor, the kind that finds fun in life's unceasing tragedy, put it in your back pocket and sit on it. Almost no one wants to be challenged by any eccentricity from somebody they don't know well enough to feel comfortable with. Hence, most men, when introduced to a stranger, wish to make small talk. Really small talk. Teeny, little, itsy-bitsy talk. The kind of tiny talk the weather guy makes with the anchor gal. If you've got a mutilated dick joke just welling up from deep down inside, take a big breath and let it out slowly. Once a new acquaintance has demonstrated an ability to actually remember your name for more than thirty seconds, *then* you can let slip with that good one about what you get if you cross Katie Couric with a gang of troll dolls. (Anon.)

- *Indulge your hunches.* A guarantee: You will never meet a guy named McLaughlin you don't like. If you meet a McLaughlin, you'll like him, no questions asked. Also, giving this much slack to anybody helps with impressions all around. (DB)
- *Hide your mark of the beast.* Disguise your intolerances. Every man jack on earth is hypocritical about something, so participate gracefully in the universal lie and keep your bigotry to yourself. For instance, just because you have a blind prejudice against white, male conservatives doesn't mean everybody does, so go easy on the mean-spirited, granny-starving honky jokes. Some guys have best friends who are Euro-American.

HOW TO CREATE A FALSE IMPRESSION

Most men—and women, for that matter—give a great deal of thought to the first impression they want to convey to strangers. Some guys, for instance, need you to know they're rich. To others, power is the impression they want to give. There are guys who want to look aloof, and guys who want to look dangerous. You can decipher most of this stuff on the spot. You know intuitively, for example, that a guy preoccupied with displaying his wealth hasn't had money for very long. And you'll probably be right if you assume a man who needs to impress with power spent much of his life begging for sex—and not getting any. Aloof and arrogant men are running scared, and, unless you're dealing with a genuine sociopath, the more hard-bitten a man looks, the easier he is to deck in a bar fight. Most of the time, though, you're dealing with strangers who have a more predictable impression to make, since most guys want to be seen as nice guys.

Even that limited ambition can run into psycho-snags, however. A lot of insecure guys figure that even though they want to be liked, they won't be liked, and so every introduction carries with it the seed of a self-fulfilling prophecy. For example: Two guys are introduced. One guy, a normal, reasonably secure guy, says, "Hey, howya doin'," and the other guy, a worried guy, answers in defensive monosyllables which say, in so many words, "Screw you, how'm I doin'. What's it to you? You hate me, right?" Most scared guys feign arrogant hipness. As a rule, it's not worth salving their fears. (BG)

IS THE FIRST IMPRESSION RELIABLE?

- *Bad first impressions are usually accurate.* If you meet some guy and he seems to be a jerk—if he ignores you, patronizes you, pulls a .45 on you, knees you in the groin—the chances are overwhelming that he really *is* a jerk.

American justice presumes innocence. You don't have to. Look at it this way: You aren't the only one who has spent your adult years refining the grand entrance you wish to make in everybody else's life. You can therefore assume that a fellow who seems boorish to you seems boorish to others, and you can also assume the guy knows it. So, boorish he is. (Anon.)

On the other hand, *really great first impressions are usually inaccurate.* Why? Because it's easy to confuse the impression you think somebody else is trying to make with the one you hope you're making. Example: What a guy! you think to yourself when you meet a brotherly soul who lets you do all the talking and actually asks your opinion about politics or money. And the chap whose hand you've just shook may indeed be a decent fellow. But really good first impressions are, among men, the infatuation side of a manly friendship, and just as infatuation in a romance soon fades, so will your inflated opinion of your new chum. Often, men with fragile but large egos want to be best friends with guys who don't need to be assertive or demanding. The resulting one-sided friendship lasts only as long as the faulty first impression that created it.

• *If your introduction is to a woman,* all bets are off. The desperate need men have to make a good first impression on a woman is matched only by a woman's need to make a good first impression on men—and on other women.

In a little survey for this section, we asked strangers about meeting strangers. Some guys were nicer to us than others. One chap was so ingratiating, we thought maybe he was a salesman or something. But no, he worked for the IRS—as an auditor, no less. Since he made a great impression on us anyway, we asked him what his secret was. He said the key to making a really good first impression is to help the guy you're meeting make a really great first impression. Then he asked us what we were being paid for this, and did we get our money in cash or by check. What a nut! Do you love a guy like that, or what? (WC, Anon.)

14. Agriculture and Livestock

The world is crowded with living things. In some places, like China, most of them are human. But in most places, when you're talking about dominant life-forms, you're talking plants and animals. Plants first:

Plants

HOW TO USE A BROWN THUMB TO RAISE A GREEN INDOOR GARDEN

You know you're Kevorkian to rhododendrons, and you know your thumb's browner than—well, it's very brown. But maybe you live in a modern, sealed modular or a high-rise condo, and all the CO_2 you spew needs a dose of home-grown O. Here's a surefire way to raise your own private rain forest without paying a fortune:

- **Get a Lazarus warranty.** Only buy plants from a huge chain of discount stores like Wal-Mart or Price/Costco. Since they guarantee the quality of all their products and stand behind that guarantee, they will give you new replacement plants every time you take the dead ones back. (WE)
- **Perform the miracle yourself.** Nurserymen don't have time to nurse sick plants back to health, just as you don't have the skill to do so. But if you can make friends with the owner of a local plant shop and explain your predilection toward plantslaughter, there's a chance he'll be sympathetic and take you up on your offer to buy all his near-death experiences at an extremely low cost. He'll be saving time, you'll be saving money, and the sheer statistical odds favor the survival of at least a small fraction of the plants you drag home. (ASD)
- **The Icon of Creation.** Keep in mind that there isn't a plant alive that was designed to live in your house, since back when plants were invented, there were no houses. We bring this up for a reason: The closer you can come to imitating a plant's natural outdoor habitat indoors, the healthier plant you will have.

The **Main Thing** to know about how to have healthy-looking houseplants is to **only buy plants that are notorious for being easy to grow and hard to kill.** Buy the healthiest-looking specimens of those species you can find. Water them once in a while, chat with them, play them Smashing Pumpkins, just to give them a thrill. When they grow out of their potted trousers, replant them in something roomier.

Here's a list of invincible domestic vegetation:

- *Amaryllis.* People used to give this name to *girls*. Better they give it to transplant survivors.
- *Yucca.* Pug-ugly, but always there.
- *Hoya,* a.k.a. *wax plant.* Easy to grow. Hard to kill. Side benefit: Some

smell like chocolate or cinnamon. You can't kill this plant, honest. Go ahead, try. It's the Mr. Bill of houseplants.

- *Philodendron.* Plant it in a closet, close the door. Join the Moonies. It'll be there when you come back.
- *Corn plant.* Lives on coffee and Pepsi.
- *Scented geranium.* A civilized survivor.
- *Grape ivy.* You can put it anywhere you want, but it will do the best in a bright patch of sunlight without being directly in the sun.
- *Boston fern.* The best thing to do is to set it on top of a small tray of moist pebbles—then let the soil dry out between waterings. Always good to have small pebbles around anyway—good for teaching a little obedience to the dog.
- *Ficus.* These are the trees you see in every office-building rain forest. Here's why they're there: They live forever, no matter what you do to them. Buy a ficus. Water it, forget it. When you remember, water it again. (LB)

Some survival tactics:

- *Underwater* instead of overwater.
- *Transplant up* to the next larger pot, not to the biggest one made.
- *Drainage counts.* Roots rot readily.
- *Don't use dirt from the yard.* Buy potting soil or mix your own (equal portions of sand, loam, and peat moss). (DR)

Meat-eating Vegetation

Looking for a houseplant that will reflect the prevailing level of domestic testosterone? Get a potful of flesh-eating houseplant. There are almost six hundred different kinds of carnivorous plants from which to choose. Hate flies? Pick up a Venus flytrap. Roach problem? The pitcher plant is Nature's cover of "Hotel California": Bugs go in, but they can't get out. Either of these plants will work for people who have angst and rage in their blood.

Here's everything you need to know about setting up your own little shop of horrors:

- *Damp digs.* **Carnivorous plants need a moist place to live at your house.** Some people use silica sand, but peat moss is the way to go: Buy some every spring, keep your plants happy all year round. (FSS)
- *Peat moss note:* You want to avoid buying peat moss that has been wetted—you're paying by the pound and water is heavy—and you also want to steer clear of peat moss that contains chemical additives. These chemicals may be good for some plants but not the carnivorous ones. Grab a hunk of

peat moss in your hand, stick your hand in a bucket of water, and squeeze; in a moment or two the peat moss will start to expand as it absorbs water. When you're playing with peat moss, wear a face mask and gloves. (RE)

Other things to try include vermiculite, perlite, and compost.

- **Finicky drinkers.** The quality of the water you give your carnivorous plants will play a major role in determining their success in life. What is good enough for you is definitely not good enough for them. Use distilled water or water that has gone through the reverse-osmosis process. Don't worry, you can drink it, too. You may want to have water delivered to your door, install a filter, or just take a big jug to one of those water-dispensing machines to be found at most supermarkets. Use the water to keep the soil moist.

- **Bug eaters need a lot of light.** Direct sunlight is good. You can also use cool white fluorescent bulbs. Put them about a foot away from the plants and make sure the full planted area is bathed in light. You can also use low-pressure sodium-vapor lights or mercury vapor lights—but if you do, get ready for a visit from the feds and their pot-sniffing hounds.

- **Carno-plants like it hot and humid.** That's why a terrarium setup is perfect. You can get a suitable amount of heat and moisture from your lighting; just make sure you don't suffocate your plants. While a glass cover is a good idea to keep small children from falling in, never seal the terrarium because, in addition to heat and moisture, the plants also like to have a nice breeze once in a while. Put your lights just outside the glass and, if you're really devoted to them, get a small computer fan and rig it so it blows much of the heat from the bulbs away.

- **Care and feeding of carnivorous plants.** Well, they aren't vegetarians. They like meat, okay? Most carnivorous plants will accept food from you but will only eat insects that are still alive, so go crazy. (FSS)

HOW TO GROW GRASS

Nothing's weirder than the suburban fascination with grass—a labor-intensive, capital-sucking, crazy crop with no known market or secondary use beyond some light mulching. Yet, when you buy into the American dream, you also get the American nightmare: Lawn Care.

The moral imperative: When you own a house with a yard and lawn, you are morally obligated to do three things with the grass:

1. Water it.
2. Fertilize it.
3. Mow it.

How to Water the Lawn

There are **four factors** to consider here:

1. *The type of grass* you have.
2. *The soil* in your yard.
3. *The weather* in your area.
4. *The location* of your lawn.

It's always better to water your lawn only when it absolutely needs it. Not only is overwatering wasteful, it also makes your lawn a target for disease. In addition, it makes the grass grow faster, and we all know what that means. (See the section "How to Mow the Lawn.")

How much **water** it needs depends on the root system. The shallower the roots, the more often you should water:

TYPE OF GRASS	DEPTH OF ROOT SYSTEM
Bahia	Shallow
Bermuda	Deep
Bermuda hybrid	Deep
Bluegrass, Kentucky	Shallow
Buffalo grass	Deep
Fescue, fine	Shallow
Fescue, tall	Deep
Rye, perennial	Shallow
St. Augustine	Deep
Zoysia	Deep

There's no charity among the blades, so if you skip a part yet soak the area all around it, the dry part will die. (GL)

Dirt data. The two ends of the whole-earth spectrum are clay and sand. Clay, obviously, absorbs less water but holds what it absorbs for a longer period. Water it for shorter periods to avoid large amounts of runoff. Sandy soil absorbs water quickly, but it also allows it to pass right through to a depth where the water is of no use to the lawn. To find out if your lawn needs watering, push a long screwdriver into the soil in various spots. You'll be able to push the screwdriver through wet soil a lot easier than you can through dry soil. Dirt will cling to the blade of a 'driver pushed into damp soil. (MMB)

Weather. This is a no-brainer. People in Phoenix water their lawns more than people in Seattle.

Location. The location of your lawn is the other no-brainer. Is your lawn in the sun or the shade? If in the sun, is it in the sun during the hot part of the day or the cool part of the day? The hotter the sun it is exposed to, the more water it will need. (GL, MMB)

How to Fertilize the Lawn

Three little words form the essential lexicon of fertilizer-talking lawn-care experts.

1. *Nitrogen.* Your grass needs it to grow and spread, but don't use too much nitrogen or the grass will grow too fast and you'll become a professional lawn mower.

2. *Phosphorus.* Helps root growth, and the stuff is crucial if you're growing a lawn from seed.

3. *Potassium.* Makes the lawn resistant to severe weather.

Some fertilizers are organic: Everything in the bag was alive once but is dead now. Lawns love this stuff.

Other fertilizers are synthetic, and plenty of people swear by them.

If you're not sure which to buy, here is an easy way to tell: Go out to your car and look at the bumper and back window. If you have any bumper stickers there that say things like "Save the Whales" or "Animals Are People, Too," then you need organic. If your bumper stickers say things like "Rush Is Right" or "Jane Fonda Is a Commie," you should buy synthetic. If you have no bumper stickers, you should buy whichever is cheaper. Pick the salesman's brain about what kind of fertilizer will work best on your grass in your part of town. He answers these questions all day so there's a better shot he'll know than that you will. If you don't want to depend on the expertise of a salesman, you can always buy a home test kit. Or, if that sounds too much like schoolwork, just buy a fertilizer that has a good mix of nitrogen, phosphorus, and potassium and call it a day. It's only a lawn, after all. Check the back of the fertilizer bag for the best time and method of application. (MMB)

How to Mow the Lawn

The big trick here is how to tell the grass needs to be cut without waiting for your neighbors to say so.

- *The rule of a green thumb* for this is you should cut the grass when it's about a third taller than the height recommended for the species. If it grows too long and you cut it, you can actually shock the grass, because you'll expose parts of the blades that have never had any exposure to sunlight before, and, bang! the grass turns yellow. A consistent height for your grass is the best bet. (GL)

- *Forget raking up lawn cuttings.* Turns out that if you keep the height of your lawn at a fairly consistent level and let the short trimmings land where they do, they will decompose and help your lawn stay healthy by providing it with lots of nutrients. However, if you cut your lawn after it has grown real long, you'll pile a thatch on top of your lawn and prevent the grass from getting the sunlight and air it needs, and, bang! the grass turns yellow. (MMB)

Here's the front-yard barber chart:

SPECIES	BEST LENGTH
Bahia	2 to 3 in.
Bermuda	1 to 1.5 in.
Bermuda, hybrid	1 in. or less
Bluegrass, Kentucky	1.5 to 2.5 in.
Buffalo grass	1.5 to 2 in.
Fescue, fine	1.5 to 2.5 in.
Fescue, tall	1.5 to 2 in.
Rye, perennial	1.5 to 2.5 in.
St. Augustine	2 to 3 in.
Zoysia	1 to 2 in. (GL)

HOW TO MOW THE LAWN REAL FAST

It can take several hours to mow a one-acre lawn on a typical riding mower. This isn't surprising, since the average mower has a top-end of five or six miles per hour, and an average cutting speed of only two or three miles per hour. How to speed up the process? Follow these simple instructions to boost your *cutting* speed up to an excellent forty-five miles per hour.

- *Change the gear ratio.* The first thing you have to do to get a higher speed is to change the gear ratio. Most machines have a three-inch pulley on the engine, and they run between a ten- or twelve-inch pulley in the back. Change the pulleys so you can put more revolutions per minute on the transmission. That means, of course, that you also have to:
- *Change the transmission.* Replace the stock tranny found on most lawn mowers with a right-angle gearbox. That allows you to have a gear ratio of 1:1.
- *Mount low friction bearings* in the back of the chassis and use a solid shaft for an axle. Mount a sprocket on the axle and a sprocket on the output of the right-angle gearbox. This allows you to set up a disk brake.

- *Reinforce the machine.* Stock chassis are made out of sheet metal. When you want to torture your machine, you have to put in some struts. While you're at it, replace all the bushings with bearings.
- *Lower the machine* a little bit to get a lower center of gravity. You can do this by altering the front axle to drop the front suspension as much as six inches. You can also install smaller tires. This will help with cornering, preventing little tufts of grass from surviving your passing blades. (KS)

If you want to get into some organized lawn mower racing, call the United States Lawn Mower Racing Association at (708) 729-7363.

HOW TO CONTROL GARDEN PESTS

One of the most overlooked gardening tools is a twelve-gauge shotgun. Let's face it, if you plant a garden and have a green thumb at all, you are also going to attract a lot of critters. If you're on a balanced diet, you can turn this to your advantage, since, if you plant the right things and have a good enough aim, you'll not only reap fruits and veggies from your garden, but also bag a little meat.

Here's the meat-to-potatoes breakdown:
- *Raccoon:* All fruit and melons, sweet corn
- *Rabbit:* Carrots, peas, beans, lettuce, beets, strawberries
- *Deer:* All vegetables, especially corn, fruit trees, shrubs, rosebushes, most flowers
- *Woodchucks* and ground hogs: Melons, peas, beans, lettuce, squash
- *Gophers:* Carrots, garlic, radishes, potatoes
- *Bear:* Corn, melons, berries, and other fruit. Honey! (EDS)

HOW S**T HAPPENS

Attention, happy composters: If you are into recycling at all, somewhere near you someone is throwing away tons of stuff that the plants in your yard and house would like to have as food. All you have to do is go get it or tip the guy who brings it to you for free.

We're talking organic waste here, from cow and chicken manure to decomposing fish to tons and tons of apple and blueberry waste. It's the smelly stuff that will make your garden grow. Here's how to get it:

First find your favorite waste. Almost anything that comes from the earth can be composted and returned to the earth as fertilizer. Someplace near you, somebody is making money from cows, chickens, horses, fish, seaweed, shellfish, cotton, carrots, celery, lettuce, tomatoes, potatoes, whey, hops, berries, mushrooms, apples, peanuts, sugarcane, or sawdust.

Next, call and find out who ends up having to dispose of the waste product. Ask if you can help take some of that waste off their hands. Don't be concerned if there's a long silence. In some cases, if you show up with a truck or just a shovel and a box, they'll give you as much as you want for free.

HOW TO GROW A SALAD

Layout for a small (six-by-four) sensible vegetable garden. Leave just a little room for working with the plants, and don't get carried away with tomatoes. You'll have more than you need, no matter what—plus they have to be moved from year to year. You'll need a sunny place reasonably near a water source—but not actually under it. If you're new to this, buy plants, not seeds, and put straw everywhere the plants aren't, to save weeding. Arrange your garden in groups of plants that play nicely with others. In this example, from top to bottom:

Top border: Rosemary and thyme plants, cabbage protectors. Add tarragon and marigolds to this mix and you can border the whole garden with a kind of bug hedge.

Potatoes, cabbage, potatoes. 'Tater leaves have a subtle scent bugs hate. Around the potatoes and cabbages: Marjoram, thyme, rosemary, chives, marigolds. Bug-beaters.

Second row: Onions, marigolds, parsley. Nematodes—the garden Huns—hate marigolds.

Third row: Basil, some lettuce, chives, cilantro. Lettuces like carrots (planted below), while tomatoes like chives. The central cluster of plants are all companion-planted—they do best if planted close together. Carrots, peas, and cucumbers don't like to be around aromatic herbs.

Fourth row: Plum tomatoes, sweet peppers, carrots, peas, hot peppers, beefsteak tomatoes. Stake the tomatoes right away.

Bottom row: Squash, bush cukes, squash.

HOW TO BEAT THE SUN

These are easy and hardy. Top row: Lavender, bee balm, butterfly bush, bee balm, lavender. Second row: Dwarf Shasta daisies. Bottom row: Dianthus pinks, carnation variety. This garden is six-by-two and shows approximate spacing between plants. It should bloom from May till September and attract huge, noisy swarms of butterflies.

HOW TO MAKE IT IN THE SHADE

This six-by-two garden will thrive in a coal mine, practically. Top row: Hostas. Middle row: Dwarf bleeding hearts (no jokes, please). Bottom row: Periwinkles. This garden will bloom in May and keep it up until a frost hits.

Sometimes, they'll even deliver—but if they do, make sure you tip the driver so he'll be happy to come back with more when you need it.

- *Figure out what you need:* Everyone's got their favorite composting method and favorite fertilizer recipe, and after you play around with the manure a bit, you will too. If you have access to wood and fish waste, for instance, you can mix them together for fertilizer that is as good as any you can buy and better than either one of the two alone: *Wood* decays slowly, but it doesn't stink. *Fish* stinks like crazy, but it decays quickly—

sometimes before you can get it home from the supermarket. But mix the two together in the right proportion—start with equal parts of each—and eventually you'll have a fertilizer that is sort of odorless and breaks down pretty fast.

If you're going to use *cow* or *chicken* manure on your garden, mix it with some leaves or sawdust or even shredded newspaper, and then apply it to the soil a few weeks before you plant.

Whey, a by-product of cheese production, can be applied directly to the soil. *Cotton gin trash* can be mixed with *horse* or *cow* manure in a ratio of 1.5:3. Or you can mix it with the waste product of *grapes* from a local winery to produce an even better fertilizing material. (MMB)

HOW TO GROW A KILLER TOMATO

Almost anybody can grow a tomato: Plant it in the spring. Water the plant. Wait. Pick the tomatoes. Big deal. But growing a great tomato requires a little effort.

- *Start early.* But not too early. The best time to transplant your tomato to the garden is before its seventh week. Do it gradually: Move the plant outdoors, but not in direct sunlight. The next day, give it a dose of sol. The next day, a bit more, and so on until you put it in a well-mulched, well-drained spot in the garden where it can get full sun.

- *Keep it neat.* Trim off any suckers, and don't let the plant spread. Keep it off the ground and well supported. Allow at least three feet between plants.

- *Keep it healthy.* Don't fool around with the plant when the soil has just been watered. Keep worms off with pesticide or, if you're going natural, with diligence. Kill slugs by leaving beer out in shallow cooking pans.

- *Let the tomatoes ripen on the vine.* But don't leave overripe tomatoes around. And don't plant too many: An average plant will yield ten pounds of tomatoes—usually within a relatively short period. (HE)

HOW TO CHOOSE A CHRISTMAS TREE

If you wish to make this a green and pleasant planet, spare yourself the plastic knockoff and go for real sap. Smells better, too.

Here's how to spot the tree of your Yule dreams:

On Pines and Needles

The type of tree you choose may be determined by where you live. But those in bigger cities will have a wider choice:

- *Pines,* with their long needles, are the most difficult to decorate using traditional ornamentation. That's the bad news. The good news is they're cheaper than most other varieties. The best: Douglas firs, which are not firs at all. They're pines in fir disguise; Scotch pines are next best; Norways, the worst.
- *Spruce* trees have needle-sharp needles that quickly fall off, but they're built like oaks, so they can take a lot of heavy-duty decorating, and their prickly needles keep dogs and kids at bay.
- *Firs* are the tree-of-choice for most. They're hardy, they keep their needles, and they maintain their shape, which puts tree ahead of man most of the time. Plus, they smell swell. Balsams are the best. Don't tell your animal-rights friends you got a fir for Christmas, though.

Longevity

The best way to make sure you have a tree with needles still on it by Christmas is to cut one yourself. Most towns have a tree lot someplace nearby where you can walk alone into the snowy woods, hatchet in one hand, chain saw in the other, emergency help only a cell-phone call away. If you cut your own a week or two before Christmas, you'll know it's fresh. (JHa)

Lot Lore

If you buy your tree at a lot, know what you're buying. The most expensive trees won't necessarily be the biggest; they'll be the ones with evenly balanced branches all around. If you're going to put your tree in a corner, you can find a bargain in a misshapen fir. Look for good color and fresh needles; to double-check, stand up the tree and give the trunk a sharp knock on the ground. If it sheds needles, shed the tree. Finally, check the trunk. If it's covered with sap and resin, it will have sealed in the moisture it had when it was cut. You'll have to cut off an inch or two to make sure it can drink when you get it home, though. (AMcLL)

HOW TO RECYCLE A TREE

If you were a pine tree, chances are Christmas wouldn't be big on your list of holidays. You spend years in splendid, semi-Alpine isolation as a home to birds, a shelter to forest critters, a respectable, dues-paying link in the food chain. Then one day, presto! Some chap with a chain saw comes to visit, and the next thing you know you're dying slowly in a parking lot surrounded by fast-talking, hard-selling Boy Scouts. And we gripe about the destruction of the Brazilian rain forests.

It's enough guilt to ruin your Christmas. An alternative: Buy a live, nursery-grown tree with the roots still attached.

- *Cost:* This gentle gesture to a green planet will set you back thirty to fifty dollars more than what you'd pay for a cut tree. That's enough money to, say, buy four packages of disposable diapers or maybe a dozen Big Macs in McDonald's ozone-eating plastic containers.

- *Benefit:* On the other hand, not only will a healthy evergreen planted in your yard after the holiday make up for the way you improperly disposed of that can of spray paint last spring, it will also *reduce heating and cooling costs, benefit birds and other wildlife,* and *add value to your property.* And, if you don't have a tree to plant, you can donate it to a park or state forest, where others will be able to enjoy it. Be sure to talk to the park manager or forest warden first, though.

- *Placement:* Before you buy a tree, figure out where you'll put it after the holiday. Most evergreens will reach a mature height of sixty to one hundred feet, so choose an open area without overhead wires. Plant the tree (see instructions that follow) at least four feet from a walkway and at least ten feet from a building. An overlooked danger: underground utilities and sewage pipes.

- *Type:* A number of factors will influence your choice of tree: soil, sunlight, moisture, climate, landscape considerations, and pollution from traffic. Consult your nurseryman or an urban forester before you decide which tree will best suit you. Example: White pine will not do well in a city because it's sensitive to salt and pollution. Trees grown outside their most suitable habitats will be prone to stunted growth or disease. Remember that locally grown trees are accustomed to the local climate. Check the needles: They should be green or bluish. No yellowish needles, no red or brown tips.

Life Is a Root Ball

Think how awkward it is to handle a prickly six-foot cut tree. Now imagine how difficult it would be to handle the same tree if a 120-pound root ball wrapped in burlap were attached to the bottom. Even a three-foot tree can have a 50-pound root ball. Here's a handy root ball chart.

TREE HEIGHT (MEASURED FROM TOP OF ROOT BALL)	MINIMUM DIAMETER OF ROOT BALL	MINIMUM DEPTH OF ROOT BALL	APPROXIMATE WEIGHT OF ROOT BALL
3 ft.	12 in.	9 in.	50 lbs.
5 ft.	16 in.	12 in.	75 lbs.
6 to 7 ft.	22 in.	16 in.	100 lbs.

You heard it here first, kids: **A big root ball is not a toy.** (SWa)

Bringing the Tree Indoors

A tree is, in the immortal words of the Troggs, a wild thing that'll make your heart sing. It'll make every Yule thing groovy, provided you take proper care of it:

- *Steady temperature.* Moving a tree from twenty-two degrees to seventy-two degrees, then back again, is stressful to the tree and can easily kill it. Before you take the tree indoors, leave it in a semiprotected area like a porch or a fire escape for several days to gradually warm it up. A cool basement will do the trick. Or the garage. Or any semipurgatorial place that will prepare the tree for the dry heat ahead. (GS)
- *Keep the root ball moist,* but not sopping wet.
- *Protect the tree* from the full force of the wind.
- When you bring the tree indoors, *keep it away from heat sources.* The coolest part of the house is the best place for the tree. At all costs, don't let forced, hot air blow directly on the tree.
- *Set the tree in a tub or deep pan with gravel in the bottom.* Keep the gravel wet, but don't let the tree sit in a pool of water. You'll drown the roots. You may have to water the tree as often as twice a day to keep the root ball moist. Don't leave the tree indoors for longer than ten days or so.
- *When you remove the tree,* make the transition to the cool outdoors gradual by putting it back on a porch for about three days.

Preparation for Planting

In the South or on the West Coast, January may be a fine time to plant trees. But in the North and in the Midwest, winter brings some extra problems.

- *Soil.* The American Forestry Association has found the soil in the average American backyard is too compacted for optimum tree growth. A solution: Till the top twelve inches of soil in a circle about five times the diameter of the root ball.

- *The hole* for the root ball should be just deep enough to accommodate the burlapped ball. Don't loosen the soil in the bottom of the hole, since if you do the tree may settle and if the roots are too deep, the tree will die. The width of the hole should be twice the width of the root ball. If the soil in your area freezes, dig your planting hole in the fall. (SWa)
  Dissent: If you take care of the tree, water it from time to time, and keep it outdoors in a cool, protected place, you can put off planting the tree until early spring. But catch it quick; if the tree wakes up from its winter dormancy, and finds it's not stuck in the ground, it'll die. (DSB)
- *Mulch* the whole area with a good organic mixture about two inches thick. Reason: Mulch prevents frost heaving after an early winter planting. Besides, mulch reduces competition from weeds (remember, to a tree, grass is a weed) and keeps lawn mowers and weed trimmers at a discreet distance. Careful: Too much mulch will produce heat harmful to a tree's roots.

Planting
Follow these simple steps:

1. *Set the tree in the prepared hole.* Make sure it's at the same level as it was at the nursery.
2. *Check that it's vertical.* A leaning tree, even in Pisa, is no architectural curiosity.
3. *Remove all strings and wires* from around the roots and stem.
4. *Pull the burlap down to the base of the ball.* Natural jute burlap will quickly decay if you leave it in the hole, but any other material is trouble, so remove all traces of the fabric.
5. *Fill the hole with soil,* then tamp it down *lightly.*
6. *Water thoroughly.*
7. *Cover the soil around the tree* with two inches of mulch.

Care
Don't let the soil dry out the first year, and watch for winter frost heaving. Other arboreal tips:

- When you water the tree, *don't spray the foliage.* It only promotes diseases.
- *Soak the ground* thoroughly once a week if rainfall is inadequate.
- As a rule, *fertilizer helps weeds more than it helps trees.*

Off the Hook

If all this root-ball-totin', tree-plantin' stuff is too much to fit into a busy holiday season, here's a thought to help you through the narrow straits of a potential ethical dilemma: If you don't buy a cut Christmas tree, some Christmas tree farmer someplace won't plant one. In fact, Strathmeyer reports that he plants four trees for every one he sells. Trees are green as money, remember, and, from a farmer's point of view, it's all crops. (SWa)

How to Select Household Livestock

WHAT CONSTITUTES A PET?

Generally, men gauge the value of pets by balancing the food value of the animal with the Keanelike softness of the animal's eyes. Goats are more charming than many dogs. But we can look into Fido's eyes and see loyalty, affection, faithfulness, adoration—all the qualities we long for in friends, women, and animals. If you look into a goat's eyes, you go mad. The devil has eyes like a goat's. So we eat goats and play tug-of-war with dogs. Cows have the best eyes, but most of us just can't get around our deep desire for burgers. Someplace, however, we do draw the line between friends and dinner. In France, for example, they eat the roasts upon which we ride down long, dusty trails, and in the Far East, people use the noggins of our simian cousins as a kind of brain-pan dip-dish.

For most of us, though, we just need a way of distinguishing a good pet from a lousy one. Therefore, the modest question of what constitutes a pet is freighted with sexual meaning and a kind of anthropological dialectic.

We can't know with any certainty how women feel about pets. But we know what men like. Historically, when most guys who counted were Egyp-

How to Tell the Difference Between a Beef Cow and a Dairy Cow: Hint: Dairy cows give milk.

tians, we thought cats were the paradigm pet. Goes to show how far we've come, yes? A hundred years ago, the pet of choice was a horse. Today, the base unit of pet equivalency for modern men is the Dog. Once you understand what a good dog is worth, the value of all other animals becomes relative to the value of one good dog. It's like knowing what an Italian *lira* is worth, or a Polish *zloty*. **If you know the value of one good dog, you can calculate the value of almost any other pet.** For example:

STANDARD DOG CONVERSION CHART

1 ficus	=	.003 Dog
1 chicken	=	.050 Dog
1 guppy	=	.075 Dog
1 parakeet	=	.200 Dog
1 hamster	=	.250 Dog
1 cat	=	.330 Dog
1 bunny	=	.400 Dog
1 lamb	=	.600 Dog
1 cow	=	.700 Dog
1 poodle	=	.750 Dog
1 mutt from the pound	=	1.00 Dog
1 border collie	=	1.20 Dogs
1 horse	=	1.40 Dogs
1 mule	=	1.70 Dogs
1 pony	=	2.00 Dogs
1 monkey	=	2.300 Dogs
1 Penthouse Pet	=	7.00 Dogs (but only for a weekend; after that, the exchange drops to one-to-one.)

From this chart we can see why more women than men are vegetarians, since, for women, many of the animals women consider cute are considered by men to be mighty good eating. However, as we can also see from this chart, the pets we normally associate with women are generally worth less than one good dog, while all masculine pets are worth at least a dog, and sometimes more. The question of how many men are equal to one good dog is left unanswered, however. (DB)

HOW TO TEACH AN OLD DOG NEW TRICKS

No corporal education: There're two ways to train your dog—the right way or any number of wrong ways. Wrong ways include yelling at your dog when he doesn't do a trick the way you want him to, hitting him when he doesn't do the trick the way you want it done, rewarding him every once in a while during the training session just because he's still hanging around while you put him through all of this ridiculousness.

Good Dog, Bad Dog

Canine ed done the right way is called positive reinforcement, which means every time your dog does something right during a training session—no matter how small a movement toward the right behavior it is—you reward him. *Under no circumstances do you reward him for any other behavior.* If you do, you ruin the effect of all previous training because with an unearned reward you will be reinforcing some behavior (or no behavior, if you give your dog a treat simply for lying there looking cute) other than the behavior you want. (GFE)

If you're beginning to see that training your dog takes some training of you first, you're catching on fast. Therefore, before we start working on your dog, let's start working on you.

Good Master, Bad Master

What you have to train yourself to do before you can train your dog is to learn to look at the trick you want your dog to do as a trick made up of many mini-tricks. In other words, **you have to see the trick the way your dog sees it.** Think of training your dog the way you learned to water-ski. Your instructor didn't throw you off the boat with two skis and tell you to grab the rope and hold on. No, he explained how to put the wet suit on. How to put the skis on, how to get into the water with the skis on, how to lie on your back while you wait for the rope to come around, how to grab the rope, how to hold the rope, how to get into position, how to put your feet when the boat starts to pull you, what to do when you get up—and what to do when you fall down. You learned to water-ski by mastering hundreds of little tasks along the way. And your positive reinforcement? The guy driving the boat telling you you were doing great even though you were getting your butt dragged all over the lake without success. The smile of the pretty girl in the bikini who was sitting in the back of the boat watching you and waiting for her turn. Finally, the ultimate reinforcement was that you finally got up.

The Sit Trick

This is dog-comp 101. **The "sit!" trick is about as basic as you can get.** But here's the bad news, pooch lovers: Sitting *up* is way too complicated for a dog to learn from a lying position. But you can teach a dog to learn a series of small tasks that, when put together, will have him first sitting—and then sitting *up.*

- ***Start with the obvious.*** For instance, if you're a dog, you have to stand before you can sit (if you don't believe me, try to get your dog to sit from a lying position). So the first thing you have to do is to get your dog to stand up.

- ***Once standing,*** if you're a dog, lying back down looks good. But if you figure out that sitting will get you some food while lying will only get you lying, you start to sit in return for that tasty reward.

Are you getting the picture? Before you can train your dog to do *anything,* you have to break the trick down into the smallest components possible.

- ***So let's say you want your dog to sit up.*** Here's how to give your dog positive reinforcement for the right behavior without reinforcing the wrong behavior:

- *Grab a bag of snacks.* You probably won't have to train your dog to get up because he will jump to his feet the minute he sees you have food. See, just by showing up with the promise of food, you have already rewarded him. And, if you think about it, you are already seeing positive reinforcement at work here: Why does your dog get up when you show up with food? Because every time you have treats, he jumps up and you feed him. You have reinforced this behavior.

- *Take a treat and hold it over the dog's head.*

- *Next, swoop the hand holding the food to the floor.* Your dog's nose will follow your hand and the food to the floor—but of course that's not the correct behavior. No reward. Do it again. No reward.

- *After several times of that, take the hand with the food and apply it to your dog's hindquarters.* Say, "Sit!" firmly and give him a solid push down. If he gives at all, give him a reward. Repeat this over and over, always saying, "Sit!" clearly each time you touch his backside.

Soon, he will know that when you say the magic word and push on his butt and he lowers it, he gets food. He'll let you push his butt down every time.

Once you have his complete cooperation when pushing his butt down, reinforce his behavior only when he lets you push his butt farther and farther down with less and less resistance on his part.

- ***Soon, the mere sight of food and the touch of your hand to his butt will cause him to sit.*** Once he sits every time you touch his backside and say, "Sit!" stop touching him. Just give the command. Repeat over and over, rewarding him only when he sits to the voice command alone. If he has trouble learning the voice command, alternate between offering the voice command and touching his butt and giving him the voice command alone. As you continue to alternate between voice command and hand and voice command, stop rewarding him regularly when he needs the help of a hand cue. Soon, the mere sound of you saying, "Sit!" will have him sitting.

- *Follow the same process to train him to sit up.* Break the task of sitting up into small steps and reward him for accomplishing each of these small steps, but offer no reward for anything else. (GFE, RST)

The Fetch Trick

Want to teach your dog to fetch? First, figure out which different tricks together constitute your basic fetch: Watching the stick fly through the air, noticing where it lands, running to the stick, picking it up, running toward you with it, dropping it at your feet.

- *Grab your bag of treats and a stick.* Hang on to the treats and throw the stick and yell "Fetch!" If your dog makes no move toward the stick, your neighbors will think you're nuts. But who cares? You know they've been trained to think that way.
- *If your dog makes any kind of move toward the stick, reward him.* If he doesn't move toward the stick, go to where the stick landed and give your dog a treat if he follows you all or part of the way. Repeat this, getting him closer and closer to the stick and rewarding him, then start rewarding him only when he moves toward the stick without needing you to lead him.
- *Pick-up sticks.* Some dogs chase a stick, but they never pick it up. If this is your dog, go with him to the stick, pick it up, and put it near his mouth. If he takes it, he gets a treat. If not, you have to break picking up the stick into smaller pieces. Try offering the treat and the stick at the same time. Eventually, he will get the point. (GFE)

The Big Trick

Housebreaking a dog is the biggest trick of all. When you teach your dog to fetch, you're teaching him to do something when you're in the mood to see it. When you housebreak a dog, you're teaching him to respond to an internal cue over which you have no control.

Don't worry; *it can be done.* Just as your dog will associate a comand with a reward and the execution of a certain set of behaviors, you can teach him to associate a reward with leaving the house or going to a certain spot whenever he feels like he has to go to the bathroom.

How?

- *First, establish a place you want him to go* when he has to go. Maybe it's a bunch of newspapers in the bathroom, maybe it's just out the door and into the backyard. How you will establish that is to first put a physical object there which he can use for forming his mental associations. Newspaper is good. Or a box. Or a tree. (GFE)

  A dissent: One caution about using newspaper as the object.: Have you ever had a great Sunday morning spreading the paper all over the floor and reading it section by section, then turned your back for a moment? (HER)

- *Next, watch your dog like a hawk.* When you see him start to drop his butt to go, grab him and race him toward the designated area and the familiar object. After he does his business, give him a reward.

  After a few days of this, don't be too quick to scoop the dog up. It helps to notice first if he is making any progress toward learning to move toward the appropriate place, even if he doesn't have the bladder control or estimation powers to get there on his own. You don't want him to associate getting picked up with getting a treat. The income has to be associated with the outgo. (GFE)

Training Notes

A few other things:

- *Short lessons:* Make sure that you don't try to train your dog for too long a time at each session. Fifteen minutes or less is good.
- *Happy ending:* Always end a training session on an upnote when the dog has just done something very well and been rewarded for it. This helps train your dog to be trainable.
- *Lo-cal:* Don't forget that the reward doesn't have to be food. To a dog, your approval and affection is one sweet deal.
- *Never too late:* Even an old dog can be taught a new trick. Age doesn't matter, even in dog years. (GFE)

HOW TO BUST A BRONC

Sometimes the slow trot of a man's life turns into something else. That's when you decide either to take control to or ride it out.

When you're working with an unfamiliar and unbroken horse, make sure all your moves are smooth and confident. Try to rein in your nervousness before you try to rein in the horse, who will be nervous enough for both of you. And remember to work slowly and patiently: Some of these steps have to be repeated for days. The routine about jumping on a wild-eyed stallion and staying there until he cries "Uncle!" is movie stuff.

1. **First moves:** Assuming the horse is accustomed to the halter, snub the horse tightly to a solid wall at least seven feet high. Teach the horse to move its hind end from left to right, first with the use of a whip (if necessary) along with voice commands, until voice commands alone do the job.

2. **Sitting on the horse:** Once the horse will follow your voice commands, calmly and confidently approach the horse on the *left* side and climb on. Sit quietly until the horse accepts your weight. If the horse is snubbed tightly to the wall, he can't throw you, but use caution, as this is a critical moment for both the horse and the rider. Remain on the horse until you feel him relax under you.

3. **The first ride:** Use the voice commands you first taught the horse to make the horse move from one side to the other. At the same time, apply outside leg pressure (i.e., kick him in the ribs—horses have no use for subtlety); repeat on both sides until the horse is moving freely back and forth at your command. Practice this for thirty minutes or longer. If the horse acts up or refuses to follow your command, it's likely his attention is wandering. A slap between the ears will bring him around. Keeping the horse's attention is of utmost importance.

4. **Circling:** After a few days, and once you feel secure with the horse's progress and he is responding well, saddle him, untie him, and put a bosal rein on him. Lead him into a twelve-foot-by-twelve-foot stall that you've made free of obstructions. Using one rein, tie the horse's head around toward the cinch of the saddle. Promptly exit the stall, closing the door behind you. When the horse moves willingly in a circle in one direction, repeat in the other direction.

5. **All aboard:** Untie the bosal rein, and, placing your left hand on the horse's neck and your right hand on the saddle horn, carefully climb on before the horse has a chance to become excited. Apply leg pressure to

Two Saddles: One, top, for work. The "western" saddle was designed to help a cowboy do his job. The English saddle, bottom, is for less labor-filled rides.

make the horse move out. Ride the horse in circles left and right inside the stall for an hour or so.

6. *Trotting:* You can teach the horse to trot by applying leg pressure and giving the horse a slap on the hindquarters with the reins. Stay with the horse until he moves comfortably and under your command. If he acts up, discipline him with a slap between the ears.

7. *Dismount* and lead the horse from the stall into a larger, enclosed area. Calmly mount the horse, then walk and trot him until he is moving like an old broke saddle horse.

8. *Lope* with the horse by applying leg pressure and a slap of the reins. Work on making the transition from walk to trot to lope smooth. There's no set time for how long this will all take, but the more you and the horse practice it, the sooner it all comes together. When you can move the horse to an open area, and he responds to your commands, he's broke to ride. Happy trails. (TH)

HOW TO MAKE A BIRD TALK

Nowhere but in bird education is the true value of conversation revealed, where you discover that what you put into the art of discourse is delivered back to you with interest. So invest wisely.

• *The bird boom:* Once upon a time, every boy had a dog. But then most of America moved into town, and the world of pets went to the birds. People are now flocking to birds. Pet birds are now an $800 million a year industry. (Think about it: $800,000,000.00. For *birds.* Per *year.*) Although the census figures aren't in, between forty and fifty million birds have a perch or two in 15 percent of the homes in this country.

• *If elephants spoke:* One major reason for birds' popularity is that people like to own animals that will talk back to them. For most people, cats and dogs have a very limited vocabulary, while most birds—cute, easy to care for, and relatively inexpensive—will converse readily.

• *Stoolies:* Talking birds are sensitive to their environment. As these birds mature from babies to adults, they bond to people. Sometimes, they even adopt people as their substitute mates. And in order to communicate with their "mates," they talk.

• *Learning curve:* Most birds can learn to chatter until they are approximately two years old. If the bird hasn't talked by then, he probably won't—a real downer if your bird is a cockatoo with an eighty-eight-year life span.

"Relaxation" is an important word for bird teachers to learn, since a calmer bird is likely to be a chattier bird. Try these tips:

- *Keep baby birds close to the ground* until they develop balance skills.
- Cultivate your own balance skills by making sure you give your bird a *nutritionally balanced diet* with foods of varying texture, color, and shape.
- *Never let anyone handle your bird roughly.*
- *Avoid fast, sudden movements* that might frighten your bird.
- *Can birdie say, "The pen of my aunt is on the table?"* If you're having trouble getting a young bird to talk to you, try picking up a learn-to-talk tape cassette from a pet shop. Just fifteen minutes a day of one of these Berlitz-for-the-birds tapes should stimulate your parrot to eloquent discourse. An untried experiment: an audiocassette of a Stephen King novel.
- *Keep your emotional life out of your bird's face.* Why? Because no matter how old the bird is, if his environment is unpleasant, he will shut up and speak nevermore.
- *A special tip for men.* Talking birds are more responsive to a female voice, so it helps to get one, if you can. On the other hand, if you're a single guy and you can't get girls to talk to you, you shouldn't expect much from a parrot either.
- **Jail bird rock:** After a bird owner teaches his bird to talk, he can look forward to decades of hearing the same words repeated endlessly, over and over. Some time ago, *BirdTalk* magazine surveyed Amazon parrots to find their favorite sounds. The most frequently sung melody turns out to be "I Left My Heart in San Francisco." Other popular tunes with birds include "Don't Worry, Be Happy" and the theme song to the old *Andy Griffith Show*. Other birds simply whistled beer commercials (particularly Budweiser's), while one didn't sing so much as he screamed the name of his owner's dog whenever he was angry at the owner. Then there was the parrot who cried, "Call a lawyer!" every time he was put behind the bars of his cage.
- **He said, "Beam me up":** If, after all the tapes and all the suppressed rage, your bird still won't talk—or, in fact, if any of your pets and livestock exhibit signs of unhappiness—you might want to consult with a pet conversationalist. Charging up to five hundred dollars a day, subspeech therapists talk to your pet through mental images and relay the pet's messages back to you. According to therapists, animals are most likely to talk about how much people bug them and how they resent owners treating them like humans. You can, of course, try this yourself. Imagine the thoughts of a weenie dog, the confessions of a cockatiel. Imagine your reply.

Now you're talking bird talk. (GS)

HOW TO CURE CAT ACNE

First things first: Overcoming cat shame.

Actually, just *having* a cat can be embarrassing. Real guys have dogs. Although it's not their fault they get named Wickety-Poo or are addressed in loathsome kitty talk ("Wickety-Poo wanna eat din-din?"), cats have a bad rap. Guys with cats become apologetic: I didn't want it, they claim; it chased me home. Or they overreact, butching up their cats by naming them Assassin or marking mouse kills NFL-style on their collars.

• *The disease:* Feline acne is one of the most familiar problems among a vet's charges. Unlike the acne in humans and canines, which is generally confined to adolescence, feline acne can appear at any age. It usually occurs on the chin and looks much like human zits: blackheads, runny sores, reddish markings.

• *Causes:* The acne is primarily caused by foreign substances rubbing off food dishes onto the cat's chin while he is eating. Other causes: the cat's own secretions or poor grooming habits—not all cats can reach and wash their chin effectively. Obese cats with inadequate hygiene are most likely to attract acne.

• *Cures:* If the bacteria grows unchecked, the infected area will fester. Shirley and the magazines suggest owners cleanse their cats' chins with antibiotic shampoos, similar to Phiso-Hex, or apply oral antibiotics. Other experts suggest changing food dishes, tossing out the plastic dinner and water dishes, which can promote bacteria, and replacing them with metal or glass bowls. Most of all, if the condition becomes serious, you should consult a vet.

• *The other option* is to emulate your parents when you developed acne. This means delivering a lecture: Tell your cat that others do not judge peers by skin blemishes and regardless, everyone outgrows acne with age. However, that method didn't work then, and it doesn't work now. (GS)

15. Outdoors

Here's some travel advice for you: Stand up, walk across the room, open the door, and go outside. But take along this book: Indoors or out, directions are everything.

How to Find True North by Using Your Copy of *A Man's Life*

Take a copy of *A Man's Life* and stand it up on edge.

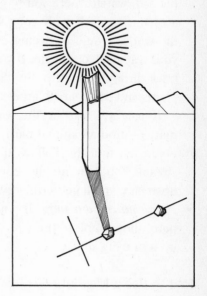

- *Put a mark on the ground* corresponding to the edge of the shadow of the top binding. That's point A.
- *Leave the book there.* Take a nap. Take a walk. Wait twenty, thirty minutes, an hour.
- *Return and put a mark* where the shadow is now. That's point B.
- *Draw a line* linking A and B.
- *Stand on the line* so that A is on your right. You're facing north.

Caution: Be wary of which book you use. Most books lack the careful accuracy of *A Man's Life*. Avoid fiction at all costs.

Ten Steps into the Woods

Okay. You know where you are. You know where you want to be. But there's a lot a man should know before he leaves hearth and home and heads off into unlisted real estate. If you stop to look it all up now, you'll never get out of the house. Instead, just head out, taking it one step at a time:

1. FIND A PATH

- *And stay on it.* If you're in a wilderness area used extensively for recreation, do everything possible to stay on the paths that have been made by others. The less off-path hiking you do, the better the wilderness will be for everybody coming along behind you.
- *Stay off it.* If you're in a real wilderness—the pristine, untouched kind—your path through the woods must be as invisible after you've passed as it was before you arrived. (MLK)
- *Mark it well.* If you're inexperienced, mark a path. Al Gore, the enviro-

veep, just after his election, took a walk in the woods and promptly got lost. For hours. It took the Secret Service to steer him along the right path. Don't count on their help, though, unless you've got Tipper in the tent. Instead, watch where you're going—really watch—and stop frequently to acquaint yourself with your surroundings. Remember, on your way into the woods, you'll be seeing everything that's behind you when you're on your way back out again. If you can follow that sentence, you can follow a track through the trees. Boy Scouts are taught to break stems on pathside plants and make small knife-cuts along the way. (RS)

If you get lost in the woods—or anywhere out-of-doors, for that matter—find an animal path, a deer trail, a cattle lane, or any obvious cut made by animals. Follow this to water. Then follow the water downstream. You'll eventually come to civilization. If you follow the water upstream, you'll get farther away from settlements. (FM)

- *Make your own way.* If you really want to get serious about marking a path, though, blaze the whole damn trail yourself. Start small, and move up to the big stuff.

How to Use a Machete

Think Sampras: Machetes are dangerous if used improperly, said one knife-wielding pathfinder. Think backhand, backhand, backhand.

Use the machete as it goes away from you. Never use a forehand. When you swing a machete, don't do it so the end of your swing has you as the target. Remember, backhand only. And if you're working with other guys, you should work more or less back to back, not side by side. That's obvious, yes? (ATR)

How to Fell a Tree

Think Bunyon: If you get tired whacking the small stuff, go for that ugly-big redwood blocking your path. Here's how one correspondent chain-saws his way through all that annoying old-growth:

- *You first notch the tree* on the side you want it to fall on. You've got a tree standing there vertically, and if you want it to fall to the right, you've got to saw a notch in there to the right.
- *You cut it about halfway through,* and angle it down at forty-five-degrees, take the notch out and then go to the other side and start cutting opposite the notch, and just slightly below it, and the tree will fall into the notch.
- *You try not to make it fall downhill,* because if you do that, you have to carry all the wood back up.

- *Then you limb it,* and then, if you've got a stove that holds eighteen-inch wood, you saw it up into eighteen-inch lengths.
- *Then you take your ax and split it,* and you throw it in the truck, stack it, and let it dry out so you can burn it in the winter.

Today, you use a chain saw to do the cutting, but in the old days we used an ax because there weren't any chain saws. So we chipped a notch and then started cutting on the other side. But using an ax is sort of like flying: You've got to have awareness. You've got to know what's going on around you. (CY)

2. WALK THE WALK

First off, recognize the **Main Thing** *about hiking: your feet.* Are they healthy? Toenails trimmed? No fungus?

Next, **you have to dress your feet for outdoor use.** Two things to keep in mind about what you keep on your feet: Keep 'em light and keep 'em dry.

Let's say you're a regular guy going out for some regular hiking or regular camping or regular backpacking. Don't get fancy. Buy a pair of medium-weight trail boots. They're as easy to find as a pair of athletic shoes. The **Main Thing:** comfort. If they feel good, give them a once-over to make sure they're made well. Buy them. Hit the trail. (JA)

On the other hand, if you plan on putting your new boots to much more demanding tests, consider the following:

- *The fit counts.* To get a good fit: Go to a good boot shop. Make sure you wear the same socks to the store that you will wear in the woods.

   Here's what you're looking for: *A snug fit around the ball of your foot and across the instep.* You shouldn't have to achieve this by yanking at the laces.

   To test for the snugness of the fit, do the following: Stand up. Have a friend or the salesman wrap a hand around the instep of the boot with one hand and squeeze—if you've got a snug fit, you're in good shape. If there's lots of extra room in there, you're going to be flying all over the place inside that boot while you walk. Good way to grow blisters. (TB)
- *Talk to the salesman* before you try on a single pair. Does he look and sound like he knows what he's talking about?
- *Make sure he measures your feet* with a thing called a Brannock Device. This is important: The Brannock will give you a better measurement than anything else on the planet. Might not be too important to you when you're buying penny loafers to wear to work, but then, at work you probably don't walk twenty miles a day with sixty pounds strapped onto your back. In addition to measuring the length and width of your foot

with great precision, the Brannock will measure ball-to-heel length, which is a crucial factor in boot fit. Ask your salesman to explain it to you—but if he can't, hoof it.

- *If one foot is larger than the other,* buy to fit the larger foot.
- *Walk on an incline* to judge whether your toes are going to slam into the front of the boots when you go downhill. You've got to have enough room that your toes don't hit the tip of the boots, but not so much room that your toes slide around.
- *Do your heels stay put?* They should. If they slip, that means blisters on the trail up ahead. (DAB)
- *Give the boots the* Man's Life *quality-control checkout.* Look your new boots right in the eyes and deep into their sole and ask some tough questions:
  1. *Are the seams nice and neat and tight?* If not, it may be a sign of inferior quality in workmanship.
  2. *Does the leather look and feel good?* You'll pay for it down the road if you buy boots made of cheap leather. Won't breathe, so it'll be like wearing East German plastic marching shoes. You'll spend all day walking in the pool of sweat that will collect in your socks.
  3. *What does the lining look like?* It should be made of a wicking material—polypropylene's good—so that when your feet sweat, the sweat doesn't stay in the boot but wicks to the outside of your socks, then out into the atmosphere for all of us to enjoy.
  4. *Are the soles the kind you want?* How well are they attached? Can they be replaced?
  5. *How heavy are the boots?* Weight really counts. You want to avoid buying the heaviest boots in the store. After all, you will pick them up and set them down thousands of times every day. Why add weight you don't need to be dragging around? (TB)
- *Keep walking around the store.* Be patient. Walk around. Walk some more. Bend over. Do a squat thrust. Stand on a bench using only the toes of the boots. Put them to a test before you leave the store. Still feel good? Okay, maybe you've found the boots for you. (TB)

3. DRESS FOR THE OCCASION

This is a walk in the woods, lads, not a stroll on the boardwalk. If you're heading up and not down, remember that for every one thousand feet in elevation you climb, the temperature will drop 3 to 5 degrees. Like, if you're at Newport Beach and you're walking to the top of Everest, take a coat because it's 150 degrees cooler looking eye-to-eye with K2 than it is watching the babes in the pipeline.

Always keep a hat, sunglasses, and sunscreen handy.

If it's a warm-weather walk, bring T-shirts, shorts, hat with brim, long-sleeve turtleneck, sweatshirt with hood, ski cap or other hat for cold and nighttime use, lightweight pants, lightweight long-sleeved shirt, rain poncho, bandanna.

If you're hiking through the cold, steely marches of Minnesota, wear your clothes in three layers—depending on how long you're going and how much you can carry. Why three layers instead of one garment that keeps you warm and keeps you dry? Maximum flexibility. Take it off, put it on.

The Three Layers

1. *Wear polypropylene* or an equivalent lightweight polyester knit like Capilene or Thermax against your skin, as if it were long underwear. These are light and warm, and they wick moisture away from your skin.
2. *A pile or fleece polyester jacket or pullover.* This is the stuff you see inside casual jackets that looks like a high-pile terry cloth. This is strictly for warmth, although it also helps wicks moisture away.
3. *The last layer protects you from the rain.* Make sure the garment you choose is made of Gore-Tex or an equivalent. These fabrics have pores big enough to breathe and let your sweat out, but the pores are smaller than water so the rain can't come in.

Let's consider **how these layers work alone and in combination:**

- *If it's hot and raining,* you put on your breathable rainwear.
- *If it's cold and dry,* you put on your light polyester layer and your heavier fleece layer.
- *If you are just sitting around* camp and relaxing, you can throw on your polyester jacket or pullover and it will not only keep you warm but also feel good against your skin.
- *Most important, having three different layers allows you to adjust* your clothing to the temperature outside in the woods and inside your body. You might start the day's hike with all three layers on, then remove the rain shell when the fog burns off, then remove the pullover when it gets warm and/or you start to get warm from the workout you're getting. Finally, if it starts to rain, you can slip your rain garment on alone or with the pullover underneath. (PER)

Hats and Headbands

One thing that can be a lifesaver is the hat you wear. Some guys prefer a fleece headband that covers their ears and keeps heat from escaping from their head, but lets them feel the fresh cool air on the top of their noggin. If the top of your head gets cold, you can throw on anything from a ski cap to a baseball cap over the headband to keep the top of your head warm, too. This layered approach gives you the same maximum flexibility that you'll need in connection with your other clothing.(PB)

A dissent: Always cover the top of your head, as well as your ears, since up to half your body heat escapes through your head—bald or not bald. Believe it or not, no matter what part of your body is cold, covering your head will help take the chill off. (PER)

What Not to Wear

You don't want to wear cotton—with the exception of cotton T-shirts. **Cotton is no friend to the backpacker.** When it gets wet, it doesn't keep you warm anymore; plus, it gets heavy and it takes a long time to dry.

Wool, on the other hand, does take a long time to dry and does get heavy, but at least it will keep you warm while the drying process is in progress. (AR)

4. CARRY YOUR OWN FREIGHT

Camping is the one form of travel where your carry-ons really do count. Once upon a time, a chap could tie up all his rations in a hankie, tie it to a stick, and down the road he went. The evolutionary chain is familiar: Metal-and-canvas back breakers gave way to aluminum-and-nylon Quasimodo boxes. Now, we have *internal* backpacks. Progress.

• *Internal packs* have padded struts built right into them. These supports are generally better molded to the body. They fit better on your back and shoulders, too, especially compared to the aluminum external frame backpacks, which required your back and shoulders to adjust to them.

• *External frame packs* have an upside too, though. First, there's the cost. You also get more pockets: There are both main compartments and little ones on the exterior. It may seem like a minor point now, while you're sitting there drinking your coffee, but when you're out in the woods and you need toilet paper *bad,* and you have an internal frame pack with only one internal compartment and one external compartment and you can't find the toilet paper, you might feel differently. External frame packs generally have two main compartments and little pockets all over the place. Smart backpackers with external frames, by the way, generally keep the essentials like TP and water close at hand in the same outside, easy-to-reach pocket on every trip.

Rule of thumb: External backpacks are better for storage; internals are better for carrying. (PER)

5. HOME IS WHERE YOU PITCH IT

Most men start their tenting careers under a blankie thrown up between two kitchen chairs. Then we get testosterone and move out.

• *Two views of life outside.* Might as well talk about this now, since it's going to come up eventually. See, the downside of camping is exactly the same as the downside of losing a war. So you can call it camping if you want, but history has another word for it.

• *This is where tents come in,* and this is also where we turn a corner on how we can look at the whole sleep-and-eat-outside experience. New-model tents are to camping what federal low-security prisons are to the corrections business. They're practically luxurious, plus they seem to float off the ground: They're almost freestanding—with a delicate filigree of ropes and pegs added almost as an afterthought—and they take about three minutes to set up and take down. (PB)

How to Set up a Modern Tent

The new tents are dome shaped. Along the outer or inner perimeter of the dome are small slits through which you slide two or more poles. Around the base of the tent, there are fittings that hold the ends of the poles. **The inertia of the bent poles around the outside of the dome holds the tent up and in place.** You may wish to sturdy your tent by putting a few pegs around the outside of it, but in most cases this is unnecessary—your weight and the weight of your gear alone will keep the tent from blowing away. (PB)

Tents Come Rated by Season

There are two-weather tents, three-weather tents, and four-weather ones. Obviously, a four-weather tent is the postman's delight. It'll get you through the worst rain, the deepest snow, the coldest sleet, and the darkest gloom of night. For the vast majority of us, a four-weather tent is overkill. **A three-weather tent will get you through almost anything but severe winter.** A two-weather tent is really a one-weather tent: You use it on a warm nights where you want to get away from the chill and the bugs and maybe a light summer rain. It's as close as you can get to sleeping under the stars naked. (PER)

Two Ways to Wet

There are two sources of water inside a tent. One source is, of course, outside: It rains, tent leaks, you're wet.

The other source is inside: Some tenting material is waterproof, all right, but that which seals the water out, also traps condensation in. The principle of staying dry in a tent is very much the same as the principle of staying dry in your clothes: The two secret words are "layering" and "wicking." The layering comes in the form of the tent, which should be made of a porous polyester material that will let your body heat out and mostly not let the rain in. Now, over the tent, you put a waterproof rain fly, which not only keeps rain out but also traps moisture as it escapes through the tenting. You're the furnace in a good tent.

The other crucial thing to look for in a tent: Tub construction or a floor that continues partway up the walls in one piece. Without tub construction, it is a lot easier for water to run into your tent. (PB, GAS)

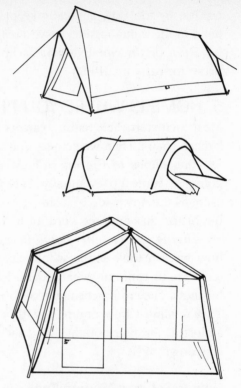

How to Check into God's Motel: These are the most modern versions of the three tent types most commonly used (top to bottom): Two-man "pup" tent, with poles. One- or two-man tent with external supports. Family wall tent, with external supports.

Where to Pitch the Tent

The ideal location is a slight incline someplace far from the site of any potential flooding. If you camp on perfectly flat ground, you'll be vulnerable to water in the event of rain. Pitch the tent so your head is higher than your feet and avoid sleeping across a slope because you will spend all night trying to keep yourself from rolling into the wall of your tent.

Pitching a tent under a tree can have a few advantages—provided you're sure the tree is strong and sturdy. One advantage is that you will have shade for part of the day, so your tent will stay nice and cool in the daytime hours. Meanwhile, if it rains you will be partly protected from the rain. If you like looking at the stars at night, don't camp under a tree with too much foliage. Watch out for lightning.

If the site allows it, handpick the view you will see out your tent door. It might be wise to anticipate the weather; if you suspect rain, avoid pointing your tent's door into the storm. Pointing your tent to the south or east will give you the morning sun, which can be a real bonus. Avoid trying your guy-lines to weaker branches of a tree—in a storm or heavy winds they will whip around and so will you. On the other hand, if you think wind will play a heavy hand in the night's weather, consider pitching your tent up against a fallen log or large rock or other natural element that can serve as a wind-break. (PB)

Tent Tips

- *Don't cook* in your tent unless you want to die. Tents aren't fireproof, and even if fire didn't get you, lack of oxygen might.
- *If you use a candle lantern in your tent,* make sure you set it on a solid flat surface in a place where you won't kick it. Better yet, figure out a way to hang it so it is impossible to knock it down or against the wall of the tent. (PER)
- *Take a ground cloth*—it'll keep water out if you have any holes in the floor of your tent. The other great thing about a ground cloth: It keeps the bottom of your tent clean. Let's face it, you can throw a ground cloth away when it gets so dirty you just can't stand it. Tents, on the other hand, cost a heck of a lot more money. (PB)
- *Pack your poles and stakes separately* from your tent to avoid puncturing it. Always carry a few extra poles.
- *Always take a piece of ripstop nylon* and a repair kit with you.
- *Seal the seams of your tent with a waterproofing agent* the first time you set it up and the first time you use it after a long hiatus. If your tent is going to leak, the seams are one of the main places it will do so.
- *Clean your tent immediately* after you get home from a trip. Once you put it back in the garage, you'll never do it and it will smell like a gym locker the next time you go to use it. As part of the cleaning, open all the flaps and allow it to air out. (PER)

Wear a Bedroom Suite

Think of a sleeping bag as a big, ugly suit. You can make yourself happy if you just get one that fits.

Mummy Bags Keep You Warmer

Sleeping bags keep you warm because they are designed to keep the air warm around your body. You bring in the heat, the bag keeps it there for you. Mummy bags are smaller and snugger, so there is less air to heat, less air to keep heated. You stay warmer. Also, the rectangular bag has a large opening, thus more cold air can get in. The mummy bag has a hood that keeps the warm air from escaping. The hood of a mummy prevents heat loss because your head is actually inside the bag and only your face is exposed if you draw the opening of the hood tight. On really cold nights, you may want to leave just your nose exposed. Still, the roomier ambiance of a rectangular bag has some virtue—and you can ditch that, too, if you can squeeze your wife inside with you.

The Stuff Inside the Bag

You've got **three choices for the stuff inside the bag: goose down, duck down, or synthetic fibers.** Ever wonder why a duck can swim in freezing water while you can only watch from inside the house? Those feathers on his back trap air and keep it there, thus he stays warm. Ditto the goose. Ditto golfers who wear synthetic fiber clothing and love to play all year 'round. The fabric of your sleeping bag is sewn in such a way that the bag is divided into small pockets. The insulating material of your choice is then stuffed into these pockets and, because the insulator is evenly distributed, you stay nice and warm all over. Like a duck. If the bag weren't divided into pockets, all the insulation would make a move for your head or your feet and the rest of you would freeze to death.

Here are the pros and cons of down versus synthetic fibers:

- *Down.* Great insulator. Light. Compressible. You can pack it small and then shake it to get air into it. The contained air is the true insulation. The downside: It's more expensive than synthetic, and it's no good if it gets wet.
- *Synthetic.* Costs less, dries fast, and keeps you warm even when it's wet. Perfect for people with allergies. But it's also heavier, takes more space, and won't last as long as a down bag. (PER)

Bag Tricks

- *Sleep sack.* Unless you get off on sleeping in nylon sheets at home, you should invest in a sleep sack, a cotton or fleece liner for your bag. It's easier and cheaper to clean than the inside of your bag, and it'll keep you a little bit warmer than the bag itself.

- *Ground pad.* Take our word here: Thickness isn't what counts. It's the material that matters. Here's the test: While at the sporting goods store, take each of the pads available—the thinnest, the fattest, the prettiest, the ugliest, the lightest, the heaviest—and grab each one lightly between your thumb and fingers. Some feel warm, some don't. Take it from us, the one that feels warm to the touch when you squeeze it is the one you want to be sleeping on. After all, what your body will be doing by lying on it all night is squeezing it, as well. If you are still worried about padding, buy another, thicker pad to put under this insulation, but make sure that when you lie your bag down, it goes right on top of this hot little pad. The insulation you have under you is much more important than the insulation you have over you. (PB)
- *Don't sleep in your clothes.* If you do, you will suffer the consequences of good logic pushed too far. Sleeping in your clothes does keep you warm—in fact, *too* warm. What happens is, you're so toasty in your jeans and sweats and socks and sleeping bag in the middle of the night that you start to sweat. The sweat makes your clothes damp. The dampness makes you cold. That sucks. For some reason, the best thing to wear to bed in a down or synthetic bag is nothing, or a pair of skivvies and a pair of socks. (SPW)
- *Washing.* When drying the bag after a wash, consider throwing a few clean tennis balls in the dryer to help keep the bag fluffy. (ER)

7. PLUMBING

You know, nothing dresses up a john like a big bouquet of red oaks and poison ivy.

- *First, find a spot at least two hundred feet from your site,* and from any body of water—lake, stream, creek, river, ocean. If you're smart, you'll make it at least two hundred feet downwind from your campsite and the trail, too. Failure to abide by this rule will result in the sudden appearance of paper rangers from the local EPA office, who will drop out of the trees and haul you off to federal court. In 1995, the EPA helped throw a seventy-four-year-old apple farmer in the clink for the rest of his life for messing up the paperwork it made him do to monitor how much of his cider waste went into the local creek. The EPA is not busy. So a lone figure such as your very self, out in the woods with serious mien and small shovel, looks like a dream come true for an enviro-dink. Therefore, do it right or do it for five to life.
- *Dig a small hole.* Make it no larger than necessary: If you're a normal guy, maybe eight inches across. If you're an academic, you might need several

extra feet in both directions. Eight inches is the magic depth; at that level there are lots of little microorganisms that will actually thank you for the treat. Do your duty. Use septic-safe toilet paper sparingly. If you're really worried about the larger environment, don't use any at all. This will cause others to express concern about your own personal environment. Bury your work.

- *Traveling in packs?* If there is a big group of you, dig a trench latrine. Same rule about the depth, just dig it wide. After each use, you should sprinkle enough dirt over the waste to keep away the flies.
- *Don't feed the animals.* Don't bury anything else in the latrine, like dishwater and leftover food, since animals may be attracted to the smell of your food. The contamination can cause death.
- *Dishwater and food scraps.* Make a separate kitchen latrine. Follow the same rules as above. Use biodegradable soap to wash dishes. Use as little water as possible. (PER, KMN)

8. KAMP KITCHEN
The Fire
Making a cooking fire is not an instinctive business for a man. Especially under difficult circumstances, building a good, useful fire is a lot like courtship: You have to coax it along, bit by bit, for if you try to get too much heat too quickly, you'll only snuff it out.

- *Always build your fire on rock or dirt.*
- *Clear the area at least three feet* in all directions of the fire site of all flammable material.
- *Start with the smallest pieces of fuel*—tinder and kindling—and then work up to larger and larger pieces of fuel until you have your logs burning. Here's the sequence: a yank of thread, a few leaves, a *match*, a handful of twigs, some small branches, a few small logs—maybe something about as big around as your wrist—then a couple of larger logs. Take it slow, and stack your fire in a loose pyramid. These principles apply to all types of fires. (TRE)
- *Make sure your fire gets plenty of oxygen.* The rule here is that the amount of air, not the amount of fuel, controls the heat of a fire.
- *The "hunter's fire."* This is a good, general-purpose fire, useful for both cooking and heating. Start by digging a shallow fire pit with two close rows of rocks or green logs on two sides parallel to one another and parallel to the wind, while the other two sides remain open. Build your fire in the pit between the rocks, which provide a place to set your pots and pans over the fire so your food can cook without sitting directly in the fire. With

two sides open that face and oppose the wind, air is allowed to come in one side of the pit and leave through the other open side, thus fanning the fire and keeping it hot and also providing a lot of heat at the side where the warmed air comes out. If you want to control the fire, you can use a windbreak of rocks at one end as a kind of damper.

- *Fuel.* The wood you burn will determine whether you have a good wood for cooking or for staying warm. The rule of thumb: The drier and harder the wood, the hotter the fire. Give your fire some time before you start cooking. The coals are hotter than the flames, so when it comes to cooking and heating, the coals are far more important. (PER)

- *A happy-camper clean-up tip.* Rub soap over the outside of your pot before you start cooking. When you are done, the soap will rinse right off and so will the black from the fire. (Anon.)

Recipes

Terry Hall, compiler of *Cowboy Wisdom,* chipped in these gastro-honkers:

SONOFABITCH STEW

    2 pounds lean beef
    Half a calf heart
    1 pound calf liver
    1 set marrow gut
    Salt, pepper
    A lot of Louisiana hot sauce
    1 set sweetbreads
    1 set brain

Kill off a young steer. Cut up the beef, liver, and heart into 1-inch cubes; slice the marrow gut into small rings. Place it all in a Dutch oven, or a deep casserole if somebody brought one. Cover the meat with water and simmer over medium coals for 2 to 3 hours. Add salt, pepper, and hot sauce to taste. Take sweetbreads and brains and cut in small pieces. Add to stew. Simmer another hour—but don't let the thing boil, ever. (TH)

BREAKFAST BEANS

    2 pounds pinto beans
    2 pounds ham hock (or salt pork)
    2 onions, chopped
    4 tablespoons sugar

2 green chilies (or to taste)

1 can tomato paste

Wash the beans and soak them overnight. In the morning, drain the water off and pour the beans into a Dutch oven. Cover them with water. Add the remaining stuff and simmer over coals until tender. Sample the beans while cooking. Add salt to taste and water as needed. Fry up a mess of eggs, over easy, with a chunk of onion. Salt and pepper the eggs. Serve up the eggs and put the beans on the side. (TH)

PRAIRIE OYSTERS

This delicate recipe is from Charles Willey, Valentine, Nebraska, 1877.

Get everything off 'em, split 'em open, and fry 'em in hot fat in a skillet until they are done good; then put salt on 'em and serve 'em hot. (CW)

SUCAMAGROWL

This dish is a good substitute for pudding or pie.

3 cups water

1 cup vinegar

2 cups sugar

2 tablespoons flour

2 pinches cinnamon or nutmeg

First, put the water and vinegar in a pot and bring the mixture to a boil. Combine the sugar and flour and stir this mixture into the boiling liquid until it is thoroughly dissolved. Let the whole thing cook over a medium bank of coals for 15 minutes and then add the spice. Have a dough ready, like a biscuit dough prepared with baking powder. Break off little chunks of the dough by the tablespoonful and drop the pieces in the simmering liquid. When the dumplings are done, serve them while they're still hot.

COWBOY COFFEE

Take one pound of jamoka coffee and wet it good with water. Boil it over a hot fire for thirty minutes, then pitch a horseshoe in. If the shoe sinks, put in more coffee. (TH)

9. TOOLS OF THE TRAIL

If your foray into Nature is a day trip, this will be an awesome exercise in overpack. But if your trip has a four-day/three-night, single-occupancy feel to it, this is your checklist.

- **First-aid and survival kit,** which includes:

  For day hikes, take matches, compass, whistle, moleskin, toilet paper, some kind of antigerm spray or cream, sunscreen, aspirin, insect repellent, Band-Aids, a first-aid booklet, a quarter for a phone call, or the cell phone.

  For casual camping, bring all of the above plus tweezers, needle for blisters, razor blade, Tums, Alka-Seltzer, Pepto Bismol, ace bandage, a compress, scissors, gauze and tape, a triangular bandage.

  For backpacking, You need to anticipate every problem, then find a set of very small solutions. Usually, you can find all of the things above, only in miniature. (Okay, except the ace bandage.) Also, make sure you take some fishing line, hooks, safety pins, a mirror.

- **Stove.** If you don't want to build a fire—or if fires aren't permitted in your neck of the woods—tote a small stove. The gas canisters are cheap and they produce a lot of heat pronto. That's good news when you're cold and want nothing more than a hot cup of coffee.

- **Water bottle.** Two choices here: You can blow a sawbuck at Al's Owl World and pick up a water bottle, or you can spend a buck-twenty-nine and grab a big bottle of water at the 7-11. Buy a big one to keep filled with water in your pack, and a smaller one to keep near at hand.

  Three more water tips:

  1. *When on the trail,* don't ever drink the last of your water—you don't know, for sure, when you'll get more.
  2. *These days, take no chances:* Purify all water unless you're in a state or federal park and you are told specifically that the water is safe to drink.
  3. *When it is really cold,* stuff your water down into your back, wrapped in clothes, to keep it from freezing. (KMN)

- **Sunglasses and hat.** Make sure the glasses are UV-safe. The best hats don't make your head itch after a while, so that rules out anything lined with polyester.

- **Shovel.** Go for the avalanche shovel at your local backpacking shop. It's light, doesn't take up much room. Lightweight alternative: a small plastic trowel.

- **The right socks.** That means two layers. A wicking sock first, which is usually made of polypropylene. These socks draw moisture off your feet and into the heavier socks you are wearing over them. Make your second pair of socks wool or polypropylene, depending on the weather. Avoid cotton socks: Unlike wool or polypropylene, which will keep your feet warm even when wet, cotton socks will just make your feet cold when they get wet—and they will, even if you're no place near water.

- **Flashlight.** Bring extra batteries.
- **Pocketknife.**
- **Rope.**
- **Poncho.** The standard GI poncho is a piece of genius with a hole in it. It's great because it gives a full range of motion with your arms while being long enough in back to cover both you and the top portion of your pack in the rain.
- **Tube tent.** A "tube tent" is a piece of lightweight plastic. Emergency? Tie a rope between two trees, drape the plastic over the rope and you're home. Takes about two minutes to unpack and put up. Throw it on the ground, and you have a great ground cloth. Cheap, too. (TP, PER)

10. LIVING OFF THE LAND

Specifically, that thin margin of land adjoining a highway. We received an alarming number of correspondence on the subject of road kill, most of which bore an if-you're-going-to-hit-it, you-might-as-well-eat-it kind of sensibility.

These recipes are too disgusting to belabor, but in the interests of thoroughness, we're providing two to tide you over until the meat wagon comes.

Note: Freshness is everything here. If you need a tool to get your dinner off the road, you may as well face the fact that you're dealing with food well past its prime.

Skin 'em. All road kill must be skinned and cleaned. The mere presence of tire tracks does not render a carcass pot-ready. For most small animals, make incisions around the neck, down the belly, and around the haunches. Then peel back the skin. Eviscerate the animal. Remove the head and tail.

Parboil 'em. All crushed critters need to be soaked in water long enough to bleach the blood out of the meat. Then the carcass must be parboiled—in which the meat is plunged into boiling water long enough to begin the cooking process. To the water you should add salt—more than you think you need—and pepper and whatever other stuff amuses you: red peppers, celery, onions, whatever's handy.

RABBIT

Cut the rabbit up into pieces. Trim along the ribs and back, and remove the rear legs.

Put all the pieces in a pot and parboil until the meat is tender.

Fry the pieces in a skillet with plenty of pepper. You can roll the pieces in flour first, if you have some handy.

POSSUM

Soak the skinned animal overnight.

Parboil the intact carcass—minus the charming head and that very attractive ropelike tail—until tender. Add plenty of salt and pepper.

Bake the thing until it's done. You can add yams or turnips to the baking pan, if you wish. In fact, the possum would no doubt have liked it that way. (PVFD)

How to Avoid Giving Blood

Mosquitoes are like kids. The minute they stop making noise, you know they're into something, like your circulatory system. A lazy guy with a fishing pole—or any man outdoors—is nothing but a big hunk o' bait for a mosquito. Here's how to avoid those needle-nosed nibbles:

- *Unplug the zapper.* Bug zappers have almost no ability to reduce the number of skeeters. They sure aren't any good for keeping them away, since they work by attracting the bugs they kill. Many bugs are thus left unzapped. Best bet: Get your neighbor to buy one.
- *Avon's Skin-So-Soft Moisturizing Suncare Plus.* Hey, big guy, go sensitive with the help of the door-to-door lady. This stuff contains citronella, a mild and natural repellent.
- *Noise machines.* The University of Illinois checked out a bunch of these things and found out that like zappers, not only did they not repel mosquitoes, they actually attracted them.
- *DEET's.* It's hard to beat this as a repellent, but use it sparingly. The stuff is potent enough to eat through your parka, and it's been known to cause eye and skin problems. Go for a 20 percent concentration; you'll get the same protection as you would with the pure stuff, but with a lot less risk.
- *Skeeter hats.* The kind with the mesh veil cost around three bucks and work like a charm. Mosquitoes see you coming in one of those camo-bridal veils, and they run away laughing. Good riddance. (AMcLL)

How to Charm a Snake

Snakes are nearly blind. But they obsess on what they do manage to see. Since they detect motion easily, you can draw a snake's attention away from you or your boot by getting it to pay attention to the tip of a moving stick. This is the same principle used in India by snake charmers. They get the snake to follow the moving object—usually the tip of a flute or whistle—and rise out of the basket. If the cobra strikes, it strikes the flute, not the flutist. (JRE)

SNAKE BITES

Good boots can make the difference between a snake attack and a snake bite.

    Good sense is what you'll need if you're snake-bit. Three tips:

1. ***Stay calm.*** Panic causes your heart to pump, and that speeds the venom to your heart.
2. ***Don't move.*** You don't want to increase demands on your circulatory system. If you must walk, take it slow and easy.
3. ***Get to a medic.*** Carving up the bite and sucking out the poison only leaves you with a mouth full of poisonous blood. Almost all snake-bit guys can survive a trip even to a remote medical facility where antivenom can be obtained.

    In general, stay healthy and fit. People who are soft and out of shape have a much worse reaction to a snake bite than those who are in shape. (JRE, Anon.)

How to Mount an Urban Camping Expedition

Let's say you're in a strange city, you have little or no money, nowhere to sleep, nothing to eat. It could happen. What do you do? Two choices: You can declare yourself "homeless." Or you can declare the entire situation to be a camping trip, downtown-style.

CITY TENTING

This is not a canvas-and-trees circumstance. "Tenting," at least when used in the context of urban camping, has a more general, shelter-oriented aspect to it.

What to Do If You've Got Absolutely No Money

- ***If you're in a large city, go to a police station.*** Take a seat. Wait for someone to offer to help you. By the time someone does, it'll be morning. Feel free to sleep while you're there. True, a precinct chair isn't the most comfortable bed in town, but it's certainly the cheapest and, compared to similar accommodations found elsewhere, one of the safest. If anyone does ask you what you're doing there, either feign a lack of English skills or say you're waiting for someone. If you're polite and well behaved, you'll be left alone. (KD)

- *If you're in a small town,* try all the doors on the local churches. Chances are, you'll find one that's open. Once inside, find a place to sleep that's out of the way and not disrespectful to a house of worship. On a couch in the rec room is fine. On a pew in the church is not. (LO)
- *If you're anywhere near a hotel* and dressed halfway decently, go there. Sleep in a chair in the lobby. (LO)

  Banquet-room ancillary: Once at the hotel, go into one of the conference rooms. Push a banquet table up against the wall. Pull the tablecloth down to the floor. Crawl underneath and sleep—but be prepared for a rude awakening in the morning when the clean-up crew comes in to vacuum. Unless it's a giant hotel, this won't be until the morning crew comes in, however. Most hotels are run by a skeleton staff at night.
- *Go to a hospital.* Look for an empty single room, or just act like someone you know is dying and pull up a couch. Best bet: The waiting room next to OB, where all those dads are flaked out waiting for all those moms.
- *Colleges are great places for an urban campout.* Look for an unlocked classroom or lounge. (AT)
- *Find an unlocked car.* Best bet: Check all the older cars and convertibles—their owners are less likely to lock their cars. You can also tell by looking whether a car is in frequent use.
- *Pick up a babe in a bar.* "Your place" is the right answer when she asks, "Your place or mine?"
- *Look in the phone book* for people with your last name. Barring that, call *anyone* and pose as a long-lost relative. (GS, KD)

What to Do if You Have Some Money, but Not a Lot

- *College dorms* sometimes have somewhere you can sleep, and some routinely rent out empty dorm rooms. Obviously, the YMCA or youth hostel is always there for a cheap room.
- *Rent a cheap car.* Depending on the city, we're talking as low as $9.95. So what if you have to pay for miles? Just take it around the corner and park. And you can probably pass on the insurance, too—unless you have violent dreams. (KD)

- **Get a job.** In most big cities, there is a huge churn in resident-managers of cheap motels and apartment complexes. Call them up. Take the job. Make it a night, or make it a career. (DP)

HUNTING AND GATHERING FOOD

Other than beating back the rats for a share of Dumpster delight—check behind hotels and restaurants—you have only two no-money means of getting dinner: You can either seek charity or engage in theft.

Charity

- **Places to get info in larger cities:** Roman Catholic cathedrals and large churches, social services agencies, beat cops.
- **Follow soup kitchen etiquette.** Wait your turn and don't badger for seconds while others are still waiting. Most soup kitchens have local protocols.
- **Find the party.** If you're dressed appropriately, you can usually find some kind of party or reception or art opening where food is being served. Hotels are great places to look, also art galleries and conference centers.
- **Sit up and beg.** Ask people as they leave restaurants if you can have the leftovers in their doggie bags.
- **Find a restaurant** (best bet: one with a working-class ambiance) and introduce yourself. Politely explain your circumstances, ask if you can work for a meal. If the answer is yes, get to work. If the answer is no, ask if you can come back at closing time and eat something that would otherwise end up in the garbage. (AT)

Larceny

If it's larceny you're contemplating, the situation better be desperate. We received *four* suggestions on various ways to steal food. Of all the things one might steal, food seems to be the most noble. You can't really imagine telling somebody that the kids were starving, so you went out and swiped a Beemer. Twinkies, that's something else. Instead of giving you a step-by-step on how to shoplift your way to the big house, we'll just point out that food is often found in restaurants and supermarkets, but none of it is free.

Cheap Eats

With a little cash, you can chow down big-time, if you take a sec to locate the blue-plate bargain. Here's one for each coast:

- *In Los Angeles,* it's the Pantry, where you can get the biggest and best breakfast you've ever seen for under $5. Dinner's damn good and damn cheap, too. (HY)
- *In New York,* it's Gray's Papaya. Two of the best hot dogs you've ever had, and only fifty cents apiece. Two dogs with a medium papaya juice are only $2.15. (DC)

URBAN CAMPING HYGIENE

Find the community stream, beat your clothes on the rocks, and wash your face. Some suggestions:

- *College dorms.*
- *College gym.*
- *Motel.* Watch for people leaving. Some of them will leave their door open or unlocked. Or, watch as people leave. Many will take their key to the office. Note those who don't. Then stroll into the office and tell them you've locked yourself out of that room. If they ask for ID, say you left that in the room too. You've got a fifty-fifty shot the clerk will hand you the key without asking you anything else. If he asks your name and then checks it against the name on the reservation, say someone from the office made the reservation. You get it: You can bluff your way through anything. (AT)
- *Hotel.* Stroll down the hallway until you hit a room with the door open and the maid's cart outside. Walk into the room as if you own it. Apologize for barging in. She'll apologize for being in your room and leave. If the maid's not there when you enter, close and lock the bathroom door and turn the shower on. You'll be left alone. If the owner of the room comes back, say you thought it was your room. (EW)
- *Private gym.* Many gyms will give you a free one-day pass to check out the facilities. If you're lucky, they'll even throw in a towel and a tour. (Anon.)

How to Outwit Fish

A trout is a fish. Fish have brains so small that fish neurosurgeons have to do their work under electron microscopes. So why, then, are so many smart men outwitted by so many dim fish? The answer to this ancient and vexing question may be found in the secret book read only by successful salesmen, right there in the section called "You Gotta Know the Territory." For a trout, the territory is a small stretch of streambed. A chap hoping to sell a trout the goods at the end of his line has to know the territory as well as his client does. Otherwise, no sale. Here's how to close:

- **Find a good stream to fish.** The best trout streams have several similar characteristics: They have a relatively subtle gradient—sometimes as little as a fifty- to seventy-five-foot drop over the course of a mile; you will not catch trout in waterfalls. They have a reliable source of cold water—a spring or a neighborhood glacier. They have a clean streambed—lots of rocks and gravel, not much sand and silt. And all good trout streams have a lot of good things for trout to eat in them.
- **In the morning, fish small areas of white water**—riffles—and shallow areas of slow flow—flats—since those are the parts of a stream where trout go for breakfast.
- **In the afternoon, fish shady banks and deep pools.** Not only do these features provide an angler with a little midday shade, they are also ideal cool-water dives for lunching trout.
- **In the evening,** you can either return to a favorite riffle or find some decent "pocket" water—the deep, calm plunge pools at the bottom of a rapids or the shallow eddies behind large boulders. (ARi)

FIVE MAINSTREAM TRUTHS

1. The current in the middle of a stream is four times as fast as the current near the banks.
2. The faster the water, the smaller the fish.
3. There's more trout food on a rocky bottom than on a sandy one.
4. The patterns of a 25-foot-wide trout stream—flats, riffles, pools—repeat every 150 feet or so.
5. Trout see you long before you see them; an aspiring angler has to stay below a 10 percent angle of vision to avoid being seen by lounging trout. (ARi, TB)

HOW TO FISH WITH FLIES

There are only two good reasons for a man to stand in water up to the point where, if you'll excuse me, men's health is an issue. Fixing pipes is one. Catching fish is the other.

Leaking overflows, flooded basements, busted drains, all call for a big-money fix. But unlike plumbing, a skill practiced by extremely well paid tradesmen, fishing is pursued almost completely by amateurs. That's because fishing is an act of complete symbolic satisfaction for most men, who come by a taste for the sport when they are young. A five-year-old boy impaling a worm on a hook and dropping it in the water with the hope of reward is participating in a pursuit so intractably manly that invariably the kid gets hooked on fishing long, long before a fish gets hooked by the kid.

There are of course many ways to catch a fish, and of all of them, fly-fishing is the least efficient. Nets are faster, worms are easier. Taking a half inch of metal and some bird feathers and tossing it in the river is not a practical proposition. Yet, it is to fly-fishing that most men, at some usually middle-aged point in their lives, are drawn. That's because fly-fishing, as a passionate pursuit, is best suited to men who have lived just enough life to recognize its limitations and its comic potential, and need some way to try to make sense of it all. In this respect, fly-fishing is natural therapy, a workout for real life, for no other activity so perfectly combines every skill a man needs in order to succeed at all that's important.

Meaty Metaphors

Here's what fly-fishing is all about, in rough order of importance:

- It's about *the technical aspects of sex and seduction.*
- It's about *salesmanship,* and about the art of closing the deal.
- It's about the *love of esoterica* and the acquisition of cool stuff.
- It's about *giving yourself that upmarket pat on the back you worked so hard for.*
- It's about *thinking hard thoughts* and coming to terms with limits.
- It's about *getting out of town* and looking up the skirts of Mother Nature.
- Also, it's about catching fish.

Sex, Seduction, and the Choice of Flies

Here's what it takes to catch a trout, fly-wise. You must first choose a fly that looks exactly like every trout's dream dinner. Trout are not experimental animals. Unlike some fish who will take a bite of a giant, shiny plastic thingamajig just to see what it is, trout only recognize the familiar as food. If mayflies are mating, and the air is thick with small, white fluffs of bug, then your fly must look like a mayfly or no trout will want it. And even that isn't good enough: It must look like a mayfly, and act like a mayfly—or, to be exact, a mayfly that has accidentally ditched at sea.

In order to mimic a mayfly in distress, it is essential that you be able to cast a nearly weightless, phony mayfly fifty feet into a likely pool and have the fly alight first, with the rest of the line following subtly, almost absently behind. If you do all that—figure out the menu, imitate its behavior, and present the whole thing with perfect delivery—then, possibly, a trout may strike your fly.

Non-fly-guys may need *a real-life parallel* here, so let's look at it the enterprise this way. Wendy is a beautiful flight attendant. She lives in Montana. So do several million trophy-sized rainbow trout. Your chances of snagging Wendy are considerably better than your chances of bumping into even one of those trout. For one thing, Wendy says she's "looking for the right man." None of the trout feel that way. For another, Wendy, already married and divorced once, says she's "a sucker for a good line." No trout in her family. In fact, the only thing fishing has going for it in this little comparison is that rejection generally occurs out of sight, so it seems as if it's nothing personal.

But it is. A nibbleless fly fisherman is a social failure, the kind of guy fish take one look at and roll their little lidless eyes. As most men instinctively know, a little practice can make the courtship of a trout a bit smoother.

How to Pick Up Fish

1. *Rig yourself a rod* (not a *pole*), go out back, stand at one end of the yard, and put a paper or plastic plate at the other. Surround the plate with a carpet of flattened trash bags.
2. *To properly cast a line,* imagine your casting arm is a clock's hour hand, where you're facing nine o'clock, and three o'clock is dead behind you.
3. *Pull out twenty feet or so of line* and lay it on the ground in a straight line in front of you, so the fly is pointing at the plate. Take ten or twenty more feet of line off the reel and let it dangle at your side.
4. *If you're a righty, hold the loose line in your left hand,* and with your right arm, move the rod slowly and rhythmically back and forth between ten o'clock and one o'clock, making sure that when it passes twelve o'clock, it's pointing straight up. Never go to nine, and keep away from two. As the rod moves, you'll see the line unfurl above your right shoulder like a giant silk thread, and you'll feel the tug of the line as centrifugal force works on it.
5. *Keep the line from your right elbow* to the tip of the rod as straight as possible until you develop a feel for what you're doing. Too much wrist too early will give you nothing but lots of tangled line in the nearby trees.
6. *Work on the rhythm of the rod.* Wait until the moment the line has unfurled behind you to begin your forward movement.

7. ***Release the line through your left hand*** a little bit at a time. Eventually, your line will play itself out.

8. ***When you feel like it, stop the rod at ten o'clock*** and watch where the fly goes. If it goes behind you, you have no sense of rhythm, and your casting motion needs a good backbeat. Most beginners go back and forth much too quickly. If it goes in front of you, you're halfway there. Once you've got the rhythm conquered, you'll want to try putting the fly in the plate. Remember, the sound you hear first should be the fly touching down on the platter. If you hear the line rustling on the trash bags, start over. (DB)

Line Control

Once you have the basic cast down, experiment with others. There are a million different ways to cast a line, but the key to all of them is getting a good feel for the peculiar dynamic of the rod and the line. For instance, a slight pull with the left hand on the line while the right arm is delivering forward thrust will give greater velocity to the line.

A personal observation:

You should be able to stand shoulder-to-shoulder with another fly fisherman and never know he's there. A good fly fisherman can land a fly on the water with all the impact of a whisper at Madison Square Garden.

Keeping track of your line and keeping your line under control are also useful skills. I used to fish with a guy who churned up the water as if he were using a small Moulinex at the end of his line. Guy married money, so he wore ten thousand dollars' worth of equipment, but he fished in a little sea of foam of his own manufacture. As an angler, he was extremely humane, in that he never caught fish, but he made it nearly impossible for those nearby to catch any, either.

Selling the Goods

You're the Willie Loman of the deep. You have to convince the trout your bug is the best bug. It's helpless, vulnerable, available, desirable. You have to get bug lust going big-time in a trout to get the fish to rise to the bait. How?

Know the market. When you get to trout-central, take a look before you go wading in. What kind of product is selling? Is there a rush on little, brown bugs with stiff wings, and no white mayflies anywhere? Then your white, fluffy mayfly is nowhere. Even if the trout spent the whole previous day eating mayflies, if yours is the only mayfly on offer, no self-respecting trout will touch it. Go for the brown-bug look. And watch the real thing as it floats on the surface. Is it a would-be swimmer, making for dry land? Or is it resigned to its horrible fate, a listless, buoyant bite just waiting for the end? A typical trout wants what all its friends have, but better, so make your fly do the proper dance of death.

Closing the Deal

When a trout strikes, you'll lose him if you don't set the hook. Trout tend to inhale food rather than chomping down on it, and they'll exhale it just as fast if it doesn't feel right. When you see or feel the trout strike your fly, give a tiny tug. The effect is like the private eye knocking down the motel-room door with a camera in his hand. The trout says damn! and runs for it. **If the hook isn't set properly, the trout's out of there.** If you made the sale, there's a no-refund, no-return squabble on your hands, in which you let the trout wear himself out complaining as you slowly, slowly bring him in. Fly tackle is extremely lightweight stuff, so a panicky yank on your part will send the fish away with a souvenir.

Dress Appropriately

There are two really great things about fly-fishing gear. First, it's fun to own lots of it—all those strange tools, little pliers, gooey gels, vests, waders, flies galore. Second, you need almost none of it on any given day. Watch a guy with a heavy metal tackle box struggle along on a hot summer afternoon, and you'll appreciate the relative sparseness of fly tackle. If you look downstream and see a guy riding low in the water because he's heavy with gear, you're looking at a man who will only kill fish by falling on them. Plus, by not having to tote heavy equipment, you'll be free to self-decorate. Some guys, for example, would never dream of fly-fishing unless they were wearing a necktie. It's just a thing.

Monofilament Enlightenment

Join the Church of Norman MacLean. When you fish with flies, you are no longer a fisher of ordinary men. By tying a fly to a line, you elevate yourself a peg or two on the big social wheel—especially if you can wangle your way into some exclusive fishing reserve. But keep your head. More than golf, more than tennis, much more than NASCAR, fly-fishing attracts snobs and others weak of will and anxious for an attractive affectation. Recently, the nation was treated to the televised sight of Tom Brokaw and Ted Turner working water on Turner's Australia-sized buffalo kingdom in Montana. Turner, the proto-cracker, outsnobbed Brokaw, the ex-farmboy, by berating the NBC newsguy's ability to tie a proper knot. This, only moments after Brokaw had interviewed Turner and Mrs. Turner, Ms. Fonda. That's called, in fly-fishing one-upsmanship, a double-knot slam. First you demonstrate your wife is superior to all others, then you demonstrate that your line is cleaner than all others. You thereby prove conclusively that you alone know what tying knots is all about.

And it also pretty much sums up what's wrong with a lot of fly fishermen, who can't quite get the hang of a sport where the competition is very subtle indeed. On TV, Turner looked like a guy who thought fly-fishing could be improved with some full-body contact. He didn't realize he'd already lost the contest, since all Brokaw did was fish. All Turner did was fish while talking about fishing.

To get this sort of thing out of your system, watch *A River Runs Through It* a dozen times, and send Orvis a check for five grand. If you still feel arrogant, remember that some fishermen consider a small chunk of trout to be excellent bait for striped bass. To really douse your flame, in fact, try fly-fishing for largemouth bass in a farm pond. That's tough work.

• ***Throw the epiphanies back.*** A guy in the middle of the woods teasing trout isn't a busy man. Too much of that sort of indolence breeds bad philosophy and a Zenlike empty-headedness that passes for bliss. Once a man buys into the whole boomer ethos of upmarket angling—as opposed to plain old fishing—something inside snaps and the quiet, rhythmic work of the rod becomes a metaphor for life as it should have been lived.

• ***It doesn't take any skill whatsoever with a fly rod to wax on the strange, dark tides of existence.*** Consequently, more fatuous literature has been written about fishing, often by aging, desk-bound, self-confessed bad fishermen, than about any other activity pursued by men with clothes on. Once, fishing stories involved lies about big ones who got away. Now, nothing gets away alive: Fish lit is full of epiphanies snagged out of the river of life and bludgeoned to death on the bank. Books in which once-middlin' writers compare the size of their insights are worthless to aspiring anglers. They're too thin to sit on, they don't burn good, and they make lousy bait.

Remember, all you're doing is trying to outsmart fish and have some fun. Fly-fishing is not a noble calling. It's golf without holes, tennis without a net, basketball without the basket and without the ball. If you're a beginner, don't let yourself be intimidated by grizzled yuppies and ancient tweedsters. Just fish and admire the scenery.

Keeping Score

Should you be so incredibly lucky as to actually catch something troutlike, you'll have a new dilemma. Hard to believe, but some guys *fish for dinner.* If you reject all modern sensibilities, feel an excess of sanctimoniousness, find yourself more than an hour from a drive-through, or if you think the trout is a potential menace to navigation, you can take the monster back to camp and toss it in a skillet. If, however, you hope to be able to tell another angler about your good fortune, you must let the big one get away.

To touch a trout, first get your hand wet. Trout have no scales, and your dry hand will injure the trout's delicate skin. (POE)

• *Catch-and-release* may be seen in various lights: Perhaps it's just a way of introducing liberal guilt into a nearly guiltless enterprise. Or perhaps it's just simple good manners among experienced fly fishermen who see the sport as a pedagogical exercise in which, with every encounter, both fisherman and fish gain in experience and wisdom, except the fish is the only one who actually swallows the hook. Either way, though, given the quickly growing number of men—and women—driven to snag trout on a feather, letting your trout swim free is perhaps the only way to make sure there are enough fish to go round. Catch-and-release is especially vital where efforts are being made to establish a native population; in many of these areas enlightened policies permit catch-and-release fishing only. Of course, *you can't hunt ducks this way,* but catch-and-release is the mark of a sporting angler who sees no need to lord it over a dying Brookie. Look at it this way: Norman Schwarzkopf is a dedicated fisherman, a master of the fly caster's art, and he's a catch-and-release guy. Just ask any trout. Or ask Saddam Hussein.

So, Yankee flyboy, *how to prove you actually caught a trout?* Put your face and the fish's side by side in a camera viewfinder and pull the trigger. Wear a hat so you can tell who's who. You get to prove you caught a respectable fish; the fish gets to go home and tell his friends lies about how he got away from the big one. (DB)

HOW TO CATCH THE LAST TROUT OF THE SEASON

This, it must be said, is a piece of information you are *certain* you possess only when you have the last trout of the season actually on the end of your line. And it must be further admitted that for some of us, the first trout of the season is also the last trout of the season, and that for some of unfortunate few, our "season" can be several years long.

Nevertheless:

- **Pressure drops:** First, no matter what part of the country you live in, *pay attention to the barometer.* Rapid falls or climbs can quickly start fish feeding or turn them off.
- **Worms work:** In rainy weather, *night crawlers will bring the last big trout out of hiding* in the cloudy water. If you're a fly-only fisherman, try beating the water with *oversized bass flies* during the last hour of daylight and during the first hour of evening.
- **Location, location, location:** *Look for rugged and inaccessible areas,* since these have the greatest likelihood of holding a trout population until the end of summer.
- **Use your noodle:** Finally, remember that by the time fall rolls around, the trout that remain alive have seen it all. They're like the best-looking women in a bar at closing time, and all the usual approaches are old hat to them by the time you show up with your tired old tricks. So don't be afraid to *vary your approach.* Try a different fly, some new bait, maybe explore a new river or lake.
- **In the Northeast:** *Use smaller lures* in shallow water as the bigger browns get ready to spawn upstream. Size-seven jointed rapalas, floating bombers, bright colors fished slow and shallow seem to work best. Try small spoons worked under banks and around log jams to find those lingering giants.
- **For Western anglers:** Western fishermen should rely first on old favorites to finesse those lingering trout. For example, fly fishermen should *use a trusty woolybugger,* the M-16 of any fly fisherman's arsenal. If that doesn't work, *try a Zonker,* fished deep and with short, jerky retrieves. Still desperate? *Use live bait.* Sculpins and freshwater leeches are often overlooked by veteran anglers, but they can be quite deadly in the fall. (TS)

HOW TO FISH ON ICE

Dead of winter. Snowdrifts. Dry branches, gray sky, the earth covered in snow crust, silence, and short light. There, in the cold, dim dawn of the year, the ice fisherman cometh.

Getting up early on a midwinter morning, going out and drilling holes in ice, then sitting in the cold all day waiting for a seven-inch perch or bluegill probably isn't what most weekend anglers have in mind. But ice fishermen are different. In fact, they're crazy.

But not stupid. First, they know the **Main Thing: *Check the ice.*** They know they need at least four or five inches of good, hard, clear ice. Of course, less ice will support a person, but thicker is better, especially when it comes to early ice. One good way to know when ice-fishing season is over: Buy an old car. Doesn't matter much if it runs. Wait until a hard freeze. Push the car out on the lake. When the car drops through the ice, spring's just around the corner.

- **Drilling.** Once you've found a safe stretch of ice, use an ice auger to drill a set of four holes for your tip-ups. The holes should be between five and ten inches in diameter; local laws will limit both the size of each hole and the total number of holes allowed.

- **Skim the ice chips** from the holes with a small ladle. For some reason, these ice skimmers are elusive devices, and you'll probably want to bring along an extra to replace the one that will undoubtedly fall through your hole in the ice.

- **Tip-ups** are simple devices, found in almost any good sporting goods store. They come in a variety of shapes and sizes, but, basically, they should all contain a spool for line and, since ice fishing is nothing but a process of carefully monitoring, from a distance, the closeness of the relationship between a fish and your bait, some sort of flag to alert the angler to a strike. A piece of leader, with a hook, a sinker, and a swivel to attach to the line, are all you need to rig a decent tip-up.

- **Set your tip-ups** for depth, then add bait. In many parts of the country, the mighty shiner—your basic sacred minnow—is the snack of choice for luring local leviathans. Fish the minnow approximately eight inches from the bottom—or, if there's a lot of underwater vegetation, and if you can see through the ice, suspend the minnow just above the weeds. After setting the trip on the flag, proceed to the next hole, and repeat the whole business.

- **A bite** will set off the tip-up's flag. Check first to see if the fish is taking the line, and, if he is, in which direction he's traveling. Quickly turn the tip-up in the direction of travel, and, as soon as possible, ease the tip-up from the water, gently applying tension to the line until you can feel the fish doing the same at the other end. Then set the hook. With luck, there'll be a bass, walleye, or northern on the line.

- **Jigging holes.** After you've set the tip-ups, choose a location for your jigging holes. Keep in mind that you have to be able to watch the four tip-ups you've set, so don't get too far from your base. One suggestion: Jig with a twenty-four- to thirty-inch rod, with only one or two eyes, and the simplest reel possible. Attach very light monofilament line and add either a small weighted jig or a Swedish pimple with a light hook. To dress up the jig or pimple, you can add a wax worm, a mousie, or a maggot to lure the fish into action. You may have to try several different locations for jigging. You'll be chasing panfish, walleye, pickerel, and the occasional catfish.

- *Break the ice* away from the holes every forty-five minutes or so, depending on the weather. Check the minnows to make sure they're still alive and that the line isn't tangled. Bare hooks do not perform well at any time of year, but bare hooks in the winter, left unchecked, can make for a very long day.

- *Keep your bait* warm, as most bait will tend to stiffen quickly on a cold day. (TS)

HOW TO CLEAN A CATFISH

Cats are kind of slick when you get them out of the water: They have skin instead of scales like most fish, and you can work yourself to death on a five-pound catfish just trying to hold on to him and skin him at the same time. They also have sharp little barbs beneath their gills. So you want to get the cat under control so you can work with it.

1. *Nail him to a stump.* The best way to skin a catfish is to find a stump and drive a nail through his head and into the stump. That'll stop the wiggling. Once you put the nail in his head, you pretty much took care of the old boy.

2. *Use your knife to cut around his neck.* You really want a good, sharp cut, so the skin comes off easy. But don't cut his head off, because if you cut his head off now, you've lost the use of your nail.

3. *Take your pliers and start skinning.* Now you see why you have to nail him to a stump. Otherwise, you can't hardly hold him. Trying to keep hold of a catfish while you work is a miserable way to try to skin one. You're trying to pull his skin off, and he's falling on the ground all the time. You really need a stump and a nail.

4. *Gut him.* Turn him over onto his belly. As a rule, you can start cutting him from the bottom and work your way toward his head, but you can do it either way. You just put your knife in there and rip the belly up as you go along. It's kind of like cutting a piece of cloth—once you get started, it just goes. Then reach your fingers in there and gut him—everything comes out. It's almost like it was meant to be that way; there's very little attachment there. A gutting rule of thumb: If it looks like something you don't want to eat, take it out.

Once you do that, *then* you cut the head off. Now, you've got a good, clean catfish. (CD)

HOW TO CLEAN AND COOK A FISH THAT ISN'T A CATFISH

No stumps? No problem. There's more than one way to skin a fish. Good thing, too, since what you do with the fish immediately after you catch it will have a lot to do with how it will taste at dinner

- *If the fish is alive,* put him on a stringer and leave him in the water. Fish begins to decompose—giving it its customary smell—immediately after death.
- *If the fish is badly injured* and sure to die, clean your fish immediately and pack it in ice. The longer you wait before cleaning a dead fish, the better chance you have of the meat spoiling. The best way to pack a fish in ice is to wrap the fish up in watertight plastic bags and then put the bags on ice. This will keep the fish dry and fresh, while putting the fish directly in ice will make the flesh soft and mushy.
- *Insert a sharp knife in the bottom of the fish,* near where the body joins the tail, and slit forward to the V-shaped area where the belly meets the gills.
- *Put your fingers into the gills* and the V-shaped area, and pull downward toward the back of the fish, removing the gills and all of the innards.
- *Look inside your incision*—you will see a red line running up the backbone. It's blood. Beginning at the tail end of the fish, pierce this red line with your thumb, and run your thumb over the length of the fish until it has been removed. (JSD)

Boneless Is Better

If you want fillets: Cut into the fish just behind the gills, cut down to the bone, then turn knife and slice through the fish along the backbone toward the tail.

- *Slice the fillet* away from the tail and the rest of the fish. Turn the fish over, and repeat the slice on the other side.
- *Remove the rib section*—again, using a knife with the blade flat and cutting along the ribs as close to the bone as possible.
- *Now remove the scales* by inserting the knife at the tail and cutting the skin away from the meat, taking care to waste as little as possible. (GH)

HOW TO GET DINNER FROM THE DEEP

High-speed trolling for marlin is to fly-fishing what Don Rickles is to Victor Borge. Forget nuance, forget stealth. Go for guts, glory, and a fast boat.

Bait

Some guys use mackerel, some use bonito. The best is a strip of mullet, a chunk of flesh so durable that you can let a pound of the stuff water-ski behind your boat for hours at a time without any visible signs of deterioration. Plus, predator-fish—tuna, swordfish, barracuda, and marlin—love the stuff. (SA)

Fighting Chair

The most important part of the boat isn't the hull or the engine or the outriggers. It's the fighting chair. If you have a monster fish on a line, you won't care if the whole boat goes belly-up, just so long as you can boat your fish before you go under. Without a decent chair, it'll never happen. Here's what to look for:

- *A socket* for the end of the rod.
- *A footrest* so you can use the power in your legs to fight the fish instead of fighting just to stay in the chair.
- *Comfortable armrests.* Think of fighting a marlin as an all-day arm wrestle, and you'll get an idea of the virtue of good, strong armrests.
- *An adjustable backrest* to fit the fisherman using the chair. Even your secretary has this one figured out.
- *A swivel* that will allow you to track the fish without standing up and running around the boat.
- *A mount* safely secured to the deck of the boat. Otherwise, you go from fisherman to bait in a second. (SA)

How to Negotiate with Seafood

Although some guys use straps and prefer to land fish from a standing position, this won't work for you unless you're in peak shape. Using the chair lets you transfer the struggle from your arms to stronger parts of your body—your back and legs.

- *Get ready:* Don't wander off from your rod. When a fish strikes, there will be no more than a ten-second lag between the time the hook is set and the time the battle begins. The fish will make its strongest run right off the bat. You need to be able to control the situation from the beginning, allowing enough line to feed without running the risk of losing the fish by quickly increasing the drag on the line. *Keep the rod tip up* not only while you follow the next steps, but in general throughout the battle. Almost all fish get away by snapping a slack line, not by snapping a rod. Let the rod bear the brunt of any unexpected lunge by the fish. The line won't take such stresses.

- *Get in position:* Position the footrest so that when you are seated, your knees are slightly bent.
- *Get braced:* Put the butt of your rod into the socket in front of the chair, and strap the main harness around the small of your back. Use the smaller thongs around your thighs.
- *Get going:* Now you're set to "pump" the fish. The elements of a pump are straightforward ones, in which you give a little and take a little more than you give. Here's the cycle: Give the tip of your rod a quick dip to lay out a bit of line, then pull back quickly, reeling in at the same time to capture slack. The fish will give a run. When this happens, reduce the drag on the reel and wait him out. He'll eventually stop. If you try to hold him, you'll just snap the line—or, worse, lose your gear. When the fish stops running, dip the tip and start pumping again.
- *Get help.* The skipper will be your best friend in this battle. He'll position the boat to keep your line to the fish as straight as possible. A lousy skipper will have you spinning in your chair. (SA, CWE)

How to Hunt

Of all the things a man is asked to do, nothing else summons ancient instincts like the idea of hunting for food. Unlike changing a flat, running a chain saw, assembling a stock portfolio, or any other mundane chore, hunting is the one thing we have in common with our oldest ancestors.

Trouble is—and maybe this is as emblematic as anything else of our disconnect from our elders—we no longer agree on how we feel about hunting. Some guys think it's just plain disgusting to stand on a hilltop and peek through the scope of a high-powered rifle at a doe-eyed doe on another hilltop a mile away and blast her to smithereens. Other guys can't imagine a better way to spend a day. Most of us are someplace in between, strung up like cheap Mexican ornaments between the eight-point antlers of ambivalence, lost in that perplexed dangle.

Let's take a look at both the upside and downside of hunting.

HUNTING PROS AND CONS

- *Guns are good.* The thing most guys like most about hunting is the firearms. If you hang in vaguely elitist circles and you just can't figure out what kind of a bumper sticker could ever shock the jaded guys you know down at the health club, join the NRA. The organization will send you a little three-inch disk you can slap right on your rear window. It reads, "Member—National Rifle Association." You put one of those babies on your Suburban and ride through the upmarket neighborhood of people who read the *New York Times,* and you generate serious apoplexy. It can be quite a rewarding feeling, actually.

But if you want to actually use the guns you own for hunting, you have to **consider the downside.** Here's a list of cautions:

- *Dork dress.* Listen, chaps, when Prince Philip and Prince Charles go out to cull the herds at Sandringham, they're dressed to kill. They wear lovely tweed hunting jackets, heavy twill trousers, really expensive boots, sweaters, and neckties, all in complementary earthtone shades. They are fully accessorized: They carry their guns with the same weathered nonchalance a veteran lawyer uses to tote his briefcase, and their field dogs trot along amiably. English hunters are like English landscapes: Philip and Charles make hunting look like an awfully decent way to spend a sunny, autumn afternoon, in which a man shoots game, drinks port, and discusses architecture with the maids. This is the England we all love, if only because cross-dressing isn't an unspoken part of the big picture. Even the dweebs of field death—fox hunters—looked damned swell in those lawn-jockey outfits, all mounted and surrounded by dogs, don't you think? All over Europe, hunters look this way, and not just because they have better taste than Americans—which, come on, they do—but also because when Euros go hunting, they don't do it in the suburbs, the way we do in America. When hunting season rolls around in America—and, most places, there's a season for all seasons—men go out in the forests of Appalachia and the Sierra looking like traffic cones, decked out in orange Day-Glo Elmer Fudd hats and matching vests. Whether it's the first lovely spring day of turkey season, a midsummer's afternoon in the middle of groundhog season, or a crisp fall day on the opening day of buck season, there are thousands of stupid-looking guys in orange clothes wandering around the landscape with guns and hangovers. And speaking of handicaps: Yankees who golf also love to hunt. Why? Wardrobe efficiency. The clothes some guys wear in the woods work perfectly well on the links. But who wants to be one of them?

- *Dork desperation.* In addition to dressing funny, a hunter must be willing to endure what to me is a massive dose of self-humiliation, self-discipline, and self-abuse in order to gain the upper hand over the local wildlife. For instance: A little garlic in your armpits or balsam fir needles in your pockets will help to disguise the smell of a human—a regular stench in any animal's book. Repels vampires, too. Plus, your after-hunting musk is going to drive women practically insane. What a hunting two-fer!

- **Hunter-general's warning.** One small upside of hunting is that even as you're trying to increase the health hazards to birds and animals, you can decrease your own, since you can't smoke while you're hunting. Deer can smell a smoldering butt a mile away. They can see it, too: Animals have sharp eyes and can easily spot that glowing cigarette and the sight of your smoke as it dissolves in the air around you, making you look mysterious, somewhat glamorous, a little dim, and terribly frightening.

- **The hills are alive with the sound of dying bunnies.** Here's something that works with animals that aren't deer: Dress up in your orange hat, grab a ghetto blaster, and go off into the woods with a full-blast tape of a dying rabbit. The woods are full of lazy animals with big appetites. Nothing combines these two characteristics like a rabbit in distress. Some good news: You don't have to make your own recording. You can buy a recording of Thumper's last moments, believe it or not, and if you play it while standing still at the edge of the woods anytime when food is hard to come by, you'll get lots of attention. Have a .22 handy or a 12-gauge.

- **The grocery impediment.** If you want to hunt for food, here are your choices: Either you can go down to Fred Sponsler's store and buy inch-point-five rib eyes, marinate them in garlic and beer, and toss them on a hickory fire, or you can bag a 150-pound buck down in a valley two miles from your car, gut it, clean it, butcher it, and extract from it a few dry, nearly tasteless roasts and some faux-baloney.

Here's what may push you over the edge:

HOW TO FIELD CLEAN AND DRESS A BUCK

1. **Cut a circle around the anus** and cut the connecting alimentary canal. Cut as deeply as you can.
2. **Lie the animal on its back** and open the belly from lower body up. Cut along either side of the penis and scrotum.
3. **Cut carefully to loosen the scrotum** and penis, then pull up on the anus—which should by now be detached—and pass it and the alimentary canal through the arch of the pelvis.
4. **Break the membrane over the chest cavity,** reach inside, and scoop out all the organs and entrails.

5. *Put the heart and liver in a plastic bag* to keep from getting blood all over your clothes.
6. *Tip the carcass onto its side* to drain the blood out.
7. *Wipe the body cavity clean* with a cloth or some dry grass.
8. *Prop the body cavity open* with a stick and let it air-dry.
9. *Next, sew up the body cavity* so that you can carry it without soiling your clothes. When you're ready to skin the deer, you can remove the stitching.
10. *Locate hair-tufted glans on the rear legs* and remove them with a knife. Some hunters say that leaving them on the carcass will taint the meat
11. *Hang the buck from a tree branch* by the neck or antlers. Using a saw or knife, remove all four legs at center joints.
12. *Take each leg and make a slit on the inside* all the way to where the belly is open.
13. *Extend the slit in the belly* to the brisket and throat, also splitting the breastbone as you go.
14. *Cut around the neck.* If you plan to mount the head, cut a little lower to preserve as much of the head and neck as possible.
15. *Skin the deer by starting high and yanking downward* on the skin. Use a knife on the tough spots. (GS)

Now, if Bob Bennett—Bill Bennett's evil twin—ever publishes a *Book of Vices,* this will almost certainly be one of the selections. For if you're like most men, right about when you get to step three, the part about how you should "cut carefully to loosen the scrotum and penis, then pull up on the anus—which should by now be detached—and pass it and the alimentary canal through the arch of the pelvis," you're in no mood for dinner, period, let alone a dinner you have to sexually mutilate. Call it detached anus syndrome, and call yourself a victim, but it just doesn't sound like the way most guys play with their food.

THE FINAL VERDICT

While we're all pleased to endorse the idea of walking through the woods well armed, and while most of us wholeheartedly advance the worth of firearms, and, for that matter, all objects of any kind that are capable of making large, obnoxious noises—save, perhaps, Senator Barbara Boxer—**the notion of do-it-yourself butchery leaves many men cold.** It's not just the moral problem. After all, most men wear leather belts and eat cheese-burgers—and besides, unless we can reclaim the entire of the earth's surface for critterdom, we have to husband wildlife just as we do other resources. That spells culling to most of us. (DB)

No. The problem with hunting—at least for some guys—is what can happen to you once you're out in the field with gun and ammo. Out there, the problem with hunting is that you might actually hit something.

HOW TO HUNT AND GRADE FOOD ON THE CHICKEN SCALE

Another problem with hunting is that for meat eaters, fish don't count. There's beef and there's chicken. After that, there's a whole bunch of stuff that sort of tastes like chicken, more or less, depending on where it registers on the chicken standard. If you're going out hunting for a specific animal—as opposed to hunting for whatever you happen to hit—we have a few specific tactical recommendations, as well as a correlative reading on the official Man's Life Chick-o-Meter. Here, in descending order of chickenlike taste affinity, is the list to take to the big meat shop in the woods:

ANIMAL	CHICK-O-METER READING	TACTIC
Grouse	Chicken delight	The best-tasting bird, bar none. Try an abandoned orchard or a berry patch. Grouse will lay low during your first pass-through. But on your return trek, they'll flush. Fire with any-gauge shotgun. With any luck, you'll hit a woodcock instead. Woodcock tastes like grouse, but better.
Turkey	Religious chicken	Really tasty. Flocks of turkey wander the countryside in big circles, going over the same pathway again and again. Once you know where their highway is, all you have to do is sit tight and wait. Since turkeys favor the edge of big, open fields, finding a parking place in the woods seems to be the ticket. Some guys go for flushing turkeys, but it's high-risk and a failed flush usually spells the end of the day for hunters, since turkeys will lie low for *days*. Reminder: Toms only. Look for the "beards" under their necks.
Pheasant	Dream thigh chicken —dark and delicate	Just-released stock pheasant often show up in farmers' chicken houses, scrounging off the hens, so if you're desperate, crash a coop and open fire. The worst that can happen is you'll be eating chicken for a long, long time. A more sporting approach: Flush pheasants out of their fave haunt, a cornfield. Takes more than two guys, though. Work in parallel. Make sure one guy doesn't get too far out in front of the others, or he'll be a ringed-neck cadaver.

ANIMAL	CHICK-O-METER READING	TACTIC
Quail	Great chicken	Use a dog, but remember that quail live in high-density coveys. So when you see the first one, take a sec to get set, because there'll soon be lots more.
Duck	Double-chick'n lick'n good	If you don't mind that gamy-just-on-the-verge-of-putrid smell, wild duck is wildly delicious. You, your dog, your buddies all hide in a blind in the weeds until your heinie is ice covered. Blow on a call. Wait for ducks. They'll show, you'll fire, but the chances aren't good for a first-time hunter.
Frog	Wingish; better than chicken	Hand-capture only. Even small-caliber ammo creates a bitter taste in the meat.
Woodchuck	Thighish-plus	Spring, and a young man's fancy turns to wood-chuck, bagging them in April before spring grasses grow so high that their dirt mounds are hidden from sight. Good scouting technique: belly-crawling across an old orchard or a hay field. In reality, no man has ever shot a woodchuck on purpose. The reason? No target. By the time you spot one, he's gone. One feeble suggestion: Whistle. This might make him stick his neck out to see if you're dating material. You have to be quick, though—or you have to have a drop-dead woodchuck outfit. Use a 12-gauge or a .22.
Deer	Pseudo-chicken	Judging from the incredible number of lucky hunters with gut-shot deer draped over hood ornaments choking the roads of Pennsylvania on the first day of buck season, all you have to do is sit up all night drinking beer, piss, scratch, and hope some roving band of guys from New Jersey will scare a wounded buck in your direction. There are two alternatives to this tactic: One is to arm your-self with a ferociously overpowered firearm and a scope from NASA and draw a bead on a deer grazing on apples someplace in the next state. The other is to painstakingly, skillfully stalk a deer, trying to defeat him on his own terms and on his own turf, but nah.

ANIMAL	CHICK-O-METER READING	TACTIC
Rabbit	Drumstick-ish, but sometimes a bit too gamy, especially on older rabbits; bunnies are best	Get on a sloping hillside and make some shuffling, scuffing racket: The rabbit's greatest form of defense is the element of surprise and the zigzag of its run. Lazyboy way: Sit in the back of a pickup and take potshots at scurrying bunnies. Wabbits aren't cwazy, though. They have NFL-style broken-field instincts, and they not only change direction, but also change speed with no warning. They're tough to shoot from a moving truck. If you bag a rabbit, wear rubber gloves when handling it. It's easy for humans to get sick from rabbits who are carrying rabbit diseases. However, even a diseased rabbit can be eaten if his meat is cooked well enough. Sick rabbit delight. Yumsters.
Squirrel	Dark meat, but iffy	Sit under a tree. Act like a nut. Kidding! The trick is to shoot the squirrel when it's on the ground. Two reasons: First, squirrel dropped from a 100-foot perch will taste more like perch than squirrel. Second, shooting slugs into trees kills the trees.
Crow	Brackish but rotten	Hey, they don't call it eating crow for nothing. If you have a crow caller or some crow decoys, you can fill up a meadow with carrion-stuffed crow meat in no time. Make sure you're shooting at the main flock, though. If you take a shot at a scout and miss, you'll never see the rest of them. One bait-and-switch technique calls for surrounding a fake owl with a bunch of fake—or dead—crows. Seems crows like nothing better than owl mugging.
Porcupine	Chicken-turning-to-cat	They can't shoot those quills, but they can tail-lash you in an instant. You're better off whacking one through the neck with an ax than you are shooting at it, though, because they just won't die: A porcupine can take a half-dozen well-placed .22 slugs before he gives up, and animals who die in distress generally leave behind a carcass with bitter-tasting meat.
Raccoon	Army chicken	Nocturnal critters, so hunt for them with a flashlight in one hand and a .22 in the other. You'll find them along creek banks and at the edge of ponds. Coon dogs chase raccoons up trees—ideal for guys who want to shoot at ducks but will settle for anything in a pinch.

ANIMAL	CHICK-O-METER READING	TACTIC
Opossum	Skunk in a chicken suit	If you're starving, but can't stomach the idea of eating that road kill out there on the state highway (see discussion earlier in this chapter), just wait it out. Eventually, a possum will amble along to scoop up what you won't. You can't miss a possum. But you might wish you could. (GS, SDE, TS, Anon.)

HOW TO AVOID SHOOTING YOURSELF IN THE FOOT

As we said above, however you feel about hunting, hunting hardware is entirely jake. Let's deconstruct the totem of the slain animal and see what kinds of tools it takes to make a man a hunter. We'll start with firearms, go through archery, and come out the other side with knives.

YOU NEVER KNOW

The bad news about guns is that you need absolutely no intention of doing evil to have evil happen. A loaded gun in the hands of a guy you can only describe as a loose cannon is trouble-in-waiting.

The best safety device to attach to a firearm is a big batch of common sense. Here's a no-brainer safety checklist:

- *Figure all firearms are loaded* weapons with broken safety devices.
- *Never point a firearm at anything*—or at *anybody*—*unless you're ready to fire.* And take a look at what's behind your target, too.
- *Don't put your finger on the trigger* of a gun until you are ready to fire it.
- *Never hand a firearm to someone else* until you have confirmed that it is unloaded.
- *Never carry a gun with the hammer cocked.*
- *Store guns and ammo* in separate, locked places where no children can get them.
- If you need to keep a loaded firearm with you or nearby, *buy the safest one that you can find,* which should be the one with the most reliable safety. (HN)

Clip that list and take it with you when you go to buy a firearm, since buying a gun is not only a consumer issue, it's also a safety issue.

You may also want to take the course in basic firearms safety offered by the National Rifle Association.

A RIFLE MAKES A GOOD FIRST GUN

As a new gun buyer, ***don't trust your first impulse*** about which gun feels best in your hands. The more experience and information you have about firearms, the more demanding your requirements will be, and the one you might have chosen first may end up being your last choice. (HN, SDE)

- ***Consider buying a .22-caliber rifle as your first firearm.*** Relatively quiet, possessing almost no recoil, a rifle capable of shooting a .22-caliber long-rifle cartridge can do almost anything you need to do with a firearm: You can kill beer cans, eliminate rodents and other pesky critters, dissuade invaders, and vanquish snakes. Even though a .22 is the smallest piece of ammo you can buy, if you fire a .22 long-rifle bullet along a trajectory about thirty degrees above the horizon, it could travel farther than a mile. (SDE)

- ***Two Trigger Tips***
  1. *Don't jerk the trigger.* You'll lift the rifle and miss your target. Instead of jerking, squeeze the trigger smoothly by concentrating on the movement of your finger, not on the movement of the trigger. This requires patience and practice. (KS)
  2. *Take a slow, deep breath,* exhale very slowly, then squeeze the trigger at the bottom of the exhale. You'll be less likely to yank the rifle during firing. (HN)

- ***Maintenance***

  Everything from the oil and perspiration of your hands to the weather to gunpowder will start breaking down the beautiful appearance of your new rifle almost from the time you get it home. Shoot back: Use wood oils and preservatives to keep your gun looking as new as possible. After each firing, follow this new-rifle cleaning schedule:

  Clean it every day for a week.

  Clean it once a week for a month.

  Clean it once a month forever. (ARi, Anon.)

SHOTGUNS

While a rifle shoots a single bullet, a shotgun shoots a whole load of shot. With a rifle, accuracy is paramount because you either hit your target or you don't. With a shotgun, the shot begins to spread out in a V-pattern the minute it is released from the barrel, so hitting a target is a kind of approximate thing, in which "close" counts, sort of like horseshoes and hand grenades. While the range of a shotgun is much lower than the range achieved with a rifle, the odds of hitting the target are much higher because you're sending out hundreds of projectiles in the direction of the target instead of just one. Because you are sending out bits of shot instead of one bullet, there is no rifling on the inside barrel of a shotgun.

Types: Shotguns come as single-shot, single-barrel automatics, double barrel with a side-by-side configuration, and double barrel with over-and-under configuration. As with rifles, you can get a shotgun that is an automatic or pump. In addition, some shotguns break open for reloading.

- *Shotguns are generally used for bird hunting* and, again because you are shooting many bits of shot instead of a single bullet, you don't sight your target. Instead, you lead it. In other words, you aim the shot along a trajectory ahead of the path of your target. The idea is that the target will fly into the shot—not that the shot will hit the target.
- *The lower the gauge, the heavier the gun.* If you're just starting out, use a 12-gauge, the big, heavy cousin of the relatively svelte 16-gauge. When you've got both of those figured, trade up to a 20-gauge. It's like shooting with a lethal feather. (ARi)

What to Shoot

When you've killed all the grouse and laid low all the pheasants, you've still got two year-round targets: skeet and trap. Think of it as hunting with a score-card.

- *Trap shooting.* Here's the bit: Five shooters stand in a semicircle and take turns shooting at clay pigeons that are tossed into the air in random directions by a catapult. In a round of trap shooting, each man fires five times from each position, for a total of twenty-five shots. If a guy hits a pigeon, he scores a point.
- *Skeet.* In skeet shooting, the targets come high (from a "high house") and low (from a "low house"). In a typical turn, a pigeon is sent out high, then low, then both, simultaneously. Each shooter gets a total of twenty-four shots, not counting the customary extra shot each guy gets after he takes his first miss. (HN, KS, SDE)
- *Some places have organized courses* through which shooters progress, taking shots at various target patterns designed to represent different types of real-life prey—pheasant, woodcock, turkey, and so on. You keep score. (KS)

Caution: Women are often better at this than men. (ALP)

In any case, the principle of leading and shooting is the same—and so is the object of the game—killing them targets.

How to Shoot a Clay Pigeon

Stop here for a minute to consider the clay pigeon. Always in season, easy to shoot, lousy to eat. Life is full of such compromises, and as compromises go, this isn't a terrible one. But what if they were not only lousy to eat, but hard to shoot? Here's how to prevent a good sport from turning into a bad deal.

- *Some safety notes.* Mind if we repeat this? Use all the gun-and-ammo common sense you've got: Don't point the gun at anybody, don't load it unless you want to shoot it, and don't put your finger on the trigger unless you're ready to pull it.
- *Armed golf.* Shooting clays is like golf with firearms. You want to start relaxed and stay relaxed. Begin by facing the area where you think it's most likely your shot will meet the clay. Then rotate your hips, like a batter, to face the launch area. Hold your shotgun with your right hand comfortably on the butt-grip; when the clay is launched, "mount" the gun by bringing it up to your shoulder and supporting the barrel with your left hand. If you haven't shot for a while, you might want to practice this crucial move a few times before you call for your first clay.
- *Clay Martians.* Once you feel relaxed and ready, yell, "Pull!"—at which time your wife, daughter, neighbor, somebody will fling a small clay target up against the sky. This is where the whole enterprise goes video, since shooting a clay pigeon is like nothing other than shooting a space invader. You watch the path of the target while swinging your gun up and along that same path of flight. At the same time, you mount the shotgun. At the moment the shotgun comes to your shoulder, you should be leading the target by a breath and a half. Now pull the trigger.
- *Be a hoser.* After you squeeze the trigger, don't stop! Think of your shotgun as a garden hose spraying a stream of water along the flight line of the clay—but in this case, of course, you're "spraying" a stream of pellets. As you fire the shot, continue leading the target; this follow-through technique will make all the difference between hit and a miss. Or between a miss and a near-miss. With a little practice, you'll be breaking clay pigeons faster than a senator can say, "Filibuster!" (PG)

HOW TO PICK A HANDGUN

The worst handgun to buy is the one you buy knowing nothing at all about handguns. The NRA and local sportsmen's organizations all offer handgun safety courses. Take one. Not only will you learn a lot about how to avoid shooting yourself, but you'll get a chance to look at a wide variety of other people's handguns.

- *Before making your purchase,* ask yourself what you are going to do with the gun. You can't get one handgun for everything. Choose a couple of priorities—target practice and security, maybe—and find something that works in those top categories.

If you're thinking of owning a small handgun for self-protection, why not buy what most plainclothes policemen use: a .38 with a three-inch barrel and no visible hammer. A gun this size and caliber is small enough to fit in the drawer of a nightstand, and, without a visible hammer, you don't have anything that is going to get caught on your clothing. (JF)

Consider loading your pistol in such a way that the first chamber is always empty. In this way, if the pistol is dropped or the trigger is somehow pulled by accident, there is no damage done. (HN)

How to Hit What You're Aiming At

Handguns are notoriously hard to control. A guy who's a good shot with a handgun may also be a lucky shot. But there are ways to make missing a little less likely:

- *If you are target shooting,* face left of the target—if you're a righty—and stand at a forty-five-degree angle to it. Place your feet shoulder-width apart, stand up straight, and point the pistol at the target. Now, with your gun out in front of you, close your eyes for a few seconds. If, when you open your eyes, you are still pointed at the target, you have found your proper angle to stand in relationship to the target. If your aim has drifted, correct your position accordingly.
- *Avoid the traditional military stance* of standing at a right angle to the target. It's unnatural and much harder to aim in that position.
- *Make sure you raise the gun high enough* so that you don't have to lower your head and neck to look through the sight. Instead, raise your hand that is holding the gun to eye level. Your arm should be straight but not rigid. Meanwhile, having too much of a bend in your arm will tire you out unnecessarily.
- *Relax.* When target shooting with one hand, try putting your other hand in your pocket. (HN, RU, PST)

How to Own Sherwood Forest

You take a dose of green politics, an affection for wishful romanticism, and a decent bow-and-arrow rig, and you've got everything you need to create Robin Hood, an Old Democrat if ever there was one. Add a bunch of federal regs and a health-care motive for stealing from the rich, and you've got a New Democrat. Either way, start with the right bow.

HOW TO SELECT A BOW

When buying a bow, the important thing to consider is the "draw weight" of the bow—the number of pounds of energy that are required to draw a twenty-eight-inch arrow. **Here's how to tell if you have the correct bow weight:** Pull the bow back to a full draw and hold it for ten seconds. If you start shaking before the ten seconds are up, you need to drop down to a lower-weight bow. Most archery rookies start with a thirty- or forty-pounder.

- *If you plan to hunt with the bow,* get one with as much weight as you can handle. The more weight to the bow, the more speed and penetrating power to the arrow shot from it. If what you want to hunt is a large animal—say, a deer—you're going to need at least a fifty-pound bow, at least in most states. (BM)

HOW TO ARM CUPID

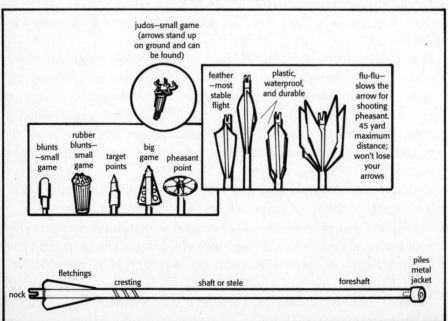

BOW CARE

Because their usefulness depends on their "freshness," or the degree to which they can maintain their shape, bows have to be used and stored with care.

- *Remove the string* when you aren't using the bow.
- *Hang it horizontally* across a couple of pegs.
- *Protect it* with furniture wax if you're going to be using it in wet weather. Dry it after wet-weather use.
- *Warm it up,* especially if you're using the bow in cold air. (KJL)

HOW TO STRING A BOW

- *One way:* Put one end of the bow on the ground against your foot and push down on the opposite end. Once the bow is flexed enough, slip the string over the end and into the notch.
- *Another way:* Use a bow stringer—a piece of rope, usually nylon, with leather pockets at each end. Slip the pockets over the ends of the bow, then hold the bow parallel to the ground, with the stringer down. Put your foot in the middle of the stringer cord, and lift up on the bow by the handle. See the flex? Slip the string over both ends of the bow and into the nocks. The advantage of a bow stringer is that it puts the same amount of pressure on both sides of the bow. (KJL, BM)

HOW TO FIND A STRAIGHT ARROW

Get good ammo. Aluminum arrows stink. If you use them when hunting, they make a racket and scare the wildlife. If you hit something hard with them, they're shot. Fiberglas is a better choice—better penetration, longer life, quieter travel.

Your choice of arrows should be as precise as your choice of bows. In arrows, as in some other aspects of life, length is everything. In fact, you can tell how long a guy's arrow is by measuring the distance, fingertip to fingertip, between his outstretched arms.

IF THE DISTANCE IN INCHES IS . . .	THE PERFECT LENGTH OF ARROW IS . . .
57–59	24–35
60–62	25–26
63–65	26–27
66–68	27–28
69–71	28–29
72–74	29–30
75–77	30–31

How to Keep Your Edge

A chap who sent in some knife-notes said to "think of a knife as an extension of your hand." If you do that, you can easily see what kinds of goofy tricks God could have got up to if He'd had even a dash of cynicism.

Other correspondents were more generous with practical advice, such as the following information:

HOW TO SHARPEN A KNIFE

Our correspondent, a well-known country musician, told us: "I can't remember ever learning how to sharpen a knife, myself—people were just always around filing or grinding their butcher knives all the time because they needed them sharp to slaughter the hogs and stuff. So learning how to sharpen a knife for me was sort of like learning to walk—everybody did it so I did it too, but I certainly don't remember taking my first step." Here's how to get sharp:

1. *Take an Arkansas hard stone*—they come from Arkansas—and put a spot of oil on it to keep the temper in the knife, to keep the friction from damaging the blade. Some guys use spit. It's best to use oil. The oil to use is called honing oil and it's made for that purpose. If you're serious, get a set of three stones, each mounted in wood. Make one a hard Arkansas, another a soft Arkansas, and the last what they call a Waschita—it's just an extra little stone that you use. They're each about four inches by sixteen inches.

2. *Take the stone and lay it down flat.* Turn the blade of the knife toward you, and bring the knife across the stone in a kind of circular motion, about a half-moon. Then reverse it to sharpen the other side. You can tell whether you're getting an edge or not.

3. ***The angle is the most important part of the sharpening,*** and that's the thing that you just have to feel and learn. If you overdo it and hold the blade at too sharp an angle, you'll make the blade flat and you won't be sharpening anything—you'll just be wearing the blade out. If you don't have enough of an angle, you'll just make the knife duller. Get the angle right. (CD)

One good reason to keep your knife sharp: If your blade is dull, you'll push harder to get the job done, and when you push harder you have less control—and that is when you are most likely to cut yourself.

Now, here's the ultimate irony: When you cut yourself with a dull blade, you do more damage than when you cut yourself with a sharp blade. The cut of a dull blade is a ragged piece of work that will take longer to heal.

HOW TO SELECT A KNIFE

Avoid collector's knives, unless, of course, you're a collector. The knife that looks good and the knife that works good are often two different knives. For instance, any blade over five or six inches long is probably too big to be of much use.

Wooden handles handle best. Knives with a solid metal handle look great, but wood is a better choice: A metal handle will get slippery when wet, and when it gets cold, it will be cold for you to hold unless you have gloves on. Wood is a much better material for making a knife useful under difficult conditions.

Here's what to look for in a knife:

- ***Durability.*** How is the handle attached to the blade? Bolts are best.
- ***Cosmetics.*** Does the blade have a lot of fancy design work on it? If so, think again, for many manufacturers put more attention into the fancy scrollwork on the blade than they do into the design of the knife.
- ***Assembly.*** Look at the guard, where the blade meets the handle. Is there a gap between the blade and guard or the guard and the handle? Shouldn't be.
- ***Finish.*** Look at the finish on the blade. The shinier the blade, the higher the quality.
- ***Operation.*** If it's a folding knife you are shopping for, listen when you open and close the knife. You should hear a little "click" when the blade snaps into each position. When the blade is closed, the handle should cover the blade completely, except for the small reveal where the nail slot

HOW TO MAKE THE PERFECT CUT

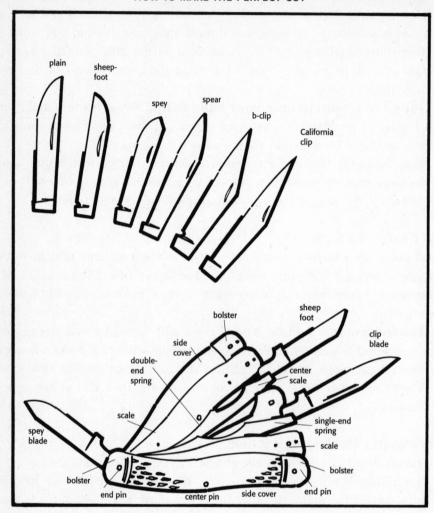

is located. When the blade is open, you shouldn't be able to wiggle the blade back and forth.

- *Size and fit.* Finally, how does the knife feel in your hand? If you're going to own only one knife, make it one with a three-inch blade.

Carbon vs. stainless steel. Stainless knives cost more than knives made of carbon steel. Although a carbon-steel blade is prone to rusting, it's easier to sharpen and keep clean, provided you follow this four-step waltz with knife maintenance:

1. When it gets wet, dry it.
2. When you put it away, oil it.
3. When you sheath it, avoid leather. Leather pits metal.
4. Once you have it sharp, keep it sharp. (CD, FT, Anon.)

Other Stuff to Do Outdoors

There are other things men do outdoors besides anthropological devolution. For instance, they play golf. To some men, golf is an end in itself. To others, it's a means to a greater good.

HOW TO GET EXERCISE ON A GOLF COURSE

First, join a country club. Then rent a set of clubs and rent a cart. Drive out onto the course. Stop at the first tee. Grab a club—make it a two-iron—at both ends and rest it across the back of your shoulders for balance. Next, take a seat on the very front of the cart. Put your feet flat on the ground so your knees form a ninety-degree angle. Now slowly stand up until your back is straight, hold that position for a second, then *slowly* squat back down until your butt is just barely touching the cart. Hold that position for a second, then do it all over again. Do two sets of ten. Then climb back into the cart and drive straight back to the clubhouse.

Why it pays to rent golf gear if you're using the course as an outdoor gym: According to the National Sporting Goods Association, the cost of outfitting a golfer tip to toe with great golf stuff: more than $2,800. Almost three grand! Fore! What? (RE)

HOW TO PLAY ELEVEN DIFFERENT ONE-ON-ONE HOOP GAMES

Basic one-on-one is a game best suited to the office. Think about it: Those feints, dodges, and awesome full-extension Nerf power-dunks over the extended fingers of Griffin from the executive suite are downright dazzling—and all the more so because you're playing with a basket duct-taped to the wall above the copier. But transport the action to the gym or the playground, and one-on-one gets old fast. It inevitably deteriorates into a dispirited sequence of mindless posting up, thirty-foot prayers, and anemic sky hooks. The trouble is no one ever posts up in a real game, unless you're Charles Barkley and you've got a big butt.

When standard one-on-one leaves you uninspired, you need to find a new game. A game that challenges you and hones your skills at the same time. Funny you should ask. Our correspondent canvassed top NCAA basketball coaches around the country for their best ideas. Here's what they had to offer. (PK)

1. One-on-One, No Post

The rules: Simple. Standard one-on-one, but with a catch—no posting up. In other words, no turning your back on either your opponent or the basket. If you do, you immediately forfeit the ball. The only way to score is to drive straight for the basket or jump up and take your shot. First to 10 wins.

The benefit: Not posting up forces you to concentrate on shooting or driving, since the focus is on keeping squared up, balanced, and organized. (Les Robinson, North Carolina State University)

2. Beat the Clock

The rules: You stand beneath the basket with the ball. Your pal sprawls out on the sideline with a stopwatch. The minute-long drill begins after you knock down a quick layup. Then you're allowed only two dribbles in any direction before you have to square up to the basket, shoot, and hustle for the rebound. Once you grab the ball, repeat the same steps: two dribbles, shoot, rebound. Swish as many as you can until your partner calls time. Then you take the watch and he's up. Each basket scores one point, and the winner is whoever scores the most in five one-minute bursts.

The benefit: This fast-paced shooting match is designed to simulate the breakneck pace of an actual game, so that players learn to make good shots at game speed. (Kelvin Sampson, University of Oklahoma)

3. One-on-One, Full Court

The rules: This is just you and your opponent, racing flat out, up and down, full court. A basket earns you one point and a trip to the free throw line for a one-and-one. Make both and earn another point; miss either and you get nothing. Play to ten.

The benefit: You're working everything here—your dribble against full-court pressure, pull-up jumpers, moves to the hole. While it ultimately builds endurance, this game centers on one crucial skill: free-throw shooting. Your heart is pumping. You're sweating buckets. If you can't knock them down under these conditions, what good are you? (Mike Jarvis, George Washington University)

4. Rhythm Method

The rules: You camp out anywhere along the three-point arc, while your opponent stands under the basket with the ball. He passes it to you and immediately pops out to stick a hand in your face while you shoot the jumper. If you make it, he quickly retrieves the ball and repeats the process as you launch different shots from about eighteen feet. If you miss, you grab the rebound, and now it's his turn to go to the perimeter. The game flows back and forth without missing a beat until someone scores ten points. Each bucket earns one point.

    The benefit: The mysterious phenomenon known as "hot hands" has everything to do with practice. The point of this game is to get you into a groove that can only come by making shot after shot in rapid sequence. (Jeff Jones, University of Virginia)

5. Close Out

The rules: Assume the same starting positions as in the "Rhythm Method." This time, however, your opponent rolls you the ball from his place under the basket and rushes out to defend once you've picked up the ball. You get two dribbles to create a shot. If you make it, you both reset and start again. Each basket earns one point, and players swap positions after missed shots. Play to ten points.

    The benefit: The offensive player gets to use his quickness to create a shot. The defender is practicing the move he would make in a real game if he were guarding a player inside, then moved out to defend the ball. (Bob Bender, University of Washington)

6. Hands Up

The rules: Your opponent plants himself on the free throw line and holds his arms straight up, keeping hands still. You dribble right at him, pull up, and shoot over his outstretched arms. After five shots, switch positions. The first player to hit ten buckets wins.

    The benefit: Stresses shooting consistently over defenders. (James Dickey, Texas Tech University)

7. Around-the-World Adjustable

The rules: Let's say you want to play your eight-year-old son, who stands just four feet, nine inches. Here's how to equalize the situation. Select five ten-foot shots for him and five corresponding twenty-foot shots for yourself. Then apply standard around-the-world rules: With each basket you make, you advance to the next position. If you miss the basket, you have two options: either give up the ball or take an extra turn. If you do elect to try again and miss, you go back to the starting position. The winner is the first player to hit his five shots going around and coming back.

The benefits: Develops your long shot. Removes the height disparity. (Tom Penders, University of Texas)

8. One-on-One Limited

The rules: This is another game for two players who are unevenly matched, a guy and his girlfriend, for example (assuming she's not Cheryl Miller). The way to make things even is to limit the areas from where the stronger player is allowed to take shots. For instance, she gets to shoot from anywhere, but he may only score if he shoots from behind the three-point arc. Further adjustments: If the skill gap is extreme, limit the better player's shooting area to two small boxes on the wings (sides of the court). If there's just a slight difference in ability, the stronger player is allowed to drive inside but not to post up.

The benefits: Mainly, you get to have a game with anyone, anytime. Hensen uses it to equalize matchups between his own players. (Lou Hensen, University of Illinois)

9. One-on-One Post Man

The rules: In this game for three players, two set up on the wings, and the third one stands in the paint (center), holding the ball. The center passes out to a wing and then immediately runs over to defend him. The ball handler drives or shoots, and all three players go up for the rebound. Score a point each for a basket. Reset after each shot or defensive stop, and rotate positions after five sequences. The first player to score fifteen points wins.

The benefit: The first benefit is having a game to play with three players. But the focus of the drill is giving the center position a defensive workout. His mission is to practice the transition from defending the ball to fighting for the rebound in a crowd. (Lefty Driesel, James Madison University)

10. Rough House

The rules: If you're feeling a bit sinister, you might try this aggression-testing favorite of Chaney's. One player must dribble in from a dead-ball stop at mid-court against a minimum of four opponents. Everyone defends as he attempts to score. Once he shoots, getting the rebound is a free-for-all. Whoever grabs it resets at midcourt, and the cycle repeats. It's every man for himself, and the first to hit seven baskets wins.

The benefit: Develops killer instinct. Chaney also uses the game to test the aggressiveness of a new recruit. He throws him to the wolves by having him face the rest of the entire team—some fourteen players, full court. (John Chaney, Temple University)

11. Beat the Pro

The rules: What would happen if you held a game and nobody came? In Beat the Pro, the inability to field a team is no problem, since you create your own imaginary opponent. The game begins with a free throw, and if you make it you get one point. If you miss, the pro, let's say Hakeem, gets three. Next, you take a series of fifteen-foot jump shots. A basket earns you a point, plus another free throw; a miss gives Hakeem two. The first player to seven wins.

The benefit: The perfect one-on-one for the friendless hoopster. At least you get a game. (Dick Kuchen, Yale University) (PK)

HOW TO PLAY THREE PICK-UP BALL GAMES REQUIRING SIX PEOPLE OR LESS

Just about the time the All-Star Game rolls around, you get to thinking about the correlation between Barry Bonds's personality and Barry Bonds's bank account, and it's enough to make you want to grab a chunk of well-turned lumber and start beating on something with it. Here are three ways to spontaneously channel that anger into something more wholesome and American, something as pure and unsullied as, say, baseball.

1. Hit the Bat

One guy's up, everybody else isn't. Guy at bat hits the ball—even a softball will do—to the field, then lays the bat down on the ground. The player catching the ball then tries to roll or toss the ball so that it hits the bat. The batter must then catch the ball as it ricochets up and off the bat. If he doesn't, the player who hit the bat is up.

2. Three Flies

One guy's up, everybody else isn't. The guy at bat hits flies to the field. Whoever catches three flies is up next. Note: The batter must hit fly balls. Grounders count as strikes. If the batter strikes out, the last person to shag a fly is up.

3. Over the Line

One guy's up, everybody else isn't. The field is divided by three lines running from the batter's left to the batter's right and ending at the foul lines on either side. One fielder plays behind each line. The first line represents a single. The second, a double. The third, a triple. Hitting the ball on the fly over the player standing behind the third line constitutes a homer. The value of each hit is determined by where it first lands. If it lands in front of the first line, it's an out. Fouls are strikes. Strikes are strikes. If the ball is hit and it lands behind the first line, it's a single, unless the fielder eligible to catch the ball does so, in which case, it's an out. Ditto for the portions of the field designated doubles and triples. The batter bats for a three-out inning, and the score is kept by determining how many runs are scored for each batter. On a hit with men on base, each imaginary runner moves up only the minimum possible number of bases. The player playing behind the single line is the next batter, and all other fielders move up one spot. (JF)

HOW TO CATCH THE LAST FOUL BALL OF THE SEASON

Want proof that God invented baseball? Science guys say the universe was the size of a Spalding regulation hardball just before the big bang. This same miracle of theoretical physics is replicated hundreds, thousands of times every season. Sometimes, these nascent universes curve up and away and land in the stands, where they become objects of veneration. How to best improve your odds of walking away with a souvenir of God's love for mankind?

- *Know your pitchers:* A fastball pitcher will generate a lot more foul balls than a guy who throws curves and other off-speed stuff.
- *Sit tight, sit right:* Hitters swing late at fastballs, so they'll either foul a pitch straight back behind the plate or they'll pop one into the opposite field stands—the first-base side for a right-handed batter, third for a lefty. *So you have two options:* Either sit in the first level behind home plate—a little to the right for a left-handed batter, or a little to the left of the plate for a righty—in order to snag a rising foul ball. Or you can sit back in the lower deck at about a thirty-degree angle from the first- or third-base bag.
- *For batters who get ahead of the pitch:* Snag those bullets from seats back along a line equidistant between the outfield wall and first or third base.
- *The best ballparks for foul shaggers:* Atlanta, Anaheim, and Detroit for balls fouled back of home plate. For shots hit foul down the lines, try

Philly, St. Louis, Houston, Yankee Stadium, and, of course, Fenway Park in Boston and Chicago's Wrigley Field.

- *If all else fails:* Head south this winter. Winter leagues offer sparse crowds, small ballparks, and slow-moving competition from other foul hunters in the stands. (CS)

16. Miscellaneous Know-How

Few things are more depressing than getting to the end of a man's life and finding nothing but a collection of odds and ends. Nevertheless, in the spirit of *completeness*, here's everything else you need to know about everything else.

How to Make a Corncob Pipe

- *Eat your corn.* Butter up a nice ear of corn, one at least two inches thick. Yellow corn works better than white. Maize—or field corn—works pretty well, too, but your talking cow chow here, so stick with what you can eat yourself.
- *Dry your cob.* You can do this either by letting it sit in a sunny window for a week or by drying it in a 150-degree oven for ten or twelve hours.
- *Cut a cross section* of the cob about two inches long for the bowl. Don't get ambitious: A three-inch bowl will be impossible to draw.
- *Hollow it out* with a pocketknife. If you're a good whittler, and you have a sharp knife (see the section "How to Keep Your Edge" in chapter 15), you can score the bowl around the top and just dig in. An alternative is to use a hole drill, then scoop out the center. Make sure to leave a wall of at least a half inch at the bottom—you don't want a lap full of hot ashes— and a quarter inch on the sides.
- *Drill a hole* in the side of the cob about a quarter inch above the inside bottom of the cob.
- *File it.* You want to make the outside of the bowl smooth. Then apply a coat of shellac. Be careful not to shellac the top or inside, though.
- *Use a short piece of bamboo* and the plastic stem from another pipe to make the mouthpiece. Taper the end of the bamboo to make it fit inside the cob tightly. Secure the stem with epoxy or Crazy Glue. Fit the plastic pipe stem over the bamboo.
- *Break it in.* Fill the bowl of the pipe a little at first, then more with each subsequent bowlful. Until the bowl is well seasoned, don't smoke the pipe hot.
- *Find a porch.* And while you're at it, find a rocker. (JBu)

How to Dance a Jig

Sure, and another St. Pat's Day office party, and there you are with a lampshade on your head and no way short of conversation to tell the world what a happy chappy you really are. The solution: our original, two-footed, one-man, completely obliterated Irish jig.

- *Get off on the right foot:* Start by hopping up on your left foot and bring your right foot over and in front of your left, so your right toe touches the floor just in front of your left foot.

- ***Then reverse the whole proposition:*** Left toe on the ground in front of your right foot.
- ***Then back where you started,*** with your right toe on the mat.
  Now the tricky part:
- ***Jump back, Jack:*** Jump backward three times, like a Bunny Hop in full-throttle reverse. Pick yourself up, man, and try again: This time, use both feet. Don't even try hopping backward with your ankles crossed, even when you're completely sober.
- ***Take it from the top:*** Start again, with the right toe in front of your left foot.

That's all there is to it. To really dress up the performance, you can tie your suit coat around your waist like a wee kilt, put one hand on your hip and the other up in the air, and make a little Gaelic whoop from time to time. Fancy Irish guys wiggle their toes a little before they bring them down to the ground. You'll look like a drunk hailing a cab, of course, but, at some point in the evening, that's what this is all about, no? (GHO'H)

How to Make a Bed So Tight You Can Flip a Quarter Off of It

- **Spread your bottom sheet** on the bed, and tuck all four corners in with a *hospital corner.* (Think of it as gift wrapping the mattress with the sheet.) Here are the four steps involved:
  1. *Pull the sheet* real tight at the bottom of the bed, then push it under the mattress as far as you can. Tight, tight, *tight.*
  2. *Go to the side,* where the sheet is hanging down. Pull the sheet out so it continues along the plane of the bed. Hold it with one hand and take your other hand and push the fabric underneath the mattress.
  3. *Make the first corner.* You should get some creases at the bottom of the bed and along the side.
  4. *Repeat this process* on the other three corners of the bed, then tuck in whatever else of the sheet is left on the sides. Always tuck the sheet *as far under the mattress as you can.*
- ***Do the same with your top sheet,*** but only at the bottom of the bed.
- ***Spread your blanket*** over the top sheet. The top of the blanket should be a few inches from the top of the bed. Tuck the blanket in the same way you did the sheet at the bottom and along the sides.

- *Pull the top of the top sheet* down over the top of the top of the blanket. Tuck this part of the top sheet, which is doubled back on itself and the top of the blanket, under the mattress as well.
- *Now, here's the trick:* The way you make the sheets and blankets tight enough to bounce a quarter off is by *pinning the sheets and blankets under the bed to the mattress.* That's why it is always better to take the top bunk in the barracks. You can crawl all over the bed of the guy below you while you do this, but if you have the bottom bunk you've got to crawl under there and get all dirty. Anyway, you pull the sheets and blanket as tight as you can under the mattress from below the bunk, and then you safety-pin them to the mattress when they are pulled as tight as you can get them. Don't be stingy with the pins either; you'll need a lot of them to get all the way around the bed and keep everything pulled real tight. (WH)

How to Make an Entrance

When most people enter a crowded room, they panic just before they walk in the door. They wonder how they look, whether there'll be anyone there they know, or whether there'll be anyone there they *like*. This is the wrong way to make an entrance.

The right way is to take two steps into the room and stop. Dead. Confidently, move your head across the room to see who is there who would benefit from your presence. Everyone else in the room will stop what they are doing to see who it is that has the confidence and authority to walk in and survey the room instead of letting everyone in the room survey him. (LE)

How to Build a Classic Snowman

At twenty below, he's a silent sentinel of sleet and snow. What a guy! Three giant balls and a borrowed top hat, the Pillsbury Dough Boy grown up, with frozen testosterone added, a classic man for one season.

Making wintertime's Mr. Right might seem almost instinctive, but there is a spark of divine sensibility required if you want to do the job properly.

- *Go for the gut.* Think of your snowman as a giant, upright, frozen bug—head, thorax, abdomen—but challenged by the apparent absence of several legs. The size of the belly is what will determine the size and shape of the entire snowchap. Here's the ratio of gut-to-torso-to-noggin: 3:1.5:1. That means you need a three-foot ball of snow to start your man off right. The middle ball ought to be about a foot and a half wide, and for the brainpan, you're looking at twelve inches or so.

- *Roll 'em!* Here's where mere mortals mess up the manufacture of their man: Pack a snowball the size of a cantaloupe as tight as God will permit. Then walk a long, long way away from the post you've assigned your winter lawn jockey. Put your melon-sized ball on the ground and roll it around *slowly,* the way kids roll Playdough, the way muggers roll sailors, packing it as you go. When you have a mass measuring about thirty-three to thirty-five inches, roll the big ball to your site. This keeps the snow around the snowman fresh and relatively untramped. Hollow out a spot on the top so that when you put the torso-ball on the belly-ball, it won't roll off. Make the next two parts some distance away from the snowman, and perch them in place atop the first ball.
- *Accessorize.* The rubrics for this are familiar, but incorrect: a corncob pipe (see instructions earlier in this chapter), a button nose, and two eyes made out of coal. In reality, the only nose permitted by federal regulations for use by temporary citizens of frozen stature is a carrot. Top hat is mandatory—a snowman is not a scarecrow; he may be frozen, but he is formal. Scarf suggested. Twig arms: akimbo, with broom or snow shovel optional. That's it. Stand back and call him Frosty. (TMcF)

How to Remake Old Friends

Sure, you've got family. But who said you can't buy friends? If you're worried about going into yet another holiday cycle without the company of good chums and trusty amigos, call OFIS—Old Friends Information Services—at (800) 841-7938. They'll find all those pals from your youth for you at only a hundred bucks a buddy. OFIS needs an average of sixty days to find somebody—much longer if you've never really had a friend. (OFIS)

How to Find a Seat

In an airplane: The exit rows of most aircraft provide the best bet for long-legged flyers. Every airline configures its seat differently: On a North-west A320 the exit rows give you nine more inches of legroom than the other sardines in tourist. Some airlines remove window seats A and F on their 737s, making 10A and 10F big enough to squeeze in a deck chair. Delta does the same thing with seats 27A and G on their 767-300s. Most airlines won't give you these seats in advance; ask for them when you check in. (WB)

In a rental car: When renting a car, choose the cheapest one available, and ask for an upgrade when you get to the rental counter. If it's late in the day, you have a great chance of getting a free boost, since the cheap cars leave the lot first. (AMcLL)

How to Park Curbside at the Airport Without Getting Hassled

When you drive out to the airport to meet an incoming pal, take along an empty cardboard box that you've put in the trunk. Here's what to do when you arrive:

- **Park at the curb.**
- *Remove the box.* Set it on the sidewalk. Stand back. Admire your work. Wait five minutes, or until you see the traffic cops.
- *Pick up the box.* Take it back to the trunk. Set it down. Open your trunk.
- *Put the box in your trunk.* Check out stews. Hum. Wait until you see the traffic cops.
- *Remove the box.* Repeat the process. (AH)

How to Read a Box of Chocolates

Of course, from time to time, everybody has the God-given right to simply go Gump—to get stupid—and to wait for trouble to knock down the door, for troubling events to dictate the course of his life. But digging into a box of chocolates isn't one of those times. When a man wraps his huge, ham-hands around a box of Godiva's best, it's no time for fooling around. A man with a serious choc-jones doesn't want to be truffled with: He wants to know *exactly* what's going to happen next.

How to tell what you'll get? Depends on where you got 'em. Godiva uses one style of coding its chocolates. Classic American chocolatiers, such as Angel & Phelps of Daytona Beach, use another.

TYPE	GODIVA	CLASSIC
Solid chocolate	Thin wafers, usually embossed with Renaissance motifs.	Molded into various shapes, like Easter bunnies.
Praline and nuts	Goofy shapes: seashells, walnuts, starfish, seahorses, little logs of hazlenut and rice, small bergs of chocolate with nut-hair on top.	Nuts are decorated with little loops on the tops.
Fruit cremes	Thick cones, often with square or rounded tops. *Exception:* the Cherry Square, which is, um, square.	All fruit cremes are round, with an "R" for raspberry, white stripes for lemon, and dark stripes for orange.
Caramels	Like ice cubes, but with slightly rounded tops	Square, topped with a straight diagonal line or a small circle.
Cremes	Various shapes, but every one embossed with one crazy thing or another: feathers, mirrors, like that. Look for the embossed tennis rackets on the Godiva "Davis Cup." Those guys.	Round, with a "V" for vanilla, a bow on the maple creme, a little sugar flower on the mint, parallel lines on French opera cremes, coconut on the coconut cremes, chocolate sprinkles on the chocolate cremes.
Truffles	Spherical, with flat bottoms, like little, melted bowling balls.	Don't make 'em. Too foreign.

The Whitman presampler: In a Whitman's world, the cremes are round, the caramels are rectangular, the nougats are square, the nuts are bumpy, and all the children are above average. (AMcLL)

How to Find the Meaning of Life

Isn't that always the way? You look and look and the darned thing was right in front of you all the time.

Perform an extremity check: To find the meaning of life, simply look at your fingers from time to time and see what they're up to.

- *If you're ten* and holding a bat and some twelve-year-old Visigoth is staring down at you from the mound, the meaning of life can be found at the exact spot where your bat will meet the ball.

- *If you're seventeen* and have somehow found your hand just inches from a small, pert breast, you may believe you have the meaning of life right there in your trousers, a long-term misapprehension that accounts for much distress in men's lives.

- *If you're twenty-eight,* fumbling with a surgical mask and standing next to a somewhat anxious young woman in a delivery room (and you're not an actual obstetrician), you'll soon be able to spot the meaning of life, because he will be the smallest person in the room.

- *If you're forty-five,* you *think* the meaning of life is hidden in a spidery weave of perks and products, ranging from the cellular phone you've got pressed against your ear to the table Vic always saves for you at Club Swank. Your ex-wife and the guy reading your electrocardiogram both think otherwise.

- *If you're sixty,* holding a fishing rod, but still otherwise gainfully employed, you think the meaning of life has something to do with fishing, but not with gainful employment. Unfortunately, you will share this epiphany with friends. At great length.

If, however, you should somehow approach the end of your life without ever having bothered to look for the meaning of it, you can, in a pinch, **use this simple mathematical formula:**

1. *Take the dollar value* of all your IRA, Keogh, 401(k), or other pension plans.
2. *Add the book value* of your savings and other assets.
3. *Divide that subtotal* by the combined ages of all your children.
4. Next, *add up how many times* a woman, not personally known by you, looked you square in the eye and smiled at you in what a reasonable man would consider to be a lascivious manner.
5. *Multiply the total number* of lascivious looks by ten, and divide by the number of divorces among your immediate family. Divide the first number by the second. Now multiply your grand total by the percentage of everything you think you can take with you.

And there you go.

This is your life, too!

Assembling all that is known about man's life on earth is a job we'll never finish—unless you help.

If you know something you think other men need to know or if there's something we've forgotten to include in this edition of *A Man's Life*, please write it down and send it in.

How? Three manly ways:

- *Send it by mail* to Man's Life Global Headquarters

  c/o Rex's Barber Shop
  116 W. Jefferson Street
  Mankato, KS 66956

or stop by for a trim and drop it off in person. You can also use this address to write for a catalog of other fine books and stuff.

- *Send it by e-mail* to MansLife@aol.com.
- *Get on the Web* and visit the sumptuous, newly painted, completely air-conditioned site of A Man's Life at

  http://www.manslife.com/

Either way, here's what you get for helping out:
- Your name in the back of the next book
- A heartfelt handshake if ever we meet
- A salutation on the Web
- A friend for life

That's it. No washer-dryer. No new car. Here's the form to use, or you can use a separate piece of paper. Include your name and address if you want, and we'll put you on our modern mailing list.

_____

_____

_____

_____

_____

Contributors

AC	Abe Carroll		DBa	Dave Barry
AH	Arno Harris		DBW	Captain Donald B. Whidman
ALP	Alex L. Pino		DC	Dylan Cuthbert
AMcLL	Ann McLellan Lardas		DD	Dick Dugger
AR	April Reinking		DE	Denise Englehardt
ARi	Art Rich		DER	Darryl E. Richards
ASD	Amy Sue Devlin		DES	Dante Elvin Stoeckel
AT	Aman Turkis		DEW	Dan E. Westchester
ATR	Andy T. Rapp		DF	Derrick Frost
AWS	Arthur W. Seddon		DFC	Dwight Frederick Cook
BAS	Brendan Alan Smith		DH	Douglas Herrmann
BB	Bob Bacigal		DKA	Darwin K. Abrahamson
BE	Bert Ellis		DM	Dana Machel
BG	Bryant Gumbel		DMcI	Donald McIntyre
BGr	Bill Grubowski		DMcIn	Dan McIntyre
BM	Brian Marshall		DP	Duane Pearson
BNS	Beck N. Shaar		DPa	Delroy Paulus
BS	Ben Stevens		DR	Diane Ravitch
BV	Blane Vuicich		DS	Dixie Szabad
CAC	Curtis Alan Cross		DSa	D. Sassano
CD	Charlie Daniels		DSB	David S. Bohner
CDa	Cliff Davidson		DSD	D. Samuel Devitt
CDA	Carl D. Astor		DV	Daniel Valenzuela
CF	Chris Fargo		DW	Dean White
CGG	Chas Griffin Gaultier		DWT	Dana W. Tuttle
CS	Cary Schneider		DY	"Diz" Yates
CSW	"Chick" S. Wolf		DZ	Danielle Zalen
CV	Clay Vega		EDH	E. D. Hirsch
CW	Clint Walters		EDS	Edward D. Steinberg
CWE	Corey William Erhard		EKH	Eric Karl Hickey
CY	Gen Chuck Yeager		EL	Ed Lopez
DA	David Allen		EMcG	Earle McGrath
DAB	David A. Bertoli		EP	Eddie Perris
DB	Denis Boyles		EQ	Emil Quentin

ER	"Elvis" Rosen	GSte	Gary Steel
ERD	Ev R. Davies	GStr	Gerrit Strathmeyer
ES	E. Styles	GW	Guy Wallace
ESD	Ezekiel Guinn	GY	Glenn Yellon
EW	Edgar Wilson	HDO	Harry Daniel Oldbrook
EWe	Edward Welker	HDS	Hayden D. Smith
EWR	Everett W. Richman	HE	Helen Elton
EWS	Elmer Walter Stark	HER	Harold Eric Rammell
FAC	Frank A. Cruz	HES	Henry S. Smith
FD	Fred Delmar	HFD	H. F. Dover
FDG	F. Darren Goetz	HG	Hank Goodman
FE	"Fitz" Evans	HGE	Hugh G. Easton
FED	Fiona E. Dickson	HGR	Howard Grant Rothman
FER	Frank Robertson	HJ	Harv Johnson
FEW	Ford E. Williams	HJT	Henry J. Takeda
FF	Fran Felson	HN	Harry Nunn
FG	Ferris Goodman	HPh	Homer Phelton
FGMcF	F. G. McFarlane	HS	Heather Sherman
FLD	Flanders L. Delvins	HT	Herb Tomas
FM	Frank Meagher	HTF	H. T. Favela
FS	Fred Schruers	HTh	Henry Thomas
FSO'R	Frank S. O'Rourke	HTR	Herve T. Rostel
FSS	Fred S. Sterling	HY	H. Yee
FT	Felix Tuckerman	JA	Janis Allworth
GAS	Gregory Andrew Selinger	JAC	James A. Clark
GDO'H	Gary D. O'Hannan	JAS	Jon A. Steele
GE	Gus Elworth	JBu	Junior Buster
GEF	Gaston E. Fortney	JC	John Cowlins
GEFi	Greg E. Fischer	JD	Joe Dillow
GF	Grant Farrens	JDa	Jack Davis
GFa	Gar Farmer	JEH	Jeff. E. Harris
GFE	Glenn F. Estudillo	JER	Johnson E. Richardson
GFL	Gale F. Landers	JF	Jake Finney
GFS	Gary S. Stein	JFo	Jay Follis
GG	Garwin Gelson	J&LG	Jennifer and Lisa Guhl
GH	Geoff Harris	JG	Jeff Gerston
GHO'H	George H. O'Hara	JGF	Janet Gennifer Franklin
GK	Gene Kramer	JGY	Jim G. Yarbrough
GL	Gary Lopez	JH	John Harper
GR	Gerry Richards	JHa	Jake Hall
GRD	Gibson Randall Dowling	JP	J. Portero
GRE	Gordon R. Etheredge	JQ	Joe Queenan
GS	Gregg Stebben	JR	Jeremy Rachelt
GSD	Greta Smith-Duncan	JRE	Jess R. Englebright
GSt	Gene Stone	JRL	Justin Richard Laramis

JS	Jody Stebben	MM	Michael Mercer
JSt	Jack Stevens	MMB	Michael Martin Benedetti
JSD	Johnnie S. Duselli	MN	M. Natali
JSE	James S. Everett	NG	Nathan Gregg
JTF	Jordan Terrance Findley	NMN	Nick M. Nyman
JTh	Jason Thorton	NO	Ned Oliver
JY	Jeff Young	NR	Nancy Romero
JYF	Jerryl Y. Farlucci	NS	Norman Schwarzkopf
KA	Karl Andrews	NSA	Nestor S. Alvarez
KCA	Kent C. Agee	OFIS	Old Friends Information Services
KD	Keith Dibert	PA	Peter Allred
KN	Ken Norton	PB	Pat Brewer
KEL	Kary E. Lewis	PDS	Parker Devlin Sanders
KEW	K. E. "Key" West	PE	Paul Edwards
KGK	Kit G. Kaputo	PER	Preston E. Ryan
KHG	Kirk H. Gibson	PF	Pete Finley
KJ	Kim Johnson	PG	Sen. Phil Gramm
KJL	Karl J. Larry	PJH	Patrick Jonathon Harper
KL	"Kip" London	PJN	Peter J. Newhouse
KLS	Karen L. Stewart	PK	Paul Kvinta
KM	Kathleen Marcus	PL	Pete Lewis
KMa	Kurt Magens	PN	Pierce Nichols
KMN	Knox M. Nelson	POE	P. O. Elster
KR	Kelly Rodrigues	PO'T	Paul O'Toole
KS	Ken Smolecki	PP	"Pop" Porter
KSw	Karl Swartz	PQ	Patrick Quillin
LA	Leo Alioto	PST	Parker S. Templeton
LB	Larry Bonds	PVFD	Paintville VFD
LE	Lawrence Edwards	RD	Rick Dawson
LEW	Lou E. White	RDL	Randy D. Lewenson
LF	Laurence Fuller	RDY	Richard Daniel Yesterman
LI	Len Inouye	RE	Red Endicott
LKO	Larry K. Olson	REM	Ralph E. Merritt
LL	Lisa Levitz	RES	Ron E. Smith
LO	Lanny Ovitz	RET	Roland E. Totter
LOP	Lee O. Polette	RFD	Raymond F. Dancer
LRE	Lewis Richard Eastwood	RFW	Rich F. Whaling
LW	Lincoln Ward	RH	Prof. Robert Hogan
MB	Marvin Berry	RHW	Russell Hamer Warren
MDW	Martin D. Wong	RHWa	Robert H. Waldman
MF	Merle Farrington	RL	Rene Lester
MG	Manny Gutierrez	RMcD	Rick McDermott
MH	Mort Hopkins	RMcE	Ronald McElway
MHC	Max H. Christian	RMcEl	Roger McElvey
MLK	Mark L. Kingman	RO	Rusty Olson

RS	Randy Straff	TES	Thomas Edward Sleath
RSA	Richard S. Adamec	TF	Tad Foster
RSE	Robert S. Eckman	TFK	Trevor F. Kingston
RSR	R.S. Roberts	TFR	Ty F. Ringland
RST	Richard Smullet Thompson	TH	Terry Hall
RT	Robert Thornton	TJM	T. J. Murphy
RTS	Rawley T. Staffer	TM	Tracy Meadows
RU	Rich Underwood	TMcD	Tim McDermott
RW	Rick Wayne	TMcF	Troy McFarland
SA	Steve Ashton	TP	Tip Petersen
SB	Steve Blanchard	TR	Tom Ramsey
SCJ	Samuel C. Johnson	TRE	Terrel R. Emsing
SDE	Steven David Estherhoff	TRW	Timothy R. Woszniak
SDW	Scott D. Weir	TS	Tom Stoner
SE	Sheldon Euler	TSB	Todd S. Bateman
SF	Sean Flanagan	TSh	T. Schwartz
SFo	Shawn Foote	TWa	Tammy Washington
SG	Stan Goodwin	TY	Thom Yasuda
SI	Stuart Ingle	TZ	T. Zwick
SJS	S. J. Sandoval	UG	U. Grauer
SP	Steve Petrosini	USG	U.S. Government
SPW	S. Peter Wharton	VCS	Victor C. Salcido
SS	Shelley Sternman	VES	Van E. Sanders
ST	Stephen Tetzlaff	VF	Vic Farrington
STE	S. "Terry" Elkins	VGS	Vernon Gerald Sloan
STo	Sara Tollis	VP	Vince Pryor
STT	Smell and Taste Treatment Center	VS	Vinnie Siedel
STu	"Sonny" Tucherman	VSDa	Virgil S. David
SW	Stephen Wiest	WB	William Booth
SWa	Skip Washington	WC	Wes Cobaugh
SWac	Steve Wacker	WE	Wade Esra
SWe	Scott Wetzler, Ph.D.	WH	Wes Hester
TA	Tim Allen	WM	Ward Melton
TB	Ted Burton	WO	Wayne Okuda
TC	Tim Connoly	WPB	Willis P. Blanton
TD	Terry Downing	YR	Yank Reese

Index